Studies in Economic Ethics and Philosophy

Springer
Berlin
Heidelberg
New York
Barcelona
Budapest
Hong Kong
London
Milan
Paris
Santa Clara
Singapore
Tokyo

Studies in Economic Ethics and Philosophy

P. Koslowski (Ed.)
Ethics in Economics, Business, and Economic Policy
(out of print)
192 pages. 1992

P. Koslowski · Y. Shionoya (Eds.)
The Good and the Economical
Ethical Choices in Economics and Management
(out of print)
212 pages. 1993

H. De Geer (Ed.)
Business Ethics in Progress?
124 pages. 1994

P. Koslowski (Ed.)
The Theory of Ethical Economy in the Historical School
345 pages. 1995

A. Argandoña (Ed.)
The Ethical Dimension of Financial Institutions
and Markets
264 pages. 1995

G.K. Becker (Ed.)
Ethics in Business and Society.
Chinese and Western Perspectives
232 pages. 1996

P. Koslowski
Ethics of Capitalism and Critique of Sociobiology.
Two Essays with a Comment by James M. Buchanan
153 pages. 1996

F. Neil Brady (Ed.)
Ethical Universals in International Business
255 pages. 1996

Peter Koslowski
Andreas Føllesdal (Eds.)

Restructuring the Welfare State

Theory and Reform of Social Policy

With 6 Figures
and 13 Tables

Springer

Professor Dr. Peter Koslowski
Forschungsinstitut für Philosophie Hannover
The Hannover Institute of Philosophical Research
Gerberstraße 26
D-30169 Hannover, Germany

Dr. Andreas Føllesdal
ARENA, Advanced Research on the
Europeanisation of the Nation-State
P.O. Box 1143, Blindern
N-0317 Oslo, Norway

Cataloging-in-Publication Data applied for

Die Deutsche Bibliothek - CIP-Einheitsaufnahme

Restructuring the welfare state : theory and reform of social policy ; 13 tables / Peter Koslowski ; Andreas Føllesdal (ed.). - Berlin ; Heidelberg ; New York ; Barcelona ; Budapest ; Hong Kong ; London ; Milan ; Paris ; Santa Clara ; Singapore ; Tokio : Springer, 1997
(Studies in economic ethics and philosophy)
ISBN-13: 978-3-642-64494-8
NE: Koslowski, Peter [Hrsg.]

ISBN-13: 978-3-642-64494-8 e-ISBN-13:978-3-642-60652-6

DOI: 10.1007/978-3-642-60652-6

Springer-Verlag Berlin Heidelberg New York

Softcover reprint of the hardcover 1st edition 1997

Hardcover Design: Erich Kirchner, Heidelberg

SPIN 10546642 42/2202-5 4 3 2 1 0 – Printed on acid-free paper

Preface

The volume at hand contains the proceedings of the conference "Restructuring the Welfare State: Ethical Issues of Social Policy in an International Perspective" held with the support of the Stiftung Forschungsinstitut für Philosophie Hannover at the Forschungsinstitut für Philosophie Hannover in Hanover, Germany, on September 8-10, 1995.

Several of the papers in the volume have been read at the Fourth International Conference on Ethics in the Public Service at Stockholm, Sweden, on June 15-18, 1994, organised by Hans De Geer and Gunilla Silfverberg at the Swedish FA Institute.

The editors wish to thank the organisers, participants and speakers of the Stockholm and Hanover conferences. They are also grateful to Anna Maria Hauk for the smooth handling of the Hanover conference, to Guttorm Aanes and Simen Bræin for their assistance in preparing the manuscript, and to Peggy Simcic Brønn for the valuable and professional management of the manuscript.

Oslo and Hanover, October 1996

Andreas Føllesdal Peter Koslowski

Table of Contents

Part IV.
Current Problems of the Welfare State

Part V.
Theory and Critique of the Welfare State

Conclusion

Restructuring the Welfare State

Introduction

PETER KOSLOWSKI

The debate about the welfare state in Europe has entered a stage where it is not anymore the question whether the welfare state in the industrialised countries of Europe should be modified or not but how it could be restructured. The costs and financing problems of social security have shifted the emphasis in the discussion from questions of legitimacy as well as extension and reform of the welfare state to questions of its survival. Questions of legitimacy and questions of adaptation for survival can, however, not be completely separated since deficits in legitimacy very often point to shortcomings in construction as well.

In this introduction four questions are formulated that guided the investigation of the volume at hand.

I. Are Welfare States Sustainable at the Present High Degree of Benefits and Public „Insuredness"?

The current problem in the European welfare states is not the question whether welfare states are sustainable at all. There seems to be consensus that some degree of social insurance is desirable. Rather, the question is how the welfare states instituted after World War II are sustainable at the present high degree of insuredness of the population. This question in turn is not only a question as to the financial means and funds of the national insurance systems, to the financial provision for the social security system. More interesting is the question whether the social insurance systems ought to be sustained in their present institutions although they create illusions amongst the insured about their wealth and their social and economic welfare.

The question can be put this way: The financial costs of the welfare state have two causes. The first cause is the increased international competition and reduced wealth of the Western nations that cannot afford the former degree of social benefits they have grown used to. If this is the case the crisis of the welfare state is a crisis of down-sizing and unavoidable.

The question more interesting to economics and social philosophy is the question whether the welfare states we are used to are inherently prone to create illusions amongst the people about their real wealth and whether these illusions can be reduced by a change of economic organisation and of the design of the institutions of social security. This problem is discussed below under the heading of „welfare state illusion": Is there an element inherent in the welfare states that creates illusions about the actual state of the people's wealth in regard to the expected future payments for pensions and to the start of retirement age?

The welfare state makes the promise to pay to its citizens a pension at a certain retirement age. If it is not able to keep this promise the plans of the individuals are severely changed and their life plans distorted. Since the individuals made the plans about their wealth creation and their distribution of wealth over the life cycle under the assumption that they will receive the pension payments promised by the welfare state there life plans are distorted considerably if the welfare state cannot fulfil these promises. A far reaching misallocation of resources over the life cycle due to illusions about the actual wealth situation will be the consequence.

The question can be clarified by an analysis of the German welfare state. The German welfare state is noted for its robustness: It can adopt to changes of the economic parameters by an adaptation of the parameters of the social security system. If the amount of the contributions to the system decreases due to economic recession the social security system can react by a later start of retirement, by an earlier start of employment in younger years or by a lower level of welfare benefits. By changing these parameters the system, in theory, will always find to a new equilibrium.

The financial equilibrium of the social security system, however, does not mean that the expectations and plans of the individuals being insured in this system are in equilibrium. The robustness of the system might be very costly in terms of a disappointment of the expectations of those being insured in the system. Even if the macroeconomic contributions/payments ratio is in equilibrium the individual economic plans that people made for their life are in utter disequilibrium since they made these plans under very different assumptions about their wealth situation than the one that is becoming reality in the payments of the social security system. The social insurance system might be over-robust, too robust to respond to the differentiated needs of the individuals.

II. Are Private Insurance Programs Better than Social Security Schemes?

As a remedy to the present high costs of the welfare state, the return to more self-reliance and reliance on private insurance systems is recommended. The politics of Thatcherism in the United Kingdom argued for a privatisation of social security not primarily because of arguments of financial crisis but for arguments of the value of self-reliance and for arguments of moral hazard in the social insurance systems.

In 1983, I contended myself that the welfare state due to its anonymity and robustness of its schemes weakens the ethics of self-responsibility and self-reliance and decreases the propensity of the individuals to a responsible conduct of life.

The experience of Thatcherism and of the privatisation of social insurance is, however, that problems of moral hazard are also present in private insurance systems. The transparency on the behaviour of the individual in its attitude towards risk and in his or her change of habits after being insured are also effective in private insurance systems. These private insurance systems are also anonymous and do not have the size at which the „large number problem" (James M. Buchanan) does not apply. The large number problem arises where people act in large groups in which they cannot control their behaviour and their adherence to the rules. Only very small groups have no „large number problem". The question is, therefore, whether there is really an inherent superiority of private insurance over social security in respect to moral hazard and to the other problems of change of behaviour towards risk when people are insured.

III. Why Do Strong Welfare States Exist in the North Western Part of Europe and not in Other Parts of the World?

Looking at the history of the welfare state it becomes visible that the most extensive welfare state arose in Sweden, Great Britain, Germany, and the Benelux countries. Since these countries also form the focus of the volume at hand it is an interesting question to ask which are the reasons that some societies develop a welfare state or social state and others do not. With this question is linked the other question whether a welfare system is the indication for a strong society or for a strong state. Some Swedish scholars argue that the welfare system in Sweden is not the result and indicator of a strong state but of a strong society since the welfare system is basically run and supported by the local community, not by the central government.

This holds also true for the foundations of the German social state or social security system. The Bismarckian system was intended not as a governmental system but as a system run by the insured themselves under a system of self-administration (*Selbstverwaltung*). Thus, the reproach often heard from American scholars that the European welfare state or social security system represents a paternalistic system and a kind of paternalism is questionable. It must rather be objected that this critique misunderstands the original blue-print of the social security systems which were intended as co-operative, self-administered systems, not as etatist systems.

If the welfare state or social security system presupposes what one could call a 'strong society' or 'strong community' what is it that makes the societies with a social security system „strong"? Are these societies strong due to a high degree of solidarity which in turn presupposes a high degree of homogeneity, of ethnic or religious homogeneity? Is the welfare state in this sense grounded in a homogenous society, in the ethnic nation state? Or is it independent of conditions of national homogeneity? Is the welfare state based on a constitution of society that leads to a strong society with weak individuals or does the welfare state enable processes of emancipation of the individuals that enable them to be strong individuals in a strong society?

The proceedings of this volume demonstrate that the introduction of the welfare state has often been linked to the idea of freeing the individual from traditional bonds of obligations in the family or in the work place. Does the welfare state lead to a situation where there is nothing between the individual and the state anymore? Are the intermediary institutions, the family and intermediary groups, marginalised by the growth of the welfare state?

IV. Does the Europeanisation of the Nation State Enforce the Europeanisation of the Welfare State and Thereby the Down-Sizing of Social Security Systems in Europe?

The European Union is the transformation of the European nation state into a supra-national commonwealth. The increasing integration of the nations of the European Union thereby necessarily weakens the national, ethnic base of the European nations. By this process, it also weakens and transforms the national, ethnic base of the welfare state and of the social security system in the former sovereign European nations. The Europeanisation of the nation state means that in the long run the sources of solidarity within the European Union coming from a national and ethnic base are weakened and that this affects the basis and the character of the national social security system.

Will the change to a supra-national European Union affect the institutional design of financing the welfare state and social security? It seems that a capitalised system of pension funds is closer to a multinational and multicultural society than a pay-as-you-go system that relies on notions of national solidarity and the like. If the pay-as-you-go system implies the creation of debt between generations it is based on feelings of solidarity between the generations that may not be able to be upheld in a supra-national state.

The welfare state based on a national insurance system is already being affected by the move to a super-national European commonwealth. The European Union is therefore a challenge to the old-fashioned national welfare states and welfare systems. Which adaptations of the welfare state are therefore necessary in order to cope with the Europeanisation of the nation state in Europe? Can the present social welfare systems be upheld in an integrated Europe? Or must they necessarily be down-sized in a European Union less closely integrated than the former independent nation states?

Part I

The Welfare State Under Siege in Western Europe

Chapter 1

Is the British Welfare System Sustainable?

FRANCES CAIRNCROSS

Britain is a good country with which to illustrate the question of sustainability of the welfare state. For Britain has tried harder and longer than most countries to restrain the growth of welfare spending. The extent to which it has succeeded says much about the difficulties of the exercise that all industrial countries will be forced to undertake in the years ahead.

I. The Growth of Welfare Spending

Britain has demonstrated, through much of this century, a remarkable appetite for public spending. The rise as a share of GDP, from less than 10% in 1890 to a peak of around 48% in 1976, was driven by the belief, common across northern Europe, that the state could perform many tasks more effectively than the private sector. The crisis of 1976 was a turning point for Britain even more important than the election of Margaret Thatcher three years later. A severe balance of payments crisis forced the Labour government to borrow from the IMF in humiliating circumstances. The Labour cabinet was forced to agree to large cuts in public-spending plans. By the time Mrs Thatcher took power, with an election commitment to "role back the frontiers of the state", public spending had already stopped rising as a share of GDP.

It has remained below the 1976 peak ever since. As a result, Britain has slid from near the top of the OECD league table for public spending as a share of GDP to the lower echelons. However the sharp dip that occurred in the second half of the 1980s has not been sustained. Since the late 1980s, public spending has begun to rise as a share of GDP – driven, in large part, by a renewed rise in spending on welfare benefits. The rise is glum news for other countries. If even a government as determined as the Tories under Margaret Thatcher cannot hold the line on public spending, who can? And once most aspects of public spending that can readily be reduced have been tackled, how are governments to deal with the core: education, health and – above all – welfare benefits?

Figure 1. Benefit Expenditure 1949-50 to 1992-93 (1992-93 prices)

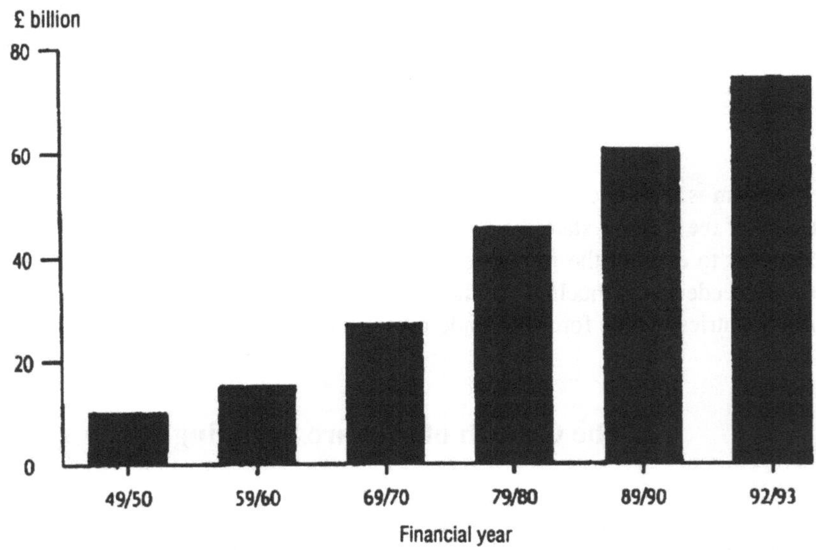

Source: Crown copyright is reproduced with the permission of the controller of HMSO.

Spending on welfare benefits has risen both in absolute terms and as a share of public spending. As a share of GDP, social-benefit spending has risen from 4.7 per cent in 1949-50, at the birth of the modern welfare state, to 12.3 per cent in 1992-93. As Tory politicians frequently point out, benefits now cost each working person in Britain £15 a day. That sort of figure is worth keeping in mind during this conference, for it is the most important single reason for worrying about the cost of the welfare state: one person's benefit is another person's tax bill – or, of course, sometimes the same person's tax bill.

Not many governments on either side of the Atlantic have been as hostile to welfare benefits as the Conservatives who have been in power since 1979. Yet hostility has not stopped benefit spending from continuing to rise. In

Figure 2. Benefit Expenditure 1978-79 to 1992-93 (1992-93 prices)

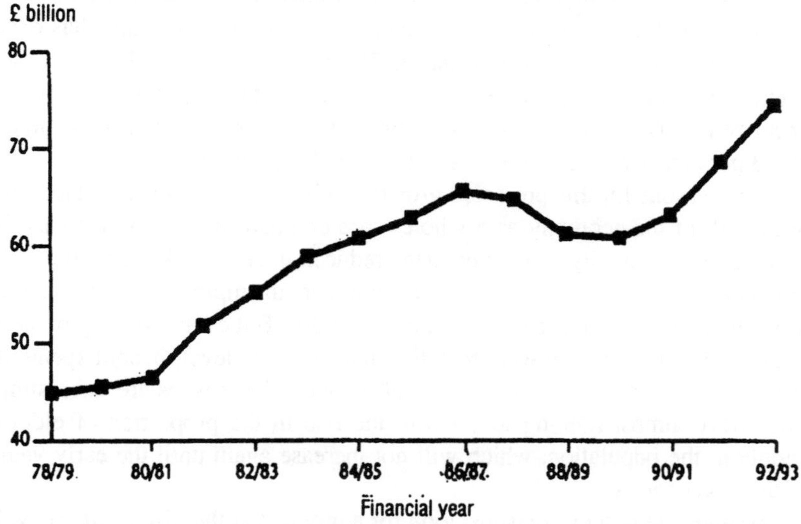

Source: Crown copyright is reproduced with the permission of the controller of HMSO.

Figure 3. Benefit Expenditure by Contributory Status 1978-79 to 1992-93 and 1999-2000 Forecast (1992-93 prices)

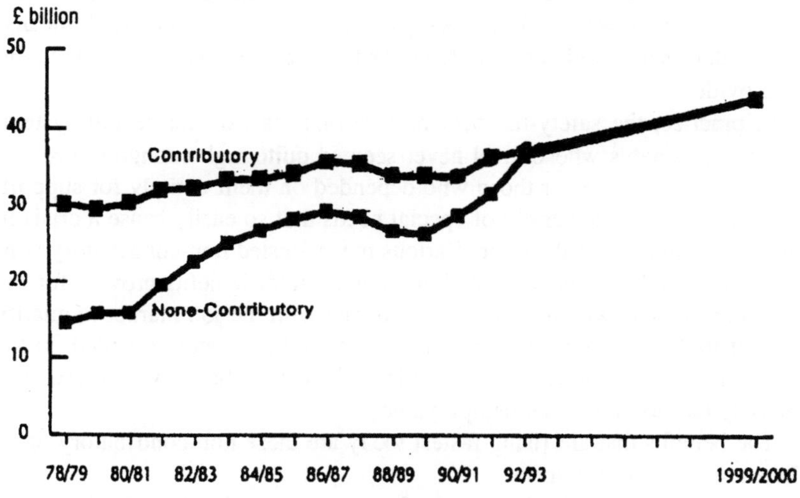

Source: Crown copyright is reproduced with the permission of the controller of HMSO.

1985 the government undertook a massive review of benefits, to try to stem the growth. A great number of reforms were introduced in the Social Security Act of the following year. Since then, the social-security budget has risen by a further 20 per cent in real terms. The rise has been partly the consequence of higher unemployment. But a forecast by the Department of Social Security in 1993 projected continued underlying growth in benefit spending of 3.3 per cent a year in real terms to the end of the century.

The reasons for this projected growth – which is above the expected rate of growth of the economy as a whole – are emphatically not an increase in coverage or generosity. Both have been reduced under the Conservative government. The growth assumes no reduction in unemployment, whose rise drove up benefit spending at the end of the 1980s. But even if unemployment at the end of the century were to fall to half its 1993 level, benefit spending in total is still expected to grow at 1.8% a year. The reasons are interesting. They have almost nothing to do with the rise in the proportion of elderly people in the population, which will not increase again until the early years of the next century.

To understand those reasons, look for a moment at the history of the welfare state in Britain. The core of Sir William Beveridge's vision, described in his 1942 White Paper, was the replacement of a system of mainly means-tested benefits with one of compulsory social insurance. Insurance contributions would be paid by people while they were in work, and would give them an income if they were sick or unemployed or when they retired. A means-tested safety-net would continue to cover the needs for which insurance did not provide.

In practice, the safety-net became a normal part of the benefit system, topping up benefits whose level never seemed quite high enough to provide an adequate existence for those who depended on them entirely for support, and meeting the wide variety of special needs that so easily cause a crisis in the living standards of the poor. Various means-tested non-contributory benefits and several non-means-tested non-contributory benefits provide for the many poor people who have too little contact with the job market to qualify for contributory benefits. The trouble with a welfare system founded on the assumption that people are employed is that most of the truly poor are poor precisely because they are unemployable.

The benefits that are rising fastest today are these non-contributory ones. There are three main culprits:

- Invalidity benefit. Paid to the long-term sick, this benefit effectively provides a higher income to those who lose their jobs in their fifties and early sixties than unemployment benefit would. It has thus become a sort of state aid to those forced to take early retirement.

- Housing benefit. Paid to cover rent bills for the poor, it often represents a transfer from one government pocket to another, as the poor tend to live in state-owned housing. When the government raises rents, housing benefit payments also increase.
- Income support for lone parents. The numbers of lone parents drawing welfare benefits has risen from 320,000 in 1979 to over 1m today. The increase reflects partly the rise in divorce, but mainly a huge growth in the number of unmarried mothers, to a rate higher than anywhere else in Europe. Most of these mothers are teenagers, and very few have ever been employed. They are one of Britain's most serious social problems, and it seems at least possible that paying them benefits is one of the factors encouraging them to have babies.

Figure 4. Total Benefit Expenditure by broad groups of beneficiaries

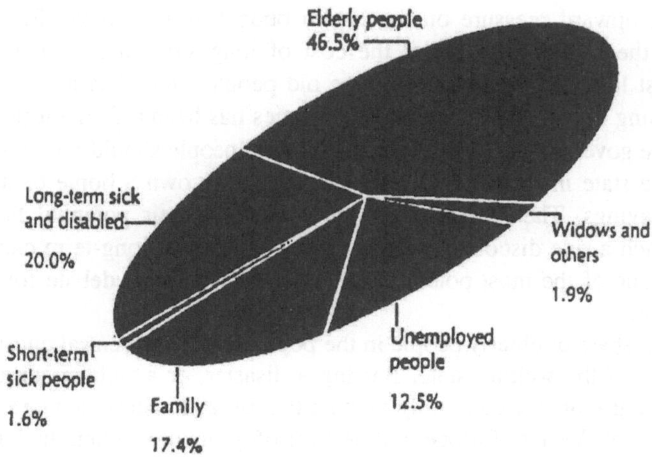

Source: Crown copyright is reproduced with the permission of the controller of HMSO.

II. The Declining Support Ratio

By far the largest group of benefit recipients, though, remains the elderly; for every lone parent, there are ten pensioners. Retirement pensions alone account for £25m of Britain's £75m social security budget. On top of that, there are a number of other benefits that go mainly to those past retirement age.

Not only do the elderly account for nearly half of all benefit spending. The older old account for much of the recent acceleration in the growth of spending on health care. Here again, Britain's relative lack of success in holding down spending is a disheartening indicator for other countries. Spending per head on health care is relatively low in Britain, and when compared with indicators of the quality of national health, relatively productive. The National Health Service, with its powerful monopoly power to determine the pay of doctors and other health workers and the cost of drugs, has proved an efficient mechanism for containing the costs of health care.

Because the over 75s will grow as a proportion of the population over the next decade, upward pressure on the health budget will continue. So will pressure on the benefits that cover the cost of long-term care, which this group is most likely to need. One in three old people over 85 is in a retirement or nursing home, and financing such homes has been a difficult political issue. The government is keen to insist that old people should not be supported by the state in residential care as long as they own a home or have significant savings. The elderly (and, more vocally, their potential heirs) argue that such a rule discourages thrift. The financing of long-term care is likely to be one of the most potent issues in British political debate for the next few years.

The rising share of elderly people in the population is the central question for the future of the welfare state. Barring a disaster, or a sudden surge in births or immigration, we can safely assume that by 2025 nearly a quarter of the population of Western Europe will be over 65 years old. When the baby-boomers start to retire early in the next century, they will look forward to a longer life than any previous generation.

Britain here has an advantage of a sort. It aged early. In 1990, Britain had a bigger proportion of over-65-year-olds than almost any other country. Over the next decade, the proportion of the very elderly in the population will continue to grow. But in terms of the total number of pensioners, Britain now has a pause.

While life expectancy has been increasing – and is continuing to increase

– Europeans born in 1990 can probably expect to live ten years longer than those born in 1950 - fertility has declined. It is, of course, the combined effect of falling fertility with rising life expectancy which underlies the problems facing the welfare state.

Here again, Britain is relatively well-placed. The fertility rate has recovered to replacement level (as, indeed, it has done in several other OECD countries). The result is that the support ratio in Britain – the ratio of 15 to 64 year-olds to those aged 65 and over – will deteriorate less than in any other large country. Today, just over four people of working age "support" each elderly person, while in Japan the ratio is nearly six to one. By 2050, the ratio in Britain will still be above two. It says something about the demographic prospect that may face us that a halving of the worker-to-old-person ratio in 60 years is a relatively modest change.

Will it really happen? Demography can spring surprises: the widespread assumption in the 1930s that fertility would not recover turned out to be wrong. The World Bank's own population projections for 2050 vary by up to 2 billion, depending on various assumptions. But there are three reasons for assuming that the support ratio will get worse, even if the outcome is less severe than these numbers suggest:

1. Fertility rates are unlikely to rise much above replacement level. The increase in the 1950s which confounded the demographers of the 1930s looks, in retrospect, like an aberration from the downward drift of the previous half century. Since then, women have entered the labour force in large numbers, greatly raising the opportunity cost of having an extra child. It is unlikely that this move into the workforce will be reversed – and indeed, if it were, the consequences for the support ratio would be dire.
2. Life expectancy is unlikely to decline, especially among the elderly. Indeed, life expectancy is probably more likely to rise for the old than the young, given that infant mortality and death rates for young people are now so low in the OECD countries.
3. Immigration is extremely unlikely to increase. We already see a growing political backlash against the immigration of the post-war era, which has been the highest ever from the poor world to the rich. The level of immigration needed to hold support ratios at their present levels would be larger than most electorates would accept.

The support ratio is therefore bound to deteriorate in all the large countries. The OECD's assumption is that spending on pensions will rise by 80% between 1980 and 2040. As pensions already account for over half of benefit spending in OECD countries, it is hard to see the prospect as anything other than unsustainable. But in Britain, again, the prospect is more manageable than anywhere else.

III. The Impact on State Pensions

In the past, Britain's pensions have been low by OECD standards – partly because the earnings-related component has been small – and the result is that Britain's relatively elderly population has received a small share of national wealth. Even as the value of pensions increased, other countries raised pensions faster.

The aggressive drive by the Conservative government to cut back future liabilities has had an effect. Indeed, since the projections in this chart were made, more government measures have reduced future obligation still further. Public pension spending is lower, as a proportion of GDP, than it is in Germany, France, Italy or even the United States.

As a result, Britain is in a unique situation. On present trends, pension payments by the middle of the next century will be lower as a proportion of GDP than they are today, and lower than contributions income too. "Time bomb?" one might say. "What time bomb?"

In fact, the problem for Britain's pensions is not that they are unsustainably high, but that they may become unsustainably low, because their cost has been cut in ways that do not focus help on those who need it most.

The single most important change to public pension liabilities occurred in 1982, with the decision to index pensions and similar benefits to prices rather than to earnings. The result of uprating in line with prices only throughout the 1980s, a period of rapidly rising real earnings, has been a sharp increase in the gap between average earnings and the value of state pensions. The single person's pension is now about 15% of average net earnings, roughly the level it was at in the early 1970s. As long as the policy is in place, the gap will continue to widen. Early in the next century, the state retirement pension will return to the minimal proportion of male earnings at which Beveridge set it.

The Conservative government has taken a number of other measures to reduce future increases in the pensions bill. In particular, it has greatly reduced the generosity of the state earnings-related pensions scheme, or SERPS, which was introduced in the Social Security Act of 1975. Britain's basic pension is paid at a flat rate. A modest earnings-related component was introduced in 1961. SERPS in its original form promised 25 per cent of average earnings, based on the best 20 years of working life. One intention was to help people with interrupted work histories, such as married women. If the scheme had survived untouched, Britain today would undoubtedly face obligations just as unsustainable as those of many other European countries.

Instead, the Tories' 1986 Social Security Act dismantled much of this monument of the previous Labour government. It changed the basis of pensions to a whole working life, rather than a mere 20 years. And the upper and lower earnings limits have both been effectively indexed to prices.

You may wonder how on earth the government got away with these changes. I think there are three reasons. First SERPs had been in existence for only eight years, too short a time for most people to have built a big stake in the system. Secondly, many people have only a hazy notion of their future entitlement. As their current living standards were unaffected, they were either mystified by or uninterested in the change. Finally, many of the people who would have been most likely to protest in other countries had occupational or personal pensions. It is to this aspect of pension provision in Britain that I would now like to turn.

IV. Private-Sector Provision

Britain's private-sector pension provision is more extensive than almost any other in Europe. Such pensions are of two main sorts: occupational, into which both employers and employees make contributions, and which usually pay defined benefits, often related to a worker's final salary; and personal pensions, which are a form of savings plan, and which pay benefits that reflect the underlying value of the individual investment.

Even by 1967, roughly half of all workers were covered by occupational schemes. In fact, coverage is highly skewed towards older workers and men – among men in their early fifties, it rises to 70 per cent. Because occupational schemes were well established when SERPS was introduced, employers were allowed to "contract out" of the state scheme by offering employees a guaranteed minimum pension above the SERPS level, in exchange for lower national insurance contributions.

Britain's occupational schemes now have some £700 billion of funds invested – more than all the rest of the European Union put together. Their effect on the British capital market is a subject beyond the scope of this conference. But the consequence of unsustainability in other countries is likely to be an attempt to encourage the growth of private-sector provision – and the impact of that on Europe's capital markets will be revolutionary. It will certainly force the pace of privatisation in countries that currently have large amounts of assets still in the public sector.

The growth of personal pensions is more recent. It received a large boost from the 1986 Act, which extended the option to contract out of SERPS to two other kinds of schemes – individual retirement accounts or personal pensions, and defined contribution schemes provided by employers. In neither case was there an obligation to provide a guaranteed minimum pension. Instead, a guaranteed minimum contribution has to be made. The government has given an extra rebate of contributions as an incentive – or bribe – to employees to leave SERPS and join a private pension scheme – with the predictable result that many employees have moved from good schemes into bad, and the pension companies have been much blamed for selling people inappropriate pensions.

Although the move to private pension schemes and to defined contribution schemes has been fraught with problems, it seems to me that this is a switch that every country will eventually have to make. Occupational schemes are a dangerous burden to place on companies, and doubly dangerous if they peg pensions to future salaries. It is surely much safer to find ways of making people provide directly for their own retirement, with a modest top-up from the state for those who for one reason or another fail to save enough to rescue themselves from destitution in old age.

The consequence of Britain's extensive occupational and private coverage is that a smaller share of the pensions burden will fall on taxpayers than in most other countries. And while the state pension scheme is financed, as in most countries, on a pay-as-you-go basis, so that today's workers pay directly for today's pensioners, private-sector schemes are funded, so that today's workers – at least in theory – save for their pensions tomorrow. Is that important? After all, in terms of real resources, pensions are likely to be paid by a transfer from workers to the retired, whether they are paid through the tax mechanism or through the financial markets.

I think that it is essential that the transfer should be confined as far as possible to the financial markets. When the taxpayer foots the bill, there are many undesirable consequences. One of them is that, however tax systems are designed, the poor tend to carry the largest share relative to their incomes.

V. Towards Sustainability

Are Britain's pension reforms sustainable? The main threat to them will be the attitude of the public to the idea that the living standards of most pensioners should remain frozen in real terms at the level of the early 1980s. For although occupational and private pensions generate a rising share of pensioner incomes, they accrue almost entirely to the top four income deciles.

The effect has been greatly to widen the gap between rich and poor pensioners. From now on, poverty in a person's working life time will lead inevitably to poverty in old age. So those groups that are detached from the job market, or on its lower echelons – the unhealthy, the badly educated, the disabled, the lone mother – will be poor for their entire lives.

Is there an alternative? Yes, but a problematic one. If the government did not pay the basic retirement pension to everyone who had made enough contributions – if, in other words, state pensions were entirely means-tested – it would be possible not only to save a vast amount of public spending, but to concentrate more help on those who have no other source of income but what they get from the state. There are, however, two severe difficulties with this approach:

- First, it would spell the end of the contributory principle. National insurance contributions would be regarded simply as another tax. It is possible that they are regarded thus already. But successive governments have felt that social insurance was a healthier basis for benefits than mere tax-financed poverty relief.
- Secondly, for anybody with low earnings, a safety net creates a moral hazard. Why save for retirement if the government will rescue you from poverty? The conflation of savings and the relief of poverty has been a constant difficulty with state pensions; but to concentrate on the relief of poverty alone as a goal would jeopardise saving.

In spite of these difficulties, means testing pensions may becomes unavoidable. For there are only two real ways to reduce welfare spending. One is to target it more closely on those who need it; the other is simply to cut it. Targeting usually involves means-testing. Means-testing invariably creates problems of boundaries. It has been bitterly attacked by Frank Field, chairman of the House of Commons Social Services committee for encouraging fraud, and discouraging work and thrift. He is right. But the only other way to make a serious reduction in the cost of a benefit – the only other way – is to reduce its value across the board. This is the path Britain has taken with pensions. Other countries will have to choose. At this fork in the road, both paths are unpleasant.

What makes the choice most urgent is the fact that, in my view, governments in most OECD countries have now reached the limits of taxable capacity. Indeed, we have not only reached it but long since gone past it: to tax workers on well below average earnings seems to me not just a moral outrage, but a sure way of distorting the job market and encouraging unemployment. But even once state pension promises are reduced, the issue of real resources will remain. Will countries be able to pay the pensions of tomorrow's workers by investing in domestic industry? Or will the rich world be forced to export ever more capital to the developing countries, so that they can pay our pensions for us, when the time comes?

There is only one way out of the real-resources dilemma – barring faster economic growth, which is improbable in an ageing Europe. That is to get old people back into the job market. It makes no sense for 69% of German 60-65 year old men, or 77% of Dutch, to be out of work. Labour-market participation has been dropping among the old for several decades. This decline is surely the outcome of the growth in pensions provision: if the elderly did not have state support to rely on, they would find work, even if at low wages. The effect is to make pensions more expensive: unemployed older workers do not pay taxes, but do draw benefits. Keeping older people in the job market is the easiest way to reduce the transfer of real resources. My guess is that, two decades from now, people will work into their seventies as a matter of course. If they do, the welfare state may be sustainable after all.

Reference

Department of Social Security: "The Growth of Social Security", London (Huso) 1993.

Chapter 2

Is the Welfare System of the Netherlands Sustainable?

KEES SCHUYT

I. Material and Moral Principles of the Welfare State

When did the Dutch welfare state begin? Did it start with The Child Labour Law (1874), which is often viewed as the genesis of social legislation? Hardly. The need to regulate ruthless economic competition was a far stronger impetus behind the child labour law. This decree is more characteristic of an incipient interventionist state than of a welfare state. Could the Disability Law of 1901, which provided important guidelines for the social security system, be the cradle of the welfare state? Perhaps, although this legislation largely concerned the individual responsibility of employees and their employers. While this very modest system of risk retention eventually expanded into the social security network, the welfare state was motivated by more than mutual guarantee funds alone. The mutual guarantee funds blossomed into social solidarity.

Beveridge's Social insurances and allied services (1942) and Full employment in a free society (1944) are probably the most authoritative historical starting points for the welfare state. For the Netherlands, the report Sociale Zekerheid (1945), drafted by Van Rhijn in London, might reasonably be considered the birth certificate of this system. While Professor Alfred Zimmern had already coined the term welfare state in the 1930s, this designation was primarily viewed as a policy programme intended as a sharp contrast to Hitler's warfare state. Aside from the direct need for social relief that resulted from the war atrocities (bombed houses, widows, orphans, divorces), the Beveridge report highlighted five long-term objectives: security for people who had lost their jobs or who were excluded from employment for other reasons (the elderly, the infirm, and pregnant women), medical care, housing, adequate educational facilities, and, most important of all: enough jobs for everyone or prevention of unemployment.

The lessons of the 1930s have taught us the material principles for the welfare state. Keynes's economic policy proclaimed that the economic crisis would subside if the unemployed were guaranteed a fixed income. A series of moral principles complemented this material basis for the welfare state: social justice manifested by an income policy that discontinued the monopoly of market relationships over the distribution of income and other social goods. The state was to participate in allocating scarce commodities wherever market distribution was clearly unsatisfactory. Despite the overall imbalance in the market sector that resulted from this correction of market failures, such concern for social justice was a major source of moral inspiration.

In 1950, J.M. den Uyl, then on of the leaders of the Dutch Labour Party, presented an illustrative example of this concern. His article 'Catholic politics and social justice' settles the score with Christian democratic perceptions of social equality and inequality. The article addressed the financial burdens of families and the resistance to income levelling among the Catholic People's Party. Den Uyl drew a distinction between dynamic and static views of society and put forward 'the assertion that this levelling is so advanced that it should quickly be reversed [. . .] in contrast to the conviction that our society requires a redistribution of incomes and wealth, both to serve social justice and to organise our society efficiently (Den Uyl 1978:25).

In 1982, Den Uyl, at that time Cabinet member, applied the same perspective of social justice in a series of articles discussing the monumental exacerbation of financial problems: 'This path of solidarity offers the sole means for keeping the welfare state affordable. Income moderation and general cutbacks must be channelled toward investments, jobs, and a shorter working week for every active individual. Jobless individuals and the elderly should not be left in the lurch. While the welfare state is definitely in need of reform, society must remain responsible for equal rights for all (women just as much as men) to jobs, incomes, and benefits' (Den Uyl 1982). Although the issue of income distribution and the affordability of benefits have changed drastically since 1950, a careful description of the material and moral principles underlying the welfare state appears in order here.

1. Solidarity: nobody should drop below the level necessary for a decent existence in a free society;
2. Social justice: the distribution of incomes and the scarce commodities derived from this system may not arise through arbitrary factors (whether at the discretion of class society, the market, or the bureaucratic competencies of citizens in the services market, which is often unfathomable);
3. Economic policy based on maximum employment for all is considered the best means to eradicate the financial problems afflicting the 'state of welfare'.

Clearly, the realisation of these three principles presents a major challenge to the policy of the welfare state. Anything entrusted to the government's financial supervision under the guise of social justice in the past three decades is due for reevaluation. Social-democratic revisionism is capable of implementing change and self-modification. In this context, an investigation is in order concerning the ins and outs of the welfare state following the noble, resolute, and dignified formulation of principles during World War II and the areas where this system has strayed slightly from its course.

These three principles remain as important and topical as ever. W. Albeda, Den Uyl's predecessor as minister of Social Affairs also assumed that: 'The basic principles of the welfare state are every bit as valid today as they were in 1950. Solidarity and justice legitimise their application. The economy is the main problem' (Albeda 1984:71).

By analysing the development of the welfare state in four periods (1945-1957; 1958-1968; 1969-1980; 1981-the present), I will embark on a quest for the heart of the welfare state, which has withstood all the criticism and problems. As both a tangible and an ideological concept, this heart signifies the core of the government's responsibility for ensuring assistance, as maintained by people who still care about the issue.

II. Construction and Expansion of the Welfare State

Very little historiography is currently available on the Dutch welfare state. Unfortunately, Wittert van Hoogland's monumental work De parlementaire geschiedenis der sociale verzekering 1890-1940 (Parliamentary History of social security)(1940) lacks a sequel on the post-war parliamentary course of social security, even though such a study would be extremely fascinating and important. Research on this topic might have averted some persistent misconceptions and misdirected reproaches. The Labour Party, which was decisive in building the welfare state, was far less significant in its subsequent expansion and arrangement. The accusations frequently heard these days that the Labour Party (and sometimes even Den Uyl himself) has let the welfare state get out of hand can, however, be qualified or refuted by means of a thorough and meticulous historical reconstruction of parliament debates from 1950 to 1980. The disability act, which is often deplored for its present excess, was the magnum opus of Veldkamp from the Catholic People's Party, who also introduced his version of the unemployment act for people without a prior record of work during his term as minister of Social Affairs in 1965. The general welfare act also became operative that year. Even the infamous linkage of benefits to the minimum wage was a sovereign remedy that temporarily relieved the constant tension between the left and the right wing of the contemporary Catholic People's Party during the early 1970s. Consequently, all these controversial accomplishments of the welfare state have not resulted solely from socialist excess, but are attributable to the policy of compromise that characterised the post-war parliamentary process. The Labour Party afforded this compromise unlimited support and welcomed it with enthusiasm, but was not the initiator.

1. 1945-1957: Reconstruction and Solidarity

Reconstruction based on a solid consensus prevailed during the years that followed the war. The government focused on raising productivity by keeping wages low and promoting peaceful working conditions. It was assisted by the elites, who represented sectarian support and acquired a following with little resistance. The discussions between the government and the social partners took place in a close circle where agreements were easily reached by today's standards. Members never reprimanded their leadership, as 'the balance of power in all three union federations lay with the upper echelons during the fifteen years that followed the war' (Windmuller and De Galan 1957:106). As a result, the emergency provisions of the act regarding the right to dismissal for controlling national wages were unnecessary.

The foundations were laid for the post-war welfare state: the provisional act for security for the elderly of 1947, the temporary act for child benefits for small entrepreneurs of 1951, the unemployment act of 1952, and, as the crowning glory of this period, the general act for the elderly of 1957 and the disability act for the unemployed of 1959. The elderly, who had experienced the bitterness of the Depression and the subsequent world war, were the first important beneficiaries of the welfare state. The circumstances necessitated an assessment method rather than a system like capital funding, where young people start saving for their old age. These preliminary attempts at a welfare state are likely to perpetuate the different views among older and younger generations with respect to state assistance. The older generation experienced the rise of the welfare state as a transition from privilege to entitlement: humiliating dependence on charity from organisations or family made way for a system of rights and obligations.

As originally intended in this first stage, the social functions of the welfare state received high visibility: relief for unemployment combined with buffers against economic fluctuations and sound investment in human capital. The first positive results undoubtedly reinforced the view that social processes could be activated and controlled. In this context, the following lines of poetry apply:

I thought it was possible.
That may very well be. You cannot force it.
A man dying of thirst will drown in the well.

(From: Hans Andrews, Sonnets of Small Madness)

Although people believed the system would work, time has shown that social courses cannot be coerced. In the welfare state, the thirst for social justice has become so great that unforeseen circumstances and effects of the assistance network threaten to drown the people in the well three decades down the road.

2. 1958-1968: Material Improvement

In the long run, the strict wage control measures created a gulf between economic options – based on increased labour productivity – and social desires. Economic opportunities, which resulted in part from the wage policy that prevailed during the 1950s, were not actually taken until the 1960s. Accordingly, material improvement and greater prosperity characterised this decade. The nation believed that every worker was entitled to own a car. It was time to express long-standing desires candidly . . . and to fulfil them. While the wage explosion of 1963 and 1964 far exceeded the subsequent rise in labour productivity, the austerity from the 1950s compensated for this excess. Civil servants also experienced tremendous improvements during the Toxopeus Round of 1964. (Twenty years later, when the salaries of civil servants were frozen, people spoke of a counter-Toxopeus Round.)

This extended economic growth and especially the profits from natural gas operations enabled considerable expansion of the government's areas of responsibility and of the range and scope of the facilities provided by the welfare state. The auspicious economic climate undoubtedly influenced the calculation of the rate to be awarded in benefits pursuant to the disability act of 1967. While the Minister of Finance did not object to eighty percent at the time, the Minister of Social Affairs would have settled for seventy-five percent.

In these years, many social security arrangements were formalised through legislation, while revisions affected existing regulations. The general welfare act of 1965 replaced the poor law of 1912/1854. The act for unemployment provisions and the national group coverage for the unemployed supplemented the unemployment act in 1965. The general child benefit law was enacted in 1963. In 1965, the national health act replaced the national health decree from World War II. The Lower House passed Veldkamp's costly general act for special illnesses. Last but not least, the disability act replaced each and every existing disablement law in 1967. The rise in optimism nearly matched economic growth. In retrospect, the estimated numbers eligible for disability benefits appear incomprehensibly low. In 1968, 162,000 individuals were entitled to support benefits. Ten years later, this figure had increased to 489,000 (seven times the number predicted). By 1992 950,000 people were receiving such assistance.

Other government affairs supplemented social security, especially with respect to funding for private welfare and health organisations. Demands from the Ministry of Welfare and Health influenced the gradual replacement of volunteers by professionals in many fields of social activity, and the national budget assumed increasing responsibility for the rising financial burden of the plethora of associations and foundations. This period of material prosperity paved the way for national spending on welfare to double during Den Uyl's administration. The increase was especially advantageous to the confessional groups in the Netherlands, given their traditional strength in this sector.

Thus, social progress to catch up with the times facilitated the changes in values and standards that characterised the later periods of the welfare state. The welfare state initiated processes and generated expectations that it was unable to fulfil in the long run. The tragic nature of the welfare state literally resembles a Greek tragedy in which the hero is defeated by the course of events he has instigated: 'The present tragedy of the welfare state specifically entails the absence of any awareness thereof (insight into limitations and finalities). Especially the welfare state's significance as the key to social justice generally promotes social claims based on such entitlements. No internal key exists, however, for honouring claims by groups based on selective criteria. This shortcoming even afflicts claims for justice among different generations. The internal dynamics of consistently justified claims will perpetuate this process. [. . .] The welfare state as a tragic hero, who brings about his own demise through his desire to be the most righteous of all heroes' (Schuyt 1983).

3. 1969-1980: The Growth of Immaterial Desires

After the wage explosion and the concurrent continuing economic growth, the focus gradually shifted from material concerns to immaterial affairs as illustrated in part by the expansion of the welfare sector. The demand for immaterial goods and services – provided free of charge by the government through professional service personnel – appears to follow and to result from consumption of material goods. As these material goods do not lead to true happiness or a meaningful existence, the demand for more has also acquired immaterial overtones. Demand for the paid services of doctors, psychiatrists, therapists, and welfare and community workers coincides with a decreasing need for the unpaid services of pastors and volunteers.

The process of secularisation, which also followed the period of prosperity in the Netherlands, entailed an erosion of traditional pillarisation. Conventional supervisory networks began to lose their influence over the conduct of individual citizens on the path to emancipation. Crises of authority and progressive democratisation sharpened the focus on immaterial concerns, made possible through the material abundance.

In 1968, a wave of democratisation in the Netherlands mirrored the situation in other countries. Democratisation and the collapse of pillarisation caused tremendous social instability. The influence of the old administrative frameworks diminished or disappeared altogether. The younger generation had grown up in a climate defined solely in terms of universal progress. Rising expectations were immediately expressed as desires and were subsequently communicated to the government as demands. These demands were cloaked in the jargon of social justice and the fight against many forms of social inequality. In the long run, however, the professional relief workers who were young and autonomous gained the most from this development.

The government of the welfare state was expected to satisfy the growing immaterial desires (welfare, legal aid, medical assistance, subsidies, contributions to the rent, and the like). This need derived great strength from the change in standards and values that had previously been regulated and supervised by the sectarian network. The parties issuing the demands joined forces in new organisational patterns that were no longer determined by ideological principles but that reflected a strong sentiment of self-interest. These gatherings were strong pressure groups. Emancipated citizens felt liberated from tight constraints, as their new freedom seemed to offer an infinite range of opportunities that had previously hardly been identified as needs. Increasing supervisory responsibilities that had been assumed by other institutions were imposed on the government as a whole. Van Doorn characterised the resulting situation as 'overcharging policy' (Van Doorn 1980).

To summarise the period between 1969 and 1980, the welfare state has already strayed significantly from its moral and material principles of 1945. Unlike the years immediately after the war, the government could no longer rely on the elites to call their supporters to order. On the contrary, a wealth of pressure and action groups demanded a formidable package of rights. By then, real economic growth had slowed considerably, the first oil crisis had taken place, and a widening gulf had emerged between social or presumed desirability and economic opportunity. This situation was diametrically opposed to the early post-war period, when economic opportunities exceeded social desirability.

4. 1981-1995: Administrative Solidarity During Economic Stagnation

The characteristics of this most recent stage in the welfare state include both the fruits of the preceding periods and the ongoing economic stagnation that increasingly eroded employment opportunities. Reversing or transforming the processes initiated during the two previous stages required time. Many relief programmes enjoyed legislative protection, citizens had become more emancipated, and an extensive network had arisen of agencies and services that were run by professional service personnel who had discovered a market demand for welfare and happiness. All statistics concerning professional services for medical care, psychotherapy, legal counsel, and social assistance thrived spectacularly after 1974, when the economic tide had already turned. Health care costs rose at a disconcerting pace until they accounted for ten percent of the national income. The Dutch National Health Service paid 1.2 billion invoices submitted by 5,500 medical specialists, while voluntary insurance companies settled 0.8 billion accounts. Health care was in danger of turning into hospital care. Financially, the provisions were spiralling out of control with respect to the correlation between the pattern of government expenditures and predefined standards and policy objectives. Loss of control would entail autonomous consequences of conduct that nonetheless have a financial impact on the institution concerned. The welfare state had become a state of facilities with costs that were rising beyond reason. While this trend would have attracted a lot of attention as an isolated phenomenon (even during an economic recovery), it was entirely overtaken and overshadowed by the rising unemployment and diminishing job opportunities. Accordingly, the affordability of the welfare state became a serious problem. The principles of the welfare state were intended to soften the consequences of temporary or permanent unemployment, and the welfare state appeared virtually incapable of living up to expectations during this crucial test. The focus returned to the groups that were originally supposed to benefit from the welfare state: the unemployed, the elderly, and young adults unable to find jobs after leaving school.

Nevertheless, concern for the moral and material principles of the original welfare state has been eclipsed by glib criticism of the course of the welfare state during the preceding period. The notion of comprehensive care from cradle to grave primarily resulted from the impression generated by the increase in services, even though these services are not the heaviest financial burden on the state with respect to social security spending.

From public and political perspectives, the term welfare state entailed a mysterious concoction of social security assistance (primarily funded by the active population), health care, education, and other immaterial goods and services financed by the government. All these government provisions are justified on behalf of social justice, despite the vast difference between a co-payment for a serious inevitable and costly operation and tuition at a day-care centre or an institution for higher professional education. In other words, a system of administrative solidarity has emerged that has reduced the basis for solidarity as the moral principle of the welfare state to an administrative norm. Professional service personnel dispassionately uphold this standard by means of assorted highly autonomous and fragmented agencies and services. These individuals have come to rely heavily on this administered relief and assistance (consider daily life in a home for the elderly). The plethora of regulations that barely scratches the surface of the overall existence of dependent persons has added the plurality of dependencies to the plurality of rights and benefits. The exact nature of the group that retains an unconditional need for government assistance is far from clear. Localisation of solidarity is becoming increasingly difficult, as the regulations that help the truly needy or people undergoing crises often also assist individuals with supplemental sources of subsistence or assistance.

The problem of localising solidarity takes on a note of urgency in discussions of the general income policy, which has linked salaries in the public and private sectors. In his contribution to the Vierde Jaarboek voor het democratisch-socialisme, P. J. Vos explains his assertion that 'professionalism and self-interest have dominated the rise of the welfare state' on the basis of the linkage issue. 'These linkages impede adaptation to changing circumstances and new objectives' (1983:5). To illustrate his point, Vos refers to the basic agreement from 1982 in which central organisations of employers and employees agreed to redistribute job opportunities through reduced working hours. Because of the linkage mechanisms, any salary adjustments based on working hours would affect the incomes of people such as the elderly and welfare recipients. Pessimistically, Vos concludes that the automatic linkage 'left so little leeway that formulating new objectives and setting new priorities is no longer worthwhile. Accordingly, organisations such as trade unions and political parties, which are in charge of legitimising the policy-making process and tendering objectives, would fall into disuse (Vos 1983:36). The inability to localise the neediest and the 'weakest [elements] of society' through any means besides administrative categories of anonymous persons is a striking characteristic of this fourth period of the welfare state. This situation may offer a guideline for redefining priorities in the welfare state and an incentive to return to the material and moral principles that inspired the welfare state.

III. Current Problems

The desire for full employment provided an important material and moral basis for establishing the post-war welfare state. Recovery of job opportunities therefore figures near (and perhaps at) the top of list of the welfare state's problems. While no simple formula is available for the best and the fastest means to achieve this recovery, economic factors and trends in the international economy are of great importance. Subjects of disagreement include the measure of responsibility attributable to the size of the welfare state (the total share of the collective sector with respect to the market sector) in bringing about the economic crisis, or at least in blocking the path to recovery.

Discussions about the employment issue are important, as this problem involves several related factors concerning the heart of the welfare state, which include the future of the social security system, the demand for minimal living expenses, the emergence of new and the perpetuation of old poverty, and, finally, the gulf that looms between two social groups, namely the people with and the people without paid employment.

The other main ailments of the present welfare state may be presented as follows:

Current problems of the welfare state:

A. Main problems: job opportunities and the extent of and relief for unemployment

B. Derivative problems:
   - B1: social security system
   - B2: subsistence level and poverty issue
   - B3: gap between people with and without paid employment

C. Additional main problem: equitable distribution of available work

   Derivative problems:
   - C1: equal entitlement of women to paid employment, independence for women
   - C2: reduced working hours and distribution of total available employment
   - C3: work for younger generations and their schooling for the future

D. Implementation problems:
   - D1: the problem arising from administrative solidarity and bureaucratic assistance
   - D2: the manner in which decisions are reached and the legitimacy of collective decision making

Solving all these problems at once is like picking a combination lock. The lock will open only after all digits have been selected in the correct order, which requires a lot of trial and error as well as patience. Because of the current interwoven nature of the problems of the welfare state, resolving the issues in one sector yields very few new perspectives for the other areas. Solutions may also conflict with one another.

Restoring job opportunities may alleviate the financial burden of social security, although these costs will also impede recovery. Furthermore, some consequences of behaviour that were unsuspected and unforeseen at the beginning of the welfare state have become noticeable in and influenced by the social security system. These effects are also slowing the economic recovery. They comprise the drastically reduced desire to save money in the welfare state, the marked decrease in the willingness to take risks (manifested by a lack of interest in independent enterprise), the deterrents from working in the private sector, and the standardisation of assistance operations, which has enabled professional service personnel to determine their duties that receive government funding according to administrative rules. Even the empirically complex relationship between the protection afforded by the welfare state and the functioning of the labour market are part of the interplay between the problems listed. In other words, distinct solutions for distinct, technically manageable problems are not the issue. Rather, a blueprint is needed for a future disposition in which the government upholds the material and moral principles of the welfare state while revitalising the economic order.

What does the enforcement of these principles entail? Does it automatically preclude proposals for reducing benefits? Are cutbacks in the beneficial system of government assistance to promote private care completely out of the question? Can nothing be done about the rise in informal (and occasionally illegal) methods of conduct facilitated in many ways by the welfare state? Is it impossible to subject eligibility for services funded by the government to stricter criteria? This series of questions – which is merely the tip of the iceberg – can easily embarrass supporters of the welfare state. Consistently successful pressure and action groups breathe down the necks of MPs even before official decisions are reached.

The citizens of the welfare state still need to adjust to the drastic economic and social changes. In his inspiring little book *Muddling towards frugality* (1978), Warren Johnson submits that, as inhabitants of the Western world, we take high wages and low prices for energy and commodities for granted, and that we will have to get used to a reversal that will persist for a long time, namely low actual wages and high energy prices and commodity costs. This prospect enables the laborious odyssey to a fruitful – frugal literally means austere as well as fruitful – society. This process also demands a quest for compassion in the welfare state. Along this search, the inevitability of unpleasant measures and tragic decisions between different groups of the population should accompany the perspective of a liveable and humane (and possibly even fruitful) society, despite all the reductions and changes.

In this blueprint, job opportunities are most likely to emerge in the labour-intensive sectors and in the service sector, even if the 'costly labour' from the welfare state ceases to be affordable. Nor will it be possible to maintain the current level of social security in the Netherlands (which is generous and sometimes even excessive compared to neighbouring countries.) The localisation of solidarity in any future social security system will necessarily be preceded by the localisation of responsibility. In the present welfare state, an overstrained transfer of responsibility to the government has culminated in an 'anonymisation' of responsibility.

Responsibilities need to be redefined. I will attempt to localise four types of responsibility.

First comes responsibility for production. The responsibility for the recovery of production therefore precedes the distribution of labour. Appealing to workers for individual contributions may restore that productivity. Improved schooling for future labour and use of everybody's creative potential at work could achieve some revitalisation without abandoning the production objective.

Second comes the responsibility for individual actions. All too often, the present welfare state has taken this form of accountability away from people and has obliterated the connection between choice, payment, and enjoyment. Neither in the case of persons, nor with industrial firms may individual choices that are expensive in many respects simply be passed on to the anonymous state apparatus. Women shall have to assume responsibility for generating and spending income. The costs incurred in the process, however, may be attributed to personal desires and choices. Accordingly, state services may become expensive with regard to these personal choices. A selectively applied direct-benefit principle is an acceptable component in the new-style welfare state.

Third comes a responsibility for allocating the scarce commodities. Aside from the personal obligation to recruit labour, the government retains a proportionately increasing responsibility for the distribution of labour and the corresponding income. Guarantees against income reductions – which will remain necessary – should not eliminate the incentive for personal contributions to an industrious society. Specifically, even if current ideas of a base income become realisable in the future, the level of this income must never diminish the desire to work. Maintaining a considerable gap between such a base income and income earned through work would encourage numerous reductions in working hours after restoring labour productivity. Many people working a wide variety of hours could participate in a production method in which a few hours of work could be combined with a low base income. The system of social security, which has become highly complex, could thus be simplified immensely without permanently disturbing the functioning of the labour market. As a result, the localisation of assistance for an guaranteed income in the welfare state may be simplified: the government will be of assistance only once the individual's primary responsibility has been defined.

Fourth comes the responsibility for solidarity with persons who have landed in desperate circumstances through no fault of their own. This responsibility is easier to localise once the three preceding responsibilities have been applied in practice. Few people will object to this joint responsibility if government assistance is offered in inescapable situations. Of course, a more principled indication of such circumstances is available. Otherwise, protection of interests on a group basis may once again give rise to government assistance according to the demands of the most powerful pressure groups. Formulating basic rights to basic facilities that have yet to be specified might delineate the minimal scope of the common solidarity. The present level of government assistance and the current entitlements to such provisions need not be considered minimum acceptable standards – especially not if we include the basic rights of Third World inhabitants among this minimal common solidarity.

Just as change is not necessarily humiliating, legislative modifications do not intrinsically infringe upon social justice. A social justice theory that has been enhanced and adjusted to reflect experience may remain the moral basis for the welfare state. In *Spheres of Justice* (1983), American philosopher Michael Walzer explains that a single conception of social justice need not govern all social sectors. The market, family life, institutions for education and training, and hospitals are all governed by different concepts of justice. If people lose track of the different measures prevailing in these spheres too quickly – which I believe has already happened in the current welfare state with its administrative solidarity that targets uniformity – concern for social justice will generate contradictory products. Deductibles are not always unreasonable. If medical care is imposed on people against their will, deductibles appear unjust. Elective treatments might, however, entail risks that should indeed be the patient's 'own liability.'

These ideas for recalibrating social justice in the interest of a frugal society preserve the heart of the welfare state. Individual responsibility and accountability for the risks and costs arising from personal modes of conduct in a single social context may coincide with government protection against all risks for which little or no blame is due to the victims. This procedure is more likely to result in a rather defensive formulation of the long-term policy objective for the welfare state than the optimistic and offensive formulations from the 1960s. Especially in retrospect, the open-ended formulation of the state's duties, with a similarly open-ended system of financing, may be considered an unrealistic and probably even a useless goal. I advocate a basic formulation of the heart of the welfare state that is still a far cry from the 'minimal state' depicted by Nozick in his well-known *Anarchy, State and Utopia* (1974).

A frugal society with different spheres of justice will reduce the state's role and will restore individual responsibility for many forms of assistance. The main responsibility shall persist: ensuring that nobody falls below a decent level of subsistence. While decency is a notch below prosperous, may not make people happy, and does not provide protection from all of life's accidents and inconveniences, it will safeguard citizens from humiliation and servitude.

Realisation of these moral and material principles will still require a major social struggle because the interests of forgotten groups are all too frequently overlooked in the course of social reorientation. All the same, these groups are easier to localise in the new style of the welfare state. Such a state deserves our unwavering support.

IV. Concluding Remarks

Should the welfare state be permanently dismantled tomorrow, new groups of citizens and political parties will join forces in creating a type of society that reflects elements of the welfare state by the following day. What might these groups do differently or better? Would they pursue the same paths as the current Dutch welfare state, or would identical moral and material principles produce an entirely different result?

I suspect that this new welfare state would operate according to the same principles because this type of society has generated a historically unique community because of its rather civilised and humane style of coexistence. The freedom inherent in a parliamentary democracy has found a strong ally in the welfare state, despite the many rough edges and imperfections. This harmony does not hold true for many old and competing types of societies.

Even if we were to continue many measures, especially the ones that arose directly after World War II, many problems would still require different solutions. Such settlements would be more austere and would entail more individual responsibility. In addition, construction would proceed noticeably slower, more gradually, and with greater regard for overall economic feasibility in the long run.

This situation would culminate a significantly different idea and realisation of the welfare state, in which the heart – the foundation for a decent and humane existence – would be preserved. Society would regain its vitality, social and individual incentives would correlate more closely with one another, voluntarism (and creativity) would have fresh opportunities, and localisation of solidarity would once again be self-evident.

One certainty remains. We would definitely want to use fewer laws in activating such a welfare state. We should probably give more serious consideration to Spinoza's advice, as quoted in D. J. den Uyl's magnificent *Power, State and Freedom*, an interpretation of Spinoza's political philosophy (1983):

> *Qui omnia legibus determinare vult,*
> *vitia irritabit quam corriget*

He who wishes to determine everything through legislation is far more likely to stimulate than to rectify evil tendencies (Tractatus Theologico-Politicus, Chapter XX).

References

ALBEDA, W.: *The crisis in employment and the welfare state* (in Dutch), Kampen (Kok Publishers) 1994.

JOHNSON, W.: *Muddling through frugality*, San Francisco (Sierra Club Books) 1978.

NOZICK, R.: *Anarchy, State and Utopia*, London (Blackwell) 1983.

SCHUYT, K.: *Between power and morals, the place of law in the welfare state* (in Dutch), Alphen aan de Rijn (Samsom) 1983.

SPINOZA, B. DE: Tractatus Theologico-politicus, in: Opera Qoutquot reperta sunt, tomus secundus, J. van Vloten et J.P.N. Land (Eds.), The Hague (first published in Amsterdam 1670) (M. Nijhoff) 1013.

UYL, D. J. DEN: *Power, State and Freedom, an interpretation of Spinoza's political philosophy*, Assen (Van Gorcum Publ) 1983.

UYL, J.M. DEN: *Insight and outlook* (in Dutch), Amsterdam (Arbeiderspers) 1978.

UYL, J.M. DEN: "Solidarity in the welfare state", *De Volkskrant*, 28.8 (1982).

VAN DOORN, J. A. A.: "The overburdening of policy" (in Dutch), *Beleid en Maatschappij* (Policy and Society) (February 1980).

VOS, P.J.: "Social democracy and the welfare state" (in Dutch), in: *The Fourth Yearbook on Democratic Socialism*, Amsterdam (Arbeiderspers) 1983.

WALZER, M.: *Spheres of Justice*, Oxford (Martin Robertson and Company) 1983.

WINDMULLER, J. P. AND C. DE GALAN: *Labour relations in the Netherlands*, Utrecht (Spectrum) 1957.

WITTERT VAN HOOGLAND, E.B.F.F.: *Parliamentary History of Social security 1890 - 1940* (in Dutch), Two Volumes, Haarlem (Tjeenk Willink) 1940.

Chapter 3

Is the German Welfare State Sustainable?

DIETHER DÖRING

I. Introduction

The term «welfare state» has a broader meaning than a state organising a high level of social security for its citizens. But creating a high level of social security can be seen as the core of welfare state activity.

- The question of sustainability is linked to social values. Goals of social policy and the instruments used to achieve them should comply with the social values dominating in the society.
- The question of sustainability is concerned with the benefit side of the system, which is intended to produce social security in case of health problems, long-term care, old age, invalidity, survivors' case and unemployment. Systems may be more or less successful in achieving defined social security goals.
- The question of sustainability is also related to the financing side. Contributions and taxes imposed are reducing personal incomes and in certain cases may influence competitiveness and employment.

The following remarks are not limited to social insurance but put a focus on it.

II. Some Remarks on the Development of the German Welfare State – Centred on Social Insurance

Comparable to other European countries the genesis of state-organised social security institutions in Germany was triggered by industrialisation and urbanisation, accompanied by a continuous growth of citizens depending on the labour market. In addition to that, the changing family profile increased the need for new social security measures. The traditional Poor Law was never considered a sufficient instrument (H. Peters 1978, F. Tennstedt 1981). Industrial workers' organisations for mutual help gained some importance, in part following the example given by craftsmen and miners already long before industrialisation started. The main purpose was to help in case of sickness, but they were not limited to this. The state, especially the Prussian state, tried already in the middle of the 19th century to stabilise and to extend them; an employers' contribution could be imposed by the towns. Concerning pensions, the earliest steps were taken by the state for life long civil servants and by corporations creating schemes for employees, mostly for white collar workers. Occupational schemes were quite often formed after the state schemes (D. Döring 1994). Within the private sector the different voluntary organisations never reached a general coverage. The highest level was attained by miners' insurance («Knappschaftskassen») with about 80%. They were made compulsory in 1854 (T. Höffner 1956).

The most important step concerning state-organised social insurance was made by the «Bismarckian» legislation in the 1880s, triggered by a positive understanding of needs, but also intended to contribute to pacification of the labour movement (F. Kleeis 1981, D. Zöllner 1981). The Health Insurance Act (1883) used the design of the mutual help organisations and established compulsory insurance. In 1884 followed the Works Accidents Insurance Act with compulsory membership established for employers. In 1889 the Pension Insurance Act passed the Reichstag, mainly centred on social security in case of invalidity; including old age but no survivors pensions. The personal coverage was targeted on blue collar workers, in part also on the «smaller» white collars. Unemployment insurance was not included in the «pack». At that time, unemployment benefits were provided by trade unions (for members only). Sometimes subsidies were paid by towns. Since the first World War the state went into this social security branch, granting at first means-tested benefits. In 1927 the modern organisation was formed, integrating labour administration and unemployment insurance.

Fundamental decisions concerning social insurance were made by state legislation, but the principle of self-administration was taken over from the mutual help organisations and applied in an altered form to the state-organised system. This division of labour in social insurance policy has been kept till today.[1] But there is a long term tendency of centralisation of decision making in state hands. This process went along with an impressive personal and financial expansion of the welfare state in Germany (H. Lampert 1980, M.G. Schmidt 1988). Some data concerning the development of expenditures and financing are given in tables 1 and 2.

III. Some Remarks on the Profile of the Present German Social Security System

The personal profile: The state-organised system in Germany has a categorical orientation; there are different institutions installed for different groups of the population. The core system (social insurance) organises on a compulsory basis the major part of dependent employees. Separate institutions exist for life long civil servants, for farmers and for different professional groups. If we concentrate on full personal membership and the acquisition of individual claims even the addition of the different institutions does not result in a universal coverage of the population?[2] Gainful employment is normally the precondition for personal membership. But even some groups of white and blue collar workers are still outside of the system, for example those employed on a low part-time basis and workers above of a certain income have a ceiling within health insurance. The major part of the self-employed are still not covered by compulsory social insurance. The not gainfully employed are given derived claims if they are family members of an insured person.

1 The self-administration system was eliminated during the National-Socialist regime. It was introduced again by Federal legislation (see H. PETERS: *Die Geschichte der sozialen Versicherung*, St. Augustin 1978, pp. 29ff).

2 The result would be different if any sort of security measures would be taken into account, including derived claims, social assistance (R. HOLZMANN: "Internationaler Vergleich von Alterssicherungssystemen: Konzepte, Strukturen und ökonomische Effekte", in: B. GAHLEN, u.a. (Ed.): *Theorie und Politik der Sozialversicherung*, Tübingen 1990).

Table 1. Social Budget (Expenditure Side)

		According to Functions			
Year	*Total*	*Old age and survivors*	*Health*	*Family*	*Others (incl. employment)*
		% of GNP			
1960	22.8	9.4	6.1	4.7	2.6
1965	25.0	9.9	6.7	5.2	3.2
1970	26.5	10.7	7.8	4.6	3.5
1975	33.9	13.2	10.4	5.0	5.4
1980	32.6	12.8	10.5	4.7	4.6
1985	31.7	12.8	10.4	3.9	4.6
1990 *)	29.5	11.9	10.1	3.6	3.8
1991	31.3	12.1	10.7	4.1	4.5
1992	32.7	12.4	11.2	4.2	4.9
1993p	33.6	12.9	11.2	4.2	5.3
1994p	33.3	13.1	11.2	4.0	5.0

* Till 1989 former Fed. Republic incl. western Berlin; since 1990 (2. half) Germany incl. new Länder.

Source: Bundesministerium für Arbeit und Sozialordnung: Statistisches Taschenbuch 1995, Arbeits- und Sozialstatistik, Bonn 1995, table 7.2

Table 2. Social Budget (Financing Side)

	Contributions			
Year	*Insurance members*	*Employers*	*Subsidies*	*Others*
		% of total revenue		
1960	19.7	31.8	45.8	2.7
1965	19.2	30.1	48.0	2.7
1970	22.1	35.5	39.9	2.5
1975	24.1	34.0	39.2	2.7
1980	24.8	37.3	35.8	2.1
1985	27.2	37.1	33.3	2.4
1990p *)	28.5	37.8	31.2	2.5
1991	28.4	36.9	32.3	2.4
1992	28.5	36.4	32.6	2.5
1993p	28.7	35.4	33.6	2.3
1994p	29.6	35.6	32.7	2.1

* Till 1989 former Fed. Republic incl. western Berlin; since 1990 (2. half) Germany incl. new Länder.

Source: Calculated on basis of Bundesministerium für Arbeit und Sozialordnung: Statistisches Taschenbuch 1995, Arbeits- und Sozialstatistik, Bonn 1995, table 7.3

Profile of the benefit side: Health insurance and the long-term care system is mainly oriented towards covering the cost load in case of risk. Monetary benefits mostly are income (contribution) oriented and in part also given on a time proportional basis.[3] Concerning monetary benefits it should be noted that there is no minimum security regulation within social insurance in Germany. The use of income and time factors for defining benefits, and the absence of a minimum regulation cause a strong inequality of monetary claims. If a certain social insurance benefit is too low to meet the needs of the concerned household, the recipient has to claim income support from social assistance, the means-tested legal scheme for minimum security. But this instrument is considered not very effective in preventing poverty, mainly because there is a considerable segment of «non-take-up» (R. Hauser 1995) especially high with the elderly, meaning that non-claimants in need remain in this position.

The profile of the financing side: The German social security system is mainly financed by contributions on a pay-as-you-go-basis. At the lower end of income contributions start at a certain minimum; at the upper end an income ceiling is applied. In between, contributions are calculated on a gross wage proportional basis. A minor part of social security expenditures is financed by state subsidy. The pensions for life term civil servants and the social assistance scheme are financed by the state budget alone. Total social security expenditure in 1992 was 27.3% of GNP (former Federal Republic only).[4] This represents a 1.,1% decrease compared with 1980. The actual figure is very near to the EU average, comprising also comparably less developed European countries.

A widespread critique in Germany is directed at the extent of financing of the present social insurance by contributions. Contributions are in part also used to finance expenditures, not covered by the insurance principle, for example labour market policy and a major part of social transfers to the new

3 This is quite obvious in the case of the pension insurance; within the unemployment insurance the time factor defines the duration of the period the benefit is paid; within workmans compensation mainly income proportional monetary benefits are given.

4 The figure for Germany including the new Länder is 32.7%; Bundesministerium für Arbeit und Sozialordnung, Statistisches Taschenbuch 1995, Bonn 1995, table 7.2; this of course reflects a somewhat exceptional historical period with massive transfer payments to the new Länder; but even this figure is not higher than in the middle of 70s.

Länder. These elements of financing by contributions not justified are topping up labour costs in Germany and therefore reducing employment chances on the labour market.

The key decisions, forming the present system were taken in the 50s and 60s by Federal social policy. Living standard security was declared the dominant goal of social insurance policy.[5] By several reform acts[6] the former German social insurance system was changed from a static to a dynamic orientation, the average monetary benefit level was largely increased (most impressively in the pension system), but on the other hand regulations for basic and minimum pensions and other regulations helping employees with low wages and short contribution biographies were eliminated (especially within unemployment compensation). German social insurance (except health insurance) was oriented more on actuarial equivalence. The task of securing a minimum was delegated almost entirely to social assistance.

Within the debate concerning the «great social reform», which took place from 1953-56, (H.G. Hockerts 1980, F.N. Ullmeier, F. Rüb 1993, D. Döring 1995) the normative basis of the dominant political faction showed up clearly: leading idea was the formation of a society, where the economic status should be mainly decided by individual economic effort, giving the market

---

5 Originally the goal of German social insurance legislation was more directed on moderating the dependency of elderly, incapable and unemployed workers on poor law and reducing poor law expenditures (see also KOSLOWSKI in this volume); ex. invalidity pension (which included, at that time elderly no longer able to take over gainful employment) gave a basic amount of about 70% of average poor law payment in bigger towns, assuming that recipients could live on it in rural areas; the basic amount was topped up by a contribution-related additional pension (D. DÖRING: "Grundsicherungs-/Grundbetragselemente in der Gründungsgesetzgebung der Rentenversicherung," *Sozialer Fortschritt* 36/7, pp. 153-157); the first design of the Pension Act 1889 even intended to introduce a uniform pension; the original unemployment Insurance Act 1927 gave high replacement rates to low wage earners, low rates to high wage earners; family additions were uniform per dependent member (D. DÖRING/R. HAUSER (Ed.): *Politische Kultur und Sozialpolitik. Ein Vergleich der Vereinigten Staaten und der Bundesrepublik Deutschland unter besonderer Berücksichtigung des Armutsproblems*, Frankfurt a.M 1989).

6 Most important: Pension Reform Act 1956/57, Social Assistance Act 1961, Amendment of Occupational Injuries Act 1964, Employment Promotion Act 1969 (P. FLORA: *Growth to Limits, The Western European Welfare States Since World War II;* Volume 2: Germany, United Kingdom, Ireland, Italy, Berlin 1986).

the power of setting the standards.[7] Within social insurance the corresponding idea was «contributive justice» («Beitragsgerechtigkeit»), which meant a decisive role of the principle of actuarial equivalence (in practice only applied to monetary systems). Beside the normative basis there were pragmatic economic policy aspects. Mainly the expectation, a sharper differentiation of monetary benefits according to individual income and contribution biography, would produce additional incentives for economic effort.

Its important to note that the reform took place in a bright economic setting; the Federal Republic had a quite continuous economic and employment growth. Full employment was reached in the second half of the 50s and persisted until 1973/74. Almost every capable adult member of society had a realistic chance to secure their means (or at least the lion's share of it) by gainful employment.[8] The expectation was that the need for income support from social assistance would decrease continuously, in the long term leaving a few «problematic» cases.

The combination of the installed social security system with full employment policy (and a collective bargaining system securing minimum conditions for workers) represented the core elements of the former Federal Republic as a «social state» («Sozialstaat»). These elements can be seen as an important means of the newly constituted partial state Federal Republic to win the loyalty of its citizen. The rivalry between different economic and political systems on German ground enforced the striving for a more generous social system (D. Döring & R. Hauser 1995).

The unemployment problems we have experienced since 1973/74 have changed the situation significantly: with a large segment of citizens not able to reach employment, the number of claimants for income support from social assistance has risen almost continuously; it reached 3.9 million in 1993 (H. Niedrig 1995). The change in the economic setting and the dynamics of citizens in need have triggered a wave of criticism and of proposals for social security reform. Although different, these proposals mostly tried to make the core system more «poverty resistant», taking into account the condition of persistent unemployment. On the other hand, we have to register

7 That means inequality of economic status is justified if defined by economic effort; but of course this orientation included a certain minimum guaranty, if a citizen was not able to gain an income sufficient for household needs.

8 There was a clear commitment to an assertive full employment policy by «Stability Act» of 1967 and «Employment Promotion Act» of 1969.

the evolution of a more «dogmatic» attitude concerning the insurance principle and the principle of income-orientation, demanding a «purification» of social insurance according to the leading principles. This attitude has been the more influential within German politics in the last decade [9] and has prevented reforms introducing minimum regulations into social insurance.

Another characteristic of the German concept since the 50s is a dominant role of the state and a reduced role of non-state activity in social security.[10] In Germany, social policy since the 50s has oriented the state-organised system toward producing the major part of living standard security. That means, commitment mainly on a field which is the playing ground of non-state activity too. Putting efforts together, state and non-state activity have contributed to a high effectiveness of living standard security especially with middle and higher incomes. On the other hand, the task of poverty prevention obviously cannot be delegated to non-state (personal, occupational) activity purely because of the necessity of income redistribution. But the role of state social policy is restricted to the case of need, if individual efforts have failed.

There is a clear contradiction between the German – popular «Bismarckian» – orientation and the classical «Beveridgean» conception of «division of labour» in social security policy: the German conception is putting state (mainly social insurance) and non-state-activity into a more additive position in producing living standard security. The task of rendering minimum security is delegated to a means-tested scheme outside of social insurance. The «Beveridgean» conception makes minimum security (poverty prevention oriented on the average case) purely the task of state policy, with living standard security delegated entirely to non-state activity. Social assistance remains important for covering needs exceeding the general minimum (some distinctive features of the two types are explained by tables 3 and 4).

---

9 An interesting example is given by the German unification process and the subsequent decisions within social policy (see W. SCHMÄHL (Ed.): *The Future of Basic and Supplementary Pension Schemes in the European Community – 1992 and beyond*, Baden-Baden 1991).

10 A widespread interpretation of this change is related to the German experience with economic consequences of wars (see P. KOSLOWSKI in this volume).

Table 3. Conceptions of Social Security

Type	*Dominant goal*	*Core instrument*	*Membership*	*Derived claims*	*Benefit*	*Core financing*	*Role of social assistance*	*Role of non-state activity*
"Beveridgean"	poverty prevention	social insurance	universal	-	national (general) minimum	contributions (not related to income)	reduced to secure indiv. needs not covered by nat. minimum (plus additional incomes)	task for acquiring living standard security (above national minimum)
"Bismarckian"	living standard security	social insurance	categorial (employees)	family members (not gainfully employed)	equivalent to income-related contribution	contributions (related to income)	securing indiv. needs not covered by income (contribution) - related benefits (plus additional incomes)	improving living standard security

Table 4. Roles in Different Conceptions of Social Security (Tendencies)

Activity Centered on		*"Bismarckian"*	*"Beveridgean"*
Poverty prevention (minimum guarantee)	Dominant instrument	Non-state*	State (social insurance oriented on national minimum)
	"Second role"	State (means-tested scheme)	State (means-tested scheme)
Living standard security	Dominant instrument	State (income-oriented social insurance)	Non-state*
	"Second role"	Non-state*	

* Private effort (occupational, personal)

IV. Problems of Future Development

1. Ageing of the Population

This is a well known perspective. Even with a certain amount of immigration taken into account, there will be a significant decrease of the total population in Germany. A decrease of about 10 million inhabitants till the year 2030 is expected (Deutscher Bundestag 1994). Within this shrinking population there will be a shift of the ratio of the population of working age to the elderly, mainly due to low birth rates since the late 60s. Calculations show the possibility of a doubling of this ratio till the year 2030. This may be changed by developments in life expectancy, by changing birth rates and – obviously – by migration, but the trend in the age structure should be taken seriously.

The consequences for the social security system (especially pension insurance) cannot be identified easily. One important reason is found in the uncertainties of employment development: persons of working age are becoming contributors within our categorical system only if they reach dependent employment (not because they reach a certain age). Another important reason is found in the uncertainty of the future average retirement age. This is influenced by state legislation,[11] but also by the future employment conditions: in cases of high employment, workers tend to postpone retirement; in cases of low employment there is a reverse trend, due to dismissals and small chances of finding employment at a higher working age.

Looking more precisely to financing, the ratio 'contributors to beneficiaries' is not sufficient to calculate the contribution load. Additionally it is necessary to know the ratio between the average level of contribution and the average level of benefit. But, despite these necessary differentiations concerning the effects of the age trend, it should be recognised that presumably there will be significant problems financing the system if the employment development will be not decisively positive (see results of different calculations in Deutscher Bundestag 1994, VDR 1995). The main impact of these problems will be on the pension system and further impacts can be expected on health and long-term care insurance.

11 The Pension Reform Act 1992 tried to postpone retirement starting in the year 2001.

2. Immigration

Germany has in fact become an immigration country.[12] Although the administration has enacted stricter controls, the present situation is likely to persist, above all because the immigration pressure will not diminish. Some reasons (I. Hauchler 1993) are economic inequalities between Germany (Western Europe) on the one hand, and the Third World and the former Soviet Bloc countries on the other hand. There are massive differences in age structure between different countries (ageing European societies and «young» populations of the Third World). Add to this the escalation of conflicts since the break-down of the old political world order. In addition to that, it should be recognised that as a consequence of European integration, an effective immigration policy is no longer decided upon by national policy alone. Within the European Union mobility is guaranteed.

Concerning the future population age structure, immigration can have a moderating effect, if immigrants have a decisively «younger» age structure. But it should be kept in mind that a positive effect concerning the financing of social insurance shows up only, if immigration leads to an increasing volume of employment (D. Döring & R. Hauser 1995). This, again, depends on the condition of the labour market and requires additionally strong efforts to qualify immigrants for labour market demands.

On the other hand, immigration can lead to additional poverty problems in the future, if a large number of immigrants cannot be integrated into employment (which means that they do not acquire claims within social insurance) or if they are too old already to acquire sufficient pension claims for old age, even if they reach employment. This is a consequence of the insurance principle. But of course this will not lead to poverty problems if these immigrants of working age bring with them sufficient pension claims to cover «missing» years.[13]

12 From 1962 -1993 there were 2.6 million ethnic Germans evacuated from Eastern Europe to the Federal Republic; 1961 -1993 20 million foreigners immigrated, 15 million emigrated again (STATISTISCHES BUNDESAMT (Ed.): *Datenreport*, Wiesbaden 1994, p. 21); an increasing segment of immigrants is coming from countries outside of the European Union.

13 The legal preconditions securing mobility of claims are well developed within the European Union, mostly with other countries by agreement. But many immigrants from outside the Union may come from countries without or with very limited social security systems, incomes and benefits may have been very low - from German/European perspective.

3. Changes in the Labour Market

Currently, the unemployment problem dominates our thinking concerning the impact of labour market conditions on social security. Unemployment leads to additional expenditures (unemployment benefits, early retirement) and social assistance and has a negative effect on financing the social security system. In addition to that three tendencies of change on the labour market are highly important for the social security system in a long term perspective:

- The reduction of the period of working life. The main cause of this is the long-term prolongation of general and professional education. An additional element is the reduction of the retirement age, due to former pension legislation and the lack of full employment.
- An increasing importance is winning part-time employment. There is a growing segment (mainly women) in part-time employment. But there are also shifts from full-time employment to part-time.
- The «renaissance» of self-employment. There is a certain segment of «new» self-employed due to a lack of possibilities to find dependent employment. But there is also a segment which has resulted from a shift of white and blue collar work places to a self-employment basis.

Some effects on the social security system, particularly social insurance:

- Claims are not reduced in health care and long-term care in case of a shortened working period. Within the pension insurance, shorter periods of working life lead to lower individual monetary claims. Claims are reduced on a time proportional basis. This reflects the shorter contribution period in case employment starts later or contribution payment to pension insurance ends earlier because of retirement. But if the retirement age is lowered, the reduction of the monetary claim does not take into account the prolonged period of benefit payment.[14] There is an additional financial problem produced by different time dimensions (concerning pensions and other monetary benefits): reductions of contributory periods and reductions of benefit levels do not occur at the same time. There are different time-lags for different monetary benefits compared with the individual contributory period. That means that the ratio 'contributors to beneficiaries' may be wors-

14 No reduction according to the actuarial equivalence principle.

ened by a continuous trend to shorter working life periods within the economy.

- An increasing volume of part-time employment may have a positive effect if it is topping up the existing segment of full-time employment. It leads to additional contributors and to more individual claims within the system. The potential of derived claims is reduced, especially for women.

  But if a sizeable segment of full-time employed is reduced to part-time, problems may occur. The level of contributions is reduced proportionally to the gross wage. On the other hand claims for health care and long-term care are not reduced. Individual monetary claims are reduced mostly on a proportional basis. Again, there is a certain time lag between the reduction of contribution and the reduction of the acquired benefit. Its duration depends on the concerned risk. In some cases a change from full-time to part-time employment may cause social security problems for the concerned groups in case of risk – especially poverty problems – if no additional social security measures are taken.

- Self employment is mostly resulting in non-membership in social insurance. If dependent employment is changed to a self-employed status, it mostly leaves compulsory social insurance: there is no contribution paid and – in pension insurance – no further claims acquired (may be on a voluntary basis). Problems financing the system may occur, if there is a massive erosion of the volume of dependent employment. The reductive effects on the benefit side occur with a certain time lag, depending on the concerned risk. Whether problems in social security with these groups will occur depends on the collective or individual social security measures taken by these self-employed groups.

4. Changing Families

In a historical perspective we have experienced already a vigorous change in the family profile. Marriage is postponed, there are more divorces, there is a large segment of non-married couples (although marriage is still the dominant form of living together) and the number of children has decreased. From 1900-1992, the average number of individuals within a household shrank from 4.5 to 2.2. About 2/3 of the households are membered only by one or two individuals. The figure for women and men living alone is growing and is presently about 1/3 of the households (Statistisches Bundesamt 1994).

The condition of the family is very important for social policy because it constitutes a pillar of social security. Families are rendering education and care. Certain poverty risks are diminished if individuals are living together: this is quite obvious with elderly married women in Germany, the vast majority of whom could not live on their personally-acquired pension claims. In these respects, the above described changes lead to a decreasing capacity of families (households) to produce social security. In addition, certain social security claims are not acquired if men and women living together do not choose the married status. This is especially important for partners not gainfully employed. Families (households) educating several children are afflicted by higher poverty risks, due to insufficient state support. Growing instability leading to more break-ups of partnerships increases poverty risks for children.

On the other hand, changes in the family have increased the number of women seeking gainful employment. This is a positive development for social security and has led to additional contributors to social insurance and increases in the range of personally-acquired claims. But it should be noted that within social insurance this does not necessarily produce sufficient monetary claims (sufficient for poverty prevention). On the other hand, gainful employment leads to a shrinking capacity within families (households) to take over care of family members; this again increases the need for collective compensation.

5. Changing Values

To describe structural changes within society and changing social values, the catchword «individualisation» is used in Germany. Concerning values, a tendency is described that goes from orientations related to community, work, discipline to a more individualistic, hedonistic orientation. Studies demonstrate that although values are changing, they are not revolutionised (U. Beck 1986, W. Zapf 1987, Ch. Brinkmann 1984, I. Ostner 1995, Statistisches Bundesamt 1994). But even from a more sceptical viewpoint it cannot be denied that there is at least an increasing preference in society for individual independence and self-determination.

Some speculation about the possible impact on social security is that there will be an even stronger preference for the insurance principle as a leading idea of social insurance policy. On the other hand, reservations against the method of giving derived claims based on marriage status will increase. Reservations can be expected from the side of the beneficiary and from the contributors side. Presumably in a long-term perspective there will be an increasing preference for a fully individualised social insurance system, including even the not gainfully employed.[15]

6. Perspectives of the European Integration

European welfare states follow different leading ideas, use different instruments, and related to them different methods of financing. Today there is a consensus between the European administrations that the core of social security policy should remain in the hands of the national states. But European social policy made in the past already has affected one important amendment of social security regulations within the different national systems, i.e. securing claims of migrant workers within the Community.

Potential effects on the social security systems within the process of European integration may be triggered by migration and by intensified economic competition within the Common Market. Both factors could lead to a certain pressure on high levels of social security benefits' respective expenditures:

- Certain regulations could produce incentives for migration, especially if attractive social security claims are given for short residence or contribution periods.[16]
- They could cause problems for competitiveness, especially if the financing of a certain social security system tops up large production costs.

15 State-organized social security with universal coverage does exist in some European countries, e.g. the Netherlands, Denmark (see EUROPÄISCHE KOMMISSION: *Soziale Sicherheit in den Mitgliedstaaten der Europäischen Union*, Luxemburg 1995).

16 There are massive differences in this respect; see results of model calculations in D. DÖRING: "Zur Alterssicherung von Zuwanderern in den Ländern der Europäischen Union", *Discussion Paper* 27, Frankfurt a.M. 1994.

Some remarks concerning recent developments:

- The migration dynamics within the community has clearly become weaker since the 80s, probably a consequence of economic development which made living conditions within the member states somewhat more equal (H. Werner 1994, OECD 1994).
- Levels of social security expenditures are becoming less different, but mainly because of a major growth in the member countries with lower levels (for example Greece, Portugal, Italy, Spain), not because of a massive decrease in the countries with a long tradition of high expenditures (for example Germany, France, the Netherlands, Denmark, Luxembourg, Belgium (Institut der Deutschen Wirtschaft 1995). This trend clearly contradicts a widespread fear that the Common Market would lead to a process of «social dumping». The trend described will probably persist in the next years; one reason can be found in the present benefit formulae of the «younger» pension systems of the southern countries producing very high relative benefit levels in the long run (D. Döring & R. Hauser 1995).
- With respect to competitiveness and employment the performance of the German economy is not too bad: Recent developments cannot be understood fully if the focus is on unemployment statistics only. The data from 1982-1994 concerning employment show a considerable increase. On the other hand, there is an even stronger increase in the number of individuals looking for gainful employment, due to immigration and a stronger tendency of women to enter the labour market. Looking to labour costs and productivity: in a long term perspective (the last 25 years) the unit labour costs («Lohnstückkosten») show a very moderate increase in Germany, compared with its main trading partners. In 1994, productivity rose by 13.5%, and unit related labour costs went down by 6.4% (C.F. Hofmann 1995). But rising exchange rates eliminated the positive effects of increased productivity (OECD 1995, Deutsches Institut für Wirtschaftsforschung 1995).

Table 5. Presumable Impacts of Selected Trends on the German Social Security System

Sector / *Trend*	*Labour market (unemployment insurance)*	*Old age pensions system (pension insurance)*	*Health care (health insurance)*	*Long term care (insurance)*	*Social assistance*
Ageing population	L	B	B	(B)	B
Immigration from EU and non-EU countries	B	(L)	B	-	B
Reduction of working period	L	B	(B)	(B)	B
Family Change	B	L	(L)	B	B
Accelerated economic change by European integration (impact on ec. growth excluded)	B	B	-	-	B

L = Decreasing burden/demand
B = Increasing burden/demand

Source: Supplemented version of Döring/Hauser 1993

V. Some Elements of Future Reform Strengthening Sustainability

- Social reform should include assertive action to strengthen employment. Besides state employment promotion and work-time policy of unions and employers, social policy should contribute to employment in the labour market through reasonable steps to moderate labour costs by finance reform. This includes at least a shift in financing non-insurance-related expenditures to the state budget.
- Social reform should tend to strengthen prevention of risks. This includes more health education in schools, more effective environmental efforts, more occupational health activities, more rehabilitation efforts concerning long-term care.
- Social reform should tend to broaden the range of compulsory social insurance by including at least all forms of gainful employment to prevent erosion of the contributory basis.[17]
- Social reform should tend to replace marriage centred elements (-derived claims) in the long run by individualisation of the contributory and benefit sides. Substituting derived claims by individual insurance claims means an extension of compulsory insurance even to those groups not gainfully employed who are mostly unable to finance contributions individually. Respective obligations of the household, the insurance membership and the state should be discussed.[18]
- Social reform should better take into account the individual capacity to acquire social security by non-state activity. Because of the effectiveness of non-state (occupational, individual) activity in creating living standard security, state policy should be more centred on (but not limited to) effective poverty prevention. If benefit cuts under

17 It should be noted that a major part of social insurance systems in the Union does include compulsory insurance for the self-employed.

18 The most discussed model centred on buiding up individual claims for not gainfully employed family members is proposed by G. ROLF/G. WAGNER: "Altersvorsorge und Vereinbarkeit von Kind und Beruf", in: G. BÄCKER/B. STOLZ-WILLIG, (Eds.): *Kind, Beruf und soziale Sicherung: Zukunftsaufgaben des Sozialstaats*, Köln 1994, pp. 289-316.

financial strain cannot be avoided within the present system they should pay attention to the vulnerability of the concerned groups.

- Social reform should tend to strengthen the conditions of members of society educating children.[19] In part this should be financed by reduction of purely marriage-related tax benefits. Raising demogrants to a level at least equal to social assistance minimum would sharply reduce poverty risks (following social assistance criteria) among children and would be a means acceptable from the family policy point of view to strengthen work incentives («Lohnabstandsgebot»).

References

BÄCKER, G.: "Der Sozialstaat - ein Auslaufmodell? Die Krise der Sozialpolitik als politische Krise", *WSI Mitteilungen*, 6/1995, 48. Jg., Düsseldorf (1995), pp. 345-358.

BALDWIN, P.: *The Politics of Social Solidarity*, Cambridge (Cambridge University Press) 1990.

BECK, U.: *Risikogesellschaft. Auf dem Weg in eine andere Moderne*, Frankfurt a.M. (Suhrkamp) 1986.

BECK, U.: *Gegengifte. Die organisierte Unverantwortlichkeit*, Frankfurt a.M. (Suhrkamp) 1988.

BEYER, J.: "Betriebliche Altersversorgung: Insgesamt rückläufige Tendenz", *Bundesarbeitsblatt*, Heft 1 1994, pp. 26-29.

BORCHERT, J.: *Renten vor dem Absturz. Ist der Sozialstaat am Ende?*, Frankfurt a.M. (Fischer) 1993.

BRINKMANN, CH.: "Die individuellen Folgen langfristiger Arbeitslosigkeit. Ergebnisse einer repräsentativen Längsschnittuntersuchung", *Materialien aus der Arbeitsmarkt- und Berufsforschung* 8 (1984), pp. 454-473.

BRINKMANN, CH.: "Finanzielle und psychosoziale Folgen der Arbeitslosigkeit", *Materialien aus der Arbeitsmarkt- und Berufsforschung* 8 (1986).

BUNDESMINISTERIUM FÜR ARBEIT UND SOZIALORDNUNG (Ed.): *Alterssicherung in Deutschland 1986*, zusammenfassender Bericht, Bonn 1992.

19 School reforms strengthening employment chances of parents, family benefit reform, reform of work-time regulations.

BUNDESMINISTERIUM FÜR ARBEIT UND SOZIALORDNUNG (Ed.): *Entwicklung der Alterssicherung in Deutschland 1986-1989*, Fortschreibung der ASID 86 in den Jahren 1987 und 1989, Bonn 1992.

BUNDESMINISTERIUM FÜR ARBEIT UND SOZIALORDNUNG (Ed.): *Alterssicherung in Deutschland 1992* (ASID 92). Vol. I: Strukturdaten zur Einkommenssituation von Personen und Ehepaaren ab 55 Jahren, Bonn 1994.

DETTLING, W. (ED.): *Perspektiven für Deutschland*, München (Knaur) 1993.

DEUTSCHER BUNDESTAG: "Zwischenbericht der Enquête-Kommission Demographischer Wandel – Herausforderungen unserer älter werdenden Gesellschaft an den einzelnen und die Politik", *Drucksache* 12/7878, Bonn 1994.

DEUTSCHES INSTITUT FÜR WIRTSCHAFTSFORSCHUNG: "Hat Westdeutschland ein Standortproblem? ", *Wochenbericht* 38 (1995).

DINKEL, R.H./LEBOK, U.: "Könnten durch Zuwanderung die Alterung der Bevölkerung und die daraus resultierende Zusatzlasten der Sozialen Sicherung aufgehalten oder gemildert werden?", *Deutsche Rentenversicherung* 6 (1993), pp. 388-400.

DÖRING, D.: "Grundsicherungs-/Grundbetragselemente in der Gründungsgesetzgebung der Rentenversicherung", *Sozialer Fortschritt* 7 (1987), pp. 153-157.

—— "Zur Alterssicherung von Zuwanderern in den Ländern der Europäischen Union", *ASEG Project Discussion Paper* No. 27 (1994).

—— "Die betriebliche Altersversorgung in der privaten Wirtschaft", in: *Forum für Philosophie Bad Homburg Haupt* (Ed.), Bern (Markt und Moral) 1994, pp. 291-308.

—— "Complementary Social Insurances, Report on Germany", in: COUSY, H., FONTAINE, M., VAN BUGGENHOUT, B., VAN STEENBERGE, J. (Eds.): *Complementary Social Insurances an International Perspective: New Developments and Challenges*, Brugge (Keure) 1994, pp. 59-84.

DÖRING, D.: "Anmerkungen zum Gerechtigkeitssbegriff der Sozialpolitik mit besonderer Berücksichtigung liberaler Vorstellungen zur Sozialversicherungspolitik", in: DÖRING, D. u.a., *Gerechtigkeit im Wohlfahrtstaat*, Marburg (Schüren) 1995.

DÖRING, D./HAUSER, R. (Ed.): *Politische Kultur und Sozialpolitik. Ein Vergleich der Vereinigten Staaten und der Bundesrepublik Deutschland unter besonderer Berücksichtigung des Armutsproblems*, Frankfurt a.M (Campus) 1989.

—— *Soziale Sicherheit in Gefahr. Zur Zukunft der Sozialpolitik*, Frankfurt a.M. (Suhrkamp) 1995.

—— "Some preliminary results of the ASEG-Project on 'Social protection of the elderly in the European Union'", *ASEG Project Discussion Paper* No. 27, Frankfurt a.M 1995.

DÖRING, D./HAUSER, R./TIBITANZL, F.: "Zur Alterssicherung vom Frauen in sechs Ländern der EG", *Sozialer Fortschritt* 6-7 (1993), pp. 142-146.

DÖRING, D., NULLMEIER, F., PIOCH, R. AND VOBRUBA, G.: *Gerechtigkeit im Wohlfahrtsstaat*, Marburg (Schüren) 1995.

EUROPÄISCHE KOMMISSION: *Soziale Sicherheit in den Mitgliedstaaten der Europäischen Union*, Luxemburg 1995.

FLORA, P.: *Growth to Limits, The Western European Welfare States Since World War II;* Vol. 2: Germany, United Kingdom, Ireland, Italy, Berlin (de Gruyter) 1986.

GAHLEN, B., HESSE, H., RAMSER, H.J. (Eds.): *Theorie und Politik der Sozialversicherung*, Tübingen (Mohr) 1990.

HAUCHLER, I. (Ed.): *Globale Trends 93/94, Daten zur Weltentwicklung*, Frankfurt a.M. (Fischer) 1993.

HAUSER, R. "Strategien einer kohärenten Einwanderungspolitik", in: DÖRING, D. and HAUSER, R. (Eds.): *Soziale Sicherheit in Gefahr*, Frankfurt a.M. (Suhrkamp) 1994.

— (1995a): "Stand und Entwicklungstendenzen der Annäherung der sozialen Sicherung in der Europäischen Union: Das Beispiel Alterssicherung", *Discussion Paper* No. 33 ASEG-Projekt, Frankfurt a.M. 1995.

— (1995b): "Sozialpolitische Optionen in der Europäischen Union", in: *Jahrbuch Arbeit und Technik, Zukunft des Sozialstaates*, Bonn (Dietz) 1995.

— (1995c): "Armut und Zuwanderung in die Europäische Union", in: DÖRING, D. and HAUSER, R. (Eds.): *Soziale Sicherheit in Gefahr*, Frankfurt a.M. (Suhrkamp) 1995.

HILLS, J., DITCH, J. and GLENNERSTER, H.: *Beveridge and social security, An International Retrospective*, Oxford (Oxford University Press) 1994.

HOCKERTS, H.G.: *Sozialpolitische Entscheidungen im Nachkriegsdeutschland. Alliierte und deutsche Sozialversicherungspolitik 1945-1957*, Stuttgart (Klett-Cott) 1980.

HÖFFNER, J.: *Sozialpolitik im Deutschen Bergbau*, Münster 1956 (= Schriften des Instituts für christliche Sozialwissenschaften an der Westfälischen Wilhelms-Universität Münster).

HOFMANN, C.F.: "Soziale Sicherung, Weiterhin arbeitsorientiert", *Bundesarbeitsblatt* 7-8 (1995), pp. 5-8.

HOLZMANN, R.: "Internationaler Vergleich von Alterssicherungssystemen: Konzepte, Strukturen und ökonomische Effekte", in: GAHLEN, B. u.a. (Ed.): *Theorie und Politik der Sozialversicherung*, Tübingen (Mohr) 1990.

INSTITUT DER DEUTSCHEN WIRTSCHAFT: *Internationale Wirtschaftszahlen* 1995, Köln 1995.

INTERNATIONAL LABOUR OFFICE: *From pyramid to pillar, Population change and social security in Europe*, Geneva 1989.

KLAUDER, W.: "Zukunft der Arbeit", *Gewerkschaftliche Monatshefte*, 12 (1994), pp. 764-7.

KLEEIS, F.: *Die Geschichte der sozialen Versicherung in Deutschland*, Berlin (Dietz) 1981.

LAMPERT, H.: *Sozialpolitik*, Berlin/Heidelberg/New York (Springer) 1980.

NIEDRIG, H.: "5 Millionen Sozialhilfeempfänger", *Theorie und Praxis der sozialen Arbeit*, 8 (1995), pp. 290-95.

NULLMEIER, F./RÜB, F.: *Die Transformation der Sozialpolitik. Vom Sozialstaat zum Sicherungsstaat*, Frankfurt a.M. (Campus) 1993.

OECD: "Trends in international Migration", *Annual Report* 1993, Paris 1994.

OECD: "Wirtschaftsberichte 1994-1995", Deutschland, Paris 1995.

OSTNER, I.: "Wandel der Familienformen und soziale Sicherung der Frau", in: DÖRING, D. and HAUSER, R. (Eds.): *Soziale Sicherheit in Gefahr*, Frankfurt a.M. (Suhrkamp) 1995.

PACOLET, J./VERSIECK, K./BOUTEN, R.: *Social protection for dependency in old age*, Leuven (Hoger Instituut voor de Arbeid) 1994.

PETERS. H.: *Die Geschichte der sozialen Versicherung*, (Asgard) St. Augustin 1978.

PIOCH, R./VOBRUBA, G.: "Gerechtigkeitsvorstellungen im Wohlfahrtsstaat", in: Döring, D. u.a. (Ed.), *Gerechtigkeit im Wohlfahrtsstaat*, Marburg (Schüren) 1995.

PLOUG, N./KVIST, J.: *Recent Trends in Cash Benefits in Europe*, Copenhagen (Danish Institute of Social Research) 1994.

RISCHE, H.: "Rentenversicherung ohne Zukunft? Anmerkungen zur Diskussion um die langfristige Entwicklung der Rentenversicherung", *Die Angestelltenversicherung*, 1 (1994), pp. 1-7.

RISCHE, H.: "Internationalisierung von Wirtschaft und Politik und Handlungsspielräume einer nationalen Sozialpolitik", *Die Angestelltenversicherung*, 1 (1995), pp. 1-7.

ROLF, G.: "Alterssicherung in Deutschland", *Discussion Paper* No. 17 ASEG-Projekt, Frankfurt a.M. 1995.

ROLF, G./WAGNER, G.: "Altersvorsorge und Vereinbarkeit von Kind und Beruf", in: BÄCKER, G. and STOLZ-WILLIG, B. (Eds.): *Kind, Beruf und soziale Sicherung: Zukunftsaufgaben des Sozialstaats*, Köln (Bund) 1994.

ROLF, G./SPAHN, P.B./WAGNER, G. (Eds.): *Sozialvertrag und Sicherung. Zur ökonomischen Theorie staatlicher Versicherungs- und Umverteilungssysteme*, Frankfurt a.M./New York (Campus) 1988.

SCHMÄHL, W.: "Zur Bedeutung des Versicherungsgedankens für die weitere Entwicklung der gesetzlichen Rentenversicherung", in: SCHMÄHL, W. (Ed.) *Versicherungsprinzip und soziale Sicherung*, Tübingen (Mohr) 1985, pp. 204-234.

SCHMÄHL, W. (Ed.): *The Future of Basic and Supplementary Pension Schemes in the European Community - 1992 and beyond*, Baden-Baden (Nomos) 1991.

— "Perspektiven der Alterssicherung in Deutschland", *Wirtschaftsdienst* 10 (1994), pp. 507-514.

— "Strategien und Maßnahmen künftiger Alterssicherungspolitik in Deutschland", *Wirtschaftsdienst* 8 (1994), pp. 390-395.

— "Familienorientierte Weiterentwicklung der staatlichen Alterssicherung in Deutschland", Zentrum für Sozialpolitik, *Working Paper* 4, Bremen 1994.

SCHMIDT, M.G.: *Sozialpolitik. Historische Entwicklung und internationaler Vergleich*, Opladen (Leske u. Budrich) 1988.

STATISTISCHES BUNDESAMT (Ed.): Datenreport, Wiesbaden 1994.

TENNSTEDT, F.: *Sozialgeschichte der Sozialpolitik in Deutschland. Vom 18. Jahrhundert bis zum Ersten Weltkrieg*, Göttingen (Vandenhock u. Ruprecht) 1981.

TRANSFER-ENQUETE-KOMMISSION: *Das Transfersystem in der Bundesrepublik Deutschland. Bericht der Sachverständigenkommission zur Ermittlung des Einflusses staatlicher Transfereinkommen auf das verfügbare Einkommen der privaten Haushalte*, Stuttgart 1981.

VERBAND DEUTSCHER RENTENVERSICHERUNGSTRÄGER: *Rentenversicherung in Zahlen*, Frankfurt a.M. 1994.

VERBAND DEUTSCHER RENTENVERSICHERUNGSTRÄGER: *Prognos-Gutachten 1995*, Frankfurt a.M. 1995 (= DRV Schriften, Vol. 4).

VOBRUBA, G.: *Strukturwandel der Sozialpolitik*, Frankfurt a.M. (Suhrkamp) 1990.

WERNER, H.: "Wirtschaftliche Integration und Arbeitskräftewanderungen: Das Beispiel Europa", *Mitteilungen aus der Arbeitsmarkt- und Berufsforschung* 27 (1994), pp. 232-245.

WORLD BANK: *Averting the Old Age Crisis, Policies to Protect the Old and promote Growth*, Oxford 1994.

ZACHER, H.F. (Ed.): *Alterssicherung im Rechtsvergleich*, Baden-Baden (Nomos) 1991.

ZAPF, W. U.A.: *Individualisierung und Sicherheit*, München (Beck) 1987.

ZÖLLNER, D.: "Landesbericht Deutschland" in: ZACHER, H.F. and KÖHLER, P. (Eds.): *Ein Jahrhundert Sozialversicherung in der Bundesrepublik Deutschland, Frankreich, Großbritannien, Österreich und der Schweiz*, Berlin (Duncker u. Humblot) 1981, pp. 45-179.

Part II

The Social Security System in the East Central European Nations of Transition and in Japan

Chapter 4

The Principle of Subsidiarity and the Transition of the Welfare States in Central and Eastern Europe

TIBOR CZÉH

I. Introduction

Our age may be characterised as the age of knowledge and information, but at the same time it has brought the end of experts, too. The world has become too confused to be under control. What is true in one field may cause serious damages in other fields. Old and new dangers are appearing: killing diseases and unknown, fast spreading insects, billionaire brokers manipulating exchange rates, religious terrorism, etc. No one is able to understand and make the whole system work properly. Although there may be some issue-areas for which a consensus may emerge among experts regarding causal laws (particularly with respect to technology, natural or biological science, or possibly some economic relationships), that may be seen as exceptions rather than the rule in creating welfare in nation states or even worse in «an ever closer union». And there is the possibility that the consensus of these experts is wrong, or what works in the EU perhaps does not work properly in another political, economic and social culture. Is there a way out of this anarchy? Perhaps the telephone-book detailed directives of the Commission? I am not sure. The way out should be certain basic principles that work as a general compass in the chaos, and the legal form of them, framework legislation and minimum norms to make the ordinary citizen able to understand the process, to make them and let them able to be responsible for their fate, their welfare and to make them able to do much more and much more freely for themselves. That should be the way out for at least the societies under the Central and Eastern European post communist, over-centralised, paternalist states. One of these basic principles that could help us is the general principle of the European Union, the principle of subsidiarity.

By 1989, the silent revolutions brought not only the hope of more democratic systems, but the hope to reach the welfare of the Western European countries. In the promises of the new political elite it was one of the main goals shown to the general public. After five years, 76 percent of the population in Hungary, and 54 per cent in the Czech Republic felt that they were absolutely or occasionally poor. The dream of the welfare state soon disappeared, but the situation need not have worsened to such an extent if the principle of subsidiarity had been applied. But instead of it we can better speak about subsidiarity-deficits both upwards and downwards.

It is obvious that the rebirth of nationalism at the highest political level caused serious damages to Hungary (for example by stopping most of our economic relations with the former Soviet Union and the other post-communist states) by not letting decisions into the sphere where the decisions could have been been with the highest efficiency and rationality (in our example to the market, the business sphere). The European integration process may play a key role in the possible rebirth of the Central and Eastern European welfare states by showing the citizens and the politicians the hope and way for a better, but much more self-made, future.

II. The Principle of Subsidiarity

In the northern Member States of the European Community there is a growing tendency to leave more and more rules and practices to be formed by the society itself. On the other side in Central and Eastern Europe the privatisation of the problems led to the so-called «wild capitalism», the split of society into rich and poor, the former winning everything from power to welfare, the latter suffering from the loss of the social state, stability of existence etc. The former experience shows that government regulation cannot solve every problem, on the contrary the totalitarian system – and its reform varieties – creates more problems than it is able to solve. This implies that the self-regulatory capacity of the society should be improved.

1. The Importance of the Knowledge of the Principle

Why is it important for our countries to know this principle? First, it is obvious if we want to join an organisation, we must know the rules of the game. Subsidiarity is a general legal principle of the Community and the inclusion of the principle in the Maastricht Treaty imposes an obligation on all the institutions which participate in the process of decision. All new proposals have to be examined in strict compliance with the subsidiarity principle.

Second, the subsidiarity principle is a democratic principle of an efficient society and economy. Openness, closeness to the citizen, democratic deficit and the question of reallocating the formerly totally centralised powers are problems and questions that are problems and questions not only in the Member States of the European Union. The principle of subsidiarity could help the government to receive greater support from the electors, by bringing the decisions more efficiently and closer to them. It emphasises that the citizens should solve the problems that they can solve with the highest efficiency.

2. Back to the Origins

Where are the roots of this principle? The concept of subsidiarity in fact is quite ancient, both a as philosophical and societal system and as a legal principle. We could go back to Aristotle, German liberalism, early Christian thinking, St. Thomas to show – and it is important to emphasise this – that the idea that society is a «community of communities» and that the division of tasks should be done as close as possible to the citizen is not new. The first well-known formulation of the principle is the Tenth Amendment of the Constitution of the United States, in which the value and inevitable right for the self organisation of society is laid down: «The powers not delegated to the United States by the Constitution, nor prohibited by it to the states, are reserved to the States respectively, or to the people.»

It is also common to date the birth of subsidiarity as 1931, that is, when the Vatican published Quadregesimo Anno, the encyclical letter to commemorate the 40th anniversary of the first social encyclical Rerum Novarum. The relevant section of Quadregesimo Anno reads as follows:

«Just as it is wrong to withdraw from the individual and commit to a group what private enterprise and industry can accomplish, so too it is an injustice, a grave evil and disturbance of right order, for a larger association to arrogate to itself functions that can be performed efficiently by smaller and lower societies. This is a fundamental principle of social philosophy, unshaken and unchangeable. Of its very nature the true aim of all social activity should be to help (to subsidise) members of the social body, but never to destroy or absorb them.»

One could say that this old Catholic social doctrine has very little to do with the current fashionable Eurospeak. But its basic values, such as personalism, pluralism, solidarity and distributive justice have found their most profound expression in the welfare state, the social market.

What other values are protected by subsidiarity? First of all the primacy of the human being over social structure, the primacy of the civil society over the state. So the state has to act only when a community's ability to act turns out to be inadequate. The state should support the smaller community rather than let a higher level or community act in its place. So the state has two roles: protective prohibition, it should not hinder the self organisations of the society in their activity, – and positive incentive, that the government and its organs must help these groups in realising their objectives.

In the Community context, the principle is enshrined in the preamble and in Article B and 3b of the Treaty on European Union. It was present in embryonic form in the ECSC Treaty, implicit in the Treaty of Rome, and spelled out in the Single European Act in relation to the environment.

Why did this principle appear in the late eighties, and why just in the welfare states? One reason is that the international system has changed: international intergovernmental organisations, like the United Nations, the European Union, the Council of Europe created a system in which the sovereignty of the member states – or at least of those that accept the rules of the game – is limited. The European integration process went on and the European Community became more and more federalist. As the borders of the states disappeared, people living in the subnational units, like regions which were always either economic, or social ethnic units, but had been sometimes divided by artificial borders, began to rethink their role in the Community. The federal states like Germany helped and accelerated this process. The centralised states had to be reshaped, not only because they were unable to respond to the challenges of unemployment, poverty, crime, inflation, but because the nation state in the modern sense is no longer the only political arena: it has lost its role of being the sole framework for the exercise of the political power.

3. Subsidiarity and Decentralisation

Here we have to make a clear distinction between subsidiarity and decentralisation.

In an economic sense the question is who or what should have the power in a modern state to levy taxes, undertake expenditures for the provision of public goods and services, or regulate the behaviour of private sector agents. The principle of subsidiarity implies that all of these categories of power should be decentralised wherever possible. Co-ordinating policies yield benefits when scale economies or spillovers between member states are important. But it has also costs. By diminishing accountability it offers scope for policies to diverge from the best interests of constituent entities, states, regions or localities. The appropriate location of power reflects the conflict between the costs and benefits of centralisation. By laying the burden of proof on those wishing to centralise, subsidiarity recognises the initial sovereignty of the lowest level and emphasises that problems of accountability of «government failure» at the centre may be substantial.

There are some points that need to be clarified. First, subsidiarity is not the same thing as decentralisation. It is a principle for allocating power upwards as well as downwards, but it incorporates a presumption in favour of allocation downwards in case of doubt.

Second, the level at which given powers are exercised need not always be an all-or-nothing matter but usually one of degrees. For instance, the relatively highly centralised Hungarian government might be assigned the power to determine overall levels of taxation, while the power to choose which kinds of tax to levy to meet the aggregate totals might be left to more local jurisdictions. Surprisingly, it is the socialist government that raised the percentage of tax – from 30 to 35 % – that remains at the local governments. And it was decided for economic and efficiency reasons. That's where subsidiarity begins to work in everyday life. The local governments are by far better informed about local needs, and the labyrinth in which money is circulating in the central budget costs a lot.

Third, the decentralised implementation of a policy whose basic features are decided centrally is not the same as decentralisation of the power to decide what the policy should be. Decentralised implementation may imply that considerable resources are employed by the localities. But decentralised power requires that these resources be controlled by some local public choice mechanism - in other words, decentralised government.

Fourth, subsidiarity may also suggest that a policy be applied in a way that is sensitive to different regional circumstances within a jurisdiction without involving either local administration or local government. For instance, central government may choose to give tax concessions to firms in a certain regionally-concentrated industry within the context of an entirely centrally designed and implemented policy.

Subsidiarity is a dynamic concept: it is far from putting the higher level action in a straitjacket, it allows it to be expanded where circumstances so required and, conversely, to be restricted or abandoned where it is no longer justified.

4. Subsidiarity Deficits and the Welfare State

Kolodziejak called subsidiarity deficit when «the national government is not able any more to act effectively with respect to some macroeconomic tasks, imposed by the Constitution, and the European Community is not yet prepared or allowed to fill the gap». In Hungary the subsidiarity-deficit is twofold: first the downward subsidiarity-deficit appears when the government is unable to fulfil its tasks relating to welfare functions and the society is not yet able to fill this gap because of the lack of knowledge and culture of the self-organised and market-based welfare, and because the population is too excessively pauperised. Second, the upward subsidiarity deficit appears when the national government wants to save its full sovereignty, though it is unable to manage a problem, but wants the targeted higher level – the European Union – to help but to help only the government itself, and no way to lower levels, and the higher level cannot or does not want to help. It is not subsidiarity to waste the savings of the EU citizens on financing inefficient central government policies and programs without the right to control the actual spending. The European Union and its constituting elements from citizens to nation states could participate in the solution of both deficit problems. As Abraham Lincoln wrote in 1853: «Nobody can be helped durably by doing for him what he should do for himself»; it is more useful to teach the citizens to fish than give them a fish. The ways to establish a European welfare state can be found from the level of ordinary citizens or their groups, through different government levels to the level of the Community. The key is the improvement of direct relations according to the principle of subsidiarity. The EU – if it wants to and is able to help – should take action on that very level, and form where and how the problem can be solved with the highest efficiency. Strict white papers for the applicant countries may be one form by reducing short termism in different policy areas, but this influence should be increased.

III. Historical Aspects of the Socialist Welfare States

Peter Koslowski says that «The modern state cannot, in its social and cultural policy, define the praxis of religion . . . but it can promote religion and philosophical ethics as the culture of knowing and finding oneself.» The peoples of the socialist countries were citizens of the same religion: communism. It did define social and cultural policy as well as all the other activities of the social being, as Islam defines the everyday life of the people living in Iran. The priests of this religion had substantial backup – the Red Army. It is surprising how the post-socialist individuals try to distance themselves from their communist past and make the world believe that there was only a minority of communists who believed in the values and goals of the system. Maybe there were few hard liners, but the whole society had to accept the values. After the collapse of the state religion, the newly elected governments could not make the whole society accept their values. The nationalist political leaders and some of the leading politicians of the EU made this situation even worse by promising the entrance of welfare, as in the developed part of Europe, if these countries changed to market economy and democracy.

1. Where Is the Self-Governing Society?

One of the basis of the communist ideology was the ability of the community - that meant in fact the Socialist Party – to take care of each citizen. In practice it meant also strict control. As the Socialist Party believed that it knew – and only the SP knew – what the citizen needed, any other idea was a crime. After the fall of the etatist system, the new prime minister, Jozsef

Antall thought that it was necessary to rebuild the reputation of the government. And he built a big one – at least if we consider its size. While the welfare state was the targeted future, the socialist welfare state collapsed with its social safety net and there was no other net: the citizens were waiting for the government to help them, the idea that they should organise themselves had been successfully erased from their heads. The culture of the self-regulatory and self-organising society is just being rebuilt. The local self governments are mainly executive bodies of the central policy and they could not become – they did not even try to be – the centre of the self-organised, self-regulated and decentralised local policy-making as the principle of subsidiarity would suggest. So the central government argues that there is no other possibility: they have to do everything.

2. The Hungarian Welfare System Between 1989-1994

The coming of the crisis of the Hungarian welfare state could be seen at the end of the 1980's, but with the collapse of the communist regime it became obvious that the welfare level was unsustainable. The growing government budget deficit and foreign indebtedness reached that high level when we needed most the survival of the welfare state. Hungary's system of transfers and entitlements is only emulated in the most redistributive OECD economies, such as Sweden or the Netherlands, all of which have considerably higher per capita incomes. The former system's paternalistic, cradle-to-grave web of benefits and services, predicated on compressed wages and high labour force participation, remained essentially intact in a different political and economic context.

The most important targeted elements of the new social policy can be summarised as the maximisation of the role of the market and the minimisation of the role of the state, the individual's and the families' responsibility for their fate, for their position in the market. This meant that the benefits were narrowed down to the «truly needy deserving poor», and there is a growing concern that nobody should be entitled to any benefit or service without compensation. In the present international political situation in the short and medium run, there is no real choice for filling the gap of the upward subsidiarity-deficit in Hungary by shifting fiscal policy duties into community action. The problem of the too-large-state above the society has to be solved by the shared responsibility of the national and lower levels. State ownership of social institutions and state provision of services were attacked partly because of the rigidity and excessiveness of bureaucracy, partly because of the limitation of choice of citizens. As the present centralising tendency makes me believe that we can give up the hope for decentralisation and increased political participation, the solution based on subsidiarity is twofold. One possibility is to eliminate public property and public production by means of so-called quasi markets. In this case, the state would continue financing, but the responsibility of operation and services, and perhaps the ownership of the institutions, would be handed over to other agents – the market or the awakening non-profit sector.

The ideology of small-state/large-individual responsibility, coupled with the concern for dwindling resources, will have a manifold impact upon social policy and society in general. First, with the increasing role of the market the systems which were integrated in the socialist era will be dismantled. There have always been institutions for the elite, but from now on the transition will result in the differentiation according to certain, mainly market preferences: first and foremost income, informal and formal relations with the members of the higher social strata, geographical position (capital, small village in a crisis region), etc. There will be separate clinics, hospitals, nursery schools, high schools and universities.

The second possible solution, in accordance with the ideology of economic efficiency, is that shrinking resources may be best utilised if the state benefits are allocated only to the needy. This individual or group targeting or selectivity is in harmony with the principle of subsidiarity. All human beings are equal, but only in the legal and biological meanings of the word. The idea of universal basic provision may not mean that a substantial part of the working population gets slightly more than those outside the market. The equality of chances means that the talented poor can be lifted from their strata by the civil society and/or the state or the market, but it cannot mean that because they can support the society with only negative product value, this negative value takes away the half of the welfare of those whose MPV is positive. A part of the society pays high taxes, and the same time pays for their own physician, for their child's nursery school, for their private insurance and are not eligible even for any family allowance, then they will consider the system unjust.

The first post-communist government inherited a welfare system that was relatively high proportionate to the GDP. Despite the declared intentions, this rate increased after the political changeover since the old needs have not changed or been augmented and even new ones appeared (like the shock of massive job losses – 1.4 million between 1990 and 1994, and the 600,000 other unemployed, though statistically counted as employed, that are sheltered in various long-term leave and work programs at public expense) that have to be immediately responded to, while resources decreased (the GDP has decreased by 20 per cent). We spent too much on social policy, which increased the deficit of the budget and led to foreign indebtedness (which is more than USD 31 billion in 1995). Although the real value of the welfare expenses decreased, this was smaller than the fall in the registered GDP. As a result, the proportion jumped to 25 per cent in 1990, then to 29.8 per cent in 1992 compared to the 17 percent in 1985 and the average of the European Union (22 per cent). The structure of the central budget expenditures has also change significantly. The share of the welfare expenditures from 1985 to 1994 rose from 38 per cent to 57 per cent, and as the World Bank report states: «About 40 percent of the population aged 15-59 (15-54 for women) is now dependent on the wages of others and on the social transfers, double the dependency ratio of 1990.» This way Hungary has reached Sweden in relative terms. The problem comes from the fact that our per capita GDP is only 2,720 USD and it is only 20 per cent of the OECD countries' per capita GDP, while the Swedish one raises almost 160 per cent of it. The question becomes: Who consumes more than the country can afford? Since the real income of the population decreased by about 15 per cent between 1989 and 1994, while the inequalities in incomes and consumption increased spectacularly, it means that 40-60 per cent of the population experienced a significant decrease in their living conditions or consumption.

The major types of pensions are old age, survivor and disability pensions. The coverage is nearly universal, and the retirement age is relatively low: 60 for men and 55 for women, (the life expectancy is very low: at birth it is only 65.1 for men and 73.7 for women). As Hungary is an ageing society the share of the retired population is increasing; presently it is 23 per cent. The benefit formula provides rather generous pensions just after retirement, so that it provides a higher pension than it could have been otherwise justified by the beneficiaries' lifetime earning record: it was calculated as a function of the most favourable 3 years from the last 5 years before retirement. Pensions are not taxable. Eligibility criteria for the disability pensions were also liberal. From 1995, pension and health insurance contribution may not be calculated as costs, but only 25 per cent of it may be deducted from the Personal Income Tax.

Family support included family allowances, child care allowances, child care fees, pregnancy-confinement allowance, maternity allowance and sick pay for the mother or father for nursing an ill child. Family allowances were paid as a monthly fixed sum for children aged 0-18. These basic income type allowances were awarded on the basis of rights, unlike the other family support measures, which are employment related. The pregnancy-confinement allowance was an altogether 5 months full salary for the mother before and after confinement, the maternity allowance is a one-time fixed sum due at the birth of the child. The child care fee was paid until the 2nd birthday of the child to the mother interrupting her employment. It was earning related, paid as a percentage of the previous salary of the mother. The child care allowance was paid as a monthly fixed sum until the 3rd birthday of the child. The financing of family support is partly contributory («insurance type»), partly non-contributory (financed out of general revenues).

The sickness provisions – sick pay, sick leave and long term disability benefits – are employment related, with the benefits tied to previous earnings. The self employed are also covered, at least those who have paid since 1989 their full contribution. The base for the calculation of the sick pay is the average earnings, 85 per cent for sickness beyond 90 days and 100 per cent in case of occupational sickness and illness resulting from an industrial accident. This formula gave the basis of the calculation of the child care fees too. The financing of sick pay and long-term disability benefits is contributory, through the social insurance fund, while sick leave (for the first ten days) was paid by employers.

Unemployment compensation has two basic forms: unemployment insurance and unemployment assistance. Since the second half of 1991, the unemployment relief basically works under «insurance» principles. This insurance contribution was raised from 2 to 6 per cent of the earnings in the beginning of 1992 (5 per cent was covered by the employer and the rest by the employee). The unemployment benefit became payable for a shorter period. During the first 360 days the benefit was 70 per cent of the last year's average monthly income, and 50 per cent during the second period. The limits of the benefit first changed from 7,000 - 21,000 Ft to 8,000 - 16,000 Ft (the lower is the actual minimum wage).

Unemployment assistance is a very low fixed amount (4,000 Ft) paid to those who lose their eligibility for unemployment insurance benefits. It is paid by the Solidarity Fund, whereas the payment of unemployment assistance is the responsibility of local governments.

Social assistance (small amounts of «crisis transfers») is also paid by local governments to the most needy families. It is awarded on a means-tested basis, mostly under the discretion of local authorities. The social official of the local government could spend the money available for that purpose on the basis of their own evaluation of the conditions of selected families. They could give either regular (full, partial or additional) or exceptional payments to families. From 1995, the seriously handicapped may deduct monthly 9000 Ft from their PIT.

3. The Consequences of the 1994 Elections for the Future of the Welfare System

The macrosocial environment of the new socio-liberal coalition was different from that of the former one. The bases of the institutions of the pluralistic democracy have been established but neither the institutional system nor the market economy have been developed. The ownership structure has undergone a considerable transformation to wild capitalism. The middle class lives in existential uncertainty, mass loss of status, long-term unemployment. The past few years reduced by half the number of those who live a middle-class existence.

The Bokros program abolished the universal social benefits from July 1995 and narrowed the circle of beneficiaries to the most needy. Again the children are the losers as the pensions float together with the minimum wage or the net incomes, the child care allowances are reduced and are not indexed. This will worsen the present state when 49 per cent of the 0-18 year old children live in the lowest income category families (while this data is only 20 per cent for the pensioners). The child care allowances are paid only until the 6th year of age.

The program abolished the universality of family allowances and child care allowances, and began to apply an income test, but only 15-18 per cent of the former beneficiaries are going to be left out of the allowances. It is a problem that 30 per cent of the incomes come from the twilight economy, and no one has information about the distribution of these incomes among the members of the society. The program introduced patients' contributions to the formerly universally free medical services. The eligibility for sick pay changed and the sum of it decreased. It is the same with pregnancy-confinement and maternity allowances, in these cases the duration was also shortened.

The Constitutional Court found certain parts of the program unconstitutional because, according to the Constitution, basic social provisions can be demanded, a too excessive part of the income may not be taken away on the basis of solidarity because it hurts the principle of proportionality, the consideration of the number of children may be discriminatory, and, finally, enough time must be given the society to prepare for the new system. The government will find the necessary steps to be taken to compensate the loss in the budget originating from the decision of the Court.

The transformation of the education is also a subject of heated discussions. As the value of knowledge generally increases, the introduction of the partly market-based system hurts the feelings of those who believe in total equality of chances. It can already be seen that those who can spend more on a child's education than the total family income of others and get really quality education for their expense, do make one of the best possible investments: they invest in the bright future of their children. According to experts this might generate much greater social tensions than unemployment or the lack of social safety net. The majority of the population gave up hope of improving living conditions, but if the impoverished strata are left without the hope of upward individual mobility through education, there will be nothing to left to connect them to social integration. I cannot quite agree with that. The principle of subsidiarity suggests the maximum possible extension of chances but it cannot mean the paternalist equalisation of chances because people, groups, organisations, and countries are different. The introduction of tuition fees at the universities will not mean any burden for the higher social strata (17 percent of the 18-35 years old attend such institutes) whose children have to pay the monthly 2000 HUF (22 DM), when many of the children of the highest strata attend the most expensive universities of the world. In fact, the financing of the universities is a bit contradictory considering that these well-to-do students study at the expense of the whole society.

In 1995, the government worked out a subsidiarity-conform tax preference system in which we can read the following: «The spreading of forms of self care and their acceptance by the society is an important interest connected with the Voluntary Mutual Benefit Funds. This motivates that they should enjoy preferences in the tax system. The measures of the tax preferences are regulated in a differentiated way among the different forms of such funds.» «An outstanding high preference is ensured for payments effected in favour of pension and health care funds.»

As the present pay-as-you-go system is unsustainable, following the advice of the World Bank the Hungarian government plans to introduce a new, three-pillar pension and old age security system. The first pillar is a universal obligatory pension, providing a flat benefit to those who reach the raised retirement age. The second is a transparently earnings-related mandatory retirement savings plan. The third pillar is the voluntary pension plans, prudentially regulated and tax-assisted.

TIBOR CZÉH

IV. Transition to Poverty?

A recent study on the social effects of the transition in Central and Eastern European countries found that in Poland and Hungary 8-18 percent of the population found themselves absolutely poor, while this rate is 9 per cent in the Czech Republic and 5 per cent in Slovakia. If we add to this rate those who regard themselves as occasionally poor, 76 per cent of the Hungarians, 73 per cent of the Polish 58 per cent of the Slovakians and 54 per cent of the Czech have experienced poverty. Though at the beginning of the transition there were no such differences regarding the future in the four countries. In 1989, 1-7 per cent of the population found it difficult to pay the housing bills and buy food for the family.

The share of the latter group, who has serious problems with the everyday costs of living, at least doubled in the past six years in all the four countries. These evaluations reflect not only the effective changes but also the different perceptions. While only 25 per cent of Czech families have bread-and-butter worries, another research study of the Brno Technical High School found that more than the half of Czech children wear smaller shoes than they should, because the per capita number of the pair of shoes per year decreased in five years by half.

The data suggest that it is not the mechanisms of the growing capitalism but that of the social allowances that shelter the citizens of a given country from poverty or its perception. The citizens of the former German Democratic Republic are the most satisfied, though there are more families with unemployed members (22 per cent), but they may get the most benefits: every fifth family receives some kind of benefit from the state. The Hungarian families are on the top in asking for social allowances – every fourth family tried in 1994 – but only two-thirds of them were successful, while 87 per cent of the East Germans' request were heard by the authorities.

Regarding the future of the welfare, the Polish are the most enthusiastic, because they and the Czech and the Slovakians feel that they are over the worst, while in Hungary the majority does not expect anything good from the future.

It is not only poverty that has increased in the whole Central and Eastern European region as a result of the shocks of the transition. No doubt, the rise of poverty has been aggravating, especially among children. UNICEF collected 29 important indexes describing other areas of quality of life, from mortality rates to education of the secondary school age population.

"Only two of the indexes showed improvement (the mortality rate of women of child-bearing age and of the age group of 1 to 4). In other respects, in 72 per cent of the possible cases, there is a conspicuous deterioration. This is not a necessary consequence of the deterioration of living standards, especially not within one or two years. Naturally, the general drop in caloric intake, or even starvation in a number of countries, are not surprising attributes of impoverishment, nor is the spread of tuberculosis in all the countries concerned. More indirect effects are the aggravating weakening of the zest for life, of confidence and of the respect of human life expressed in the rapid drop in the number of marriages, the increase of mortality in young adults and above all, the almost general fall in birth-rate (by no means typical only of Hungary), and the increase of crime, including growing juvenile delinquency and the number of murders. At the same time, as a result of pressure on social policy and the conscious dismantling of major systems, the level of social benefits is deteriorating everywhere with the possibility of access narrowing." (Ferge, 25. 1995, p. 55)

A World Bank report on the chances of the return of the former welfare shows that even in the optimistic scenario, the 1989 standard of living would not be restored in the countries predicted to grow fastest – Poland, Hungary and the former Czechoslovakia – for more than ten years. The pessimistic forecast extends the period of recovery to 20 years or more. All the while, inequalities continue to increase, but the society must wake up sooner or later: the responsibility for their life is theirs, and that of the state is only subsidiary. The new welfare state will much more depend on self-made welfare, therefore we have a lot to do in organising this kind of society.

1. Hungarian Poverty

The communist model, based on the fusion of a monopolistic party with the state and its total control of economy, society and thoughts, tried to reform from within, but it failed. By the 1980s no credible «reform socialism» survived, and communist regimes had exhausted their legitimacy. When challenged by massive popular demonstrations, they had neither moral credit nor a credible model of political economy with which to fend off demands for freedom, human rights, free elections, democracy. There was only one, but much more important, factor that our scholars previously did not count: it was the communist model of the welfare state. After the second elections in the region, the «democratic» world was shocked by the fact that the winners were the communists, and the reason for that is the package of benefits of the socialist welfare state: price controls, cheap bread, invisible poverty, full employment, subsidising of culture, etc. The communist regimes did provide a level of material satisfaction that many people became reluctant to give up. The population's nostalgia for this era brought the communist leaders back.

However, poverty did exist at that time too. The estimations varied between 7.3 and 11.0 per cent. According to the analyses of the Hungarian Household Panel, 35 per cent of the interviewed persons in March 1993 lived in a household having a per capita income lower than the subsistence level.

One can define the following household types as vulnerable groups in Hungary in 1993, groups for which the poverty risk is clearly higher than average, notwithstanding which of the relative poverty concepts is used and which adjustment for incomes is applied:

- households headed by a person of lower education,
- village households,
- households headed by an unemployed person,
- lone parent households,
- female headed households,
- household headed by a person aged less than 30,
- household having 4 or more children.

V. From the Social Charter to the Self-Regulated Society

The principle of subsidiarity exists because the experience of the centre to solve problems may create more problems than it is able to solve. It represents also a general philosophy of government that touches upon the basic relationship between government action and civil society. At any governmental level the latter has to be encouraged by political institutions. Even the general goals of the Treaty are endangered if the self-organisations of the civil society are in opposition to them. If a Community directive through government legislation is not acceptable for the societal actors it is likely to be much less effective than that version when they rely on these self-organisations.

As the countries of our region are applicants to the EU and we still have duties in developing democratic practice, letting grow a responsible society, it would be of high importance for us and for civil society to get to know the possibilities of self-regulation within the bounds of Community law. It can only help our integration process if we implement practices that improve democracy and welfare, and that can diminish the deficit of the central budget and the fear of the recently appeared new political elites of losing too much power to the EU institutions.

The Community Charter of Fundamental Social Rights aims to develop Community social policy. Subsidiarity appears in one of the considerations in the preamble: «. . . whereas, by virtue of the principle of subsidiarity, responsibility for the initiatives to be taken with regard to the implementation of these social rights lies with the Member States or their constituent parts and, within the limits of its powers, within the European Community,» immediately followed by the reassuring statement, that «the solemn proclamation of fundamental social rights at European Community level may not, when implemented, provide grounds for any retrogression compared with the situation currently existing in Each Member State.»

What does it mean for the Central and Eastern European transitory welfare states? First, it means that it is an instrument of Member States to protect the national character and development of the welfare state. As these states tend to lose their welfare character it is less important. Second, it means that the Community has competence in this field. According to the principle of subsidiarity, the Community «shall take action . . . as the objectives of the proposed action cannot be sufficiently achieved by the member States and can therefore . . . be better achieved by the Community», or simply: the countries of this region are waiting for the help of «Uncle EU» in all its possible forms. On the EU's side it would mean an annual 6-10 billion USD transfer, a 14-20 per cent increase in the EU's budget. In practice, this sum is a serious obstacle in the process of the integration of the CEE-countries. (From the point of view of the real welfare states there is the possibility of social dumping, that is the prospect that firms operating where social wages are low may be able to undercut prices of competitors, forcing higher cost firms to either go out of business, relocate to low social wage areas, or pressure their governments to reduce social wage costs and ask for the help of the EU.)

Thirdly, the Social Agreement between 11 of the Member States added by Protocol to the Treaty on European Union expands the possibility of self-regulation between management and trade unions. Article 4(2) of the Agreement provides for a choice of law in case a collective agreement is concluded, and the explicit option of implementation through self-regulation. The European Court of Justice has helped the extension of competencies of the

Community and the self-regulation too. The Court has already accepted self-regulatory measures under certain conditions. The first recognition that an area covered by Community law might be dealt with through self-regulation came quite implicitly. In a case concerning the registration of domestic physicians, the Court accepted the referral of an arbitration tribunal to the Court, thereby acknowledging the fact that the Community obligation in question was implemented through regulations of a professional organisation.

Therefore the civil society in Central and Eastern Europe has the right and exceptional possibility to implement European norms or create their own, to organise their activity and to make the state accept it as a part of the country's integration process. But it would be possible only in that case if the Community forced the nation states of this region to legislate consistent with the principle of subsidiarity and leave more and more room for the society to organise their lives themselves within these frames.

References

ANDORKA, RUDOLF, MICHAEL F. FORSTER, ZSOLT SPÉDER and ISTVAN GYORGY TOTH: *Poverty, Inequalities and the Incidence of Social Transfers in Hungary, 1992-1993,* Budapest (TARKI) 1994.

AUGUSZTINOVICS, MARIA: "A nyugdijrendszer válsága". *Kozgazdasági Szemle XXXIX* (1992) 7-8, p. 631.

GAZSO, FERENC: "Government in an Unstable Social Environment", in: *Question Marks: The Hungarian Government 1994-1995,* Centre for Political Research 1995.

GYORGY, TOTH ISTVAN: "A joléti rendszer az átmenet idoszakában" (The Welfare System in the Transition Period) *Kozgazdasági Szemle XLI* (1994) 3. sz., pp. 313-340.

MINISTRY OF FINANCE ACT: "The Modification of the Personal Income Tax 1995", LXXXII 1994.

STEYGER, ELIES: "EC Law and Self-regulation" *Journal of Common Market Studies,* 31 (June 1993), p. 181.

VILAGGAZDASAG, HETI: "Bomlásveszély" (Danger of Collapse) 1995, *Május* 27, pp. 9-12.

VILAGGAZDASAG, HETI: "Labilitási csomag" (Instability Package) 1995, 07.01, pp. 97-99.

VIOLINI, LORENZA: "Subsidiarity and the Welfare State in Italy", Conference Paper 1994.

Chapter 5

The Social Security System in Japan

Yoshifumi Fushimi

In spite of the 1994 reform, further drastic reform seems to be indispensable for the Japanese social security system with regard to its theory and practice. Major points of the 1994 reform are as follows (see Takagi (1995) for further reference):

For Pension Insurance Systems

1. Raising the age to start receiving old-age benefits from 60 to 65 years old in the employees' pension (between 2001 and 2013 for men).
2. Instead, another pension (second-tier earning related benefits) is served to a person until 65 years old.
3. The old age employees' benefit is revised so that the total sum of benefits and increase in wages encourage the willingness to work.
4. Indexing benefits level in accordance with the trend of net wages excluding taxes and social insurance premiums.
5. Raising the insurance premium by stages to accumulate a certain fund level for securing a sound pension budget for the long term.
6. Insurance premiums are based on bonuses as well

For Medical Care Insurance Systems

1. Reforming the benefits related to nursing and custodial care provided by nursing attendants.
2. Promotion of home medical care.
3. Reviewing the benefits of providing meals for inpatients.
4. Improving medical services related to the care environment.
5. Reviewing the benefits related to pharmaceuticals.
6. Establishing a custodial care service system.

The issue of justice between generations is especially keen in the society where the ageing of the population is so rapid, which will bring about unbalance of benefits and burdens between generations. In addition, strong conflicts of interest exist among different social insurance schemes that were independently initiated but integrated partially by the measures of financial adjustments since the 1980's. The spread of disincentives to participate in the social insurance System, which is observed especially in the pension system, must also be taken seriously.

The social security system in Japan has been characterised by a social insurance approach, primarily covering income security and medical care. But today there is a growing need to adjust the social security system to meet the increasing demand for welfare services, like long-term care for the elderly and child care under the decline in family size and an increasing number of working women.

To discuss these issues, I shall briefly explain the characteristics of the social security system in Japan (section I), then discuss the conflicts among different social security schemes including intergenerational problem (section II), and finally address the disincentive problem in pension insurance (section III).

I. Characteristics of the Japanese Social Security System

The Japanese social security system is characterised by the social insurance approach to income security and medical care. In fact, the benefits paid by pension and medical care insurance schemes amounted to 83.1% of ILO-defined total social security benefits in 199O, with 46.2 % for pension and 36.9 % for medical care. In this system, Japanese employees with standard working careers (currently, 35 years of insured periods with average wages) are promised old-age pensions that are equal to 68% of the average wages, except bonus, of the active working generation. The medical care insurance schemes provide people fairly equal access to medical services whichever social and economic class they belong. In fact, there is no significant difference in the admission rate to the medical facilities among patients of different social classes. The equality of access to medical facilities seems to have contributed to the attainment of the longest life expectancy at birth in the world.

The second characteristic of the Japanese social security system is that both pension insurance and medical insurance includes a wide variety of different schemes, although there is an universal insurance system in the sense that everybody is covered by some public scheme. The Japanese social insurance system has developed by three major steps. First, social insurance began as mutual aid schemes for employees in the workplace at the beginning of the twentieth century. Second, these schemes were expanded into employees' insurance schemes covering all employees, to which the German model of social insurance system was applied. Third, social insurance schemes for nonemployees, who had not been included in the employees insurance schemes, were introduced and finally evolved into a universal social insurance system in 1961, but a number of separate social insurance schemes based on occupation, industry and area remained as they were.

List of the insurance schemes (as of the end of March 1992)

(Medical insurance)	*Insurer*
Employees' health insurance	
For small-scale firms	State
For large-scale firms	1,823 units
For day labourers	State
Seamen's Insurance	State
Mutual Aid Associations	
For central government employees	27
For local government employees	54
For private school teachers and employees	1
National health insurance for farmers, self-employed, & no job	3,254 Municipalities and 166 vocational units

(Pension insurance)

National pension
Employees' pension
  Employees' pension insurance
  Central government employees
Nippon telegram and telephone corporation employees
  Japan railway's employees
  Japan tobacco inc. employees
  Local government employees
  Private teachers and employees
  Agricultural, forestry and fishery institutions employees

From the financing aspect, the Japanese social security system depends largely upon contribution because of the insurance approach. It should be noticed that the contribution base is limited compared to the tax base. The contribution base includes usually only wages and salaries from enterprises and earnings of the self-employed, which makes financial operation of the social insurance system difficult. Further, when the system is managed by a number of separate schemes, disparity in financial status is remarkable. A small social insurance scheme with rather homogeneous membership is inevitably weak and easily affected by economic and social changes.

Another financial source of the social security system is state subsidies. But, under the current policy of reducing the government deficits, it was not easy to increase subsidies for the social security system during these 10 years without raising taxes. Thus, the measures of financial adjustments between different schemes have been introduced both in pension and medical insurance systems.

In medical insurance systems, Health Service Systems for the Elderly was founded in 1982. It covers those aged 70 years and over as well as disabled aged 65 - 69, for whom medical care insurance schemes are applicable. Of total costs of this system, 70% are shared by the insurers, 20% by state subsidies, and 10% by local governments. The medical service program for retires founded in 1984 also brings about inter-scheme transfer.

In the 1985 pension reform, the flat basic pension, common to the whole nation, was introduced under the National Pension. Although equality in both benefits and burdens in the basic pension was realised, it has brought about huge inter-scheme transfers. Insured persons of employees' pension insurance schemes still remain in their schemes, although they are also insured in the National Pension at the same time and their premiums are borne by their employees' pension schemes.

The process of financial adjustments characterises the current social security system in Japan.

II. Conflicts Among Different Schemes and Justice Between Generations

When the social insurance system is managed by a number of separate schemes, financial adjustments among them must be naturally taken if they are to cope with the socio-economic changes that Japan is facing.

To keep the autonomy of each social insurance scheme, the measures of financial adjustments should be limited to common risks for persons covered. However, there are two principles in the operation of financial adjustments. First, net inter-scheme transfer should be zero in the long run. Second, amount of inter-scheme transfer should not exceed the extent to which the autonomy of the social insurance scheme is spoiled.

In fact, inter-scheme transfer under the Health Service System for the Elderly is just a one-way transfer from the Employees' Health insurance schemes to the National Health Insurance schemes (the former includes growing industries and less elderly, the latter includes decreasing number of insured and increasing numbers of elderly). Further, the transferred amounts between schemes have been increasing as a result of the expansion of the scope of benefits and the progress of the ageing, so that the percentage of inter-scheme transfer to the Elderly system exceeded 20% in most of medical insurance schemes. Under these circumstances, there is a threat to the existence of the medical insurance system as a whole. The insurers of employees' insurance systems strongly resist further increases in the outward transfer, and at the same time they are gradually losing the governability of insurance systems operations. The National Health Insurance, which has more elderly insured, has already lost their governability. This will cause the moral degeneracy as an insurer of a social insurance system. A drastic countermeasure is urgently required so that the principles of social insurance can function properly.

Introduction of the basic pension has had similar effects as the Health Service System for the Elderly although the amount of the transfers from separate schemes to the basic pension scheme are more than two times. But the pension insurance system seems to be more regulated than the medical care insurance system with respect to insurance principle. All persons receiving basic pensions are insured by the National Pension Scheme even if some of them are insured by other employees' pension insurance schemes at the same time. This seems to give the insurer the legitimacy of advocating a solidarity principle for maintaining the National Pension Scheme.

There is another cause of inter-scheme transfer; "The Special Law on the Adjustment of Expense Burden among Employees' Pension Schemes" has come into effect in 1990 primarily to assist the Japan Railway's Employees' Mutual Aid Association and the Japan Tobacco Inc. Employees' Mutual Aid Association, which were both financially weak. These burdens are shared by other employees' insurance schemes among which the Employees' Pension Insurance is a major contributor. But this assistance does not satisfy the common risk principle, although this was a result of the privatisation of these industries. The violation of the principle causes conflicts among the employees' pension insurance schemes and makes it difficult to consolidate them into a unified scheme.

However, the council on the consolidation of public pension schemes summed up the basic view on the consolidation and submitted a report to the Prime Minister in August 1995. The report proposed following three principles:

1. The base of pension finance should be increased.
2. The burdens for common risks throughout public employees' pension schemes should be equally shared by each scheme as much as possible.
3. The Japan Railways Employees Mutual Aid Association and the Japan Tobacco Inc. Employees Mutual Aid Association, which are not already functioning as independent pension schemes, should be properly liquidated in the consolidation process.

Based on this report, the government will submit a bill to merge both associations into the Employees Pension Insurance in 1996.

The financing method of social insurance will change the effects of the inter-scheme transfer. If a pay-as-you-go system is taken as the financing method, the inter-scheme transfer will affect directly the account for the year. On the contrary, if a funded system is adopted, we can ignore the effects of the inter-scheme transfer in a certain period of time. For the transfer can be adjusted by using the reserve and its real burden will be transferred to the next generation. As Japanese employees' pension insurance schemes partially adopt the funded system, the present insured feel little pain from the inter-scheme transfer, which will however make conflicts between generations worse.

It is pointed out in Employees' Pension Insurance finance, that most parts of a premium, about 80% of total, is used for redistribution between generations, transfers from the younger generation to the old generation. The 1994 financial recalculation of Employees' Pension Insurance shows that the premium rate will eventually reach about 29.6 % in 2025, which indicates that future generations will bear much larger burdens (present premium rate is 16.5 %), while benefits will be the same between generations in a sense of the percentage of benefits to net income of the working generation. This situation will not change much even if a drastic reform is taken so far as we retain the social pension system. Therefore, philosophy of justice between generations must be established.

When we think about justice between generations, we must take into account inheritance from the previous generation, including even private bequests. For a person lives in a society which the previous generation has established. We need a rule of an optimal distribution of resources between generations. Professor Ihori (1965), using Barro's model, suggested that positive economic growth can be attained as far as bequest motive exists, even if the pension system is based on pay-as-you-go system, which is alleged to cause the growth rate to decline.

III. Disincentives in Pension Insurance

The 1992 survey on the public pension insurance participation reported that about two million of eighteen million non employees were not insured.

In addition to those not insured more than two million insured persons do not pay premiums to the National Pension. There are several reasons for the non-entry and defaulters; carelessness, complicated procedure of application, unawareness of public pension, and lack of trust for the National Pension. Here, I take up these disincentive problems.

The National Pension promises an insured the payment of 65,000 yen per month in old-age basic pension if he or she has paid the premium for 40 years, which is planned to increase up to 21,700 yen per month in the future from the present 11,100 yen per month in real terms. The younger a generation, the less beneficial is the system. Looking at the results of the 1993 Delphi survey on pension reform, the percentage, of those who rely on private saving rather than public pension is higher in the younger generation. Since the non employees must submit notification forms when they apply to the National Pension, their application depends on their deliberation. These circumstances are supposed to create disincentives to participate in the National Pension. Disincentives can also work for rich people because 65,000 yen is not attractive to them. No significant difference was found in the average family expenditure between insured and not insured according to the 1992 survey, although not insured were expected to be found more in the low income group.

Different composition in terms of qualification of the insured in the

National Pension may cause disincentives. There are three types of insured; non employees, employees, the dependent spouses of insured persons under employees' pension schemes. It is very difficult for all to be aware that they belong to the same pension scheme and have the sense of solidarity as the insured of the public pension insurance system. All people aged 20 to 59 who live in Japan, compulsorily join the National Pension system, and the insured of employees pension schemes are automatically registered as those of the National Pension. But, the self-employed who must submit notification forms for their application would not become readily aware of this significance. It seems to be one of the reasons for the existence of many young non-entries living in urban areas.

The nature of a basic pension as the benefit from social insurance should be re-examined although one-third of contributions for the basic pension is paid by the national treasury.

IV. Discussion

The above discussed issues on the conflicts of interest and the disincentives of participation are strongly associated with the issue of justice between generations. The conflicts of interest among different insurance schemes are caused by the financial adjustments which resulted in making a huge transfer from the working generation to the old generation. The disincentive to participate in the pension insurance system is observed mainly in the young generation. Facing the rapid progress of the ageing, these problems must be overcome by further reform of the social security system. The present medical insurance schemes should be reorganised to properly aggregated new schemes so that each scheme can maintain its governability. As for the pension insurance system, the reduction of the insurance part of the basic pension should be considered. This means that either the pension finance should rely more on the national treasury, or the benefit level of the basic pension should be cut off. In this connection, the use of the consumption tax for the pension finance, which is planned to be raised in the near future, should be examined (see Takayama 1995).

Further, the reform should meet newly growing demands. The report "Welfare Vision in the 21st Century" compiled by the Council on Welfare Vision for an Ageing Society of the Ministry of Health and Welfare pointed out the increasing demand for welfare services like long-term care for the elderly and child care due to the decline in family size and an increase in the number of working women. Thus, the report proposed the introduction of a social insurance system for custodial care for the elderly. This new system will produce various interactions with the existing social insurance systems. For example custodial care services now covered by a part of medical care services will be shifted to the new system explicitly designed as custodial care, and will possibly rationalise the medical care insurance system. It is important to design a reform so that social insurance systems as a whole work consistently. For this purpose, the establishment of philosophical base for justice between generations is badly needed.

References

BARRO, R.J.: "Government spending in a simple model of endogenous growth", *Journal of Political Economy,* 98 (1990), pp. 103-125.

IHORI, T.: "Pension and social security systems, savings and Bequest", *Review of Social Policy,* No. 4 March (1995), pp 1-23.

MINISTRY OF HEALTH AND WELFARE: *Report on the survey on peoples public pension insurance participation*, 1992 (in Japanese).

MINISTRY OF HEALTH AND WELFARE: *Report on Delphi survey on pension reform*, 1994 (in Japanese).

MINISTRY OF HEALTH AND WELFARE: *Welfare vision in the 21st century*, 1994 (in Japanese).

TAKAGI, Y.: "Social security reform and its viewpoints", *Review of Social Policy,* No. 4 March (1995), pp 45-65.

TAKAYAMA, N.: "The 1994 Reform Bill for public pensions in Japan: Its main contents and related discussions", *International Social Security Review,* Vol. 48, 1/95 (1995), pp 45-65.

THE SOCIAL DEVELOPMENT RESEARCH INSTITUTE: *The cost of Social Security in Japan*, 1993.

Part III

The Rise of the Welfare State in History and Theory

Chapter 6

State and Citizenship in the Age of Globalisation

PETER BALDWIN

Back in the years of major Social Democratic influence in northern Europe there circulated a theory of the welfare state proposing a geographical explanation of its spread and variations: the factor determining the generosity of social benefits in any given country was proximity to Stockholm. Already Copenhagen and Oslo were departures from the alembicated purity of the Swedish welfare state. By the time one got to London or Bonn and then further afield to Paris, Rome and Madrid matters were distinctly less well organised. Washington and Ottawa, not to mention Tokyo, were scarcely within the pale of what could properly be considered a welfare state, with Sydney and Wellington slightly anomalous cases that should have been located, by this standard, perhaps somewhere near the Azores.

Although, of course, never meant more than facetiously, this geopolitical view of the welfare state did highlight an anomaly in discussions of social policy. Here was a part of the world – northern Europe in its widest formulations, Scandinavia in more focused ones, Sweden alone in the narrowest – that, although it played no more than a peripheral role in most other respects, in this question had assumed a kind of intellectual great power status. In discussions of the welfare state, northern Europe and especially Sweden represented the pinnacle of welfare evolution. Moreover, these nations were trailblazers, not merely anomalous developments in the greater scheme of things. Theirs were not unreproducible fortuitous developments like that unique combination of vertiginous topography and well-formulated banking laws that has helped Switzerland to security and prosperity, but which hardly holds out much hope of emulation. The north European welfare states were signpostings to other nations of a common route that could be followed. What America in the hands of Tocqueville had been for democracy – horrifying for some, liberating for others, but nonetheless a harbinger of the future for all – northern Europe and especially Sweden of the mid-twentieth century became in terms of the development of the welfare state (Ruth, 1986). Like it or not, all nations would move in this direction, the state would take over larger spheres of responsibility for the well-being of its citizens, the market be increasingly restricted by the dictates of the public good, the private give way to the social.

The historical trajectory of the welfare state in this understanding thus divorced perfected development from geopolitical importance in a manner uncommon to the gestation of social scientific concepts. Iceland may be home to the oldest democracy, but is still treated by general political histories in what the brothers Grimm would have described as a step-motherly fashion. The Rumanian Iron Guard may have been a more perfect example of fascist ideology than Mussolini's party, but rarely merits more than a paragraph in histories of the interwar era. Nothing helps focus the attention like geopolitical clout, as historians of small countries have regretfully had occasion to remark time and again. And yet Sweden, since the Thirty Years' War otherwise firmly settled in the suburbs of European events, has been able, because of its exemplary social political development, to command considerably more attention than its geopolitical importance would suggest. For those who dislike the direction of evolution indicated by its history, Sweden has provoked allergic reactions disproportionate to a country that most people outside of Europe would be hard-pressed to locate on a map (for example, Huntford 1971). And conversely, from supporters of a Social Democratic style of welfare policy, Sweden's role as a beacon of development has also been exaggerated. The same may be said more generally, if we look at the welfare state in a global context, of northern Europe and its well-developed systems of social policy and the extent to which they hold lessons for the rest of the industrialised world.

The Social Democratic view of the welfare state and, more broadly, of the development of modern society, proposed a metanarrative based on the actual historical development of certain otherwise peripheral nations that were held up as exemplars of a broader stream of evolution eventually to be followed by the geopolitically perhaps more important, but socialpolitically laggard nations. Much like the unilinear theory of industrialisation, based on England's experience and formalised in Rostow's three stages, or the unilinear theory of democratisation based on the experience of England, America and France and formalised in the Marxisant theory of the bourgeois revolution, so too social science of a particular political inflection tried to distil from the historical experience of Sweden, Scandinavia and northern Europe laws of social evolution with pertinence to the rest of the globe. For the moderate left of nations outside of northern Europe, the Social Democratic model of the welfare state has functioned something like what used to be said of Paris in the eighteenth century: that it will not make you happy, but will prevent you from being happy anywhere else (the Comte de Sade quoted in Lever 1993, p. 92). The aspiration has been for developments elsewhere to resemble those to the north. Stockholm was the beacon, however flickeringly remote its beam, however hopelessly unapproachable for foreign vessels its shores.

I. The End of North European Primacy

This siren song of the north European welfare state has, however, lost its timbre in recent years, and that for at least two reasons: First, the Social Democratic model itself has come under intense fire. The Danes have consigned the Social Democrats to the sidelines for many years and seen much of the luxurious underbrush of their social policy pruned back. The Swedish Social Democrats were replaced by Conservatives, temporarily but ignominiously, and have come back to preside over the cutbacks required by huge deficits and unprecedentedly high unemployment. The Norwegians alone, always the cowboys of the North, remain the last true believers in a separate Scandinavian route, while Sweden and Finland join Denmark along the primrose path of compliance that leads to Brussels.

Much of the blame for the hard times faced by the Social Democratic model of the welfare state can be laid at the door of economic globalisation. Globalisation has deprived each nation of much of its economic autonomy and forced a reform of social policy in a more market-oriented direction, even among those nations that had been paragons of welfare statism.[1] With the increasing mobility of capital and production that picked up steam in the seventies and eighties, all countries have had to play by largely convergent economic rules. Interest rates and levels of inflation have had to stay broadly in line with international levels. Holding inflation down has taken precedence over keeping employment up. Production costs, including of course indirect labour expenses, have been under pressure to converge with the least pricy, equally productive labour available on the international market. The upper-end outliers, high cost producers that compete abroad like Scandinavia

---

1 For globalisation, see: SCHWARTZ, 1994a; SCHWARTZ, 1994b; ANDREWS, 1994; NOTERMANS, 1993; MOSES, 1994; MOSES, forthcoming. I am indebted to JONATHON MOSES for guidance through the now extensive literature on this subject.

and Germany, have been the ones to feel this pressure most insistently.[2] The opposite extreme, the rising Asian nations with modern technologies and low wages have, of course, benefitted most. The countries of the middle, including the US, have had a harder time weighing the pros and cons.[3]

The second reason why northern Europe is no longer the locomotive of social policy development is that it has become increasingly clear that other nations are simply not following the Scandinavian path, or indeed any other foregiven route, to the welfare state, but are instead striking out in their own directions. Economic globalisation may be exerting similar market pressures on all nations and yet, ironically, at the same time that a certain overall uniformity is taking hold, a thousand welfare state flowers are blooming. At no previous time has the multiplicity and divergence of social policy been more clearly recognised. The Social Democratic view placed all industrialised nations at some point along a common road whose goal was the social policy pinnacle of security from the cradle to the grave or, to update a hoary metaphor, from the brood box to the life support system. All nations were assumed to be at quantitatively different points along the road leading to Stockholm. If they could not all actually be expected to reach this welfare Mecca, at least they were all, from different removes, genuflecting in the same direction. It is this one-track view that is now crumbling. Even scholars of a Social Democratic persuasion have recently taken to elaborating different models of welfare state development, none of which is reducible to another. Different fates, in other words, for different states, with value judgements about which is better or worse left to political evaluations that stand at a certain remove from the scholarly analysis rather than being embedded in it, as was the case with the Social Democratic approach (Baldwin, 1992).

The result is that the field of welfare studies is awash in typologies, Linnaean categorisations that testify to a plethora of different social policy possibilities, rather than any one overarching unilinear development. What started out as strict monotheism then developed into the usual scholarly trinity and has since ended up with as many typologies as the English have religions

2 The chapter by GÖRAN THERBORN in PFALLER et al., 1991, was probably the last expression of the traditional Social Democratic belief that Sweden was immune to the pressures of the international economy under which all other nations were suffering.

3 Many of those who most vociferously feared the loss of jobs southwards in NAFTA, Perot's famous sucking noise, are the same sorts who welcome Mercedes' decision to flee the high costs of home in order to produce in the leaner circumstances of North Carolina. One person's labour exploitation is another's healthy business climate.

and the French sauces. Among European welfare states alone there are at least a Scandinavian model, a British model, a Christian Democratic model, a Bismarckian social insurance model and a Mediterranean model.[4] Soon we will be adding various East European models, which, along with the other systems in the world outside Europe and North America, will complete the Babel of paradigms. The tendency among welfare state studies is decidedly nominalist and the motto of the field at the moment seems to be a variant on Buffon's claim that "the more one increases the number of one's divisions... the nearer one comes to the truth, since in reality individuals alone exist in nature" (quoted in Toulmin and Goodfield, 1965, p 174). But if unilinearity and eventual convergence are no longer seen as the case within Europe why should they be in a more global accounting? Or, more precisely, why should the goal of convergence throughout the world necessarily be found in the well-developed welfare states of northern Europe? This is the challenge thrown down by Richard Rose in a very stimulating global approach to the welfare state (Rose, 1991). His main point is to reintroduce the question of geopolitical importance. The Social Democratic view of the welfare state proposed northern Europe (in Rose's accounting France, Germany and Scandinavia) with its well-developed state structures and high social spending as the model for all nations. In fact, he argues, if one looks at the social policy systems that are home to the vast majority of the industrialised world's citizens, then the anomalies are not the other nations, but rather precisely those European countries whose social policy relies so heavily on the state. The Social Democratic model which claims for northern Europe a pre-eminent position is based on a normative evaluation of what the welfare state should be. But, viewed globally, the northern European welfare state is obviously not the norm; demographically and geopolitically speaking, the majority of those countries with social policy are not of this variety. Given the rollback of Social Democratic forces in northern Europe over the last decade, the problems posed by the stiffening globalisation of economic competition and the demographic issues thrown up by gerontocratisation, the tendency, if anything, is away from the sort of Nordic welfare state that achieved its apex during the 1970s. So what standard is it by which the Social Democratic model can still be portrayed as the goal towards which all welfare states are, or should be, moving, however slowly, however far their present remove?

---

4 BALDWIN, forthcoming. One scholar, once a believer in a unilinear development, has now declared himself ready to accept practically as many different models of welfare state development as there are industrialised nations (ESPING-ANDERSEN, 1993, p 136).

Rather than take the most elaborate welfare states – those that spend the most public monies and rely most heavily on the state's intervention – as the standard, Rose now introduces geopolitical significance as the criterion by which to measure such development. His claim is that if we wish to understand the kind of welfare state in which most of the industrialised world lives rather than the sort that is home to a few Scandinavians and north Europeans, then we should be expending our energies instead on what he calls the American-Pacific model – one, that is, where the state plays a lesser role and more is provided through the market, the family or other private means. One need not accept Rose's politics, nor even his obviously all too blunderbuss new American-Pacific category, to see that his challenge is one to which welfare state theorists must respond. Rose has phrased in extreme terms a common tendency among observers of social policy, he has formulated globally what has already been adumbrated in the European field alone. The issue is whether there is one set of standards by which social policy can be measured or whether each nation approaches a certain set of largely common problems from its own vantage point, solving them according to its own dictates, needs, ideologies and traditions. In the broadest sense, one not broached explicitly by Rose, the question is whether in an age when all metanarratives are being challenged we can still speak of a uniform, unilinear mode of development in this realm as well. Can there be a single welfare state in the era of postmodernism, or only a panoply of different ones?

In the days of a unilinear standard of welfare statedom, most systems of social policy other than the north European were dismissed as scarcely up to snuff. With the gradual realisation that waiting for other nations to become welfare states in the Swedish manner might well become an exercise in Godot-like patience, it became increasingly plausible to deal with the non-Nordic systems on their own terms rather than waiting for them to change their spots. From this point began the slide down the typologically slippery slope that has led to the current nominalism of welfare state studies, with a category for each national experience and little attempt to press different systems of social policy into larger common conceptual frameworks. The question is whether, having abandoned a largely inapplicable Swedocentric standard for other countries, we have arrived at the opposite extreme where no common standards exist any longer. If each system of social policy addresses problems common to all industrial societies in ways that reflect each unique social, ideological, demographic, economic and historical set of circumstances, then can we say that some do so better than others. Or rather, if we do, on what basis?

II. Varieties of Welfare

There are, globally speaking, at least three major families of welfare states, that is to say, ways of approaching the issues dealt with by social policy. In Europe, both western and eastern, the state is looked to for most solutions. Private and occupational efforts still play a role, as does charity, but it remains comparatively minor. In the burgeoning economies of Asia, at the other extreme, matters are reversed: the customs and institutions of civil society are expected to bear the brunt of social provisioning, with personal savings, occupational provision and support within an extended family intended, for example, to take the place of fully-developed statutory pension systems. The Asian nations appear so far to have achieved what the west did not: to bring through the crucible of industrialisation the institutions of civil society largely unimpaired and still able to fulfil their traditional functions. In the United States, an in-between system holds its ground: in certain respects – pensions, disability, unemployment – it is organised through the state and fits comfortably by most quantitative measures into the bottom half of the spectrum of European systems. In others – health, family benefits – it relies more on the efforts of civil society. These three approaches to welfare treat various social problems in quite different manners.

The question in such circumstances of welfare pluralism, is whether and, if so, how we can compare these various systems, what sorts of evaluative judgements we can make among them. As long as, say, infant mortality and whatever other chosen standards of public health are comparable, does it much matter whether a nation provides medical services by means of a nationalised system (Great Britain), a mix of various forms of compulsory insurance (Germany) or a basic national system supplemented by occupational provision (Japan)? If to be a welfare state a nation must be like Sweden – one, that is, in which the state is called on to solve the bulk of social problems – then only Sweden and a few others are or will become welfare states.[5] This is winning the argument by definition. If, in contrast, we see welfare states as something broader, something perhaps like Gerhard Ritter's definition of a *Sozialstaat*, a system whose legitimacy is founded on an ability to satisfy its citizens' desire for prosperity and security, then there is a broader interaction of state and civil society that needs to be taken into

5 This is the reasoning implicit in FRANK CASTLES' argument that Australia has achieved many of the same social ends as Scandinavia, but has done so in different ways (CASTLES, 1994, pp 31-46).

account (Ritter, 1989). Similar problems may be solved in different countries in different ways, by different combinations of state and civil society. Moreover, it may be that the concept welfare state should be seen as but one variant on a broader category of welfare society. Some nations achieve welfare through the state, others through the institutions of civil society.

As long as certain conditions of well-being are fulfilled, should we worry about how these are achieved? Obviously there are cases in which certain problems are simply not solved rather than being differently solved. Health care in the US is better organised for prison inmates than for ghetto residents, yet incarceration is scarcely a reasonable way to see a physician. The US faces a health care crisis that cannot just be treated as another way of approaching the problem. Health indicators for the white population are excellent, for certain minorities, in contrast, of third world standards. Similarly, since Hong Kong is now considering introducing a statutory pension system, thus taking the first step down the slippery slope to what Asian boosters like to portray as western decadence and sloth, the unprovided-for aged are presumably becoming a problem no longer adequately addressed by the informal practices of civil society. But in other sorts of cases, a significant element of cultural variation is involved. Many Americans think that the right to stockpile weapons is a cornerstone of their civic freedom and that without the protection of Saint Uzi, totalitarianism would be upon them; the average German apparently believes that the right to drive at breakneck speeds on the highways is an essential democratic liberty. Are there not similar differences in conceptions of social rights? Perhaps many of us would not wish to live in the well-ordered police state, however plushly upholstered, that is Singapore. But at some point, once we get away from the extremes that make for good debates but bad policy, we begin to deal with matters of cultural and ideological preference and taste.

Significant differences in the ideology of delivering welfare distinguish even systems that in other respects appear to be quite similar. In Germany, for example, it is in many ways not the individual who is the primary focus of social policy, but the family. The parents of even adult recipients of public assistance are liable, depending on their income, to reimburse the state for sums expended (BGB, § 1601. See "Schlimmer als Lindenstrasse," *Spiegel*, 38 (1992) p. 116). Thus, in a way that is not the case in Scandinavia nor in the Anglo-Saxon world, the family is responsible even for individuals over whom in other respects it has no control. The state agrees to administer the solution, paying public assistance in the first place, but foists ultimate accounting for the problem off onto civil society.

Or consider the way the three main varieties of welfare state take different approaches to reproduction. In Asia, the issue is dealt with largely through civil society: a family wage is paid to men, few women work once married, children are born and raised within a strong family structure and the issue generally does not percolate to the level of state intervention, except in the negative sense that in some nations strict limitation of family size is encouraged or enforced. In Scandinavia, at the other extreme, the state is heavily involved in what, from the Asian perspective, would be considered the basic responsibilities of parenthood. In many ways the traditional role of the father as breadwinner has been shifted to the state, with dramatic results for reproductive behaviour. With job security, family benefits and access to day-care, it is perfectly feasible for women to raise children alone, or at least without a partner whose obligations of parenthood are sanctified by marriage, and many births occur outside the venerable confines of the nuclear family. In America, similar circumstances – high illegitimacy rates – are cause for a degree of alarm unknown in northern Europe. Part of the problem is that such illegitimacy tends, Murphy Brown notwithstanding, to be more concentrated at the bottom of the social hierarchy than in Scandinavia. Part of the issue concerns American puritanism and a basic moral belief in the illegitimacy of illegitimacy that is still widespread.[6] But the main dilemma is that the US has no system other than Aid to Families with Dependent Children (AFDC) of dealing with the problem. Conservatives think that reproduction should remain the responsibility of civil society; liberals argue that the state must play a larger role in the family structure of the late twentieth century. Caught between the absence of any agreement on having the state intervene in such respects and the weakening of the traditional family, the North American debate circles in often shrill tones around issues of compulsory birth control, sterilisation and now – almost unbelievably – state-run orphanages. The basic debate, thus, is not whether there is a problem and whether it should be solved, but which part of the larger social system should be responsible for reproduction: state, civil society or some mixture of the two.

---

6 Although here it should be clear that conservative social values and illegitimacy are perfectly compatible. In Bavaria, for example, a conservative Catholic society by almost any measure in which it is still normal for children to live within shouting distance of their parents and grandparents, rates of illegitimacy have been abnormally high since records began. This obviously has more to do with old peasant customs where marriage was something arranged after the birth at a time when opportunity and circumstance coincided propitiously, than it does with the breakdown of the modern family in some guise or another.

The differences between national approaches to welfare are great and in more ways than is often appreciated, incommensurable. At the most basic level, not all countries face the same problems in the same way or to the same degree. Take housing: if much of the population owns its own home free and clear by the age of retirement, as is the case in the Anglo-Saxon world, then the pension system will be under less pressure to replace a high percentage of wages than in a nation where most remain renters, as in Germany. Housing policies, or at least tax breaks for ownership, serve as a partial substitute for other, more direct, forms of social policy. In other respects, certain basic social problems faced by every industrialised nation can be dealt with in quite diverse ways. Consider unemployment: some nations, like France, were able to ignore the problem until well into the post-war period, partly because their still only semi-industrialised economies made the issue less pressing than elsewhere.[7] Others, the majority of welfare states, have simply insured against the loss of wages due to involuntary redundancy. Instead of merely passively insuring, still other nations have intervened in the economic process itself to calibrate the supply and demand of jobs to each other. The Swedes have tended to tackle this from the supply side, seeking to retrain redundant workers and make them employable again. In the east bloc, matters were approached from the demand side, with the promise of a job, whether needed or not from a market point of view, for each person. Finally, one could foist the problem off onto civil society in various ways: pressuring women to withdraw from the workforce and free up jobs for men, as happened everywhere after 1945; encouraging the young to prolong their education and thus not be counted as disappointedly seeking work, as happens throughout Europe today where higher education has become for many students a form of outdoor relief and where, for example, in Germany the average university finishing age is above 30; promoting traditions of lifetime employment, as in Japan where featherbedding in private firms has left unemployment less of a problem than elsewhere.

Not only do different societies take different approaches to common problems, in some cases they may refuse to take an approach at all. There are certain forms of social policy that contradict basic ideological presuppositions within given cultures. Take family allowances. Because they are an ideologically charged issue, the importance of family benefits within the welfare mix varies dramatically, even within the allegedly so homogeneous

7 Unemployment insurance in France dates from only 1958 (LAROQUE, 1969, p 183).

European circle of welfare states.[8] Family benefits can be formulated in various ways and made to serve different ends. Seen as a wage supplement to compensate for the cost of rearing children, they are an antipoverty measure that seeks to distribute resources according to specific needs in disregard of merit. As such they have come into contradiction with the interests of unionised workers to be paid the highest possible wage for their work. Trade union interests in wages sufficient to rear and maintain dependants have clashed with the concern of employers to use family benefits in distributing wage increases in a targeted manner according to need rather than across the board. The great disparity between the French and British approaches to family benefits, as Susan Pedersen has shown, arose because in France such measures were favoured by industrialists and conservatives, while in Britain the strength of the male trade unionist movement hampered any similar introduction of a system of resource allocation that undercut direct wages in favour of indirect remuneration through social benefits (Pedersen, 1993).

But things can vary even more sharply. Why are there no family benefits along the lines of the European model in the US? Partly the answer is that the problem addressed was simply less pressing – that, as in Britain when the issue was being discussed in the late nineteenth and early twentieth centuries, American workers were being paid, by comparison with the French, a family wage. But is there not a deeper sense in which family benefits are in some ways wholly incompatible with most varieties of American political ideology? It is not that children are wholly ignored as a social problem. AFDC is targeted at children of the socially weakest and deductions for dependants and their care channel comparatively generous tax relief to the parented middle classes. If family benefits are motivated by demographic concerns, as they were when introduced in France and Sweden, they give voice to a certain kind of ethnic chauvinism that an immigrant nation could scarcely second and sometimes to a class preference incompatible with an egalitarian ideology.[9] Implicit in family benefits is the attempt to produce more of "our kind" and to reduce the need to admit and rely on nationally and ethnically different groups.

---

8 In 1983, family allowances, as a percentage of total benefit expenditure, varied from a high of 24% on Malta to a low of 0.3% in Switzerland (ILO, 1988, table 8).

9 In Sweden, for example, family measures were supported by the parties of the centre and right for reasons of eugenic and völkisch nationalist concern and in hopes of shoring up the fortunes of the insufficiently fertile middle classes. See: HATJE, 1974, pp 178-83; RAUSING, 1986; KÄLVEMARK, 1980, pp 55-57; MYRDAL and MYRDAL, 1934, pp 202-03.

There is also a sense in which family and especially maternity benefits raise troubling questions for feminists, at least in the way they are often formulated. However generous these benefits, there is evidence that, focused as they are on the role of females as reproducers, they hinder women's interests as producers. Employers, locked into long-term and expensive commitments for continued wages and job security during birth and infanthood (in Germany for up to three years), may well be reluctant to hire women of childbearing age. There is a strong likelihood that the continued low rate of female employment in Germany and France is encouraged by such measures, although obviously there are other factors involved here as well. In Scandinavia, where family benefits tend to be financed by the state rather than by employers and the immediate disincentive not to hire women of a certain age is thus reduced, rates of female employment are the highest in the world. At the same time, one of the peculiarities of the situation here is the extent to which women, having been shunned by the private sector, are predominantly employed in the public.[10] Having created a problem in the first place by pricing female labour out of the market, the welfare state is called on to solve it by hiring women directly.

Or take more generally, as an example of ideological and cultural attitudes that require different approaches to social policy, the liberalism that characterises all frequencies of the American political spectrum and forbids many of the statutory interventions taken for granted in Europe. The division between those for and against statutory social policy runs, of course, largely between left and right. But even the American left has been so liberalist, so concerned with a punctilious defence of civil rights at the expense of communal efforts, that it too must bear much of the responsibility for the inability, indeed the lack of desire, to implement a European-style welfare state in the US. This is not to criticise a concern with civil rights as such, but to emphasise that there are consequences and trade-offs to such a focus, and that one of them is to hamper the techniques of control necessary in order to dispense benefits that, while generous, do not also give away the store.

The intermittent American debate over a national identity card, for example, gives voice to fears of a police state that, from a continental European point of view, are exaggerated. The result is that, for perfectly obvious func-

10 ESPING-ANDERSEN, 1990. This skew has had consequences most recently in the Norwegian decision not to join the EU, where many women apparently voted no in fear that Brussels would limit the Norwegian welfare state and thus their employment opportunities.

tional reasons, the legitimisation function required in modern societies is instead foisted off on odd sorts of documents never intended for such tasks: drivers' licenses, credit cards and the like. (That the perquisites of citizenship should depend on one's relationship to an automobile is, I suppose, very American.) The one nation-wide and universal official document that does exist, the social security card, is usually specifically disallowed as proof of anything, since it testifies to little other than a brief correspondence with a Washington address. To enrol a child in public school – to claim, that is, and therefore prove entitlement to one of the basic appurtenances of citizenship – one brings, of all things, an electricity bill. In a nation where seatbelt laws are barely enforced, where perfectly commonsensical interventions like helmet laws for motorcyclists pass by the narrowest of margins when at all, it is unclear how the sorts of controls required by a full-fledged benefit system could be implemented. Or take the reaction that would doubtless erupt in America if certain sorts of control techniques were ever implemented, even in conjunction with generous measures. Maternity benefits in Germany tend to be financed by employers; in return, women are legally required to give notice if pregnant. Employers may ask female job applicants whether they are pregnant and they, in turn, are liable for damages if less than truthful. Employers can require, as a condition of employment, that women undergo medical examination, including a determination of pregnancy. Working women who breast feed are allowed an hour daily to nurse, but must in return prove on demand through medical examination that they are in fact lactating.

III. Citizenship and Access

Finally, consider an issue that, in California, has raised all the neuralgenic tensions implicit in different conceptions of welfare statism and, more generally, the potential contradiction between the generosity of social benefits and access to them. Proposition 187 would restrict public education and non-emergency health care to legal residents. Among its many problems is that it proposes to force teachers and others whose task this should never be to undertake a job that rightly belongs to the immigration authorities. The major unfairness of the proposition is that, in the middle of the game, it reformulates a series of unwritten rules. The Californian economy profits from the labour of illegal aliens and therefore, despite the letter of the law, tolerates their presence through an informally acknowledged claim to a quasi-official existence. Having done so in fact, it is unjust that long-settled, but officially unrecognised aliens, be deprived in midstream of such social services. Prop 187 is in fact a unilateral renegotiation of the rules of citizenship, passed because of an unpleasant combination of recession and racism.[11] But clearly the controversy generated has had less to do with its various infelicities of implementation and more with the basic principle here enunciated that social benefits, such as they are, should be restricted to those with a legal right to residence. However unfortunate the intent of Proposition 187, it would be naive not to recognise that it introduces a practice considered perfectly normal elsewhere, that it rests on a principle taken for granted everywhere in Europe and, as some commentators have pointed out, also in Mexico. The concept of illegal alien is scarcely known in Europe. No one without proper permission and authorisation is allowed to enter, much less remain here, and certainly not to enrol their children in school. Access to benefits not requiring some sort of market equivalence is regulated by the immigration authorities.

The crucial issue is not the limiting of access as such, which seems a fairly self-evident measure of economic rationality, but the definition of citizenship that gives access to benefits. Different qualities of citizenship give varying degrees of access and thereby have implications for the generosity of the social benefits granted. One of the major changes attendant on the development of the welfare state has been the evolution of the concept of social citizenship. Roosevelt's Four Freedoms, TH Marshall's whiggish analysis of the progress of rights, from civil to political and finally to social: such are the conceptions of citizenship at the core of the modern welfare state. Political rights anchor the unmediated right of individuals to participate equally in the decision-making process of the community regardless of their status or market position. Social rights are thought of as an analogous distribution of a certain level of bread and butter resources independent of virtue, wealth, pedigree or talent.

For certain sorts of benefits there is no question that social citizenship has helped justify a new level of access and availability. The British National

---

11 Although, one is almost relieved to note, this alleged racism is shared among almost all ethnic groups other than Hispanic, and not found just among whites. This, of course, raises the question whether racism, when ubiquitous, is racism any longer. If a majority of voters who belong to every ethnicity except the one that, for arbitrary geographic reasons, happens to be most directly implicated (and even here a large percentage of Hispanics voted for the proposition) supported the measure, then can we really speak of racism as one of the motivating forces?

Health Service most nearly puts into practice the theory of social citizenship, willing as it is to patch up anyone unfortunate enough to fall ill within the boundaries of the United Kingdom. No other health system, all with their various requirements of citizenship, membership or contribution payment barring admission to everything but the hospital emergency room, is so ecumenical. Primary education, in turn, is a benefit that in every industrialised nation is equally universal, while secondary and higher education of one variety or another is largely accessible to all of sufficient talent and motivation willing to make reasonable sacrifices. But beyond such realms in which social citizenship has left a distinct imprint, it is a concept fraught with difficulties. There remains, half a century after Marshall first formulated the idea, a tension between the market distribution and the social allocation of resources. Social rights are still not as unqualified as their political equivalents. There remains a strong sense in which even social benefits must be "earned" in market terms to be considered legitimate (Klausen, 1995). Social citizenship is an attempt to remove the stigma of what used to be considered public assistance or charity, to change public attitudes so that the fact of membership in the community is regarded as entitling one, irrespective of any market-based claims, to certain benefits. For most social benefits other than education, and in some cases health care, the criteria of entitlement rest not on social citizenship, but in fact on some sort of market exchange. In systems based heavily on the social insurance principle, as in Germany and France, payment of contributions is the price of admission, but even in more heavily tax financed systems, like the Scandinavian, those who pay for the goods know perfectly well who they are and have been expressing their dissatisfaction through Glistrup-like protest parties at having to support those who are primarily recipients.

The concept of social citizenship has in fact little pertinence to the distribution of, monetarily speaking, the bulk of welfare benefits: pensions, unemployment, health insurance, disability. Such matters tend to be a factor of the recipient's relationship to the labour market and in most countries benefits reflect one's position in the market: the longer the working life and the higher the wage, the more generous the payment. Social citizenship instead concerns largely the margins of the welfare state: the sorts of benefits that are distributed regardless of any effort made in return, ones that are often dependent on a test of means. It is here that the issue of citizenship, not in the social sense, but in the broader one of official and legal membership in the national community, has come to intersect recently with the question of access to welfare benefits. Political citizenship, or at least legal residence, is often the condition of access to such social rights. Citizenship in the general sense determines social citizenship.

Consider the debate in Germany where, thanks to its peculiarly ethnicist definition of citizenship, the issue has been posed most acutely. Because hundreds of thousands of east Europeans with long-distant family relationships to Germany, but no current cultural contact or familiarity, have had the right to citizenship and its perquisites (including various forms of public assistance not conditional on previous contribution payment or criteria other than legal residence and need), the non-market based elements of the German welfare system have been severely tested.[12] To this have come the claims to residence and similar benefits that could be staked under Germany's previously liberal asylum laws by arrivees claiming political persecution at home. The breakdown of Communism in Eastern Europe and the Yugoslav morass have in effect called the German bluff of widespread access for certain specifically defined groups to the rights of citizenship or legal residence. As long as the ethnic Germans of eastern Europe could not travel, as long as the Balkan and other crises had not yet sent thousands seeking asylum, the Germans could be generous. Once the proverbial pigeons came home to roost, matters changed and access to political citizenship and residence was tightened. The asylum laws have now, as elsewhere in Europe, been reformulated to choke off the flow and the newspapers report regularly on unpleasantly violent incidents as asylum seekers whose petitions have been denied are forced to return home.[13]

The citizenship issue has presented a nettlesome problem because the German definition of membership in what conservatives like to call the *Schicksalsgemeinschaft* is unusually dependent on ties of blood and descent. A debate is currently underway that pits most of the Greens and some elements of every other party in favour of a new definition of citizenship that would include at least elements of the *jus soli* criteria employed in most other nations against their opponents who favour retaining the old system in which family and "blood" ties are the primary determinants of citizenship. In its

12 A *Spiegel* cartoon many years ago showed foreign minister Genscher relating a nightmare he had just awoken from, wherein the 40 million Americans of German descent had also all wanted *Heim ins Reich*.

13 A recently passed referendum in Switzerland would allow foreigners without residence permits to be jailed for up to three months "preparatory incarceration" when they commit crimes or "do not reveal their identity." Foreigners can also be forbidden to leave or enter certain areas within the country. *Tagesspiegel* (5 December 1994), p. 1.

broadest sense, in the hands of conservative ideologists like Ernst Nolte, Botho Strauss and Rainer Zitelmann, this debate concerns more than just access to social benefits, or even citizenship in the narrow sense of a passport; redefining a neonationalist sense of identity is at stake here. And yet, as with Proposition 187, social benefits granted certain people who are not generally regarded as members of the community have been the issue sparking protest and reform. Nor are the Germans and Californians alone in this. In many nations, the wagons are being drawn around in protection of already won rights for those *sur place*, keeping others away from the enjoyment of social benefits. In Israel, it has been the alleged tendency of young Russian immigrants to park their pensionable parents in the Mideast while they themselves go off to America to earn a living that prompted Labour Minister Ora Namir to broach the possibility of a "selection," with all its Auschwitz connotations, of immigrants, rather than allowing every Jew the incontestable right of citizenship. Similarly, the claim of thousands of Indians to be Jews and hence potential Israeli citizens threatens to overwhelm the welfare system.

Political and social citizenship thus run at cross purposes. The simple rule governing the interaction of social benefits and political citizenship is that the wider the scope of welfare, the less encompassing citizenship can be; the more open membership in the political community, the more restricted access to social measures must be. Citizenship, or at least legal residence, is the hurdle to those aspects of the welfare state that are not based on market reciprocity and for which barriers are not therefore built automatically into their very functioning. For those benefits that are quids without quos, the watchdog of the welfare state is the immigration authority. In civil society-based welfare systems, this problem remains comparatively minor. Access is effectively restricted to those who are members of whatever informal communities redistribute resources. Whatever citizenship-based benefits exist are carefully guarded by a definition of membership that excludes almost all not born to it. Japanese definitions of citizenship, for example, are more restrictive than even the German. We tend to forget, however, how clannish in this respect, how Gemeinschaftlich, the European style of social policy is. The Social Democratic view of the welfare state with its overemphasis on the role of the labour movement, which in turn has a long history of exaggerating its cosmopolitanism and supranationalism, has tended to downplay this aspect. But surely it is no coincidence that the most elaborate and generous welfare states were developed in the most ethnically, religiously and socially homogeneous of European countries. The peasant and petty bourgeois background, not the proletarian, of Scandinavia has been the source of its social policy solidarity. Premarket communitarianism explains much of the luxuriance of measures that have treated all as members of a large family, measures that in effect equated citizenship and membership in the Gemeinschaft. Even in Germany, where we obviously get a wrinkle as far as the religious question is concerned, much of the story concerns the continued influence of a kind of antiliberalist, premarket thinking that has been very influential on the right.

The official public relations of a Gesellschaft tend to remain more tightly woven in with the informal connections of Gemeinschaft in Europe than in North America. Take, as but an example of an admittedly vast and nebulous topic, the gulf in attitude between the attempt, however successful, in the US to eliminate from job applications all personal information that might bias an employer one way or another (with the major but benignly-intentioned exception of affirmative action criteria) and the requirement that applications of almost every sort in Germany be accompanied by a photograph, or the rule that every child be given a first name that makes its gender apparent.[14] The debate over sexual harassment and its variations among nations also has its roots in such differing relations between public and private. Provoked by the Clarence Thomas-Anita Hill debacle, the European, and especially French, attitude toward such issues in America tended at first to be the snickeringly contemptuous approach that here was yet another example of American puritanism (Guttman, 1993, pp 205-06). But since then, as it has become increasingly clear that the main issue was less sex than power, and that the whole debate indicates the elevation of another realm of formerly private connections to the status of public relations, this too is an issue that is being increasingly debated and legislated across the Atlantic.

The nature of citizenship and the generosity of social benefits are intimately connected. Different definitions of community have consequences for welfare policy. Where citizenship has been most Gemeinschaftlich, a welfare state has hardly been required and the concept of welfare society is more

14 No Knabe namens Sue here. University of California policy on letters of recommendation, as an example, states that "Written material forwarded to an employer will contain no information which identifies a candidate by race, colour, ancestry, national origin, marital status, religion, sexual orientation, physical or mental handicap, medical condition (cancer-related). . . special disabled or Vietnam era veteran status, or within the limits imposed by law or University regulations, because of age or citizenship." In contrast, the slogan on Fotofix automats in Berlin exhorts self-assured applicants to enclose a photograph with their applications, that is, even in those instances when they are not required.

useful. Issues that elsewhere have become the state's problem are still those of the family, the firm, the voluntary community. Within the realm of the welfare state, properly speaking, things also vary greatly. Strict control is imposed at the borders of the community, limiting access to those welfare states that are most solidaristic and generous; conversely, less generous benefits are given in tandem to the more porously accessible American definition of citizenship. The concept of the welfare state has been fragmenting to the point where convergence on any common system of social policy seems unlikely. Each nation is increasingly implementing social policy according to its own dictates, of which definitions of citizenship are an important element, and each is likely to continue tailoring such measures according to local needs and criteria. Economic globalisation has thus, despite the common economic game rules it is foisting on all industrialised nations, led to a multiplicity of different approaches to the welfare state and undercut the intellectual importance of the north European model.

IV. The Multicultural Welfare State

There is another aspect to globalisation, broadly understood, that has implications for the welfare state: the cheek-by-jowl juxtaposition of different cultures that is one of the consequences of the era of mass migrations in which we live, the tendencies usually summed up in the hapless phrase multiculturalism. If the solidarity of the most generous welfare states, if the very concept of social citizenship has been dependent on a feeling of communality, whether created temporarily by the war, as in Titmuss' famous explanation of the Beveridgean revolution in Britain, or conveniently provided in an ethnic sense by geography and demography in northern Europe, then it is likely that multicultural tendencies will test and fray this sentiment of common purpose. Will the growing presence of Muslims in Europe mean an increasing demand for female physicians in the health insurance system?[15] Will circumcisions, now recognised as a cultural preference rather than a hygienic precaution, no longer be covered by American health insurance policies? Such possible consequences of multiculturalism for social benefits narrowly speaking are, of course, hardly insurmountable. But what about

15 As the contact between native women and Western medicine did in India during the late nineteenth century (Arnold, 1993, p 214).

requests, of the sort now addressed to European health insurance physicians, by women who wish to be reinfibulated postpartum?[16] Most of the consequences of multiculturalism have so far been felt in the broader realms of educational and cultural policy: when Algerian school girls in France demand the right to cover their heads in the classroom; when Muslims in Germany insist on being excused from sex education and on having separate sports for boys and girls; when Sikhs in Los Angeles stand on their claim to wear ceremonial daggers to school.[17] But there may well be a larger sense in which cultural fragmentation will have implications for the sentiment of common solidarity on which social citizenship is based.

Can we expect the same sort of groupthink possible in a culturally and ethnically homogeneous population also in one that is divided by cultural habits and practices? The distinction between smokers and non-smokers is already a major actuarial issue in America and will become one soon across the Atlantic. If non-smokers are beginning to fret at the health costs imposed on them by their inhaling fellow insurance members, can disputes between Big Mac gorgers and granola munchers be far behind, or between joggers and the sedentary.[18] And if such comparatively minor differences in habits between members of a common middle class culture can have major actuarial implications, then surely the same can be said of differences in multicultural practices and norms. If multiculturalism is to mean more than just window dressing in a fundamentally homogenous culture, the garlic in the otherwise bland meatloaf of drive-by cuisine, the banda station in the FM spec-

16 Or what about the arguments used to squash the Mexican National Institute of Public Health's campaign to educate consumers about the dangers of lead-glazed ceramics, that this was an attempt to suppress national cultural traditions? *Harvard Magazine* (January-February 1995), p 12.

17 The head covering issue in France has now expanded from primary and secondary schools, where one might begin to formulate an argument in favour of prohibition, to universities where it seems to bespeak a return to old-fashioned parietal regulations. In December 1994, the dean of the Faculty of Law at the University of Lille II forbade two first-year students from wearing head coverings because of the threat this allegedly posed to public order. *Deutsche Universitäts-Zeitung* (3 February 1995), p. 9.

18 Each "healthy" group of course conveniently forgetting what society as a whole saves in pension and disability costs through premature deaths. In any long-term and global cost/benefit analysis, it is likely that the most economically rational policy would be to encourage unhealthy practices. Long live the future Minister of Filthy Habits!

trum of easy listening – if, in other words, it means that real, and therefore often mutually distasteful, differences in personal habits and customs persist and are brought into jarring juxtaposition in the increasingly internationalised major metropolitan areas – then there will be consequences for the general sense of cultural solidarity and commonness and, from this, for the system of social policy, broadly understood. Much social policy is based on certain unspoken cultural norms and practices that are increasingly hard to take for granted. Generous sick leave with no waiting days, for example, assumes that the healthy will not abuse the system by calling in ill. But pain thresholds, a sense of what is required, how much indisposition an individual can reasonably be expected to bear and a general notion of what one is entitled to from the state all vary, both differing between cultures and evolving within one over time. The rising rate of sick days in Sweden (now the highest in the world and, by comparison, ca. seven times the Japanese) is not, presumably, due to a weakening of the Swedes' constitutions, but to a changing sense of what is tolerable and expected, as well, of course, as what the system will allow. In an Eliasian sense, if controls are not imposed internally they must come from without, but contrary to the development of the Civilising Process from external to internal ones, the development in social policy seems to be towards stricter external controls. It will be interesting, for example, to see how long Germany and Scandinavia can continue their systems of public transport based on the honour-cum-surprise-checks method before adopting the control-at-entrance (and sometimes also exit) methods found everywhere else. The honour system is based on communal groupthink, a sort of mass transit superego that avoids the free-rider problem in its most literal sense and keeps passengers in line with an unspoken but obviously firmly engrained cultural ethos that will be increasingly hard to maintain as the homogeneity of these nations is muddied.[19]

The solidarity and generosity of the post-war European welfare states were based on the premise that their populations were stable and homogeneous. It is precisely the unspoken assumptions that could be taken for granted under such circumstances that are increasingly being eroded. How these encapsulated and exclusionary welfare states deal with the issues of mass

19 Already now there are major problems in Berlin with *Schwarzfahrer* who give false identities and thus cause fines to be levied on innocents (usually friends or family of the culprits, whose names and addresses they know offhand). A system based mainly on informal processes of control is thus spilling over, in an era when such informal commonalties are breaking down, into major formal control problems for innocent bystanders.

migration and multiculturalism will be interesting to observe. Perhaps the welfare states of northern Europe, founded in circumstances of ethnic and cultural homogeneity and only subsequently faced with the problems of plurality, will have an advantage in their ability to integrate new immigrants, at least the few who are admitted, on the same terms as those formulated for the original members of the community. In northern Europe the onslaught of immigration, whether "guest workers" in the seventies or asylum seekers in the eighties and nineties, has provoked well-publicised chauvinistic excesses. But at the same time, the first generation of native born outsiders – often distinctive in their pigmentation, but conversing in the unmistakable twang of their local surroundings – is coming of age.[20] In the long run, these nations will need to reach an accommodation with their new status as destinations of immigration whether they like it or not. Demography, the increasing geroncratisation of the population, will require ever greater immigration over the next decades if the locals refuse to reproduce themselves. Every chauvinist with 1.56 children who wants to keep X-land for the Xs will have to tolerate more foreigners if he hopes to collect his pension once a chauvinist senior citizen.

Conversely, it may be that America, whose system has had long practice in accommodating new arrivals, will continue finding it difficult – to the extent it intends to remain a country of more open access than most – to institutionalise greater social solidarity than is already the case. Certainly the consequences of ethnic fragmentation for its social policy has been a theme as old at least as Sombart.[21] But on the other hand America can hope to play to the strengths of its system. American social policy have traditionally emphasised equality of opportunity rather than of outcome. All individuals were, in theory, to have comparable chances to demonstrate their mettle, with the outcome – fraught as it naturally was with sharp distinctions between the successful and the not – thereby legitimated as the result of individual differences in talent, ambition and energy rather than, as in the old world, that of inherited social station and status. In those aspects of social policy where equality of opportunity has been most consistently implemented, the American system holds its own with those of northern Europe or anywhere else: in education, especially higher, or in access of the handicapped to a normal public existence.

20 The first Germany-born MP of Turkish descent, Cem Özdemir, (whom the Germans still insist on referring to as Turkish-born [*geborener Türke*] because he has no automatic rights to German citizenship) was elected in late 1994.

21 And has now been pursued in QUADAGNO, 1994.

How the general dilemma between social solidarity and the increasing heterogeneity of modern culture, the cultural balkanisation that is an outcome of mass migrations, labour mobility and, generally speaking, globalisation, will be dealt with is one of the fundamental questions we face in the waning years of the millennium. Multiculturalism, broadly understood, forces the issue of how the social community is defined and where it ends. Social policy is the most important practical expression of the self-definition of a society, the nature of its community. Whether we can fashion a multicultural sense of solidarity or whether liberal bourgeois democratic societies will fissiparate even further – whether, in other words, there can be a post-modern welfare state that is more than the sum of its actuarial parts – will be one of the main questions requiring an answer.

References

ANDREWS, DAVID M.: "Capital Mobility and State Autonomy: Toward a Structural Theory of International Monetary Relations", *International Studies Quarterly*, 38 (1994).

ARNOLD, D.: *Colonizing the Body: State Medicine and Epidemic Disease in Nineteenth Century India*, Berkeley (University of California Press) 1993.

BALDWIN, P.: "The Welfare State for Historians: A Review Article," *Comparative Studies in Society and History*, 34, 4 (1992).

BALDWIN, P.: "Can We Define a European Welfare State Model?", in: BENT GREVE, (Ed.): *Comparative Welfare Systems: The Scandinavian Model in a Period of Change*, London (Macmillan) Forthcoming.

CASTLES, F G.: "Comparing the Australian and Scandinavian Welfare States," *Scandinavian Political Studies*, 17, 1 (1994).

ESPING-ANDERSEN, G.: *The Three Worlds of Welfare Capitalism*, Oxford (Polity Press) 1990.

ESPING-ANDERSEN, G.: "The Comparative Macro-Sociology of Welfare States", in: LUIS MORENO, (Ed.): *Social Exchange and Welfare Development*, Madrid (Consejo Superior de Investigaciones Cientificas) 1993.

GUTTMAN, A.: "The Challenge of Multiculturalism in Political Ethics," *Philosophy and Public Affairs*, 22, 3 (1993).

HATJE, ANN-KATRIN: *Befolkningsfrågan och välfärden: Debatten om familjepolitik och nativitetsökning under 1930- och 1940-talen*, Stockholm (Allmanna) 1974.

HUNTFORD, R.: *The New Totalitarians*, London (Allen Lane) 1971.

ILO: *The cost of social security,* Geneva (ILO) 1988.

KÄLVEMARK, ANN-SOFIE: *More Children of Better Quality? Aspects of Swedish Population Policy in the 1930's,* Uppsala (Historiske institutionen) 1980.

KLAUSEN, J.: "Social Rights Advocacy and State Building: TH Marshall in the Hands of Social Reformers," *World Politics,* 47 (1995).

LAROQUE, P.: "Social Security in France," in: SHIRLEY JENKINS, (Ed.): *Social Security in International Perspective,* New York (Columbia University Press) 1969.

LEVER, M.: *Sade: A Biography,* New York (Farrar, Strauss and Giroux) 1993.

MOSES, J. W.: "Abdication from National Policy Autonomy: What's Left to Leave?" *Politics and Society,* 22, 1994.

MOSES, J. W.: "The Social Democratic Predicament in the Emerging European Union: A Capital Dilemma," *Journal of European Public Policy,* Forthcoming.

MYRDAL A. and GUNNAR M.: *Kris i befolkningsfrågan,* Stockholm (Bonnier) 1934.

NOTERMANS, TON.: "The Abdication from National Policy Autonomy; Why the Macroeconomic Policy Regime Has Become So Unfavorable to Labour," *Politics and Society,* 21, 2 (1993).

PEDERSEN, S.: *Family, Dependence and the Origins of the Welfare State: Britain and France, 1914-1945,* Cambridge (Cambridge University Press) 1993.

PFALLER, A., I. GOUGH and G. THERBORN (Eds.): *Can the Welfare State Compete? A Comparative Study of Five Advanced Capitalist Countries,* Houndmills (Macmillan) 1991.

QUADAGNO, J.: *The Color of Welfare: How Racism Undermined the War on Poverty,* New York (Oxford University Press) 1994.

RAUSING, L.: "The Population Question: The Debate over Family Welfare Reforms in Sweden, 1930-38," *Europäische Zeitschrift für politische Ökonomie,* 2, 4 (1986).

RITTER, G. A.: *Der Sozialstaat: Entstehung und Entwicklung im internationalen Vergleich* , 2nd ed., Munich (Oldenbourg) 1989.

ROSE, R.: "Is American Public Policy Exceptional?", in: BYRON E. SHAFER (Ed.).: *Is America Different? A New Look at American Exceptionalism,* Oxford (Oxford University Press) 1991.

RUTH, A.: "The Second New Nation: The Mythology of Modern Sweden", in: STEPHEN R. GRAUBARD, (Ed.): *Norden: The Passion for Equality,* Oslo (Norwegian University Press) 1986.

SCHWARTZ, H. (1994a): "Public Choice Theory and Public Choices: Bureaucrats and State Reorganization in Australia, Denmark, New Zealand, and Sweden in the 1980s," *Administration and Society,* 26, 1 (1994).

SCHWARTZ, H. (1994b): "Small States in Big Trouble: State Reorganization in Australia, Denmark, New Zealand, and Sweden in the 1980s," *World Politics,* 46, 4 (1994).

TOULMIN, S. and J. GOODFIELD: *The Discovery of Time,* Chicago (University of Chicago Press) 1965.

Chapter 7

Origins of the «Social State» in German Philosophy and «Staatswissenschaft»

STEFAN KOSLOWSKI

In Germany, the origins of the «Social State» can be traced back to three different intellectual traditions: the socialist ideal of a transparent rational community of workers is as fundamental to it as are conservative defensive strategies against the social revolution. Standing alongside these sources have been, from the very beginning, deeply-rooted ideas of the «Caritas» of "Christian personalism." These superficially contradictory basic concepts came together for the first time in today's welfare state, based on the German constitution: the modern-day welfare state presupposes the acceptance of state and society as two forms of organisation, autonomous in principle, for the political and economic co-ordination of the human community (H. Zacher).

I. Philosophical Sources

With the «Grundlagen des Naturrechts nach Principien der Wissenschaftslehre» (1796) and «Der geschlossene Handelsstaat» (1800), J.G. Fichte transmits the social and political upheaval initiated by the French Revolution to German idealistic philosophy. Fichte refers to the «Discours sur l'origine et les fondements de l'inégalité parmi les hommes» and the «Contrat Social.» He builds on an individualistic ethical theory of the contract, combines it with the revolutionary motivation of the «German Idealism» and establishes the first German theory of the State: The State embraces all forms of social life and defines liberty in a material way. "It is the destiny of the State, firstly to give everybody what is his, then to establish him in his property, and only thereafter to protect him" (J. G. Fichte 1971, p. 399). It is not the protection of individual liberty that is focused upon but the duty of the State to care for the community – seen as a universality owned by the State. The State of the Age of Enlightenment cares for basic needs, and only then are its citizens permitted by «public servants» to decide what kind of activity they are «allowed» to do. Orientated to the autarky of the ancient polis, the enlightened State aims ". . . to help to give everybody as much of what belongs to them as part of mankind and then to keep it; . . . thus the State of the Enlightenment is as much a closed commercial state as it is a closed empire of laws and individuals" (p. 420). Fichte's model of a rational state provides for a socialist community. Public benefits and the right to free employment gain the upper hand over the right to own property and the co-ordination of the market. His doctrine ". . . places the primary and original property, the basis of all else, in a exclusive right to a destined free occupation. According to our theory, a property right to possess land does not exist"(p. 441f.). It follows that the State has to administer the national prosperity, allocate employment, forbid all non-governmental foreign trade, establish an internal currency and protect the weal of the nation by bribery of foreigners, economic espionage and territorial conquest. In short, the previously postulated rule of the State being governed according to Law is removed and the separation of State and society is disavowed; the development of mankind supersedes the individual as the purpose of State business. «In fact, Fichte's 'geschlossener Handelsstaat' is nothing other than the first great reflex of the French socialist ideas in a great German mind; it is the first German Utopia, but without consciousness that it is only a Utopia" (L.v. Stein 1975, p. 44). In a way, «der geschlossene Handelsstaat» anticipates a timeless topos of socialist theory.

The knowledge that society and State, market and policy are divided in principle, but are, in reality, constantly interpenetrating forms of co-ordination in the human community opens for the Hegelian «Philosophy of law» a way to understand that the State has an obligation to public assistance. With the egalitarian commercial society, social contradictions arise which demonstrate, that ". . . with the excess of wealth, civil society is not rich enough, i.e. is not possessed of enough property in real wealth to check the excess of poverty and the breeding of rabble" (G.W.F. Heger 1970). The State mediates between the common weal and the social conflict of interests. For Hegel the State is legitimised "... regarded in the abstract, chiefly in the interpenetrating unity of the universality and the particularity... and therefore... in action, determined by general laws" (p. 399). Although the Hegelian theory of the State partially contains rudiments of the modern Welfare State, such as an internal control over State authority (cf. 295 Rph.), its enforcement remains vestigial and its purpose false: His project, to integrate the philosophy of the State into the identical system of the idealistic philosophy, i.e. not only to combine freedom, law and social equalisation, but, beyond that, to see in the State a phenomenon predicated by the self-realisation of the «Weltgeist», on the whole destroys the system of Hegel's political philosophy, inasmuch as the «Rechtsphilosophie» is constrained by the differentiations introduced into it only to sink back again conclusively into the unknown development of the future – seen as a «substantial deity» beyond its phenomena. This hidden pantheism in the linear system of Hegel's dialectical method made him into an author «par excellence» of socialist theory: «The great importance of Hegel lies in his understanding of the general life of the world and of the personalities as a whole, that unfolds itself organically in its moments, and in which therefore the particular is nothing of itself and everything exists only as a moment within this universality. According to this absolute communism mankind itself is the only real personality; in which the particular is a vanishing part, and all are essentially equal inasmuch as, that they ... as individuals are of equally little significance"(L.v. Stein 1846, p.239) Insight into the complex interplay of individual, society and State constantly remains extraneous to German Idealism.

The way that social conflicts are not the consequence but the cause of political grievances is seen in the area around the idealistic philosophy by Franz v. Baader: ".... almost everywhere there exists a revolutionary potential easy to activate in society nowadays... [that finds]... its more deep-laying root ... by no means ... in an incongruence of relationship between the forms of government and the governed ... but in an incongruence which has arisen in the evolutionary stage of society these days, between the propertyless or poor class of folk and the propertied class in relation to their income ...." (F.X. Baader 1854, p. 129). A view over the so-called Christian and enlightened Europe shows that "... still, for most part, the civilisation of the few exists only by reason of the non-civilisation, even brutality, of the many, and that one has already approached much nearer to the ancient inhuman slavery and helotry, than was for example the case in the Middle Ages, the barbarity of which, by the way, presumably none acquainted with history would seek to defend" (p. 132).

Mechanical labour and cartels of employers do not only lead to the impoverishment of the «proletarians»; the power of capital wealth has shown, in addition, that, "... just as the proletarians exchanged their former bondage for social outlawry ... some administrations changed their former subjection to dynasties and lords for an ignominious dependence on puny argyrocrats, who mutated from being chamber servants to rulers of the treasury cabinets . . . and have, indeed already concentrated themselves into a world power" (p. 133). Baader recognises the explosive effect of the social-political grievance as a social challenge to society in a State, where "... the representation of the interest of the poor labouring people ... is scorned" (p. 136). As one of the first, he draws the attention of the "... audience ... to the big problem that is facing society in these times, the adoption of the proletarians into [society St. K.] . . . and this, until now . . . remains not only unsolved, but is seen as an absolutely insoluble problem . . . ." (p. 139). Beginning with the insight, that it is absurd, "... wanting to solve the conflicts of the civil society . . . without the spirit of religion . . . " (p. 18); in Baader's theocentric thinking the «Caritas» demanded of Christian charity replaces the chiliastic program of German Idealism.

II. Christian Charity and Social Mission

The writing of Wilhelm Emmanuel Freiherr v. Ketteler are grounded in Christian caritas like the reflection of Franz v. Baader. Returning to Thomas Aquinas and the medieval scholasticism, the later bishop of Mainz preaches that the Catholic church "... does not acknowledge an absolute property right for man over earthly goods, but only a right of using the order established by God. Then the Church protects the property right in a way that she says, that ... for the interest of order and peace, the established division of goods, as it has evolved between men has to be respected"(E.W. Kettler 1977, p. 32f). Liberalism like Capitalism, freed of religious and moral limits, proclaimed an absolute freedom and self-determination for man, but in fact they both destroyed humility and charity and therefore the load-bearing pillars of community. «Whether we have to go through the terrifying drama of a mankind, released from all higher law of the [divine St. K.] order, remains to be seen. But it is certain that, if this time is coming over us, it will surpass all, that earth has seen at any time, since human beings inhabit it» (p. 16). Like

Baader, Ketteler sees in the «soziale Frage» (p. 35)[1] the touchstone of State authority and legitimacy. But differing from the liberal Catholic Baader, Ketteler stands firmly on the rock of Peter. According to him, the origin of evil lies in the hubris represented by liberalism, which apostasises mankind from God for the sake of deifying their property: "The world has apostatised from Christ, it has refused redemption in Christ, it has become a slave to the mastery of its passions, and that is the last, deepest and truest origin of our social suffering and conditions" (p. 40). Consequently the «curing» of such a failure of social conditions is an obligation not only of social interest groups but, above all, of religion. «He, who believes in an eternity, wants to put his capital out to interest, which is paid out in heaven. That opinion can generate only avarice and hard-heartedness» (p. 60). ". . . if there is no universal court, where all suffering and joy is thrown into the scales and compared, one to another, before mankind . . . : so let us throw the paltry practice of justice here on earth overboard too, for . . . the idea of justice among men is a folly. However, this is not so really. . . truly there is an eternity, in which each man personally receives what he personally has sown here, reward for the just, punishment for the unjust" (p. 6f). "Whether the Church speaks to an innocent child . . . or to the perfectly wise, she always does this only by reason of the same assumption of mission, that she has received from the Son of God, and thus from a superhuman authority, to teach human beings . . . " (p. 8f). In the face of a society, in which the traditional concepts of religion and morals no longer symbolised anything, [2] the appeal to Christ in men, i.e. a "Christian mind" was not sufficient. Industrial poverty, the «pauperism», had already led to a situation where individual private charitable care was no longer sufficient to ease want. «The employers stand in a world market and ask: Who wants to do the job for the least wage? and the workers outbid each other in making the smallest demands, according to the measure of their misery . . . . At last, naturally, this leads. . . to privation of the most

1 "The political movement finds its overwhelming sympathy for the poorer people only because of the desolate and unnatural conditions of their victuals. . . . Thus, if we want to recognise our times, we have to get to the bottom of the social question. Those who grasp this, recognise the present times; for those, who do not understand this, the present time and the future remain an enigma."

2 Already by 1848 KETTELER had had to recognise: «We live in times of delusive Christianity. Still so many men belong superficially to the Church, that are separated in belief from her. The consequence is depravity in the marriage, in family life and the destruction of the family spirit, which we have to deplore» , p. 71.

necessary needs in food, clothing and accommodation . . . . No illusion is any longer possible, that the whole material existence of almost all the working class, thus by far the greatest part of men in modern States is exposed to all the ups and downs of the market and varying prices of goods, for the existence of their families, i.e. with their daily care for bread for man, wife and children. . . This is the slave market of our liberal Europe, tailored to the model of our humane, enlightened, anti Christian liberalism and freemasonry" (W.E. Ketteler 1977, p. 379). Ketteler was already an early supporter of the co-operative unions and the «productive associations», (p. 450) yet at first he rejected all kinds of State socialism. Disappointed by the negligible response that his proposals to the rich found, the bishop of Mainz finally saw that his working associations could not be financed by private alms only and ". . . that he could not do justice to the social tasks without State support and legislation" (E. Iserlon 1977, p. 408). The year 1869 can be seen as the moment of the birth of the Church's social policy, insofar as Ketteler made many demands of the labour movement his own. In a speech on «the labour movement and its aspirations in its relationship to religion and morality», (W.E. Ketteler 1977) he supports not only ". . . this justified endeavour to obtain a different payment for human labour than for work done by machines, which means the same as to give back to human labour and to the worker their dignity, which the principles of liberal political economics had robbed them of. . ." (p. 413); he also outlined a social-political program that transcends charitable care and pointed ahead far into the future. The aspiration for wage rises, orientated to economical rentability and productivity, is flanked by a requirement for shorter working hours, respect for Sunday rest, the guarantee of rest-days and the ban on work done by children, girls and women. All these demands were claimed – with the reservation: «It is not the struggle between employer and worker that has to be the aim, but a just peace between both" (p. 415). These propositions were combined with the admonition that all this ". . . will only be crowned by a lasting success, if it remains in profound connection with religion and morality" (p. 413). "Everywhere we would see that the demands of the working class, as far as they are justified, find their true support in religion and morality" (p. 426). Wilhelm Emmanuel v. Ketteler initiated the tradition of the German social Catholicism.

Although the German episcopate accepted Ketteler's initiative in the same year,[3] it found an echo only in 1891 with the official social pronouncement of

3 c.f. «Referate für die bischöfliche Konferenz zu Fulda», 1869.

the Catholic Church authorised by the ecclesiastical hierarchy: With the encyclical «Rerum novarum» by Leo XIII, Rome freed itself for the first time from its defensive struggle against modernism and the «social question» became a central part of the Church's task. Now social conditions of the workers were seen as a genuine new challenge to Church and society: A sufficient wage was demanded for the subsistence of the workers' families "... as the rightful property (of the one) who has done the work" (Leo XIII 1977, p. 36). Besides a just wage, the right to join combinations of workers (trade unions) and an obligation on the State to undertake orientated intervention in the economy, limited by principles of subsidiarity were demanded. Today this is valid still: "State intervention is allowed only as far as it is necessary to mitigate harm and prevent danger, but no further into the private life of its citizens" (p. 52). The form and content of «Rerum novarum» were as characteristic of the neo-aristotelianism of the «neoscholasticism» as was the encyclical «Quadragesimo anno» by Pius XII., published in 1931; this writing establishes as much the right and the duty of the State, to protect private property rights as it does the necessity to limit them. "If ... State authority limits private property for the sake of the common weal, this indicates no hostility towards the owners but is an act of friendship; for it thus prevents harm caused by the establishment of private property, leading to intolerable things not to be borne and, thus, the danger of private property digging its own grave" (p. 109).

The evolution of the social doctrine taught by both Christian confessions in Germany is firmly connected with these important documents. The ecclesiastical social doctrine "... is a compilation of key subjects, which was developed as an answer to the challenges of the day" (W. Kerber et al. 1991, p. 31). After World War II, in West Germany, principles of this «Christian personalism» were integrated into the concept of the Welfare State of the unitary federal state (Konrad Hesse): According to the principles of subsidiarity, concrete property rights are protected by constitutional law, while jurisdiction and administration of the law protect the political liberty of the individual against economic power and governmental arbitrariness. The disparate aims of property rights and social rights form a constitutional and administrative system that partly dates back to the originally ecclesiastical principles of concordance, founded in the "Confessional era" (M. Heckel 1983) during the XVIIth century. Under the doctrinal primacy of the "unity of the constitution", the administration has to establish a balance between the social inequalities caused by the dynamics of a competing economy. In this way, the temporal State has changed from a «liberal» moderator to a «social» organiser of society's antagonism, a view not disputed in the present-day German doctrine regarding the State.

III. The Way to a «Social State» in German «Staatswissenschaft»

As one of the first in German «Staatswissenschaft», the lawyer and historian August Ludwig Schlözer saw charity as a public task and primarily as an obligation of the state. As a liberal and critical companion of the philosophy of the Enlightenment his concern was that "... civil and State society have to be separated from each other and that some ideas have to be formed for a science of its own, without which no tested State law is thinkable" (A.L. Schlözer 1793, p. VI). In respecting the freedom of the individual, the State finds its highest purpose "... in the weal of its citizens insofar as it be possible to maintain, support and promote it by a State association" (p. 17). Agriculture, commerce and trade were seen as tasks for an «industrial policy» of the State (p. 20) and the State administration was to settle social grievances.

As early as the beginning of the Nineteenth century in Germany, industrialisation, combined with the population explosion,[4] aggravated the social antagonism; very soon structural poverty, «pauperism», was quickly recognised as a challenge to be met by the State. "One sees the wonderful contrast between the wealth and the glamour of the capitalist ... and the boundless dirt and misery of those who formerly worked in these mills and lie there now, crippled in mind and body... in dreadful idleness... " (H. Luden 1811, p. 221). The State should not "... be unconcerned, whether labour and its fruits are separated, so that one part of its citizens is producing, while the other is consuming, or whether they are so unified, that each one gets the use he wants and needs for a full education" (p. 221f). Therefore it is necessary that the government "... tries, firstly, to minimise all kind of poverty among its citizens, because ... this could everywhere become disadvantageous to the purpose of the State" (p. 395f). According to Luden, the aim of the State was to guard the freedom of the individual. For their protection two things should be done: « Firstly, he [the individual St. K] must be certain of his rights; secondly the space of action, which is allowed to him in this space, must be big enough for him to be able to live fully within it and, because he is always developing ...: this space has to widen or change itself in a way, so that at all times he remains free to live his life to the full. Without the one

4 c.f. HENNING, F.-W.: *Die Industrialisierung in Deutschland 1800 bis 1914*, Paderborn (UTB Schöningh) 1976, p. 17.

and the other, the unsociable nature of man will soon become predominant . . . . Without the first, there is no culture possible, without the other, there is no development in culture" (p. 8); thus the State would be ". . . a union of human beings who, among themselves, wish so to modify their relationships, that their complete rights – or their common liberty – should be preserved with joint enforcement against each violation, and that each member should be able to be sure of the security of such rights, which permit him freely to live his life to the full" (p. 10). Security under the law and provision for existence were seen as an indivisible uniform purpose of public action. Even the understanding of the culture of the State in our times was anticipated in a nutshell: population policy, public assistance, health care and education were recognised as tasks for the social policy of the State (p. 409f, 416, 422).

The works by Lorenz v. Stein comprised concepts, systematically arranged, that had arisen in English, French and German political science during the transition from the 18th to the 19th century under the conditions of the industrial and political revolutions; moreover Stein combined these thoughts, part of the huge heritage of French socialist ideas with the philosophical rationalism of the 17th and 18th century in England, France and Germany and with the German Idealism. Yet his model of «Staatswissenschaft» is bound to a «close to earth» scientific empiricism:

In the egalitarian society of commerce, State and society were, in principle, to be separated and the State was obligated to the weal of each individual. The solution of the «social question» (soziale Frage) – a term, created by L. v. Stein (1842)[5] – "did not lie, by any means, in an impossible ablution of the distinction between social classes and of the differences between men in the general; . . . but it lay . . . in the relationship between the interests of labour and capital. Therefore labour and capital, mutually generating and conditioning each other, according to their innermost essence, have a solidarity of interests" (L.v. Stein 1959, p. 203). Stein's writing built on this insight. It conceives Society and State as genuinely "timeless" tasks of social philosophy, which had become a general study of legal and administrative science. It refers back to the Philosophy of the Enlightenment, taught by Hugo Grotius, Samuel Pufendorf and Christian Wolff, linking it with the older German doctrine of public law and subjects both to the primacy of self-determination of the individual, demanded by subjective idealism.

5 "Just as at the end of the last century, one rank of the people rose up against the state, so nowadays one class of it has it in mind to overthrow society, and the next revolution now can only be a social one."

This system based at first sight on contradictory theories, legitimises and limits the purpose and tasks of a «social state»: It is in equal measure as much an answer directed against socialism and communism as it is against the "eudaemonistic" Welfare State: While the eudaemonistic principle of the Welfare State leads to the dictatorship of a police state, socialism "makes all individuals . . . as representatives of the species, equal" (L.v. Stein 1846, p. 239), failing to recognise that individuality and private property rights belong together and leads to the tyranny of a crudely rationalistic central planning commission. In contrast to this the «social state» understands itself to be the fulfilment of the German liberal doctrine of the «Rechtsstaat»: Avoiding the nuisances that result from a doctrinal Liberalism, the «social state» acknowledges the liberal axiom ". . . that the validated order of State life, and therefore that of the administration too, has to be determined only by law, established through an organised intention of the State" (L.v. Stein 1975, p. 21), and connects it with the social mission that ". . . each man rises by himself . . . from a lower class to an upper one . . . ." (L.v. Stein 1876, p. 140). Stein's project leans toward the perception that the State ". . . is representative only of individuals, who already have their position in society. . . ." According to his idea, the state is the ruler, but in reality, he is the ruled (L.v. Stein 1959, p. 51). This knowledge causes a change of paradigm in the theory of the State: Contrary to the doctrine of the State and philosophy before his times, Stein already takes his stand amidst the industrial society ". . . and wants to build an overarching State onto it" (E.-W. Böckenförde 1958, p. 149). Therefore (St. K.) the doctrine of the State has only first to accept the fact that " . . freedom given by law certainly only becomes valid law by means of a Constitution, but that it can only be generated, in fact, by the '-State civic society' (staatsbürgerliche Gesellschaft)" (L.v. Stein 1975, p. 30). It is not sufficient to write the equality and liberty of individuals into the constitution and ". . . to look for the core of public law only in a negative limitation of all governmental rights by the constitutional institutions; so that, the power of legislative process and of scientific research is exhausted in questioning how these restraints may be brought about most effectively, before reaching the much more serious question, concerning what could and should be the content of these governmental rights, in order that they might be empowered to find their just limits by this necessary content only" (p. 299).

Stein takes over the «material equality» postulated by socialism; yet he combines with it the right to individual self-determination. Stein's concept transfers the chief importance of the constitutional State to the guarantee of equal rights and not to individual liberty and he combines the social mission with the constitutional State. This social mission has a decisive importance for the evaluation of the administration . . . . Thus, for Stein, the important point . . . "of activity in the service of the community is a characteristic of administration" (E. Forsthoff 1973, p. 46). For "amidst all the directives, movements and contradictions in society, it is namely the State that remains the personal unity of all . . . . Its greatness, its power and development . . . arise only there, where progress in all areas of life is common to all, without being influenced by social distinctions. The higher nature of the State . . . always cares first for those, who are subordinate and under dominance, because of their intellectual, economic and social dependence. Grounded in this, her nature . . . the principle of the social administration in a higher sense arises, which is the end purpose of administrative doctrine" (L.v. Stein 1975, p. 31). "The inner administration of the State, therefore, comprises the totality of all those real activities of the State, the mission and last aim of which is realised through the individual development of all individual personalities belonging to the State – that is to say in the widest meaning of the term"(L.v. Stein 1975, p. 5). Whereas liberalism mistakes the co-ordination of the markets that were freed by the egalitarian economic society for the political co-ordination of general ends as a whole, socialist theory forgets that ". . . the science of the State, which it only notices in order to damn it" (L.v. Stein 1876, p. 247), is nothing other than ". . . the philosophy of the deed, elevated to an organic system of living inequality and of its own practice" (L.v. Stein 1972, p. 270).

While believing in a holistic universal idea of «Staatswissenschaft», this kind of intellectual investigation has reached a differentiation within the social sciences that requires a knowledge of ". . . the interaction between the weal of the people, State economics and administration . . ." (L.v. Stein 1885, p. 3) as much as it has to correspond to the «democratic principle." Into this complex framework the ideal of a social state can gain only normative meaning as a "general principle" or "mission"; in other words: the promises of the liberal constitutional State are taken up by the "social administration." «For, by the powerful element that forms society, which lies precisely, after all, in a good administration, the administration will generate the best constitution through itself. These are and remain the starting points for the science of the State in our times and in our future" (L.v. Stein 1876, p. 49).

Interpenetrated by a philosophical idea, the social State becomes a reality, above all, through the "administration." Therein lie the dangers and the good points: the State administration can only distribute what has been produced beforehand in society. Therefore, the possibility always exists, as a potential possible structural danger mainly within the welfare administration, that "... the State separates itself from the interests and missions in life of individuals, and, instead of seeing them as an end, uses them as means" [6] (Stein 1975, p. 48).

The «social state» sees itself thus far as heir to the socialist principle of solidarity as well as to Christian «Caritas." As it is responsible equally to the democratic principle, which appears in State and society as a participatory right and as negative freedom for the individual, the State has to remedy social inequality caused by economic life. Therefore "... the entire essence of public assistance, in which the development of individual fortune forms the basis for rising from a lower to a higher class, is a task for the administration" (p. 50); In this perspective "... the inner administration ... sets no limits at all for its social tasks" (L.v. Stein 1885, p. 156). From this arises the main problem of the timeless challenge to and the "endangerment" of the «-social State»: If the given income receipts do not correspond to the limits of social expenditure, that is to say if the administration costs more "... than it is worth – thus, first of all, individual production loses its power to increase capital ... through these payments to an unproductive administering State, and will then go under itself .... What is sure is that it must be the highest economic principle of a State administration not to demand more in payment from its citizens than the value that it is producing itself, and afterwards it has to allocate these ... sums to each part of the administration in such a

6 One has to mention that in contrast to today's «social politics» Stein was always aware that: "... there is no substance of the administration, no matter for it, that is personally owned by the state, which he could give the administration .... Therefore, the state in its administration has nothing at all to do on the whole with property of its own, but with things, produced by the acts of individuals that participate in the community. In fact its (the state's – St. K.) administration is on the whole the reciprocal action of all, one with another, subject to an individual self-determination, that was brought to a personal form within the community; this personal aspect of a harmonious development of mankind appears firstly in the subordinate spheres, such as the economy of the state and the administration of justice, being concerned with the material substratum of goods in the former case and with the negative element of external inviolability in the latter and, finally, in the administration elevating itself to the positive life of the harmonious development of the individual by the whole" (ibid., p. 47). Beside Stein's tribute to the holistic concept of German Idealism, one should see that, at the time, his understanding of the problems of administration, caused by the unlimited nature of its functions, was almost unique.

manner that just as much money is applied as it is able to use for the needs of the community as the case may be under given circumstances" (p. 26).

According to Stein, the State fulfils its social tasks only if it respects the autonomy of the social development and social science that mirror and accompany it: furthermore, financial science – emancipated from ancient «cameralistics» – has to complete its mission: it must ". . . figure out the measure of the attainable limits for this social mission" (p. 156). Although the social principle demands from the State a «benevolent administration», the latter finds its limits at the one point, where a benevolent administration threatens the private autonomy of the individual and the State starts to attack the basis of its own existence; ". . . because it is indeed the sum precisely of these single individuals, who, taken for themselves, are only what they have worked for and call their own by their own doing. Therefore this State benevolence has to find its limits, where it threatens the autonomy of the free personality" (L.v. Stein 1975, p. 58). Hence, there follows the "subsidiarity" of a benevolent administration as a principle of the «social State»: Since ". . . the State is never allowed under any circumstances to effect, via the administration, something other than the production of the conditions of personal, economical and social development, which an individual cannot produce by himself and then to leave to the individual and his free self-determined act to build and develop his own life by using these conditions" (p. 59).

The «eudaemonia of the Welfare State» and the «social question», which was insufficiently understood by communism and socialism, came together in a complex theory. The edifice of the social State was not built on an abstract principle that eliminates the individual, society and State. Within the administration system, as in society and politics ". . . each part of them has its own policy, even if it is determined by personal, economic and social conditions" (p. 61).[7]

7 Cf. KOSLOWSKI, ST.: *Die Geburt des Sozialstaats aus dem Geist des Deutschen Idealismus. Person und Gemeinschaft bei Lorenz v. Stein,* Weinheim (VCH/Acta humaniora) 1989, and ST. KOSLOWSKI: «Die Staatswissenschaft als 'Philosophie der Tat'. Das Zusammenspiel von individueller Freiheit, Gesellschaftsmacht und staatlicher Verantwortung bei Lorenz v. Stein», *Archives for Philosopy of Law and Social Philosophy,* Vol. LXXVIII (1992), pp.35-67.

IV. The Road to the Temporal Welfare State

Stein's expositions regarding the possibilities and the limitations of the State within an industrialised society are connected with the insight of post-Hegelian philosophy that, in general, a life accompanied by rules does not become simpler, but instead indicates a growth in complexity. "Mankind individualises itself more and more in a richer and deeper way; and this liberation of individuality on all sides is the fundamental content of history" (I.H. Fichte 1832, p. VII), wrote Immanuel Hermann Fichte in 1832. He views the «Janus-headed» comprehensiveness of the drive to modern industrialisation: "But the more manifold and the more particular the way the individuals stand beside each other, the less the individual decides and, henceforth, only whole epochs, the totality of basic trends will count and act, and only with a comprehensive view, no longer constrained by its own dullness or prejudiced arbitrariness, will be possible to understand the times and oneself within it" (1832).

In the industrialised society, the single individual and society are increasingly separated from one another; machines determine the rhythm of life, compel men to mobility, dissolve the existing pattern of class domination and its "personal legitimisation», while the new collective identity of social classes replaces feudal-hierarchical systems of reference. The rise of fixed social classes might be the cause, in the long run, of the biggest one of them, i.e. the proletariat ". . . without any force and external shock to the ordering of the State, being able to abolish, in a strictly legal way, by means of the gradual destruction of independent capital, all the inequalities that had arisen by a diverse distribution of goods in humane society" (L.v. Stein 1885, p. 149). Although Stein's social-scientific analysis of the origin and direction of the creation of social classes as well as his systematic ordering of society, law and economy in a social state could not be maintained in times «where causality had the sceptre» (Gustav Schmoller), nevertheless he had justly foreseen tendencies towards a step-by-step settling of social class interests and of compensation for social struggles by technological innovation and education: The insight that ". . . what one understands by 'the final objective of socialism' in general [actually St. K.) . . ." (E. Bernstein 1898), meant the movement towards the Welfare State was constantly present among the «pragmatic wing» of the German social-democratic party; it first appeared explicitly in the so-called «Revisionismusstreit» (controversy on revisionism) within the SPD, which was influenced mainly by Eduard Bernstein.

Beginning with a Marxist analysis of society, a critical review of its, in the meantime, dogmatised doctrine had shown "... that the class of capitalists increases.... The roots of society are changing, but its formation does not become simpler" (E. Bernstein 1909, p. 31). «The rising class movement,» already described by L. v. Stein, was also seen by E. Bernstein. Although social inequality was increasing, one had to realise that even "... right at the bottom, amongst the workers, there is yet a certain rise to be detected" (p. 74). This is the theoretical background for Bernstein's suggestion to modify the social democracy from being a social-revolutionary movement into a left-wing reforming people's party. "Thus the perspective that we see lying before us, from now on demonstrates that the way of the working class, as it were leads not only forward, but also upwards at the same time, with not only an increase in numbers but also a rise in its economic, ethical and political level, an increasing ability and engagement as a participant ruling factor in the State and the economy. In this sense of the perspective, revisionism, translated into politics means reformism" (p. 41f).

Since the late 19th century, alongside political controversy, concepts of democracy, constitutional state and welfare state were drawn to each other ever more in social sciences too; firstly by J. Ofner: "Elementary democracy requires the social state, an organism similar to the constitutional state, but not, like this one, limited to maintaining what belongs to me and to you ... but a social state taking on public assistance as an object to protect a just distribution of benefits and burdens in their totality, based on the equality of all" (I. Ofner 1894, p. 76). In consequence, the term «sozialer Rechtsstaat» (social constitutional state) was coined, influenced mainly by H. Heller.[8] Nevertheless, even within the SPD, the influence of social-democratic lawyers was negligible during the first German republic.[9]

While Stein had scientifically developed the prospects and limits of a social state based on an universal philosophical conception, German social democracy, admittedly, demanded socialism, politically and socially, but, in its gradual transition to being a people's party, it was one that, in practice, was step by step on the road to bringing about the social state. German "State and law philosophy," following Kant and Hegel, remained, as before, a phi-

8 cf. HELLER, H.: «Rechtsstaat und Diktatur», in: HELLER, H.: *Gesammelte Schriften*, 2, 1971, p. 450; PILOTY, R./SCHNEIDER, F.: *Grundriss des Verwaltungsrechts*, Teil 2, 4/5, 1930.

9 c.f.: LÖSCHE, P. and WALTER, F.: *Die SPD. Klassenpartei – Volkspartei – Quotenpartei*, Darmstadt (Wissenschaftliche Buchgesellschaft) 1992, p. 67.

losophy, the theory of which had flowed "... from a doctrine about the content of the State to a philosophical deduction of the concept of the state, the basis of which is again for most the concept of the Law, which embraces the State and all other aspects of life as a whole .... It became a totally abstract philosophical system, which set, as its ultimate and highest aim, the development of a pure concept of State and Law ... but one in which it no longer engaged itself in things that the administration of justice or internal administration demanded of it; it became 'impractical' in the ordinary meaning of the term ... for it in no way... solved ... all the questions and contradictions in this constitutional State for those who had to live within it" (L.v. Stein 1975, p. 26f). [10]

10 The conception of a «Wirklichkeitswissenschaft» by L. v. STEIN remained committed to the understanding that man was a self-determining being and, therefore, one that acted in a responsible way. It demanded from philosophy a 'positive' fulfilment of idealistic promises; in short a return was demanded to the realities of daily life. His 'view over the fence' brought him to a realization of where, in the era of specialization, the experts in universality, i.e. the philosophers, might slip off to; namely to that place where, "... our philosophy threatens to become a little lost in a spiritual microcosm of dialectical processes." And he demands in vain of philosophy, "... that after it seemingly has lost sight of the concept of property for the most part, nevertheless it asks itself, what is the meaning of 'administration', philosophically speaking. Just one more time only – and we would be standing on the threshold of mighty successes!" (STEIN, L.v.: *Handbuch der Verwaltungslehre,* Teil I, Stuttgart 1888, p. IIIf). As equally fruitless as his invitation to philosophers were his efforts to suggest philosophical thought to specialists in administration science and national economists. In 1867 Gustav Schmoller had already foreseen the merit and the futility of Stein's pioneering efforts in a review of the first volume of Stein's Verwaltungslehre : «The critique ... is, in the main, correct and far superior to the narrow horizon of most of our teachers of state law. ... Stein, who proceeded from philosophy to his theory of the state, dares to take the same road with the national economy and he ventures the same leap from a mechanical causal explanation to just a teleological one; ... with that, he creates a true system for the first time, but his experience is that by far a great majority of national economists so little understand his books, that they may as well be written in Chinese. ... The firmer the exact and historical basis becomes, on which Stein built his teleology, the more valuable it becomes; but, whether or not our times want to hear it, just because he is taking another scientific direction, he has effected something truly great» (SCHMOLLER, G.: «Lorenz v. Stein», *Preußische Jahrbücher,* 19, [1867], p. 245ff < 249 and 269>). It is precisely this that lends the works of L. v. STEIN a timeless actuality, which goes way above their significance in dogmatic history and the history of philosophy.

V. A Short Review of Theoretical and Ideological Efforts to Rebuild and Legitimise the Public Assistance System in Germany After World War II

With its «Grundgesetz» (fundamental law) the Federal Republic of Germany gave itself a political and juridical system committed to federal, democratic and social principles.[11] Thanks to its deep horizontal and vertical differentiated «social administration," the new political order proved good at an expensive price – which was seen far later. Stein and Heller had still recalled that "... everywhere the institution of a state generates similar effects, which have an objective significance for the life of society as a whole" (H. Heller 1970, p. 20), that is to say that the State should by no means be understood simply as an annex of social processes. It is true that, during the reconstruction and development of the economic and social public life in Germany, leading economic politicians were agreed that the new system should not mean "... a return to the liberalist forms of business, as shaped in past history, and to an irresponsible filibustering of times gone" (G. Ambrosius 1977, p. 160), but in contrast to Stein, Heller and the best of 19th century's «Staatswissenschaftler» (scientists of the state), the neo-liberalist economic theory and the «liberal socialism» propagated by the SPD, namely Karl Schiller in these times, believed in Keynesianism and therefore in the «Globalsteuerung der Wirtschaft»[12] but had kept – Liberalism and Socialism alike – the superstition that "... the economy stands for the true reality, as a causal and load-carrying basis; all other social functions, namely politics, were seen only as an ideological covering of an economic situation, as realities of a secondary order, that basically were to be explained as epiphenomena of economics" (H. Heller 1970, p. 213). This «German Model» contributed to the undoing of family and social ties and unintentionally generated new drives 'toward individualisation.[13] Caused by an interpretation that saw the State only as

11 Cf. *Grundgesetz*, art. 20 I, 28 I, 79 III with «perpetual guarantee of validity»; cf. Herzog, R.: «Demokratie und Sozialstaat», in: Maydell, B.v./Kannengießer, W. (Eds.): *Handbuch der Sozialpolitik*, Pfullingen (Neske) 1988, pp. 79-84 (80).

12 Cf. Schiller, K.: «Sozialismus und Wettbewerb», in: Schiller, K.: *Der Ökonom und die Gesellschaft. Das freiheitliche und das soziale Element in der modernen Wirtschaftspolitik.* Vorträge und Aufsätze, Stuttgart (Gustav Fischer) 1964, pp. 15-34 (28).

13 Cf. Höffe, O.: «Das Prinzip Gerechtigkeit», in: Maydell/Kannengießer (1988), pp. 66-78 (76ff).

one «social function» – even though as one standing out from the others – the Welfare State limited itself more and more to the development of social security pay-outs in order to "generalise" the cost of the "disintegration" of natural relationships in life, the unions and other "social milieus." Thus new drives towards individualisation were generated. The State social security system ranks below the primacy of economic efficiency and leads to a situation where the life-style of different social classes is homogenised «beyond rank and class,» but this superficially safe social world is linked to huge unintended psychological and social side-effects. The individual and the people in general are likewise «short-circuited»: ". . . the risks of employed labour are made uniformly milder and at the same time generalised by social administration. In the course of economic-technical change, ever-widening circles among parts of the population are drawn into its systems and they develop ever more distinctly their egalitarian effects, beyond the bounds of income and education" (U. Beck 1983, p. 52). This homogenising of different social levels is connected with an increasing loss of tradition, which for its part causes a decrease of «integrating» solutions for social problems in family, friendship and neighbourhood units. All this is accompanied by a loss of collective identity. ". . . in the Welfare State mass democracies individualisation occurs just as an expression and the conditions of a framework of social processes, which make individualisation (in the sense of individual autonomy) more and more impossible" (p. 55).

For the relation between the philosophical ideal and the reality of the contemporary Welfare State means that today's «social state» is endangered by its own success: At the end of this development, "quantitatively total state of weakness" may remain, which increasingly has to tackle more social tasks and becomes overwhelmed by them, because it no (longer) has the political power to reject them as a State task. Another problem is the dependence of the State on an expanding economy, whose (increasing) output is necessary to get the means for tasks guaranteed by the social State without intervening in the existing order of things. This leads to a partial identification of State and economy and to a sudden turn-around in economic-social positions of power and influence to (indirect) decision-making power (E.-W. Böckenförde 1987).

If the economic interest and weal of the individual is not only the purpose of State transferred payments but, beyond it, the sole end of the State communalizing, collective identities are undermined and faulty tendencies, which arise from «social rights», defined only monetarily, are intensified. The farthest horizon of these faulty tendencies is indicated by this, that it leads to an illusion of security, caused by the normative promise of money payments in assistance. "In the meantime, it is clear that the Law cannot fill the cash-box. Thus the Law is on the bumpy road back from the boundaries that were pushed far forward with a maximum of promises, given under optimal conditions" (H.P. Zacher 1983, p. 73). The price for this illusory security for a maximum of social protection is high. The loosening of the links between social rank, income and individual life-style, thanks to social administration, has thus not only mediated less abstract forms of large political communities, such as the State and its social administration, but has dissolved them. Politics mirror this loss of joint action below the primacy of individual horizons in life: democratic, i.e. publicly articulated, positions of power are used, ". . . to loosen the political title of the 'social' from what is '-social' in actual fact, and while calling on the political title of the "social" interest in a relationship beyond their true social urgency. . . (thereby) . . .the relationship between the social purpose of the State to democracy approaches an especially critical point. From where may the legal title of 'social' draw the power to pit itself against the political enforcing power of an interest and against the political title of 'social' (H.P. Zacher 1987)? Aspects of social security are instrumentalised by politics; great benefits with massive transfer effects attendant on their distribution right across the disparate social levels are held permanently at disposal. Politics ". . . distributes individual uncertainties in such a way that a calculable uniformity arises" (H. Barbier 1988, p. 398f), and the costs of social security systems vanish behind the «veil» of social administration. This development is intensified by an «illusion of the welfare state» (P. Koslowski) : The individual notoriously overrates the value of his contribution to the social security system. "Corresponding to the illusion on national debt, there arises, too, an illusionary problem with today's pension insurance. . . . The decrease of the reproductive rate of the 'human capital children' is partly conditioned by the social assurance system and its inversion of the obligation regarding care. The system of care for the aged rewards childless marriages" (P. Koslowski 1994, p. 344); and this at the expense of those responsible for payments at present. "The contributors. . . namely, ignore the fact that with fewer children and therefore fewer payers, later on they will hardly get the equivalent value, which is proven according to today's calculations" (p. 352). Connected to that is a "rationally" based "maintenance-egoism" that privatises the burden of children and socialises the usufruct of children in the old age pension scheme, just as in health insurance it lets the costs of individual health provision vanish under the collectively calculated payments.

This kind of social policy, orientated to individual interests and group egoism, injures the collective «ethos» and diminishes the common weal. "The national economy remains poorer than it would be with a more careful use of its tight resources and appropriately greater increase of capital" (H. Barbier 1988, p. 401). Political coalitions no longer strictly follow vertical conflict lines of social inequality or horizontal ones of confessional loyalty; neither are they even able to formulate general aims, transcending individual interests. "In this perspective it becomes explicable how,in parallel with the disappearance of social class lines, naturally caused inequalities acquire a new meaning and determine the public disputes" (U. Beck 1983, p. 69). Thanks to the benefits of the «Sozialstaat», individuals have reached a homogenous life at different levels of social class for the price that individuals are atomised in their subjective experience. Therefore they lose the ability to generate a universal interest, which could create a collective identity, represented by the State. After the loss of a given collective identity, the State, legitimised for the most part by far more than co-ordinated functions for the commercial society, cannot take a "community-forming ethos" for granted. At the end of the social vision remains as a challenge and task for the future safe-guarding of liberty, a society of individualised classes, dependent on care and incapable of shaping the community and, thus, the State.

VI. Summary

An historical and intellectual review shows that the plan of realisation of the Welfare State principle builds less upon philosophical concepts than upon religious, liberal-conservative and social-democratic ideas. As early as the beginning of industrialisation in Germany, political theory recognised that State and society follow different principles of co-ordination (politics and market). The purpose and task of the State is the promotion of the individual in the midst of the surrounding society.

For Lorenz von Stein, socialist ideas of the public good, enlightenment philosophy, and the Utopia of German idealism flow together into the systematic development of the Welfare State principle. Through administration is realised the freedom and equality of the citizen within society demanded by the constitution. Governmental achievements are limited to the economic capacity of the society, which is why financial science must ". . . also establish the measure of the attainable for these tasks" (L. v. Stein).

With the transformation of the SPD to a left-reform people's party, governmental concepts of social reform replace social revolutionary ideas. As liberal socialism maintains, the constitution results in a balance between neoliberal thinking and the Keynesianism adopted by the SPD. The global direction of the demand-oriented economy is combined with the extension of the social system to the «German Model." Individual risks of life are generalised at the price of the disintegration of social milieus. Against the veil of huge transfer payments, the union of social classes, economic productivity and individual life styles are dissolved. As a result of «social rights» being defined only monetarily, undesirable consequences increase. Social politics, oriented to individual interests and group egoism, injure the collective «ethos,» lead to the isolation of individuals, and place burdens upon the general prosperity. As a challenge to the social state, the incompetent society of individualised dependent classes stands as the end of the welfare vision.

References

BARBIER, H.: «Die Notwendigkeit und Schwierigkeit von Reformen», in: MAYDELL, B.v., KANNENGIEßER, W. (Eds.), *Handbuch der Sozialpolitik,* Pfullingen (Neske) 1988, pp. 398- 405.

BECK, U.: «Jenseits von Stand und Klasse? Soziale Ungleichheit, gesellschaftliche Individualisierungsprozesse und die Entstehung neuer sozialer Formationen und Identitäten, in: *Soziale Ungleichheiten, Sonderheft* Vol. 2 of «Soziale Welt», Göttingen 1983, pp. 35-74.

BERNSTEIN, E.: *Der Revisionismus in der Sozialdemokratie. Ein Vortrag. Gehalten in Amsterdam vor Akademikern und Arbeitern. Mit einem Anhang: Leitsätze für ein sozialdemokratisches Programm,* Amsterdam (Martin G. Cohen Nachfolger) 1909, p. 31.

BAADER, F. X. V.: «Über das dermalige Missverhältnis der Vermögenslosen oder Proletairs zu den Vermögen besitzenden Classen der Societät in Betreff ihres Auskommens sowohl in materieller als intellectueller Hinsicht aus dem Standpuncte des Rechts betrachtet» (1835), in: *Franz v. Baaders sämmtliche Werke,* ed. by Hoffmann, F., Vol. VI, Leipzig (Herrmann Bethmann) 1854, pp. 125-144.

BÖCKENFÖRDE, E.-W.: *Gesetz und gesetzgebende Gewalt. Von den Anfängen der deutschen Staatsrechtslehre bis zur Höhe des staatsrechtlichen Positivismus,* Berlin 1958, p. 149.

BÖCKENFÖRDE, E.-W.: «Demokratie als Verfassungsprinzip», in: ISENSEE, J. and KIRCHOF, P. (Eds.): *Handbuch des Staatsrecht der Bundesrepublik Deutschland, I: Grundlagen von Staat und Verfassung*, Heidelberg (C. F. Müller) 1987, pp. 887-952.

FICHTE, J. G.: «Der geschlossene Handelsstaat», in: *Werke*, ed. by I.H. Fichte, Vol. III, Berlin (Walter de Gruyter & Co.) 1971, p. 399.

FICHTE, I. H.: *Über Gegensatz, Wendepunkt und Ziel heutiger Philosophie*, Heidelberg 1832, p. VII.

FORSTHOFF, E.: *Lehrbuch des Verwaltungsrechts. Erster Band: Allgemeiner Teil*, München 1973, p. 46.

14TH MEETING OF THE «BIZONAL ECONOMIC COUNCIL", 21/ 4/1948, p. 441. Quotation after AMBROSIUS, G.: *Die Durchsetzung der sozialen Marktwirtschaft in Westdeutschland 1945-49*, Stuttgart (dva) 1977, p.160.

HECKEL, M.: *Deutschland im konfessionellen Zeitalter*, Göttingen (Vandenhoeck & Ruprecht) 1983.

HEGEL, G. W. F.: «Grundlinien der Philosophie des Rechts oder Naturrecht und Staatswissenschaft im Grundrisse», in: *Werke*, ed. by Moldenhauer E./Michel, K. M., Vol. 7, Frankfurt a. M. (Suhrkamp) 1970, § 245.

HELLER, H.: «Rechtsstaat und Diktatur», in: *Staatslehre*, ed. by Niemeyer, G., Leiden (A. W. Sijthoff) 1970, p. 20.

HENNING, F.-W.: *Die Industrialisierung in Deutschland 1800 bis 1914*, Paderborn (UTB Schöningh) 1976, p. 17.

HÖFFE, O.: «Das Prinzip Gerechtigkeit», in: MAYDELL, B. V., KANNENGIEßER, W. (Eds.), *Handbuch der Sozialpolitik*, Pfullingen (Neske) 1988, pp. 66-78.

KERBER, W. ERTL, H., HAINZ, M.: *Katholische Gesellschaftslehre im Überblick. Hundert Jahre Sozialverkündigung der Kirche*, Frankfurt a. M. (Josef Knecht) 1991, p. 31.

KETTELER, W. E.: «Die Arbeiterfrage und das Christenthum» (1864), in: KETTELER, W. E. FRH.V.: *Sämtliche Werke und Briefe*, in: Iserlon, E. V. (Ed.): part I, Vol. 1: *Schriften, Aufsätze und Reden 1848-1866*, Mainz (Hase & Koehler) 1977, pp. 367-516.

KETTELER, W. E., Frh.v.: «Die großen socialen Fragen der Gegenwart. Sechs Predigten gehalten im hohen Dom zu Mainz», in: KETTELER, W. E., FRH.V.: *Sämtliche Werke und Briefe*, Iserlon, E. V. (Ed.): part I, Vol. 1: *Schriften, Aufsätze und Reden 1848-1866*, Mainz (Hase & Koehler) 1977, pp. 22- 87.

KETTELER, W. E., Frh.v.: «Die Arbeiterbewegung und ihr Streben im Verhältnis zu Religion und Sittlichkeit», in: KETTELER, W. E., FRH.V.: *Sämtliche Werke und Briefe*, Iserlon, E. V. (Ed.): part I, Vol. 1: *Schriften, Aufsätze und Reden 1848-1866*, Mainz (Hase & Koehler) 1977, pp. 406-428.

KOSLOWSKI, P.: «Der soziale Staat der Postmoderne. Ethische Grundlagen der Sozialpolitik und Reform der Sozialversicherung» (first published in 1990), in: KOSLOWSKI, P.: *Die Ordnung der Wirtschaft. Studien zur praktischen Philosophie und politischen Ökonomie*, Tübingen (J. C. B. Mohr) 1994, pp. 332-379.

KOSLOWSKI, ST.: *Die Geburt des Sozialstaats aus dem Geist des Deutschen Idealismus. Person und Gemeinschaft bei Lorenz v. Stein*, Weinheim (VCH/Acta humaniora) 1989.

— "Die Staatswissenschaft als 'Philosophie der Tat'. Das Zusammenspiel von individueller Freiheit, Gesellschaftsmacht und staatlicher Verantwortung bei Lorenz v. Stein", *Archives for Philosophy of Law and Social Philosophy*, Vol. LXXVIII (1992), pp. 35-67.

LEO XIII.: «Rerum novarum», in: *Texte zur katholischen Soziallehre. Die sozialen Rundschreiben der Päpste und andere kirchliche Dokumente. Mit einer Einführung von Oswald v. Nell-Breuning*, ed. by Bundesverband der katholischen Arbeitnehmer-Bewegung, Kevelaer (Butzon & Bercker) 1977, p. 36.

LUDEN, H.: *Handbuch der Staatsweisheit oder der Politik. Ein wissenschaftlicher Versuch*, 1. Abtheilung, (Jena) 1811, p. 221.

OFNER, J.: *Studien sozialer Jurisprudenz*, 1894, p. 76.

SCHILLER, K.: «Sozialismus und Wettbewerb», in: SCHILLER, K., *Der Ökonom und die Gesellschaft. Das freiheitliche und das soziale Element in der modernen Wirtschaftspolitik. Vorträge und Aufsätze*, Stuttgart (Gustav Fischer) 1964, pp. 15-34.

SCHLÖZER, A. L.: *Allgemeines Staats-Recht und Staatsverfassungslehre* (State law and the Doctrine of the State Constitution), Göttingen 1793, p.VI .

STEIN, L. v.: *Die Verwaltungslehre, Teil 7: «wirtschaftliche Verwaltung»* (the doctrine of administration, part 7, economical administration), reprint Aalen (Scientia) 1975 (original Stuttgart 1868).

STEIN, L. v.: «Der Begriff der Arbeit und die Principien des Arbeitslohnes in ihrem Verhältnisse zum Socialismus und Communismus», *Zeitschrift für die gesammte Staatswissenschaft*, 3 (1846) pp. 233-290.

STEIN, L. v.: *Die Geschichte der sozialen Bewegung in Frankreich von 1789 bis auf unsere Tage*. Vol I: *Der Begriff der Gesellschaft und die soziale Geschichte der französischen Revolution bis zum Jahre 1830 (1921)*; Vol. III: *Das Königtum, die Republik und die Souveränität der französischen Gesellschaft seit der Februarrevolution 1848*, both volumes reprint Darmstadt (Wissenschaftliche Buchgesellschaft Darmstadt) 1959.

STEIN, L. v.: *Die Verwaltungslehre, Theil 2: Die Lehre von der innern Verwaltung. Einleitung. Die Lehre von Begriff, Inhalt, System und Recht der Verwaltung*, Stuttgart 1866, reprint Aalen (Scientia) 1975.

STEIN, L. v.: *Gegenwart und Zukunft der Rechts- und Staatswissenschaft Deutschlands*, Stuttgart 1876.

STEIN, L. v.: *Die Verwaltungslehre, Theil I, Abth.1: Das verfassungsmäßige Verwaltungsrecht. Erster Theil. Erstes Gebiet. Die Regierung und das verfassungsmäßige Regierungsrecht*, Stuttgart 1869, Aalen (Scientia) 1975, p. 30.

(1921); Über Gegenwart und Zukunft der Rechts- und Staatswissenschaft Deutschlands, in: Forsthoff, E. (Ed.): LORENZ V. STEIN, *Gesellschaft – Staat – Recht*,

STEIN, L. v.: *Lehrbuch der Finanzwissenschaft*, Teil I, Leipzig (F. A. Brockhaus) 1885, p. 3.

ZACHER, H.P.: «Chancen und Grenzen des Sozialstaats – Rolle und Lage des Rechts», in: KOSLOWSKI, P./KREUZER, PH./LÖW, R. (Eds.): *Chancen und Grenzen des Sozialstaats. Staatstheorie – Politische Ökonomie Politik*, Tübingen (J. C. Mohr) 1983, pp .66-89.

ZACHER, H. F.: «Das soziale Staatsziel», in: ISENSEE, J. and KIRCHOF, P. (Eds.): *Handbuch des Staatsrechts der Bundesrepublik Deutschland, I: Grundlagen von Staat und Verfassung*, Heidelberg (C. F. Müller) 1987, pp. 1045-1111.

Part IV

Current Problems of the Welfare State

Chapter 8

Do Welfare Obligations End at the Boundaries of the Nation State?[1]

ANDREAS FØLLESDAL

I. Introduction

Welfare states tend towards egalitarian principles of distribution of social opportunities and wealth. Their citizens hold that a just society should not only secure a decent standard of living for all, but also prevent large inequalities of shares of power and wealth.

This domestic egalitarianism does not exclude a concern for foreigners: to the contrary, it is often coupled with a commitment to global regimes for the prevention of misery and deprivation. The basic needs of all should be met (Stokke 1989, Noel 1995). However, obligations across borders seem to be less demanding: foreigners can not reasonably claim equal income and wealth. The political borders of the state thus seem to delineate a sphere of individuals whose interests ground special, though not exclusive, claims on their shared institutions. This chapter focuses on this Priority of Compatriots. [2]

The Priority of Compatriots is challenged on two fronts: the problems of

1 I gratefully acknowledge discussions with other participants in the ARENA research program and participants at the Oslo conference on «The Europeanisation of the Nation-State?» March 28-29, 1995: THEO BARTH, ALEXANDER CAPPELEN, KAI DRAMER, LARS FJELL HANSSON, KNUT MIDGAARD, JOHAN P. OLSEN, ANNE JULIE SEMB, DAN SMITH, BJØRN OTTO SVERDRUP, ULF SVERDRUP, FREDRIK SEJERSTED, HENRIK SYSE, and BENT SOFUS TRANØY; as well as the participants at the Hannover conference and participants at the seminar on normative theory at the University of Uppsala, Sweden.

2 BEITZ 1983, 593.

application and of justification. First: The Priority of Compatriots take the system of sovereign states for granted. However, the scope and political significance of state borders is shifting, rendering the principle difficult to apply. Globalisation of trade raises perplexing questions about distributive justice within and across state and regional borders. Political events on several continents change the legal and normative impact of state borders. The changing role of political borders forces us to reconsider the distributive significance of borders generally, and those of the nation-state and of world regions in particular.

To illustrate, consider three important practical reasons for asking about the scope and content of welfare obligations with regards to the European Union.[3]

- There is deep disagreement about the legitimate ends of the EU. Some claim that increased market efficiency is the sole purpose and legitimate end of the EU and the treaty governing the European Economic Area (EEA): the citizens within the EU and EFTA, now the EU and Iceland, Liechtenstein and Norway. Pareto improvements follow in the wake of the four freedoms of the flow of goods, persons, capital and services. Distribution of these added benefits should take place simply according to prior endowment and bargains, with no further concern for where on the Pareto frontier the participants start out or end up. Others have held a different view, including even the secular saints of European integration, Paul-Henri Spaak, Robert Schuman, Konrad Adenauer, and Alcide de Gasperi. They insist that a united Europe should also provide some guarantees for individuals' welfare (MILWARD 1992, 318-344). We must consider and assess the grounds offered for these conflicting judgements.
- We disagree about the extent of any such distributive commitment. EU documents talk of 'convergence' of living standards and 'solidarity', but these terms must be specified: is the aim only to eradicate dire poverty, or also to go beyond that baseline, towards equal living conditions for all Europeans?
- The Principle of Subsidiarity will be central in the future development of the EU.

3 Recent philosophical contributions to a normative political theory of Europe include ACKERMAN 1994 and SCHEFFLER 1995.

> The Community shall take action, in accordance with the principle of subsidiarity, only if and in so far as the objectives of the proposed action cannot be sufficiently achieved by the Member States and can therefore, by reason of the scale of effects of the proposed action, be better achieved by the Community.
>
> (Treaty on European Union Article 3b)

To apply the principle of subsidiarity properly, we must be clear on the legitimate ends of the EU and those of the member states. Will the EU institutions focus exclusively on market efficiency, leaving the distributive tasks solely to member states? The EU would then respect formal sovereignty, but may leave states unable to fulfil the legitimate claims of citizens. Or the EU regimes may have to assist, by regulating and providing regional transfers aimed at equality among citizens of different states – invading formerly internal issues of domestic policies of states, in favour of a centralised federation without much leeway for national governments in the field of social policy.

In addition to this practical concern, the Priority of Compatriots challenges our moral commitment to the equitable treatment of all. We may be witness to, and perpetrators of, the perpetration of unjustified bias, like sexism and racism. But this time based not upon arbitrary 'natural' differences, but on the social construct of the sovereign state. Or can we justify that the social construct of national borders diminishes the claims others have on us? If indeed we accept the Priority of Compatriots, we must consider what grounds there are for granting such normative significance to state borders: Why should the basic needs of foreigners count, but not their further claims, e.g. to equal shares? [4] John Rawls' A Theory of Justice (1971) offers what is perhaps the most convincing defence of the liberal egalitarian welfare state. However, his contribution takes as its prime subject domestic justice, leaving aside the implications for global distribution. Even in «The Law of Peoples» (Rawls 1994), a contribution to international political theory, he addresses sovereignty rather than issues of distribution. A thorough understanding of the grounds for Priority of Compatriots will enable us to determine and assess the normative significance of changing scopes of sovereignty in Europe and elsewhere.

In this chapter I consider how and why shifting notions of sovereignty may affect the scope of application and content of principles of just distribution. I defend the Priority of Compatriots; the scope of our welfare obliga-

---

4 For a recent illuminating discussion of the legitimate scope of egalitarianism, cf. TEMKIN 1995.

tions may legitimately be affected by state borders. For our purpose we take for granted the egalitarian commitment of many welfare states, and pursue the international implications of this commitment. In section II, I summarise various arguments offered in favour of the Priority of Compatriots, only to set them aside as ill suited for our topic. In section III, I present several arguments against domestic inequality. Section IV argues that a further claim to equal shares is a reasonable demand to make among citizens of democratic welfare states. In section V, I bring the arguments against inequality and for equality to bear on the issue of global and regional distribution. I conclude that legitimate global regimes must secure the satisfaction of the basic needs of all, but not necessarily secure equal shares for all participants. Section VI considers some normative issues arising within the European Union, where states have partly pooled their sovereignty. I suggest that the shared institutions of the EU support claims to equal shares among the inhabitants: the same egalitarian arguments appear to hold among them as hold among fellow citizens of a state. Among citizens in the EU, justice thus requires equal shares of political power, of social opportunities, and of life income and wealth, due to the nature of their social co-operation under the four freedoms. Thus a legitimate EU may not be limited to maintaining a free market: 'real' convergence and solidarity within the EU must go beyond the alleviation of poverty, towards securing equal standards of living. State sovereignty must therefore be restricted for the benefit of central institutions aiming to secure equality.

The claims to equality I sketch do not exhaust the normative relevance of political borders. In conclusion, in section VII, I therefore note countervailing considerations and further important areas of normative reflection regarding a theory of global distributive justice. Our concern for equality comes into conflict with another important interest – democratic self-governance, leading to a diversity of equally just social arrangements.

II. Why Should Political Borders Matter?

The distributive significance of borders can be justified normatively by two main strategies: the Priority of Compatriots may be regarded as a basic principle at a foundation level, or it may be a 'mid-level' distributive principle, in turn justified by appeal to other moral principles. I shall suggest that the latter is more illuminating for our purposes.

Foundational Arguments

The philosopher Alasdair MacIntyre represents one family of foundational arguments: The nation state as prerequisite for personal identity and flourishing. MacIntyre argues that the Priority of Compatriots is justified because the society shapes and maintains the individual's identity and status as a moral agent (MacIntyre 1984, 11). The nation is a project, a morally distinctive community among individuals with special obligations towards one another, justified by stories of a shared history and shared goals.

One of MacIntyre's points is worth stressing: social institutions have a pervasive impact on our lives, because human nature is pliable. Institutions shape our plans, aspirations and preferences, for better and for worse (Wollstonecraft 1792).

However, MacIntyre's approach fails to answer our questions. MacIntyre does not provide criteria for identifying those states and societies which are deserving of patriotic support by their citizens, including criteria for legitimate distribution. Moreover, MacIntyre's account, at least as developed so far, pays insufficient respect to foreigners and to the shifting roles of the state and of European institutions in shaping the identity of individuals. Furthermore, when conflicting stories and prophesies are offered, how should we assess them? Finally, what should we make of those political borders which cut across nations? These urgent issues are worthy of pursuit, but beyond the reach of MacIntyre's arguments.

Michael Walzer sometimes expresses another foundational argument in favour of Priority of Compatriots. The nation state is the bearer of shared meanings, and hence serves as the ultimate arbiter of value (Walzer 1983, 28).[5] Walzer's account allows us in principle to acknowledge obligations to foreigners, though he is hard put to account for the existence of values which hold outside the own society:

> The only plausible alternative to the political community is humanity itself, the society of nations, the entire globe. But were we to take the globe as our setting, we would have to imagine what does not yet exist: a community that included all men and women everywhere. We would have to invent a set of common meanings for these people, avoiding if we could the stipulation of our own values. And we would have to ask the members of this hypothetical community (or their hypothetical representatives) to agree among themselves on what distributive arrangements and patterns of conversion are to count as just.
>
> (Walzer 1983, 29-30).

5 Though he is also prepared to agree that there may be values and norms which do not depend on the prevailing views of society (33).

The political processes in Europe would allow Walzer to argue from shared meanings: There are shared institutions, and some shared meanings, expressed in the European Convention of Human Rights and various EU treaties. Alas, Walzer is silent on some of the issues which confront us, such as the distributive significance of changing and emerging social institutions, where meanings are changing and emerging. There are no shared meanings and understandings as of yet – indeed, our deliberation is motivated by the desire to settle some of these disagreements about principles of distributive justice for global or regional institutions.

A more fundamental problem with Walzer's view is that normative argument should allow critical assessment of the social phenomenon of sovereign states, of social institutions and of accepted practices. Current acceptance by the population is not the final arbiter of legitimacy. To be sure, critical normative argument starts out with broadly shared values and commitments, but these shared meanings only provide a starting point, not the endpoint of theory (Cohen 1986). Starting with those moral convictions and principles in which we have great confidence, we must seek to shape them into a coherent argumentative structure which may be brought to bear on those issues on which we are more uncertain, or find ourselves in disagreement with others.

These brief sketches suggest that these foundational arguments fail on two counts. They leave unclear why equality should be secured among compatriots, and they fail to allow a critical stance for assessing existing and emerging social institutions. Our purposes are better served by regarding the Priority of Compatriots as a mid-level principle. This principle must then in turn be justified by appeal to grounds acceptable to all, since a commitment to equal respect requires that the interests of all must always be taken into account.

Mid-level Arguments

Various lines of argument hold that the states system – and, by extension, a regionalised world order – is the most effective way to answer to the fundamental moral obligation of respecting all affected parties. Thus Robert Goodin offers an Assigned Responsibility Model. National boundaries is a good way to divide up «the general duties that everyone has against everyone else world-wide» (Goodin 1988, 681).[6] Another argument in favour of the Priority of Compatriots insists that special treatment of compatriots is itself an important interest. Thus David Miller (1988) suggests that our psychological attachments may ground the Priority of Compatriots. Jean-Jacques Rousseau may have made a similar point, when he argued that citizens must perceive that they receive special treatment, if they are to comply with the social institutions:

> Do we want peoples to be virtuous? Let us then start by making them love their homeland. But how are they to love it if the homeland is nothing more for them than for foreigners, and accords them only what it cannot refuse to anyone?
>
> (Rousseau 1755/1978, 221).

Such arguments – if successful – might justify preferential treatment of compatriots, but none of these approaches seem to justify the distinctly egalitarian trends among compatriots expressed by the Priority of Compatriots.

I shall therefore pursue other arguments, still interpreting the Priority of Compatriots as a mid-level principle. We remain committed to the fundamental principle of equal respect for all persons, committed to treating all as equals, but I shall deny that equal respect always requires equal concern for the similar needs of all. To be sure, the basic needs of all must be met. Thus the vital interests of foreigners must temper any further weight we accord compatriots. There are acceptable reasons for weighting the further interests of compatriots more than the interests of others. In particular, I suggest that co-operation under social institutions generates special claims among the participants. John Rawls has explored such arguments «of reciprocity» regarding issues of domestic justice (1971, 1971b, 1993). Several others have sought to extend those arguments to international relations (Richards 1982; Beitz 1979; Barry 1989; Pogge 1989), but, unlike them, I suggest that state borders affect the standing of foreigners' claims to equal shares.

6 «The duties that states (or, more precisely, their officials) have vis-à-vis their own citizens are not in any deep sense special. At root, they are merely the general duties that everyone has toward everyone else worldwide. National boundaries simply visit upon those particular state agents special responsibility for discharging those general obligations vis-à-vis those individuals who happen to be their own citizens.» (Goodin 1988, 681-82)

III. The Cases Against Inequality

Egalitarian welfare obligations do not end at the boundaries of the nation state, but that they are legitimately affected by such boundaries. I first briefly discuss three grounds for lamenting inequalities, and in section IV offer a more detailed account of a fourth, more positive argument, in favour of equal shares of benefits.[7]

Preventing Misery

From the moral point of view, a set of institutions must be acceptable to all affected parties. If this normative commitment is to have any substantive content, surely acceptable institutions must engender and distribute benefits so as to meet the basic vital needs of all. To be sure, the world order we live in fails dismally on this point: large economic inequalities within market economies prevent wage earners from acquiring food, and differences in relative political power perpetuate abysmal prenatal health care for the poor.

To rephrase: we can object to large inequalities engendered by social institutions, based on the paramount importance of what we may think of as our central interest in meeting basic needs. However, this objection does not amount to a general argument for equality. It is really only an argument against drastic inequality regarding certain specific goods, insofar as these inequalities engender misery.

Preventing Domination

In addition to basic needs, individuals have a legitimate interest in maintaining control over their own lives – in particular if the alternative is that such control is wielded by others. Large inequalities of wealth prevent the less privileged from exercising control over their lives and subjects them to the bargaining power of the powerful in various spheres of life.

It is objectionable if some individuals can control the lives of others, e.g. by drastically restricting their attractive options, or by leaving them at the mercy of the powerful. Domination and subjection occurs when others can limit my range of options, or my ability to choose according to my interests. Such distribution of control adds avoidable risk to those risks we already

7 I here draw on SCANLON 1988, and TEMKIN 1988, 1993.

face through nature and luck, and the inequalities which engender domination fail to accord each individual proper respect as equals.

However, this objection to inequalities among individuals is also limited to those inequalities which yield outcomes that are clearly detrimental to some individuals' lives. For instance, if others have very high incomes and much wealth, or own all employment opportunities, my interest in controlling my own life is easily subject to their will, and is further restricted by the spill-over of economic power onto political power. These effects of inequality of wealth constitute grounds for objecting to social institutions, but only insofar as they allow differences in wealth to effect our control over other spheres of life. Arguments from domination thus serve to ground claims to equality – or rather, restrictions on inequalities – of certain goods and powers. Such arguments are contingent on the impact of such inequalities for the distribution of control over individuals' lives, and apply against certain inequalities.

Equal Power for Fair Procedures

A further ground for equality stems from our interest in controlling the social factors that shape our lives. Many social procedures and mechanisms require for their fairness a roughly equal distribution of procedural input levers. Consider how many adversarial procedures must work in order to generate legitimate outcomes. If legal trials are to regularly identify the guilty, both parties must be represented by competent counsel. Political campaigns competing for attention must not be able to crowd out competitors in the media. I submit that such arguments for equal levers based on the need for even playing fields in various procedures may be offered in favour of:

- equal rights to legal representation during trials
- universal political rights, including equal rights to influence government policies and attaining offices through majority rule
- freedom of the press
- freedom of association and speech
- limits on expenditures for political campaigns
- access to those educational institutions that are gate keepers to professions and other prominent social positions.

We may indeed conceive of political power, social positions of power including access to political offices and to certain kinds of education, and income and wealth as procedural levers which affect outcomes. Democratic institutions should disperse these levers of political influence broadly and equally among all parties to these procedures, insofar as relative shares of these levers often matter for the distribution of output benefits. We must be sceptical about procedures that permit unequal shares of procedural levers when these inequalities skew the control over outcomes in favour of some individuals.

This argument for equality of procedural controls comes into play when relative shares of input levers are important for the output of the procedure. To sum up, several arguments against certain kinds of inequality can be offered on the grounds that they violate individuals' claims to equal respect within social institutions.

IV. The Case for Equal Shares

The final reason for claiming that the social institutions should secure opportunities for all to obtain an equal share of political power, opportunities, life income and wealth, draws on a particular view of social institutions and how they can be said to exist only by the participation of others.

Behaviour which is regulated according to public rules I call social practices. For a social practice to exist there must be a set of rules, generally complied with and acted on by the participants in the practice, and this fact of general compliance must be common knowledge. We may talk of social institutions as the practices that are maintained by the use of legal powers. When a social institution is in place, sanctions enforce the public rules and hence provide public assurance of general compliance; and authoritative interpretations apply the rules to new or difficult cases. Three aspects of these social institutions are important for our purposes: They affect our life prospects deeply; they generate 'goods internal to the practices', namely legal powers; and these goods are created or constituted by the joint participation of all in upholding these institutions.

The Impact of Social Institutions

Social institutions distribute important kinds of power among citizens, and thus have a large influence on our lives. The system of law, the educational system, markets, the health care system and other social institutions create and distribute opportunities for joint action. They reward certain abilities, permit certain conceptions of the good, reward certain kinds of effort, generate certain kinds of formal powers, and set side constraints on how the fruits of co-operation shall be distributed. These constraints and background conditions thus have pervasive effects on citizens' plans and lives. Institutions provide the backdrop against which individuals make plans and live their lives.

The roles and positions I am born into affect my conception of myself, what I come to regard as appropriate roles, ambitions, duties and actions. Institutions even affect how we value the possibilities that we have. Social institutions such as the system of health care, the educational system and the markets for goods and services give us opportunities and thus expectations. These expectations make us adjust plans, values and conceptions of the good.

Mary Wollstonecraft stressed the role of social institutions in facilitating – and subverting – capacities to reason and deliberate. If my expectations are sufficiently low, I will be satisfied with amazingly little. Thus how social institutions should distribute power – goods and burdens, possibilities and formal powers – among individuals becomes an extremely important question. This is especially true for political power. The agenda for day-to-day bargaining among political parties is limited both directly, e.g. by constitutional constraints, and indirectly, affected by signals from influential groups whose consent will be needed to make agreements (Bachrach and Baratz 1962). Political and law-making power – the power to establish, maintain and change the social institutions – is thus of the utmost importance, and one central topic when assessing whether the state, or a world order, is legitimate.

Legal Powers: Products of Co-operation

Within domestic institutions, a wide variety of legal powers are constituted by the rules of rights of social institutions. Political power, rights, and even income and wealth can be regarded as aspects of the rules which regulate social practices. Money exists, to take an example, only within a social practice regulated by rules defining legal tender; ownership, freedom of speech, and political rights are likewise aspects of social institutions. Individuals and groups can be said to have such goods – such rights – only when there are rules in place that are generally complied with by the others who are subject to the rules. For instance, an individual who validly lays claim to certain objects as her property must show that she has acquired these objects according to certain public rules regulating entitlements. Insofar as she has complied with these rules, the objects are clearly hers, and not anybody else's. But her claim of ownership is only true – and can only be made sense of – because these rules of ownership are publicly known and generally complied with by those participating in that practice. While her entitlements are hers, the entitlements are nevertheless entitlements only because others regulate their actions according to public rules.

The social institutions which specify various allocations of rights are products of co-operation, created by the participating individuals. A wide variety of legal powers are constituted by social institutions, i.e. by the general compliance with laws within a state which all citizens uphold. Someone enjoys these powers and controls if and only if the participants in the practice generally recognise and act according to the rules specifying these rights. Individuals and associations can further their interests by means of these rights only when the duty-bearers do their part in the social institutions.

A right, in this view, is therefore a benefit of co-operation among a group of individuals; the right exists only when they participate in the social practice specified by that right. When we rely on our rights and legal powers to further our interests, we benefit indirectly from the participation of others in social institutions.

Legal powers are thus goods that are products of co-operation. When considering how institutions should distribute these goods, all participants in social institutions must be granted an equal claim to the political and other legal powers that arise. «Equal shares of products» is an appropriate standard.

This complex view of social institutions provides an argument that citizens have equal claims on how social institutions should regulate the distribution of political power, income and wealth. This grounds a claim on social institutions, that they should engender equal shares of these benefits – unless unequal shares of certain goods may benefit all, e.g. due to incentive effects, leaving open the institutional questions of whether the preferred institutions should involve high levels of redistribution and administrative bureaucracy. This is congruent with John Rawls' theory of domestic justice, which insists on equal shares of political and civil rights, and equality of opportunity and income and wealth, but allows for unequal shares of economic goods only if such inequalities also increase the share to the worst off.

V. Domestic Equality, Global Inequality

I have presented four reasons against domestic inequalities of various kinds, and for equal shares of goods. Similar claims against inequality and for equal shares do not apply with the same force when applied to global distribution among states.

Within the states system as we know it, governments enjoy broad formal powers of external sovereignty, as guaranteed by international institutions. There are few if any decision-making bodies above it, and states will generally not intervene forcibly or dictatorially in one another's internal affairs. (Bull 1977, 70) Thus, the government and, in a democratic state, the citizens, are formally free from external agents to influence the social institutions that shape their lives. This is not to deny, of course, that the range of alternatives is often restricted by natural facts and the actions of other powerful agents. Still, I suggest that formal external sovereignty affects the standing of arguments for equality.

A legitimate world order must clearly constrain global inequalities of income and wealth. Market shares, oligarchic trans-national corporations, and structural adjustment policies affect a state's ability to determine its international and domestic policies. Citizens enjoy less control over outcomes when they have little purchasing power relative to foreigners in international markets. However, international inequalities in income do not determine the domestic distribution of control over non-material goods. Furthermore, domestic legislation can often insulate domestic political institutions from the impact of international economic inequality. For instance, legislation may prohibit foreign funding of political campaigns, and bar the immigration of foreigners who outbid domestic applicants to education and employment. Governments can regulate access to international markets. Hence state sovereignty can serve as a buffer to reduce the impact of international life income inequalities, preventing domination and avoiding unfair procedures.

So the claim to reduce international inequality of income and wealth, while bolstered by the concern to avoid misery and domination, is not supported by the arguments from domination and unfair procedures, as long as states enjoy formal external sovereignty. Moreover, foreigners do not maintain the domestic social institutions of sovereign states. So they cannot claim that they participate in shared institutions to the same extent as compatriots do. The Priority of Compatriots then is justified: in an ideal-type state system the arguments against inequality and for equal shares do not apply with the same force as among compatriots.

VI. Equal Shares Among Europeans

I have argued that there are few grounds for requiring regimes to ensure equal shares of benefits of co-operation among citizens of different states at the global level. However, the changing content of state sovereignty affects this conclusion. In particular, I wish to argue that Europeans co-operate under social institutions precisely so as to render claims to equal shares appropriate.

Shared Procedures

Changes in the EU make it more urgent to remove the inequalities which lead to domination and the perversion of procedures. The four freedoms are gaining importance:[8]

- An Economic and Monetary Union will have pervasive impact on individuals' lives.
- Citizens are becoming more vulnerable to economic activity in other EU states, and must compete with foreign goods and workers.
- Intra-European capital mobility seems to be on the increase (Tsoukalis 1993, 337; CEPR 1993, 70).
- Furthermore, domestic legislation cannot insulate domestic institutions and citizens from the power of other states.

States can therefore no longer serve as shock absorbers between their citizens and the surrounding world.

Pooled Sovereignty

The argument for equal shares of products of co-operation also applies to institutions within Europe. European regimes are maintained with mutual pooling of sovereignty:

8 Even though labour mobility appears to be low (CEPR 1993, 72-77).

- Individuals may petition the European Commission on Human Rights, and the European Convention for the Protection of Human Rights and Fundamental Freedoms (ECHR) generates European constitutional case law.
- The EU can make law for member states, creating and maintaining regimes at the European level. Domestic parliaments cannot insulate domestic political institutions from superior courts.
- Individual member states no longer enjoy a right to veto on many issues (1986 Single European Act).
- Under EMU, governments will abandon the use of exchange rates as a policy instrument.

In light of these changes, I submit that citizens of the EU must be said to jointly maintain the social institutions of all member states.

These characteristics of the EU have several normative implications. Welfare obligations go beyond national boundaries in Europe. Claims to equal shares of economic benefits at the European level are plausible, due to the interconnected institutions of European states. European markets cannot be allowed free reign without considering distributive aspects also. Markets – domestic, regional and global – are legitimate only within social structures that maintain background distributive justice over time. Domestic markets should not be allowed to run rampant, in ignorance of the long-term distributive impact of market transactions among those with tradable goods and services and those individuals who can offer nothing to the market.

Thus we should insist that arguments of solidarity, convergence and structural funds must be an integral part of attempts at creating an acceptable European market. Unacceptable inequality at the European level cannot always be resolved by internal redistribution within each state, so regulation and international transfers may be needed. Discussions of subsidiarity must consider not only how economic efficiency is best served, but a broader range of distributive concerns and interests of citizens.

VII. Conclusion and Challenges

In conclusion, I wish to make two comments pertaining to the implications of this view of welfare obligations beyond the nation state, again illustrated by the EU.

When Is it Legitimate to Not Join Co-operative Ventures?

What are the normative implications of this view for distribution within Europe? The general drift of my argument might suggest that all European states should join the EU, moving towards an ever «closer and just union among the peoples of Europe». I have discussed the conditions which legitimise co-operative arrangements must satisfy. Similar conditions might seem to hold for the regime established by the European Economic Area Treaty, insofar as citizens become more mutually dependent and reduce national sovereignty. However, this conclusion would be premature: the criteria for just co-operative arrangements do not answer the very different question of when justice requires us to set up and maintain social institutions. When is co-operation morally required? Surely, the commitment to respect all as equals suggests that provision of aid may be called for even at some disadvantage to ourselves, but co-operation is not a general requirement of justice. Membership in mutual beneficial societies may not be a matter of justice – unless, for instance, free riding is at issue.

Furthermore, it is not clear that the EU satisfies the conditions of a legitimate regime, thus shifting the issue to one of 'non-ideal' justice.[9] Four grounds for this worry are worth mentioning:

- It is not clear that there is, as of yet, a regime or general practice within Europe: 'variable implementation' is rampant, invalidating claims based on shared efforts in upholding a practice.
- The treaties of the EU seem to violate principles of distributive justice among its participants, as I have explored here.
- The EU appears to fall short of whatever requirements of democratic accountability are appropriate for social institutions of that sort.
- Finally, there are reasons to doubt that the current EU policies are compatible with the claims of those outside Europe: migrant workers, refugees, and citizens of bordering states and of the third world.

Whether the EU is the best available vehicle for discharging our distributive obligations is thus an imminently discussible issue.

9 POGGE (1995) offers a recent contribution to the perplexing issue of 'non-ideal theory'.

Resolving Conflicts Between Equality and Sovereignty

The need for inter-state transfers should not be overstated: it is not simply a matter of arriving at similar GDP per capita, since domestic distribution may be unfair. It is unclear – to say the least – why global or European institutions should require citizens of other states to assist the poor of a state, instead of requiring redistribution within each state, i.e. insisting that all states become egalitarian welfare states. This is not to insinuate that international transfers are always illegitimate, but simply to underscore that sovereignty regarding domestic matters can come into clear conflict with transborder claims to equality.

Once we move beyond a global concern for basic needs, it becomes increasingly important, yet more difficult, to determine the limits to permissible variations concerning domestic institutions, within which populations should be free to determine their fates by participatory procedures. It appears that we must temper individuals' claims to equality with their claims to sovereignty. Sovereignty also makes it difficult to measure living standards across state borders, e.g. within Europe. How should we measure equality of shares at the regional and global levels? We must deal with significant differences in national arrangements since we need indicators of unacceptable inequalities.

Again, consider the European case. There are several shared features of the welfare regimes of all European states, and there may be a trend towards convergence of European welfare regimes (Cochrane 1993, 240), in part due to intra-regional mobility of workers. Nevertheless, there are national and regional variations, e.g. concerning who cares for children and elderly, how pension systems are funded, and what counts as 'low' wages given different social institutions and modes of public provision. Surely, some existing practices may be unjust, violating individuals' concern for equal respect. But we may well have to accept that some of these differences, enacted democratically, are not a matter of more or less just arrangements, but of equally just ways of maintaining a public order. These differences render it difficult to determine the relevant sense of 'equal' share (Daintith 1995, 152). How can we determine whether individuals living conditions are equal under such different circumstances?

An important task in working towards a legitimate world order is therefore to develop indicators of living standards so that we as citizens can check whether justice is served; respecting legitimate claims to benefits as well as claims to control our own fate.

I have argued that welfare obligations do not end at the boundaries of the nation state. Still, the Priority of Compatriots can be justified as consistent with a commitment to the equal worth of all. State borders modify the claims we can make on social institutions, but I have suggested that the changing significance of state sovereignty affects the conditions of legitimacy for global, regional and domestic institutions. Our normative commitments under changing world orders require careful, systematic deliberation. Our need for a theory of global justice should be obvious.

References

ACKERMAN, BRUCE: «Political Liberalisms», *Journal of Philosophy* 91 (1994), pp. 364-86.

BACHRACH, P. AND M. S. BARATZ: «The Two Faces of Power», *American Political Science Review* 56 (1962), pp. 942-52.

BARRY, BRIAN: *Theories of Justice*, Berkeley (University of California Press) 1989.

BEITZ, CHARLES R.: *Political Theory and International Relations*, Princeton (Princeton University Press) 1979.

BEITZ, CHARLES R.: «Cosmopolitan Ideals and National Sentiment», *Journal of Philosophy*, 80 (1983), pp. 591-600.

BULL, HEDLEY: *The Anarchical Society*, New York (Columbia University Press) 1977.

CEPR: *Making Sense of Subsidiarity: How Much Centralization for Europe?* Monitoring European Integration 4. Centre for Economic Policy Research Annual Report. 1993.

COCHRANE, ALLAN: «Looking for a European Welfare State» in: A. COCHRANE and J. CLARKE (Eds.): *Comparing Welfare States: Britain in International Context*, London (Sage) 1993, pp. 239-68.

COHEN, JOSHUA: «Review of Walzer's *Spheres of Justice*», *Journal of Philosophy*, 83 (1986), pp. 457-68.

DAINTITH, TERENCE: «Regulation, De-regulation and the Forms and Ends of Justice in the European Union», in: E. PAASIVIRTA and K. RISSANEN (Eds.): *Principles of Justice and the Law of the European Union* Brussels (The European Commission, DG XIII) 1995, pp. 143-166.

GOODIN, ROBERT E.: «What is So Special About Our Fellow Countrymen?» *Ethics*, 98 (1988), pp. 663-86.

MACINTYRE, ALASDAIR: *Is Patriotism a Virtue?*, Lawrence (University of Kansas) 1984.

MILLER, DAVID: «The Ethical Significance of Nationality», *Ethics* 98 (1988), pp. 647-62.

MILWARD, ALAN S.: *The European Rescue of the Nation-state*, London (Routledge) 1992.

POGGE, THOMAS W.: *Realizing Rawls*, Ithica (Cornell University Press) 1989.

— «Three problems with Contractarian-Consequentialist Ways of Assessing Social Institutions», *Social Philosophy and Policy* 12 (1995), pp. 241-266.

RAWLS, JOHN (1971a): «Justice as Reciprocity» in: S. GOROVITZ (Ed.): *Utilitarianism: John Stuart Mill, with Critical Essays*, New York (Bobbs-Merrill) 1971, pp. 242-68.

— (1971b): *A Theory of Justice*, Cambridge, Mass. (Harvard University Press) 1971.

— *Political Liberalism*, New York (Columbia University Press) 1993.

RICHARDS, DAVID A. J.: «International Distributive Justice», in: J. ROLAND (PENNOCK) and John W. CHAPMAN (Eds.): *Nomos 24: Ethics, Economics, and the Law*, New York (New York University Press) 1982, pp. 275-99.

ROUSSEAU, JEAN-JACQUES: «Political Economy», in: R. D. MASTERS and J. MASTERS (Eds.): *On The Social Contract*, New York (St. Martin's Press) 1978. Original 1755.

SCANLON, THOMAS M.: «Notes on Equality», unpublished paper, Cambridge, Mass. 1988.

SCHEFFLER, SAMUEL: «Individual Responsibility in a Global Age», *Social Philosophy & Policy* 12 (1995), pp. 219-36.

TEMKIN, LARRY S.: *«Inequality», Philosophy and Public Affairs* 15 (1986), pp. 99-121.

— *Inequality*, Oxford (Oxford University Press) 1993.

— «Justice and Equality: Some Questions about Scope», *Social Philosophy and Policy* 12 (1995), pp. 72-104.

TSOUKLIAS, LOUKAS: *The New European Economy*, Oxford (Oxford University Press) 2nd. ed. 1993.

WALZER, MICHAEL: «Spheres of Justice – an Exchange», *The New York Review of Books*, 1983 July 21, pp. 43-44.

WOLLSTONECRAFT, MARY: *Vindication of the Rights of Women*, 1792.

Chapter 9

Meeting Needs Versus Respecting Autonomy – Dilemmas of the Welfare State

ELISABETH LILJA

I. Introduction

The practice of the Swedish welfare state can be characterised as very contradictory. On the one hand, this practice can guarantee a certain degree of welfare, security and life without suffering. On the other hand the same practice can control the individual. This contradiction has become more evident over the last few years through cutbacks in spending on social programs. This has been regarded by some as a crisis of the welfare state and the end of its future. But cutbacks can also serve as starting points for a new debate about the dilemma of the welfare state, and can initiate the development of a deeper knowledge of its practices and how to deal with its contradictions.

The contradiction of welfare state practice has become more evident over the last years through claims that have been raised for greater freedom. People who raise these claims think that the welfare state still has an authoritarian character.

Democratisation up till now has involved rights to participate in decision-making process and to express opinions. Demands for freedom arise out of the desire to acquire more individual control and take full responsibility for oneself. The democratisation of the welfare state in response to these demands has centred largely on matters of principle and intent, and not so much on the actual practice and experience of it.

The contradiction in the practice of the welfare state is a modern phenomenon. As late as the early 1950's the contradiction was still invisible. Then the practice of the welfare state functioned in accordance with maintaining the norm that everyone ought to work and earn their living. In addition to this, little was done to help sick and old people who were unable to do anything about their poverty. The contradiction you find in the same practice today has arisen as a result of democratisation and the change in perspective regarding human beings and human needs of welfare, security and freedom. As a result of this change a new relation has developed to these human needs.

Today the contradiction of welfare state practice has become greater and turned into a dilemma. This dilemma shows itself in acting to meet human needs of welfare, etc., both on an individual and a social level. The dilemma on the individual level is that actions that are taken to meet human needs of welfare, security and freedom also can be experienced as a kind of control. The dilemma on the social level is that the same actions in the end can reproduce inequality in society. The aims of this practice are to create greater equality in living conditions, greater security, less suffering, and more freedom. The welfare state is a means to create such improvements in living conditions both on the individual level and in the society as a whole. But the scheme by which these aims are made operative involves on the one hand that you tend to replace individual responsibility and autonomy with collective responsibility. On the other hand the practice of the welfare state involves a valuation of people's life styles. The choice to act or not to act involves a discrimination between good and bad life styles, good and bad conduct. Thus barriers are erected between what are seen as weak groups – those who can't or won't be allowed to take care of themselves – and non-weak groups. The result of this way of acting is that these actions may meet the needs of welfare, security and a certain kind of freedom, but that they also can create social inequality and engender feelings of manipulation in individuals.

In its actions the welfare state gives expression to a certain moral code. Up until the mid 1960's this moral code could be characterised as a work-ethic and welfare practice dealt with fostering the norm that everyone ought to earn their living according to their ability to work. On the individual level, valuation of people's life styles was made for the purpose of preventing conduct that could endanger the person's ability to work, the well-being of others and of their environment. From the middle of the 60's the moral code began to change as a new practice started to develop. This new practice centred on the idea of community work, where the aim was to act together with people to improve their everyday lives. In the 1970's social planning also started to develop as a method to create conditions for good social life, especially in newly-built areas. Today the ethics of the welfare state is rather ambiguous as there is still the task of improving individuals' conduct and life styles. So the dilemma intensifies – and the entire process of actions that develop in the social welfare system, in order to meet human needs of welfare, security and less suffering, can be characterised as a tightrope walker pulled on the one side by the necessity to try to satisfy needs of equality in welfare and security, as well as less suffering, at the same time the possibility of controlling people's life styles and on the other side by the need of the individual or group for responsibility and freedom to act to satisfy their needs. As a result it is often said that this dilemma is the end of the welfare state as a means to meet human needs of welfare, security and freedom.

The future of the welfare state is represented by a choice between two alternatives: either the individual gains full freedom and responsibility for his welfare needs and the welfare state is abolished or we continue to develop the welfare state. The future looks bleak. If this dilemma exists, then apparently we either dismantle the welfare state or further develop it along the same lines, and pay the price of control and manipulation. Instead of being caught in this dilemma, I think it is important to analyse its basis from a historical and a philosophical perspective. In this way a better understanding of the dilemma can be a road to new knowledge about the welfare state today and in the future. Perhaps we will then see that we don't have to choose between two equally unfavourable alternatives, but that different approaches can be found that will make such a choice unnecessary.

II. The History of Ethico-Pragmatic Concept of Social Justice in Practice: The Swedish Case

There has always been poverty in society, but poverty hasn't always been regarded as a social problem. The turning point in attitudes towards poverty is contemporary to changes in values towards work. In Europe this turning point is the Renaissance. Then man, for the first time, discovered the possibilities to act and change the world. When man became conscious of his potentialities, poverty became shameful. If you were poor, it was your own responsibility due to your own ability to work (A. Heller 1981). According to Luther it was simply your duty to work and earn your living. When this attitude spread, poverty became a social problem. This relationship of poverty and work was dominant till our own century and was the basis of poor laws. At the end of the last century, with the emergence of a more humanistic attitude, attitudes towards poverty started to change. Demands were raised that society as a whole should be responsible for poverty and that something should be done to improve the living conditions of poor, old and sick people. These humanistic values got support from the worker's movement and democratic movements. But it was not until after the Second World War that these values were established as a basis of a new social policy and welfare state practice.

In 1932, the Social Democrats won elections in Sweden. By the end of the 1930's the Social Democrats started to work out a new social policy. New poor laws were ready by the end of the 1950's. In addition to a new social policy and new poor laws, a new administrative system had to be implemented on all levels in society. The welfare state was invented as an answer to demands for social justice and equality in welfare and demands for greater freedom. At the same time it was a cultural project. The redistribution of wealth was a necessary but not sufficient condition for the good life. Still the aim of the welfare state was not to make people happy. The idea was not an utilitarian one of maximising people's happiness. The guiding idea rather was to create a home for the people, where everyone could be a member and feel at home. It was a pedagogical and pragmatic approach to the question of the good life.

Gunnar and Alva Myrdal had a great influence on the program of the new social policy. In elaborating this program Myrdal tried to do this in a way that would avoid the traps of utilitarian welfare economics. His pragmatic approach was to work out a program of social policy that was founded on an analysis of the values and attitudes of ordinary people at that time. But the goals in the program were not equivalent to these values, neither were they goals in an absolute sense: «The valuations should, as far as possible, be `rational`, in the sense that they represent the valuations people would have if they had a better knowledge about reality; second, that they must be valuations not only of the elements in the present situation but also of elements in all the possible future developments» (G. Myrdal 1958). The policy then should only fix the direction towards which social action should be taken. A list of reforms were suggested that were founded on a positive valuation of a high standard of living, of the family, children and marriage. The aim was to make it possible for people to marry and have a family with children without having to accept an unduly depressed standard of living. In addition to this provisions had to be made in housing, in medical care and in education. What was suggested was a plan for a new social policy and that was to be implemented through social engineering. That was the ideal.

On a more concrete level, it was envisaged that people's needs for security and welfare should be satisfied through an insurance system. This system was to be obligatory and to include all of the population – that is the working part. Various insurances were to be one's security in times of illness, job disability, unemployment, old age, death of parents, widowhood, and single motherhood. The strategy was that insurances should be paid in proportion to one's income and cover the normal insecurities of life. In this way the majority of the population would get a basic level of security and welfare or at the best a possibility to satisfy these needs. At the same time, it was also an important goal to satisfy the need of freedom for the majority of the people, i.e. to break paternalistic bonds.

In one municipality that I have studied the old Social Democrat politicians can point out exactly when this process started – the day after the election in 1934. It was the day when members of the working class for the first time got an opportunity to influence local policy. For the first time they got an opportunity to use their municipal government as a means to improve their living conditions and to begin to do something about the worst of those conditions. Until that day in 1934 the manager of the local factory had held all this power. He had been the chairman of all the decision-making assemblies and had all the local administration in his hands. Even the municipal office had been situated in his own house. In 1934 he lost all this power and the municipality became an organisation in the hands of the workers and the majority of the population. Now the workers were responsible for the decision making and for local administration. They rented a flat as an administrative office and started their efforts to improve the everyday lives of factory workers, of old people, and children. The most urgent problems were bad housing, unhealthy, cold and small flats without running water, no garbage collection system, no electricity, bad roads and a generally dull environment. Behind all the needs for improvements in welfare and security in everyday life, there was a strongly felt need for freedom, to break the paternalistic bonds to the local manager, who in a very real sense ruled in the name of the factory owner and decided where people worked, where they lived, where they shopped for food, and so on. Most of the workers' needs up until that time had been satisfied through the will of the manager. Now the majority of the population got an opportunity to satisfy their needs through the development of the welfare state. At the same time, though, it must be said, the manager also got rid of the responsibility he had had before to provide for the needs of the labour force (to build houses and so on) – the workers had to pay for all their welfare themselves.

Notwithstanding all of this, we still find that the norm that everyone had to work to earn their living was maintained through the insurance system. The amount of welfare one could get was set in relation to the income one earned. The main principle was that your income could in effect be transferred to periods when there was none. It can therefore be argued that the basis of the social policy, whose implementation began in the late 1940's and 50's, was a compromise between democratic claims for welfare, security and freedom and claims for economic rationality. The social policy was referred to as a «social investment» according to a rational «social plan». It was a «productive» social policy (A. Myrdal 1941). Viewed from the perspective of those who still were defined as poor, the development of the welfare state moved along a contradictory line. They were still under the protection of the welfare state and social authorities.

Three new poor laws were established in the 1950's. The goal in this part of the social policy was to change the character of the state help one could get from a «gift of grace» to a «social right». A «free estimation» of people's needs was now replaced by an examination of people's income. This was a more stable ground to decide on. Such an examination could give a certain guarantee that the help would be the same in all municipalities in the country. The goal of the policy was to achieve equality and justice in the distribution of welfare throughout the country on the basis of uniform regulations used by all local authorities. The possibility of getting help was also improved because the right to send poor people away, which the local authorities had had before, was abolished. Other important changes were the improvement of economic subsidies as a form of aid and the introduction of social work as a method of improving people's living conditions and attempting to prevent poverty and suffering in society. If the reason for poverty was unemployment, the local social authority now could help people get an education or a job. If a person drank too much, the social welfare authorities could try to help the person get rid of this habit. The idea was that social welfare practices should develop from being a passive spectator to become an active social agent. An important improvement in the three poor laws of the 1950's compared to the old poor law was that one didn't lose one's legal capacity if one got help. There were even procedures for complaint and appeal.

If we move from the 1950's to the current day, and analyse the practice that has developed in local social authorities, we find a democratisation in values and forms of action. In current legislation, values such as human respect are inscribed alongside goals and practices that should be implemented to meet human needs of welfare, security and freedom. In this legislation we find a major interest of the individual and his everyday life. This represents a great change in the recognition of human needs. There was little interest in the poor individual at the beginning of the century, but interest slowly grew as attitudes towards work and poverty changed. The current legislation, where human needs of welfare, security and freedom are the focus, is the result of almost half a century of changes in the practice of the welfare state. These changes started in the late 1930's. Then the ideology was that poverty in society was a collective responsibility. The society as a whole was responsible for realising the norm that all individuals should have possibilities to live decent lives. The goal was to create a welfare society and the goal of welfare was linked to the goal of social justice. These intentions were the basis of the welfare state and the new social policy, which was codified in the new social legislation in the 50's, which in turn led to the development of new practices.

It was a rather slow process and it was not until the middle of the 1960's that this change in values also changed forms of action. Before this time the change in values had a major impact on the intentions, and the needs of welfare and security were recognised. From the middle of the 60's needs of freedom also began to be recognised and at the same time forms of action started to change. Social authorities started to work together with individuals and families to try to improve living conditions. This new relationship to the needs of freedom was expressed in the more respectful treatment of those who applied for help and by a concern on the part of the authorities to act together with citizens. The individual was also encouraged to take more responsibility for himself and to act together with others in the same situation in order to affect changes. In the middle of the 60's municipalities began to get resources for these kinds of practices. The number of educated social workers grew significantly and budgets increased. In the 1970's community work was established as a method to improve living conditions on the local level. In the 80's these methods of community work were entrenched in social legislation, as were methods of social planning.

Despite all of this, the practice of the Swedish welfare state still has an administrative character. As a social worker you still have the old traditional task of controlling people's life styles and trying to correct destructive ones. In the light of the changes in values and the relations to human needs of welfare, security and freedom that has developed in practice, one would expect that the possibilities to meet those needs through this practice should have increased. But at the same time the contradictions in this practice have become more evident and have grown into the dilemma now confronting the welfare state. During the 1960's up until the middle of the 1970's, practice developed to meet human needs of welfare and security. As a consequence, a contradiction developed between these new tasks and the traditional tasks of control. During the last decade actions have developed to try to meet the needs of freedom and these actions often contradict practices that have developed to meet the needs of welfare and security. In the practice of the welfare state today you can distinguish between actions to control and correct life styles on the one hand and actions to meet the needs of welfare, security and freedom on the other.

From a historical point of view, it is evident that through the foundation of the welfare state the needs for freedom could, to some extent, be satisfied. The foundation of the welfare state meant improvements in the possibilities for freedom and dignity as old paternalistic bonds with employers were broken. At the same time new borders were established between weak and non-weak groups, and new paternalistic bonds were forged. The majority of the population gained greater freedom and at the same time improvements in the satisfaction of their needs for welfare and security, while a minority emerged dependent on social authorities. The gradual implementation of social policy and the reformation of the administrative system created possibilities that never existed before to do something about poverty. Especially important were the resources that were created on the local level in municipalities. These resources could be used to improve welfare of old people, of children and others in need. Today there is a certain guarantee of welfare that is important to many individuals. But social work today also involves a kind of «welfare-making», that categorises and defines who is «weak» and in need of help and who is not. The forms of actions within the welfare state have changed from unpaid labour done by politicians to wage labour done by professional social workers and social planners. The way of acting has changed from traditional administrative judging and discriminating to investigating, need satisfying and social planning. Today a social worker/planner is an expert whose aim is to try to satisfy people's needs through actions. The model of action is usually a model of instrumental rational reason. The practice includes a kind of discrimination. The choice to act or not to act revolves around evaluating people's life styles and conduct. This discrimination is a function of the ethic that is upheld and maintained. Earlier this ethic was principally a work ethic, but today it is a compromise between this and democratic values of welfare, security and freedom. The fact that the «welfare-making» practices are implemented by employed professionals within local social authorities also means that these actions have to be optimal and rational according to administrative, legal and professional rules. Consequently, today there are contradictions between the «welfare-making» function and the forms of actions that have developed. The problem is that the professional social worker is playing three different parts at the same time: the creator of welfare, the wage labourer and the administrator in the local social authority.

III. The Contemporary Dilemma of Welfare State Practice

The basis of the contemporary dilemma of welfare state practice is the ethico-pragmatic concept of social justice that has developed and its special kind of relationship to needs of welfare, security and freedom. The ethical and pragmatic elements include a theory of needs.

1. The Ethical Element

In the light of historical perspectives, it is evident that the kind of relation to needs of welfare that has been established is an economic one. Needs of welfare and security have been measured and estimated in quantitative categories. In fact it was an aim in the 1950's to break the old tradition of estimating needs qualitatively. The aim was to get a more stable ground from which to discriminate and to express welfare needs in terms of quantitative social indicators such as subsistence level, income, etc. This was to be a method of improving equality and minimising discrimination against poor people. It was also seen as a method that would be able to avoid ethical questions. The argument was that there couldn't be consensus about the needs of welfare, security and freedom in a pluralistic society. If you still wanted to implement a policy to improve welfare, solutions could at least be developed along economic or instrumentally rational lines. This economist perspective was sufficient in practice up until the middle of the 1960's, when democratisation started to have an impact also on the welfare state practice. The welfare state was then criticised for being too passive in its effort to improve people's living conditions. Especially the social workers were accused of passivity; they only administered welfare, without trying to change poor people's everyday lives or their deprived environments. Since then, the lack of attention to the qualitative aspects of human needs has become more and more dissatisfying. The qualitative aspects have become as important as the quantitative ones in judging and deciding who is poor and who is not, and in determining improvements in the welfare system.

The usual way to discriminate today, besides relying on economic perspectives, is to use a negative perspective. The argument is that though consensus about the needs of welfare, security, and freedom can't be reached in a pluralistic society, it is possible to determine what is not welfare, security and freedom. This negative perspective makes it possible to argue for a person's right to get a part of the collective resources through the welfare state. The negative perspective allows the argument that a person «suffers from injustice» and that something has to be done to improve their living conditions. But this method has been criticised as unworthy of human beings. It is a method that can take away human dignity, decrease self-confidence, and in the end can emphasise inequality instead of the opposite. The work a social worker has to do according to the law is to investigate and formulate arguments for the decision to act or not to act. There is a tendency on the part of the social worker to screen off interest in the individual who applies for help, even to ignore positive resources in their life. In short, this negative perspective is a bad solution to the ethical problem. If it can help one to discriminate, it is definitely useless when one has to act and start to implement changes in living conditions. A precondition of acting is that there is some intention and some means according to which one can perform the action. The negative perspective can help one to decide to act, but not how to act.

2. The Pragmatic Element

The «how to act» has been looked upon solely as a question for the professional social workers and planners to solve, and the usual solution has been to adopt a model of action that is instrumentally rational. According to this model of action, welfare, security and freedom are goals that can be fulfilled. In this model persons and their needs are treated as objects in relation to other persons. The result of this way of acting and treating human beings as means, or objects, can be that feelings of manipulation and uncertainty are aroused. The dilemma is that these results can come out of actions that are taken in order to create just the opposite.

Is it possible to solve the dilemma and to act in a way where inequality is not reproduced and the freedom of some people is not sacrificed? Is it possible to act without manipulating persons for whom we want to do something good? In light of the analysis of this dilemma, I have concluded that the rational model of action that has developed has to be changed. I have also concluded that simply an economic and negative perspective of the needs of welfare and security is insufficient, if the aim is to do something about the quality of living conditions. Ethical questions can't be neglected.

The first set of questions about models of action suggests the critique of instrumental reason. The second set of questions, about the ethical foundation of action, raises questions about what qualitative values could be added to an economical perspective of needs, given that the society is pluralistic and that we can't defend a welfare state that tries to force the same life style upon everyone. If we want to act without manipulating, is it possible to try to meet needs of welfare and security and freedom in practice at the same time? Is it possible to argue for social justice out of respect for human beings – in a way that humiliation and sacrifices don't occur?

A discussion about the contemporary dilemma has to include an analysis of the view of poverty that the welfare state presupposed. My earlier, historical analysis of poverty suggested that this perspective was intimately linked to the value of work.

Poverty became a negative concept when work came to be regarded as something that was a duty and what you had to do to earn your living. The practice of the state was then confined to ensuring that people really worked and did their duty. The industrialisation and democratisation processes changed this perspective. Poverty was gradually recognised also as a social responsibility. Poverty was reinterpreted.

3. Reinterpretation of Poverty

Today, once again, there is pressure for the reinterpreting of poverty. Needs of welfare are estimated negatively and quantitatively. There is still a tradition of paternalism; the «weak» don't know what is best for themselves; they can't take care of themselves, etc. This perspective is part of a long historical tradition, which runs from the landowner's view of their subjects, through the factory owner's view of workers, to the present situation, where there seems to be possibilities to change the negative view of welfare to a positive one. Today the concepts of poor and poverty have been replaced by «weak groups», welfare, and equality in welfare. The crucial question is: Is it possible to have a view of welfare needs that is positive, where the individual is active; creating/recreating themselves in relation to the environment as both subject and object? We require today a view of needs that is not linked to our ability to work; a perspective of welfare as something personal and social at the same time.

Yet, is it possible to have a positive view of welfare needs in modern society, which can be characterised as the dissatisfied society? Furthermore, does it make any sense to talk about «weak» groups in such a society? I think that these questions have to be analysed in light of a general analysis of the characteristics of human needs and everyday life in modernity. I think Agnes Heller's analysis of human condition in modernity, her theory of needs and analysis of the dissatisfied society are fruitful for this discussion. Her analysis is interesting because it furnished a theory of needs that assumes that needs are founded, in practice, in a social context. This means that only socially produced needs exist; even «natural needs» have a «socially produced» character (A. Heller 1976, p. 31). This is one of her essential points. This means that needs can not be defined or treated like objects. There is no abyss between the individual's need and the need structure in society; on the contrary, our needs are personal and social at the same time. Furthermore human needs have an active character; they change as society changes and they change society. Our needs are historical. Heller's second point is that needs are a category of value. My interpretation of this is that our needs are reflected as values and intentions in our actions.

What is interesting with Heller's analysis of the dissatisfied society is that she has caught the dynamics within the modern structure of needs. This need structure is distinguished by an internal contradiction between needs that stimulate increased production, increased consumerism, increased power and domination and on the other hand needs for freedom, equality and the alleviation of suffering. The contradiction between these two need structures expresses the tension between the developmental logic of capitalism and industrialisation, on the one hand, and the developmental logic of democracy, on the other. The value of progress is the highest values in both. Both sides can relate to this value. It is this value of progress that implies dissatisfaction in both cases, "but propels the actors in two different direction" (A. Heller 1983). The contradiction is caused in practice because actions that are taken to satisfy needs of increased production, consumerism and power are in most cases different to actions that are taken to satisfy needs for freedom, equality and the alleviation of suffering.

Heller's analysis also helps us to understand the dissatisfaction in modernity. Dissatisfaction is caused because the value of progress is a universalistic value, and as such it can not serve as a specific guide-line in practice. It cannot «constitute any particular way of life, as earlier particularistic and hierarchical value systems could and did» (1983, p. 366). Dissatisfaction is also caused because there are no limits to progress. «In modernity, it is success that people normally seek. Lusts are oriented towards the «more» of the «same»: more power, more fame, more wealth. As there are no consensually accepted virtues to achieve or to practice, there is no «way of life» at all, and the qualitative difference between the sublime and base is replaced by the quantitative difference of more or less success» (1983, p. 367). The distinction between «life» and «the good life» cannot be applied in modernity. Still there are some possibilities in this as the universalistic need structure at the same time creates radical needs, whose satisfaction is sought for in opposite direction to the success orientation. Even if these radical needs cannot form a way of life, they can serve as a guide-line to action, as they come about through reflection, and interpretation of universalistic values (1983, p. 368). In short, the need structure in modernity is very contradictory. On the one hand people develop unlimited needs that are alienated; on the other hand, there is a development of radical needs. Both sides of the need-structure cause dissatisfaction; needs for more welfare, more power, etc., raise this feeling because these needs are unlimited and the forms of satisfaction are alienating. Radical needs on the other hand cause dissatisfaction because they cannot be satisfied within the existing structure of society; they demand that the structure be changed.

In light of this let me return to my question about «weak» groups and welfare-making as a legitimate basis of welfare state practice. In what respect is it possible to talk about «weakness» in a society where everyone is dissatisfied? I think the time has come when we have to abandon the use of concepts of welfare in general and «weak» groups to legitimise welfare state practice. I think this has to be replaced by an analysis of value structures as a basis of action. Such an analysis has to focus on the values related to needs and different forces behind these values. In modernity we can expect to find «weak» groups on both sides of the need structure. The needs for more freedom, equality and less suffering can however only be related to logic of democracy. The crucial question turns out to be; if and in what respect the logic of democracy and the need for less suffering, more equality and more freedom have penetrated on the one hand values in society and on the other hand practices, intentions and means for action in institutions like the welfare state. On the individual level I think it is important to analyse possibilities to satisfy these needs in role-playing and forms of actions. This makes it possible to look upon welfare-making from the poor man/woman's point of view. I have made such an analysis of the role of single mothers since the Second World War. The results show that the possibilities to act in this role have changed a lot due to the changed valuation of the role in society. Single motherhood was still shameful in the 1950's and a woman had only very limited possibilities to live a good life both economically and otherwise. Today there is no condemnation in this way of single mothers, though the role has low social status. Today economic realities are much better and single mothers can get support from the social environment and the welfare state.

The crucial question today seems to be: whether the woman has chosen the role herself or whether she has ended up in it, because she didn't have a choice. If the woman has chosen the role herself, she seems to experience the possibilities she has in life, she has self-confidence, etc. If on the other hand she has not chosen the role, she seems to experience limitations.[1] According to Kierkegaard this is the existential choice; to choose a role is in fact the only choice there is in modernity. You can choose role, and thereby you also choose your destiny. Kierkegaard though doesn't see the possibilities that Heller points to in her analysis of the human condition in modernity. According to Heller you also can make an existential choice and that turns our contingency into our destiny. This can be done by trying to satisfy our need for

1 The image of the choosing being is closely linked, historically, with the birth of the image of the creative, rational man during the Renaissance. This is also the birth of the individual (HELLER, A. 1981) During the Renaissance, man (meaning all humankind) for the first time discovered his possibilities to act and create his own destiny. Man experienced a relationship between his own intentions and actions on the one hand and their consequences on the other. In a world where man experiences the fact that he can make his own destiny and his own world, norms and values become important. Earlier man's destiny was predestined and all actions, good or evil, developed in relation to God. Now this thinking changed and man developed an ethics as a conscience, and his relationship to God became a personal relationship. Man was born as a subject responsible for his actions. At the same time poverty became shameful. When man discovered his creative power the possibilities to develop seemed endless. Fulfilment would be to become like God. There seemed to be no limits to power, prosperity and happiness. The only limits turned out to be lack of knowledge about the world. The importance of developing theories in natural science was stressed.

self-determination. When we try to satisfy this need, we become conscious about restrictions in our environment and start to raise claims in order to change them. The core of the welfare/poverty question seems to revolve around the question of existential choice. The real dilemma is: Is it possible to act in a way that such choices are easier to make?

IV. The Ethical Foundation of Welfare State Practice

In the contemporary theoretical discussion about the welfare state and social justice there seem to be two irreconcilable opinions about the dilemma of the welfare state. Some, like Nozick (1974), recognise the dilemma but sees no solution to it. He even argues that there ought not to be any solutions to it. Others do not recognise that a dilemma exists (Rawls 1971). An interesting exception to this dichotomy is Heller (A. Heller 1987), who suggests an incomplete ethico-political concept of justice. It is a concept where the ties between existential and social philosophy are looser and not fitted together in a metatheory. Hers is a theory of justice suited to a pluralistic democratic society.

Nozick (1974) recognises the dilemma in the welfare state practice and characterises it as a dilemma where the freedom of the individual is sacrificed. This dilemma can only be solved when the individual gets his freedom back from the state. For this to happen the contemporary extensive state would have to be dismantled again and reduced to a minimal state. There cannot, according to Nozick, be any solution to the contemporary dilemma because the minimal state is a precondition for the individual getting back his freedom. Nozick's utopia is a minimal state, whose only function should be to protect individuals from force, theft, fraud, lack of enforcement of contracts and so on; namely the function of retribution according to criminal laws. Every function beyond these would limit the freedom of the individual. In *Anarchy, State and Utopia* Nozick argues for a liberal concept of freedom, where the individuals are free to do what they wants, as long as they do not limit somebody else's freedom. The foundation of this concept is the freedom to decide about his own property. Nozick doesn't concern himself with democratic freedom; the freedom to take part in decision making in society, even if the individual is without property. Neither is he concerned about differences in possibilities that are caused by inequality in possession of property. He is concerned solely with liberal freedom, but even in this respect, and, contrary to Nozick, I think that the foundation of the welfare state has actually increased the possibilities for a majority of the population to realise liberal freedom. The creation and development of the welfare state became, as I pointed out, a means to break traditional paternalistic bonds to landowners and factory owners; those who possessed the property in society. This meant that people no longer had to be dependent on someone else's good will in every sphere of their lives.

Rawls (1971), who elaborates a theory of justice and a procedure that will secure justice in society according to a principle of fairness, on the other hand doesn't recognise any dilemma in his scheme. As in conventional welfare state practice ethical questions are subordinate to the question of form and procedure. His main interest is to elaborate a procedure that can guarantee justice. For Rawls, «All social values – liberty and opportunity, income and wealth, and the bases of self-respect – are to be distributed equally unless an unequal distribution of any, or all, of these values is to everyone's advantage» (Rawls 1971, p. 62). This justice is concerned with a «thin good» that everyone can agree upon, and if it can be realised, then the good society will also be realised. He also presupposes that every individual is equal in rights and abilities to participate in the procedure and will agree to conform to, or at least not press claims that directly violate, the principles of justice. Other presuppositions in Rawls' theory are that society is stable and that individual ends are realisable because people's life-plans are in harmony. In this theory people are rational individuals, who make rational choices according to a life plan. This is in fact a norm in Rawls' image of the just society; that everyone has a life-plan and that the choices, that are made are all rational ones. In these rational life-plans you find the «thick good» – that is the various kinds of values of the good life, individuals want to realise. The «thick good» is complementary to the «thin good» and as all life-plans are in harmony, the good lives of individuals and the good society coalesce. There is no dilemma in Rawls' theory of justice. The goals of justice and goodness can be realised at the same time in society as a whole and in the individual. It is evident that Rawls' ethico-political concept of justice is even more complete than that which has developed in practice of the contemporary welfare state. The ethical questions are solved by Rawls, because every individual has his life-plan and the values in it are in accordance with values of the «thin good» in the concept of justice. If Rawls' theory could be implemented any aberrant tendencies in the individual would be suppressed by the norm of acting rationally according to his life-plan.

The basis of Heller's (1987) incomplete ethico-political concept of justice resides in the fact that this is a pluralistic world with different ways of life existing simultaneously side by side. In modernity there can't be a single ideal way of life. Therefore, she suggests a normative foundation for different ways of life. Her incomplete ethico-political concept of justice posits «the simultaneous existence of ways of life all bound to one another by ties of symmetric reciprocity» (A. Heller 1987, p. 220). This can be realised if certain norms are held in common and «if they are 'equalised' by common norms» (1987, p. 220). Symmetric reciprocity is the golden rule of justice and if this is applied, it excludes certain kinds of social relations in society – for example «relations of superordination and subordination, hierarchy and domination» (1987, p. 222). On the other hand, it includes «social intercourse, communication, mutual understanding, co-operation and the like» (1987, p. 222). The incomplete ethico-political concept of justice consists of two different elements: the ethical and the political. These elements together form an ideal and best possible socio-political world. According to Heller the supreme political good is «equal freedom for all» and the supreme social good «equal life-chances for all». These are the essential values in the concept. When it comes to designing a procedure and suggesting institutions that could guarantee these values in society, Heller says that the only institution that could be pointed out is the procedure of symmetric reciprocity. Other institutions could not be advocated, because they are all designed to fit certain values and forms of life. Instead, she invites everyone to make suggestions to realise the «golden rule» of justice in accordance with their social ideals, traditions, cultural backgrounds, etc. Heller's suggestion of such an incomplete ethico-political concept of justice is an interesting and challenging effort to avoid getting trapped in a complete ethico-political concept like that of Rawls.

Heller's theory of justice is not a theory addressed to the welfare state. But since this is the concrete institution that exists and its practice tries to implement an ethico-political concept of justice, I think it is important to look at it in this perspective. What she says is that if we want to stick to the value of equal freedom for all and equal life-chances for all in the welfare state practice and try to implement this, we have to act in accordance with the principle of symmetric reciprocity. To act in this way excludes manipulation and domination, instead we should act to facilitate communication, mutual understanding and co-operation. As a consequence of this, a guiding principle in discriminating and making decisions to act should be to maintain symmetric reciprocity on the social as well as on the individual level. This should mean intervening and trying to change life styles that in the end would lead to treating others as means and tools. To discriminate in this way should not mean being destructive and increasing inequality in society, on the contrary. To practice symmetric reciprocity on the individual level should mean acting without reducing someone to a means or an object. This is the only way to act in order to succeed in fighting poverty and humiliation: to act out of respect for human dignity and life itself; to treat persons as human beings. To fight poverty in this way is to fight to maintain human rights and to fight for freedom. The values that must guide this kind of action are freedom and life. If the practice in the welfare state could be changed in this way, the contemporary contradictions, between actions that are taken to meet human needs of welfare and security on the one hand and the needs of freedom on the other, would be eliminated. In fact the only way to fight poverty is to fight for freedom at the same time.

References

HELLER, A.: *The Theory of Need in Marx,* London (Allison & Busby) 1976.
— *Renaissance Man,* London (Schocken Books) 1981.
— «The Dissatisfied Society», *Praxis International,* vol 2 no 4 (1983).
— *Beyond Justice,* London/New York (Blackwell) 1987.
LILJA, E.: «The Modern Planner as a Seducer», *Geo Journal,* Vol. 30 no. 4 (1993).
MYRDAL, A.: *Nation and Family,* London 1941.
MYRDAL, G.: *Value in Social Theory,* London 1958.
NOZICK, R.: *Anarchy, State and Utopia,* New York (Basic Books) 1974.
RAWLS, J.: *A Theory of Justice,* Cambridge/ Massachusetts (Belknap Harvard) 1971.

Chapter 10

Forward to the Nineteenth Century: Has Growing Old Gracefully Become a Luxury?

PETER CURWEN

I. Introduction

The Twentieth Century will soon be history. It has witnessed enormous advances in economic and social welfare within Western Europe, which has created the expectation that each successive generation will enjoy a higher standard of living than its predecessor. The primary purpose of this chapter is to examine whether this expectation has become unrealistic, at least until well into the next century.

The chapter explores a paradoxical situation. As societies become ever wealthier, their populations live, on average, increasingly longer lives. In principle, this could yield enormous benefits as working lives are extended in parallel. In practice, however, longevity comes at a price because, firstly, the tendency is, if anything, for working lives to be reduced rather than the reverse and, secondly, because ever-larger resources are needed to maintain living standards for the ever-larger number of retirees. Again, in principle, the retired could be held entirely responsible for their own living standards, but in practice the creation of the welfare state has generated the expectation that post-retirement living standards are only partly the responsibility of the individual.

So who else is responsible? Clearly, within a welfare state system the answer is the community of which the individual forms a part, where that community normally takes the form of a nation state. For obvious reasons, however, resources can only be generated by those who are economically active, namely those between full-time education and retirement (net of the unemployed) traditionally taken to be those aged between 16 and 60 in the case of women, and between 16 and 65 in the case of men.

Historically, individuals did not, on average, live all that long beyond retirement, and the birth rate exceeded the figure of 2.1 per couple needed to maintain the aggregate population size (after adjusting for unmarried people). Hence, there were more than enough economically active individuals to ensure that living standards would continue to rise across the population as a whole. However, it has become apparent over the past decade that this happy equation no longer holds true. No only do people live longer and retire earlier, but young people stay in education and training for longer periods and the birth rate has fallen below replacement levels throughout Europe. As a result, successive generations of the economically active are set to shrink in size while the absolute number of the economically inactive is set to grow continuously.

It follows, therefore, that unless the economically active can so increase their productivity that they can simultaneously improve both their own living standards and those of the retired, then the living standards of at least one group must decline. Since, logically, the economically active are unlikely to choose voluntarily to maintain the living standards of the retired in preference to their own, a situation of inter-generational conflict necessarily arises which, if resolved at the expense of the retired, could consign many among them to an old age characterised by the very kind of poverty that the welfare state was brought into being to alleviate. Conceivably, their lives in the twenty-first century could be more comparable with their nineteenth century predecessors than with those in the twentieth century.

Such an hypothesis may be deemed to be unnecessarily alarmist. Clearly, if action is taken in the near future to deal with what is self-evidently a long-term problem, all may yet be well. One must remember, however, that politicians are more interested in the forthcoming elections than in anything that might transpire when they have left office, so it is unwise to rely upon the political process to inflict short-term pain for long-term gain.

II. The Scale of the Problem

A recent World Bank Study (World Bank, 1994) estimates that the number of people aged over 60 will increase from 0.5 billion in 1990, equivalent to roughly 9 per cent of the global population, to 1.4 billion in 2030, equivalent to roughly 16 per cent of the global population. Over one half of this increase will take place in Asia. Only 14 per cent will occur in industrial countries, with which this paper is concerned. However, it is in these latter countries, which currently have the highest proportion of older people, and which are growing relatively slowly, that the retired enjoy relatively high living standards and where the pain of adjustment is likely to be correspondingly severe.

Looking specifically at the 18 Western European members of the OECD, the position is that the number of people aged 65 and over will rise from 50 million (15 per cent of the population) to more than 70 million (20 per cent of the population) between 1990 and 2030. During the same period, the number of people of working age will actually fall because fertility rates, notably in Catholic Southern Europe, are declining rapidly. Specifically, in Europe:

- Two out of three over-65s who have ever lived are alive today.
- The world's oldest country is Sweden where 18 per cent of the population are aged 65 or over.
- The number of over-65s will outstrip the number of children aged 14 and under in roughly 25 years.
- Once a man reaches the age of 60 he can expect to live, on average, to 78, whereas a woman can expect to live, on average, to 82.
- Well over 12 million people are currently aged over 80, of whom roughly 4 million are incapacitated in some way.

The result is that by the year 2030 there will be fewer than three people aged between 15 and 64 in Western Europe for each person aged over 65, compared to five today.

However, the situation varies considerably between countries within Europe. The UK, for example, is least affected in the long run. The current ratio of 4.5 between those of working age and pensioners is set to rise slightly until 2010, after which it is forecast to fall to 3 by 2030, at which level it should stabilise. In Germany, by comparison, the current figure of 4.5 is forecast to decline steadily until it reaches a figure of 2 in 2040, after which it should show a modest rise. This profile is similar for France and Italy, other than that they both start from roughly 5 and decline steadily to roughly 2.5 before rising slightly. Only in the UK, therefore, is there any realistic prospect of a ratio higher than 3 before 2050.

Interestingly, the profile in the USA is similar to that of the UK except that the current ratio is over 5 and is forecast to plummet to little more than 3 between 2010 and 2030, so the system will come under severe strain in the medium term even though the longer-term prognosis is not too severe. The country which will suffer most among the advanced countries is Japan, where the current ratio of 6 is forecast to become little more than 3 by 2010, and to fall, and remain, below that level after 2030.

It goes without saying that demographics is an inexact science, and it is accordingly quite easy to claim that fertility rates have bottomed out and that the situation will not deteriorate as rapidly as forecast. Equally, it is possible to argue that immigration represents a partial solution, since immigrants tend to be relatively youthful and to have fertility rates above replacement levels. On the other hand, Western Europe is, if anything, becoming increasingly reluctant to welcome immigrants, and in the short term at least, they tend to be a drain on the host country's resources because of the associated demand for subsidised education and health care.

An alternative way of representing the above data is in terms of `dependency ratios', which measure the number of persons aged over 65 as a percentage of those aged 15 to 64. In effect, the ratio of 4 cited above would accordingly yield a dependency ratio of 25%, and the figure 3 cited above would yield a dependency ratio of 33%. A lot obviously depends upon the specific years taken for the purposes of comparison, but if 2040, which is forecast to be the time when the above figures reach a minimum, is compared with the situation today, then dependency ratios are set roughly to double in many European countries. For example, according to the OECD, Germany rises from 23.7 to 47.1; France from 21.9 to 39.2; and Denmark from 22.2 to 43.4. Some countries do better, among them, as indicated above, the UK which rises from 23.5 to 39.1 and Ireland which rises from 18.4 to 27.2. On the other hand, Spain rises from 17.0 to 41.7; Italy from 20.4 to 48.4; and the Netherlands from 17.4 to 48.5.

Finally, it is important to remember that, although our concern here is with the fiscal consequences of ageing, the burden of the welfare state is simultaneously rising in other respects. This is shown in Table 1.

Table 1: Social Expenditure. Burden per person aged 15-64 years. 1980 = 100

	2000	2010	2020	2030	2040
France	101	105	117	129	133
Germany	112	119	131	157	162
Italy	102	109	120	135	143
UK	98	101	106	118	117
Japan	112	133	138	136	150
USA	97	100	118	133	132

Once again, it is evident that the UK gets off fairly lightly, if such an expression can be applied to a near-20 per cent rise in inflation-adjusted expenditure. The countries currently considered to be most successful from an economic perspective, such as Germany and Japan, must cope with far more severe long-term fiscal problems.

III. Ageing and Health Care Costs

An ageing population has serious implications for welfare systems in two main respects, the first of which is the relationship between ageing and health care costs. Health care costs in Western Europe currently account for between 7 and 10 per cent of GDP, although some smaller countries have lower ratios. With the exception of Sweden and Ireland, every country's ratio is higher than it was in 1985, in many cases by between 1 and 2 per cent. There is every reason to suppose that these ratios are set to rise still further, since a combination of rapidly-rising labour costs, increased use of expensive technology and drugs, and changing demographic profiles are straining the capacity of health care systems to meet the demands placed upon them. In the case of the USA, which may or may not be viewed as providing a pattern of health care towards which Western Europe will evolve, the ratio already stands at 14 per cent.

It is, perhaps, ironic that one of an advanced society's primary aims has always been to ensure that its citizens live long and healthy lives. Until fairly recently, that worthy objective was difficult to deliver. Large numbers of children died at birth or in their infancy, and relatively few people lived beyond the age of 70. However, as indicated above, longevity has now essentially been achieved, with both men and women in Europe surviving, on average, to roughly 80 years old. This does not mean, however, that health care systems must provide for many more people overall, since fertility rates are so low and aggregate populations are consequently static. Rather, it means that these systems must accommodate much different age profiles, with proportionately large numbers in the group aged over 60.

Beyond that age human bodies begin to show signs of wear. Hence, although fewer than 5 per cent of Europeans in their sixties are severely incapacitated, this percentage is 6 to 7 times higher for people in their eighties. Not surprisingly, therefore, the older age groups consume a disproportionate share of health care and account for a disproportionate share of health care costs. It follows that, as Western Europe ages progressively until 2040, health care systems will come under immense strain even if there are no other upwards pressures upon costs. In practice, it is well-known that healthcare costs rise much faster than prices in general, so whereas it is indeed a noble objective to keep people alive as long as humanly possible, it is a highly uneconomical strategy!

For obvious reasons, where health care is provided within a welfare framework, (that is, largely free at the point of consumption), the healthy must pay the taxes that are needed to subsidise services for the unhealthy. This has long been regarded as an acceptable form of inter-generational transfer, since each successive generation can look forward to being subsidised in its turn by the next. Nevertheless, it is unclear to what extent this represents an open-ended commitment, given a probable rise in the ratio of health spending to GDP in Western Europe to more than 10 per cent by 2020.

Indeed, in some countries such as the UK, it has been clear since the creation of public national health care systems that the rate at which the demand for health care is outstripping its supply can only be accommodated by some form of rationing. Traditionally, this rationing has taken the form of queues, with only the very wealthy abl to 'jump the queue' by paying large fees in cash. However, the increasingly wealthy middle classes have found their own method of 'jumping the queue' by taking out private insurance, thereby paying twice for health care, once through taxation and once through insurance. This has affected an improvement in supply, but has unsurprisingly left queues for those unable to bear the not inconsiderable burden of insurance premiums. This trend has led, as indicated, to spiralling health care costs in the USA, and although the US system is unlikely to be adopted wholesale in Europe, its costs are the subject of great concern.

It must also be borne in mind that health care insurance is the province of the healthy, since no insurer will accept known and expensive risks at affordable premiums. The retired, by implication, are often uninsurable, and their disproportionate care costs necessarily fall upon the public purse. Hence, the healthy middle-aged not merely have to pay for an increasingly expensive public health service that they prefer, wherever possible, not to use, but also pay high insurance premiums which, because they are healthy, are effectively written off'. This is understandably putting the inter-generational compact under strain, given that it was initiated at a time when health care systems were almost entirely tax financed, and taxpayers may ultimately rebel against paying so much for the health care of the older, largely uninsured, age groups.

IV. The Pension 'Time Bomb'

Van den Noord and Herd (1993) offer an analysis of projected pension spending by the public sector as a percentage of GDP. Although this excludes private provision, their figures nevertheless show countries such as the USA, the UK and Germany currently in the 5 to 7 per cent bracket, with France at just below 10 per cent and Italy well above that figure. More importantly, all of these countries are set to reach much higher percentages by 2030, with France peaking at roughly 15 per cent and Italy at roughly 22 per cent. Add in private provision, together with the 10 per cent required for health care as noted above, and it immediately becomes apparent that health care and pensions represent what is often referred to as a 'time bomb' waiting to explode in thirty years' time if no action is taken to contain it.

As in the case of health care provision, it is evident that pensions at a level comfortably above the poverty line are an expression of a society's more noble objectives, and one which it is impossible to secure until a country attains a very high level of GDP. This level has now been achieved throughout Western Europe, and it is no longer at issue whether these countries can afford to provide pensions. What has become an issue, however, is whether the state should be responsible for maintaining pensions at an absolute level, in which case pensioners' living standards will decline progressively relative to those who work, or whether it should raise pensions progressively in line with workers' earnings.

In order to understand why the latter option, which is not merely morally superior but, at least until recently, was considered to be affordable, no longer finds favour in countries such as the UK it is necessary to begin by returning to the point in time when state pensions were first introduced. Presumably in the quest for electoral support, state pension schemes were normally introduced for everyone who happened to exceed a particular age at that point in time without requiring the recipients to have made any prior contributions. In effect, these pensions represented a bribe rather than the implementation of a noble objective because, as is well known, 'there is no such thing as a free lunch'. In practice, the implementation of these pension schemes on a 'pay-as-you-go' or 'unfunded' basis meant that the first cohort of pensioners received a direct transfer paid for by taxes levied on the next generation at work. The latter, in turn, while believing that they were funding their own pensions, actually had their pensions funded by the following generation and so forth.

It is obvious that the pensions of the current generation at work are a future liability for society since the state has made a promise to pay. However, since they do not need to be paid for currently, it is technically unnecessary for governments to include them in their national accounts, and, unsurprisingly, they choose not to do so. Were they to do so, the level of national indebtedness would be shown to be vastly greater than is officially acknowledged.

Naturally, it can be argued that this is merely a distraction; that if each generation is happy to provide pensions for its predecessor then all will continue to be well. Under certain circumstances, namely where the number of workers and pensioners remain broadly in ratio, there is indeed little cause for concern. However, as explained above, the ratio between workers and pensioners is changing in an adverse manner, effectively requiring each worker to finance more pension liabilities than before while at the same time creating fewer workers to finance their own pensions when they retire – a recipe for eventual inter-generational conflict if ever there was one.

Crudely expressed, if each successive generation of pensioners grows larger while their pensions remain constant in inflation-adjusted terms, and each successive generation of workers grows smaller, then a financial crisis becomes an inevitability. As demonstrated in the earlier discussion, this problem must first be addressed by the OECD countries, although one minor saving grace is that the dependency ratios does improve after the year 2040, so if the crisis does not occur before that time it may never occur at all.

Unfortunately, whereas the pensions 'time-bomb' has not been public knowledge for very long, the very fact that it has 'come out of the closet' is likely in itself to make things worse. This is because, as the burden of paying for pensions grows, attempts to transfer this burden onto the generation at work will cause taxes to rise which in turn will leave fewer workers to pay yet higher taxes and so on.

The simple fact is that this is not going to work, and it is precisely because this is the case that must follow logically that governments must begin to consider reneging on their promises through such means as raising the minimum pensionable age, removing indexation adjustments or means testing, as discussed below. Understandably, such a prognosis is less than acceptable to countries which have spent decades building up their welfare states and which contain strong anti-poverty lobbies, although, as has seemingly become the custom in Europe, the UK is prepared to go where other countries fear to tread.

V. Issues

Interestingly, attempts within Europe to strengthen the welfare state rather than the reverse have produced somewhat unexpected results. The quest for gender equality in pensions is a case in point. As a result of a number of cases brought before the European Court of Justice, it is now firmly established that there must henceforth be gender equality in pensions where previously women retired typically at the age of 60 compared to 65 for men. The objective of the exercise was to bring the pension age for men down to that for women, partly in recognition of the fact that increasing numbers of men were anyway retiring at 60, or even 55, even if that meant that they had to wait until 65 to claim their state pensions. However, the judgements of the Court made it clear that the precise age of equalisation was a matter for national governments rather than the Court to determine (see, for example, the *Financial Times*, 29 September 1994), and what most of them determined was that the pension age for women should be raised into equality with that for men.

It can be argued that equalisation offends natural justice because women live longer, and hence should retire later than men, but that would imply the need to raise the pensionable age for women to 70, which governments are understandably reluctant to implement. Nevertheless, there can be no doubt that equalisation has much eased the burden of state pension provision when the intention was to the contrary.

A second issue is arguably more fundamental. It has always been assumed that the underlying reason for state provision of pensions is that the retired are one, if not the most deserving, of the groups requiring state assistance. In a world where the great majority of members of this group earned comparatively little while at work and were thereby prevented from saving, and owned no assets to speak of, such an assumption made sense and was supported by research.

It is clear, however, that the retired are no longer a homogenous group. Many among them are extremely affluent, having built up substantial pension rights in occupational and/or private schemes, and own considerable wealth, albeit often in an illiquid form such as housing. Others, reliant entirely upon the state for their income and with negligible wealth, are in much different circumstances. Only the latter group are arguably comparable with the 'new poor', who particularly include families with young children, especially where the father is departed, unemployed or has a low wage.

Obviously, few individuals are willing to forgo voluntarily even the modest state pension rights which they believe they have 'paid for' out of the taxation or social security contributions. In all probability, the most affluent are unlikely to complain much even if stripped of these rights, and the more awkward problems are likely to arise among those who believe that the state pension right does make some difference to their lifestyles. In particular, there is unlikely to be much enthusiasm for private provision among those with modest incomes if they believe that the state stands ready as pension provider of last resort. In other words, why provide a modest pension for oneself if the state must, for reasons of equity and the eradication of poverty, provide a minimum fall-back provision for those who have failed to provide for themselves. The benefits of adopting such a position are enhanced by schemes such as the "Care in the Community" provisions in the UK which, under certain circumstances, strip individuals of almost their entire wealth if they need full-time nursing care.

A further issue which arises in the context of private provision is that implied by the underlying principle of insurance. It is an awkward fact of life that no-one knows when it is going to end. As a result, it is almost impossible to calculate how much is needed in a private pension plan to ensure a decent lifestyle throughout retirement. State pensions are open-ended, working on actuarial principles based upon huge numbers of the retired to ensure that provision is sufficient on average. For the individual, however, the length of retirement is essentially a lottery which may elicit a variety of responses. On the one hand, an individual may choose to set very little aside, preferring instead to enjoy life in the present. On the other hand, an individual may set so much aside that it is not all consumed during retirement, thereby depriving him/herself of a high quality of life pre-retirement.

In addition, individual choices may be distorted by inadequate information about, for example, the cost of living in retirement or the probabilities of surviving to certain ages. Equally, such choices may be distorted by poor or unscrupulous advice from so-called professionals, as recent experience in the UK has borne out.

Unfortunately, we do not know whether, even if properly informed, individuals will set sufficient amounts aside. The empirical evidence, such as it is, provides contradictory results. Furthermore, the past may be a poor guide to future behaviour since circumstances may change quite radically. An example would be the recent collapse of house prices in the UK, since rapid asset price inflation during the 1980s had created a general expectation that capital gains on houses would provide a cushion of wealth to fall back on through trading down to a cheaper property on retirement and using the difference to finance retirement.

A further point is that the providers of private pensions are large institutions, which have much greater market power than individual clients. This would appear to suggest that the state is preferable as a provider since it is even more powerful than the institutions and can achieve economies of scale and spread risks. In particular, whereas individuals are prone to suffer when periodically changing jobs or becoming unemployed, since such events may make it difficult to maintain contributions, a state scheme could readily allow for such eventualities by averaging over huge numbers of contributors.

Finally, it is crucial to bear in mind that if an individual is set free to make his or her own arrangements, that individual becomes wholly responsible for the end-result. If contributions are invested unwisely, the only person to suffer is the contributor. Where the state has overall responsibility for a scheme, all pensioners are treated alike, whether well or badly as the case may be.

These points appear to weigh heavily in favour of state-run schemes. However, such schemes are themselves subject to severe drawbacks. For example, whereas an individual can set up a private scheme to make payments at literally any age, and in any amounts, a state-run scheme necessarily has a predetermined common retirement age. This has become an increasingly important factor because, as mentioned above, budgetary pressures are driving up the official age of retirement at precisely the time when individuals are increasingly opting for early retirement.

A further objection to state-run schemes is that, whereas there is an implicit assumption that governments in advanced countries cannot go bankrupt, they can constitutionally change their minds and, for example, renege on pension promises. This is more of a risk than it may appear to be at first sight. The UK government, for example, unexpectedly ceased to index pensions to average wage inflation, switching to indexation against the customarily lower consumer prices index. Unfortunately, however, even private schemes are not wholly immune from such a drawback since, for example, pensions are almost universally subject to tax breaks and these can also be withdrawn at the government's whim.

The ultimate virtue of private provision to its adherents is that it restricts, even if it cannot altogether prevent, the government interfering with rational individual choices. They hold that, suitably informed, the individual should be left to strike a balance between current and future consumption and, if mistakes are made, the individual, as in other spheres of life, should be left to bear the consequences.

Obviously, irrespective of its virtues in the general case, this cannot provide a universal solution since the state must retain some responsibility, perhaps suitably means-tested, for those unable reasonably to save for their old age. This suggests that private provision combined with a state fall-back represents the optimal long-term solution even though this is subject to the reservations expressed above and is most unlikely to reduce the overall burden of financing pensions which will basically be transferred from one source to another.

A word of caution is also needed concerning the concept of means-testing, previously mentioned. Currently, a basic (and it can be very basic) state pension is almost universal in advanced countries. This very universality causes it to be regarded as a 'right' which is financed in some mysterious way that does not directly concern the recipient. If it is means-tested, therefore, it becomes a socially-divisive factor. Those entitled to claim it will feel that they have been identified as incapable of financing their own pensions, with probable consequent low rates of take-up. On the other hand, means-testing also sends out a clear message to individuals who could provide a basic pension for themselves that, by saving absolutely nothing, they can ensure that someone else pays for it.

Awkwardly, this discussion begins to point towards the virtues of compulsion. However, it is surprising how acceptable this idea is becoming to radicals of all political complexions. They hold that everyone should be obliged to make regular minimum payments into a state-approved scheme, other than the small minority who are truly destitute. This is not simply a statement of principle. Some countries, such as Australia and Singapore, already have such a system in place, although one as yet unresolved issue is whether a mandatory state scheme is to be preferred to a mandatory private scheme. All this may suffice to make libertarians take fright. However, the alternatives, which are set out below, are less than convincing if compulsion is entirely excluded.

VI. Solutions?

Historically, the response to underfunding would have been to provide more money. Hence, the traditional solutions would have been:

- To raise taxes and transfer the proceeds into the state pension fund.
- To borrow via an increase in the national debt.

At the present time, neither of these solutions has much appeal, either from a financial or electoral viewpoint. Under the conditions specified in the Maastricht Treaty, member states of the European Union are expected to have a national debt/GDP ratio of less than 60 per cent, and to run budget deficits of less than 3 per cent of GDP. Currently, few states meet both these conditions, and indebtedness is generally on the rise rather than the reverse. Raising taxes will not cause either of these ratios to deteriorate, but higher taxes, especially where these are ring-fenced until they can be drawn upon at some point well into the future, are unlikely to strike a sympathetic chord among the electorate. This suggests that a preferable solution would be:

- To cut future pension liabilities

As indicated above, almost all countries now accept that this must form part of a solution. However, there is understandably little enthusiasm among politicians for unilateral reductions in the amount on offer. Hence, the UK government's approach, involving pension increases but ones which, because they are indexed to prices rather than earnings, actually cause the real spending power of the pension to drop gradually, is likely to be favoured. On the other hand, it should be noted that, according to van den Noord and Herd

(1993), the problem of under-funding in France could only be resolved in this way were pensions to rise at no more than 60 per cent of the rise in earnings, and that the equivalent figure for Canada would be 20 per cent. Clearly, such figures will not be acceptable to the increasingly vocal pressure group that pensioners now represent. Hence, it might be preferable to:

- Raise the minimum pension age

As previously noted, most advanced countries have either already taken this step or have it under consideration. Nevertheless, it is a retrograde step, given the desire for early rather than late retirement, and is difficult to make compatible with a tendency at times of high unemployment to dismiss older, and typically more expensive, workers in favour of those newly entering the work force. In any event, for this solution to work in the absence of higher taxes would require the retirement age to be raised to 81 in Canada and to at least 75 in the UK, Germany and Italy (van den Noord and Herd, 1993).

What this indicates is that none of the traditional approaches can be expected to work in isolation. Whether they would work in combination is obviously a moot point, given that no country has so far implemented the full set of policies, although the UK has proceeded further than others. Again, the electoral consequences must not be downplayed. Governments operate on, usually, 5-year cycles. What happens thirty years hence is of little concern. In some ways, therefore, it is an electoral curiosity that the UK government is floating radical solutions at precisely the time when it is already so unpopular that it can ill afford to irritate the electorate any further.

VII. Case Studies

Case Study 1: The UK Pension System

Although, as indicated above, the UK pension system is under less pressure than most others, the government has been unusually active in taking steps to reduce its future liabilities. For example, as previously noted, it has reneged on its commitment to uprate the basic state pension in line with earnings and switched to uprating in line with retail prices which habitually rise more slowly. As a result, the basic pension has fallen to the equivalent of roughly 15 per cent of average gross male earnings, the lowest figure since 1970. Had the uprating been linked to prices since 1945, the pension would be worth approximately $30 per week, so it is evident that by the year 2030 it will probably be worth considerably less than 10 per cent of average gross male earnings (Disney, Johnson and Whitehouse, 1994).

Furthermore, the state earnings related pension (SERPS) has been scaled down under the 1986 Social Security Act. Not surprisingly, therefore, state provision looks to be singularly ungenerous by the standards of many of the poorer EU member states let alone the wealthier ones. On the other hand, the government has been pushing towards a system where individuals who are capable of so doing become obliged to finance their own pension provision, leaving the state responsible only for the rump of the effectively destitute who will be provided for in good part via means-tested income support and housing related benefits.

Although such an approach might seem to be radical in other European countries, this was not the perception in the UK given that company pension schemes, which go hand-in-hand with an opt-out from SERPS, had long been a feature of the UK system. Insofar as it was seen to be radical, this was because the government advocated opting-out from company schemes and into purely personal pensions. For obvious reasons, this opt-out has to be treated with great care by individuals since there can be no guarantee that it will leave people better off. It has, however, been a popular option, and the government actuary estimates that there are now six million individuals with personal pensions of various kinds. Unfortunately, unscrupulous individuals and companies took the opportunity to make unsubstantiated, if not positively fraudulent, claims about the virtues of personal pensions compared to company schemes, and the government has been obliged to unravel the consequent mess, a Herculean task which is as yet incomplete.

This is unlikely to have delivered a mortal blow to the cause of personal pensions, but it is no minor setback and other countries would do well to avoid the pitfalls exposed by the UK experience. Nevertheless, the controversy has at least served to force certain fundamental issues to the forefront of the discussion. In particular, there is the issue of 'defined contribution' versus 'defined benefit'. Company schemes in the UK have largely been of the defined benefit variety – that is, the pension is related to the recipient's earnings in the years prior to retirement. This has caused problems both in relation to the security of the funds placed in the scheme, as the Maxwell scandal has ably demonstrated, and also in relation to those who move from company to company, leaving part of their pension behind them as they go.

Both of these defects can ultimately be remedied by changes in the law. This approach may also be needed to deal with the further problem which has arisen in the context of companies taking 'contributions holidays' – that is, temporarily ceasing to pay their share of the pension contributions made on behalf of employees. This technique has the obvious benefit of boosting declared profits, but is superficially justifiable at times when, due for example to an unusually high return on investments, the pension fund has more than sufficient funds to cover its liabilities. However, there is no guarantee that this situation will not become reversed, and it plainly affects adversely the company pensioner who, without consultation, has his or her pension curtailed below what would have been achievable were contributions to have been maintained.

For these reasons, defined contribution schemes have become increasingly popular. These accrue returns in relation to what is paid into the scheme rather than to the income of the employee at retirement. On the whole, such schemes would have yielded a higher return than most defined benefit schemes over the past decade, but it has to be recognised that this outcome cannot be guaranteed, and that if the individual invests unwisely the consequences fall entirely upon that individual and are not averaged out over all of a company's pensioners.

The debate is important, not least because it possibly affects the employability of contributors. Defined benefit schemes normally create ever-larger liabilities for companies as workers move up salary scales with age, creating the temptation to fire older workers before they become 'too expensive'. Naturally, companies will never admit that this factor influences decisions about who is employed, but it is bound to be taken into consideration.

Defined contribution schemes are accordingly likely to displace defined benefit schemes for increasing numbers of younger employees in the UK. Nevertheless, it should again be borne in mind that this will have little effect upon the circumstances of those employees whose incomes are too low for the nature of the scheme itself to make any real difference.

Case Study 2: The Italian Pension System

If the approach in the UK discussed above can be said to be 'progressive', then the approach in Italy can at best be said to be 'blinkered', although the government has tried hard to give the opposite impression. As previously indicated, the situation in Italy is particularly problematic. In 1990, the national pension scheme, INPS, required a state transfer of L 54,112 bn., equivalent to 24.7 per cent of its outgoings. In 1995, the figures were L 72,000 bn. and 26.5 per cent respectively. Currently, there are roughly 1.1 contributors per pensioner, a figure which has declined from 1.22 in 1990 and 2.8 in 1965, and is set to worsen further if reform of INPS is postponed.

Italians neither like paying taxes nor contributing to their own pensions. It was generally acknowledged that there were huge numbers of the self-employed who, by declaring much higher incomes in the years prior to retirement, were able to withdraw in pensions vastly more than their lifetime contributions. Other groups have taken advantage of pensioni di anzianita, or seniority pensions, which allow a full pension to be drawn after 35 years of contributions even though the pensioner may be in his or her early fifties. Given that such pensions may be equivalent to 70 per cent of final salary, and index-linked, it is evident that on average they must be hopelessly out of balance with the recipients' contributions.

The situation has been widely accepted as untenable for some time, but political instability has meant that each successive government has been either unwilling, unable or both, to take on the vested interests in preserving the status quo. Unusually, the technocratic Dini government chose in 1995 to stake its reputation upon, among other things, pension reform. It subsequently reached agreement with the unions to a reform that links pensions to contributions during the pensioner's working life and to his or her life expectancy at the time of retirement. Furthermore, seniority pensions will be phased out.

On the face of it, such a reform package may appear to be extremely radical, but the fine print tells another story. In particular, it should be noted that only those entering the workforce for the first time will be wholly subject to the new rules, which means that the reforms will not be fully implemented before 2030. For this reason, the initial savings to INPS and other state-funded schemes are forecast at under L4,000 bn., rising to L10,000 bn. in 2005. Unfortunately, however, INPS outgoings are rapidly approaching L300,000 bn., so the savings will barely be noticed in practice.

This would not matter so much were these savings seen as a preliminary gesture to be followed up by substantive reform. In practice, the unions regard them as major concessions. For those approaching retirement, such an attitude is doubtless welcome, but for those newly entering the workforce the situation is potentially explosive as they will be obliged to finance pensioners' incomes at a higher level than they are simultaneously financing their own. This should provide an interesting test of inter-generational solidarity.

Case Study 3: "Care in the Community"

The purpose of this third case study is to remind readers that the dilemmas of old age are not simply pension related, but also have to do with the cost of illness and incapacity in old age. The traditional response, which remains the orthodoxy in such countries as Australia, Canada and Sweden, is to regard these costs as a burden upon the welfare state but, as previously noted, this implies that health care costs will rise inexorably as a proportion of GDP. For this reason, other countries, such as Austria, Belgium and Japan, restrict state obligations to those deemed to be unable to pay for themselves, whereas others such as France and Germany try various other combinations (see *The Economist,* 16 July, 1994). It was in response to this dilemma that the government in the UK brought in the National Health Service and Community Care Act of 1990. The key provision, implemented progressively since 1993, is the Care in the Community system which set out to permit disabled people to remain living in their own homes rather than being transferred to hospital wards. This was expected to produce savings, given the high costs of providing long-term hospital beds.

However, the Act distinguished between "medical care" and "social care", which is concerned with daily living costs. Medical care is free on the National Health Service whereas social care is not. Thus, when an elderly person is transferred into a nursing or residential home that person must, if so able, pay personally for the care provided. Specifically, anyone with an annual income, inclusive of pensions and social security benefits, in excess of £3,000 and who possesses wealth valued in excess of £8,000, must contribute towards the cost of care on a sliding scale. This cost is unlikely to fall below £200 per week and may be considerably more.

Whilst such a person cannot be obliged to sell his or her house, its value is counted as part of wealth unless a spouse or elderly or incapacitated relative remains in the house. Refusal to sell the house simply means that the appropriate sum will be appropriated by the local authority at a later date when the house is eventually sold, and giving the house away will not be permitted if it is clearly with the intent of avoiding payment for care.

This has understandably caused a good deal of outrage among the elderly. They argue, firstly, that if a person has contributed taxes to pay for medical care over possibly a forty-year period, that person should be entitled to free care when old and disabled. Secondly, they argue that those who have savings have almost all of them, including their property, forcibly expropriated, whereas those who have no savings receive the same quality of care.

Currently, over 360,000 UK citizens live in private nursing and residential homes, of whom fewer than one third pay fees. Thirdly, they argue that their savings constitute the inheritance for the next generation who are thereby deprived of what should `rightfully' be theirs in the course of time.

According to the Association of British Insurers, the inflation-adjusted costs of long-term care are likely to rise by roughly two-thirds between 1990 and 2040. Such an increase is clearly beyond the means of the state to finance. The response of the UK government, in the face of the rebellious elderly, has been to propose alternative radical measures, including long-term health insurance, the diversion of part of pension funds to a date beyond retirement when they can be drawn upon to finance residential care and the exemption of the family home in calculations of wealth. Such ideas are either untenable, insofar that the middle-aged are unlikely to want to pay out huge premiums into an insurance policy to cover such care and, should they be compelled to do so, are likely to rebel politically on the grounds that is just another disguised tax, or too expensive for the state to finance willingly.

However, the government adheres to the view that individuals will be obliged, one way or another, to finance much more of their lifestyle post-retirement. There remains, as indicated, just one major fly in the ointment. The elderly are growing in numbers and political power. In 1994, the elderly in the Netherlands formed their own parties and successfully contested the May elections. There is, as yet, little sign of such behaviour in the UK, but the government has been heavily criticised for the Care in the Community provisions, and now realises that they were too radical for its own good.

VIII. Conclusion

One thing at least is abundantly clear from the above discussion, namely that someone must pay if the retired are to enjoy their expected standard of living over the coming decades. One thing, however, that remains abundantly unclear is who that someone is going to be. Historically, that someone was the subsequent generation, but imposing the entire burden which has built up over several generations upon one, or possibly two future generations is likely to create a situation of inter-generational conflict.

In any case, given the size of the problem, it is unlikely that one generation could afford to deal with the problem by itself. Naturally, governments prefer not to be too explicit about the specific numbers, and they are in any event very much subject to the specific assumptions made in any particular model.

One interesting approach is that proposed by Alan Auerbach of the University of California at Berkeley, known as 'generational accounting'. This seeks to make the scale of the problem as explicit as possible in order to force governments to take remedial action of some kind. In essence, this approach seeks to identify the value of the taxes paid, and benefits received, over the lifetime of an 'average' individual in a particular generation.

Certain underlying assumptions obviously have to be made. For example, Auerbach assumes that benefit levels remain unchanged, and that taxes are raised to the point at which the present value of all future taxes is equal to the present value of future spending plus the current stock of debt. These higher taxes are then assumed to fall entirely on each of a sequence of subsequent generations.

Not surprisingly, the current retired generation is shown to be a substantial net recipient over its lifetime, whereas subsequent generations are shown to be massive net payees, with the biggest burden falling upon the group aged currently in their twenties. Rolling that generation forward to retirement produces rather frightening consequences in that, whereas the current average tax rate in advanced countries is normally between 35 and 40 per cent, this might need to rise, depending upon the assumptions made, to twice that level. Calculations by the OECD confirm that such a jump is indeed possible, although there is potentially a huge discrepancy between individual countries. Some, such as Germany and Sweden, show quite modest increases, whereas the position in Italy where a five-fold increase is projected, appear to be unsustainable.

In principle, the key conclusion is accordingly only too obvious, namely that if the burden is to be shared out at all equitably then it must be spread out over as many generations as possible. In other words, if the situation is fudged for electoral reasons, and the Italian case study above indicates that it is indeed being fudged in some countries, and decisions pushed back into the next century, the adjustment process will be extremely unpleasant. Which generation will then bear most of the burden is a moot point, but individuals of all ages will be well-advised to reassess their lifetime finances for themselves if no explicit state action is forthcoming before the end of the millennium.

In practice, the omens increasingly point to the introduction of some kind of compulsory programme of saving which cannot be drawn upon prior to retirement, with the individual left to decide how much supplementary saving to undertake. This is a far cry from the original conception of the welfare state but, for example, at the time of its inception too little account was taken of the distinction between an individual's need to save towards his or her own lifestyle post-retirement, to provide for unpredictable events such as the need for residential care and to provide, as appropriate, for transfers to those incapable of providing for themselves – and all within the context of an ageing society. No wonder children, a private and very expensive good, have gone out of fashion. Perhaps, therefore, the best and most radical solution is to nationalise the costs of their upbringing.

References

CUTLER, D., POTERBA, J., SHEINER, L. and SUMMERS, L.: "An Ageing Society: Opportunity Or Challenge", *Brookings Papers on Economic Activity,* 1 (1990), pp. 1-72.

DISNEY, R., JOHNSON, P. and WHITEHOUSE, E.: *Pension Policy in the UK: An Economic Analysis,* London (Institute of Economic Affairs) 1994.

JENSEN, S. and NIELSEN, S.: "Ageing, Inter-generational Distribution and Public Pension Systems", *Public Finance,* 48 (1993), pp. 29-42.

JENSEN, S. and NIELSEN, S.: "Population Ageing, Public Debt and Sustainable Fiscal Policy", *Fiscal Studies,* 16 (1995), pp. 1-20.

JOHNSON, P. and ZIMMERMAN, K. (Eds.): *Labour Markets in an Ageing Europe,* Cambridge (Cambridge University Press) 1993.

VAN DEN NOORD, P. and HERD, R.: "Pension Liabilities in the Seven Major Economies", OECD Economics Department Working Paper, Paris (OECD) 1993.

WORLD BANK: *Averting the Old Age Crisis,* New York (Oxford University Press) 1994.

Chapter 11

The Unpaid Work of Mothers and Housewives in the Different Types of Welfare States

ANNEKE VAN DOORNE-HUISKES

I. Introduction

Are European welfare states converging in terms of the way unpaid household work is divided between men and women, or do European countries in fact differ considerably on this point? That is the central issue that will be addressed in this chapter. European data on the distribution of household work between men and women lead to different conclusions (Section II). One observation is that, although increasing numbers of women have jobs outside the home, household work is still largely women's work in almost all Western nations. This "stalled revolution" (Hochschild, 1989) is an intriguing social fact for which there are different sociological and economic explanations (Section III). The gender perspective complements the classic explanations. Definition processes, some more subtle than others, appear to contribute to the traditional division of domestic tasks between men and women in many countries in Europe (Section IV).

There are differences as well as similarities among Western countries in the way men and women spend their time. The division of household tasks between men and women is more unequal in some countries than in others. The present chapter will explore to what extent such differences in inequality are related to differences in the type of welfare state. The discussion will make use of Esping-Andersen's typology of welfare states and feminist criticisms of this typology (Section V). Although there are differences – minor ones — among countries in how men and women divide up unpaid work, the most important conclusion of this chapter is that in all of the welfare states, it is primarily women who are responsible for caring for the home. Until now, institutional welfare-state arrangements have done little to change that situation. Such arrangements seem to have had a greater impact on paid work and on the extent to which women have become integrated into society. The Scandinavian welfare-state model appears to offer the best conditions for equality between the sexes (Section VI). It is highly unlikely, however, that this model will be adopted by the other European welfare states. The various countries differ too much in terms of their socio-cultural and historical contexts. Furthermore, we may question whether the Scandinavian model can survive given recent global-economic developments. Less government intervention will, in all likelihood, lead to even greater social inequality between women and men (Section VII).

II. Time Spent on Household Work in Different Countries

Very little international-comparative data is available on shifts in the amount of time spent on household work. An Irish study entitled Changing Use of Time (1991) indicates how much time women in Canada, Denmark, the Netherlands, Norway, the United Kingdom and the United States spent on unpaid household work at specific times. The study splits unpaid work into routine domestic chores, child care, odd jobs and shopping, and travel. Between 1970 and 1985, in each of the countries investigated, the average amount of time women spent on routine domestic chores appears to have declined by about an hour and a half. This change has been adjusted for so-called "compositional effects". In other words, the decrease in the time spent on domestic work cannot be explained by the fact that women in 1985 were more likely to engage in paid work than in 1970. Neither can the decrease in domestic work time be ascribed to a reduction in family commitments. That means that the amount of domestic work has been declining for women, even when we adjust for structural changes in women's employment and family status. At the same time, men's domestic work seems to have increased in this period.

A French study on how women spend their time (1991) also shows that men contributed more to household work in 1986 than in 1975 and that women contributed less. The contribution that women in dual-career households made to "genuine" household work, however, was still almost three times as great as the contribution made by men. Wyatt (1992) observed the same phenomenon in the United Kingdom. The more hours that women work outside the home, the more unpaid work men do in the home. But men tend to spend their time working on tasks that do not have to be performed every day. Women continue to do the typical routine household work, such as cooking, laundry and cleaning. Van der Lippe (1992) investigated the distribution of paid and unpaid work between men and women in households in the Netherlands. Her analyses also demonstrate that there is a slight redistribution of household tasks between partners when women work (longer hours) outside the home. Her conclusion is an interesting one: partners redistribute the household tasks not so much because men begin to do more inside the home when women increase their working hours outside the home, but because women reduce the amount of time they spend on household tasks when they increase their working hours outside the home. That is why men can contribute more to household work without there being a substantial rise in the overall number of hours spent on these tasks.

In Table 1, a general picture is given of the way time is used by women and men in several countries of the European Union. The table, based on information provided by the Multinational Time Budget Archive (Gershuny, Jones and Baert, 1991), was taken from the study Scarcity of Time of Women in European Union Countries, carried out by Van der Lippe at the behest of the European Union (1995).

Paid work includes employment, travel and education. Family and household tasks include chores, child care and do-it-yourself activities. Personal care includes meals at home, sleep and other personal activities, and personal medical care. Leisure time includes both indoor activities (television, radio, reading books, papers and magazines, other hobbies, talking, and relaxing), and outside activities (going out to restaurants, pubs, cinemas, and the theatre, sports and games, visits to relatives and friends, and civic duties).

Table 1 shows the trends that were already mentioned in the first section. Despite the increase in the paid work done by women, domestic work is still also done primarily by women. In the last decades, however, inequality between the amount of domestic work done by men and by women has decreased slightly. These tendencies are most clear in the countries that have relatively recent figures: Denmark, the Netherlands and the United Kingdom. This could mean that similar developments have taken place in other countries as well.

Table 1 Time use, in hours per week, by men and women aged 20 to 59 in several European countries

		paid work		domestic work		personal care		leisure time	
		female	*male*	*female*	*male*	*female*	*male*	*female*	*male*
Belgium	1965	15	52	44	9	77	73	32	34
Denmark	1964	17	47	32	3	71	67	48	51
	1987	31	44	22	11	70	66	45	47
France	1965	20	51	47	13	79	78	23	26
	1974	22	44	40	13	78	77	28	34
Italy	1980	18	46	42	8	74	72	35	42
Netherlands	1975	9	39	37	12	75	71	46	46
	1980	12	38	34	12	76	71	46	47
	1985	14	37	35	16	74	70	45	45
UK	1961	21	48	35	9	78	75	34	39
	1975	18	45	33	10	77	75	39	36
	1985	20	38	33	16	75	73	40	38
West Germany	1965	20	51	43	11	78	75	28	32

Source: Multinational Time Budget Archive; Van der Lippe (1995)

Differences among countries in the division of unpaid work between men and women are not very clear. In fact, similarities among the European countries in this area are more striking than dissimilarities. What can be said, however, is that in Denmark neither women nor men devote as many hours per week to domestic chores as people in other countries, but Danish men's contribution to household work is relatively high. The low number of hours Danish couples spend on household chores indicates a relatively high availability of public help and facilities. I will return to this matter later. First I will focus on the continuing dominant role of women in unpaid work in all countries, despite the increase in the number of women doing paid work. Hochschild has called this phenomenon a "stalled revolution." How can this stalled revolution be explained? In Section III, I will give a brief overview of economic and sociological arguments. Insights from both disciplines are needed to clarify how the mechanisms that determine the division of unpaid work between men and women work.

III. A Stalled Revolution: Sociological and Economic Explanations

One of the earliest sociological explanations for the gender division of paid and unpaid work within the family is the theory of role differentiation. Parson's name is inextricably connected with this theory (Parsons and Bales, 1955; Parsons, 1959). Role differentiation in families can be considered as a specific case of the more general pattern of structural uniformity in small groups. In this pattern, two roles emerge: that of the adaptive-instrumental leader and that of the integrative-expressive leader (e.g. Hiller, 1989). In family terms, the instrumental leader has to earn money outside the home, while the expressive leader stays home to take care of the members of the household. In the middle of this century, little imagination was needed to answer the question of which person was most suitable for each role. This division of labour was considered efficient, functional and more or less inevitable in the family. Blood and Wolfe (1960) also stressed the efficiency of this division of labour between women and men. Much of the progress of the modern economy, they argued, was due to the increasing specialisation of its division of labour (e.g. Hiller, 1989). With this argument, they came in line with Becker's proposition for maximising the economic well-being of the family (1965). I will elaborate more on Becker's proposition later.

Because of the dominance of these so-called functionalistic thoughts, sociological research on time allocation has emphasised norms, values, role expectations and role attributions as behaviour-regulating mechanisms. In this approach, processes of socialisation guarantee that the functional prerequisites of societies transform themselves into the personal needs of individuals. And if these socialisation processes do not always result in the full transformation of societal needs, there are always – according to socialisation theories – sanctions and other mechanisms of social control to redress deviant behaviour.

Another important approach to the division of paid and unpaid work between the sexes in sociological research is the so-called relative-resources theory (Hiller, 1989). Blood and Wolfe (1960) stipulated that the partner with greater resources – in terms of education, occupation and income – would have more power in the relationship. Blood and Wolfe worked under the premises that people would try to avoid unpleasant work and that household work was primarily seen as unpleasant. They contended that the partner with greater power would be more able than the partner with less power to minimise his or her contribution to household chores and childcare duties. Empirical evidence on this relative-resources theory is not convincing. Also the general assumption that household work is considered unpleasant, could be challenged.

Economic theories on the division of paid and unpaid work between men and women within households, are based predominantly on the so-called new home-economics approach. In this approach, market goods and the time household members spend both at home and in the market are seen as combined to produce household commodities. An example of this type of commodity is the "home", that is, a pleasant place or atmosphere in which family members like to live. A household can be considered as a "small factory", trying to maximise output, given constraints of time and money (e.g. Van der Lippe and Siegers, 1994). The goal of the family is to maximise utility. It will, therefore, create the division of labour that gives the highest utility, or the most pleasant set of household commodities for the family.

Becker has argued that households would allocate the time of their members according to each member's potential contribution, that is, according to the financial earning power of the partners. If the male partner is relatively more productive as a paid labourer and thus can earn more and is relatively less productive as a household labourer than the female partner, the male partner will specialise in paid labour and the female partner in unpaid labour at home. It could, of course, be the other way around, although this is empirically less probable. The household productive capacity is, therefore, important as well as the greater or lesser earning capacity of the respective partners in the market. If both partners have the same productive capacity in paid work but both agree that the woman will be more productive in domestic tasks, then a specification of tasks along traditional lines will still occur.

Evidence from research shows that these types of decisions have accumulating effects (De Jong & De Olde, 1994). If, at a certain time, the partners divide their tasks along a true or untrue estimation of their household capabilities, this estimation will become reality later on. Specialisation processes transform an expectation or assumption at point T1 into reality at point T2. If the female partner reduces her participation in the labour force in order to meet the needs of the family, she will lose some of her professional skills and experiences. These losses, in turn, later legitimise the division of tasks which has been developed in households between male and female partners.

In their research on division of household tasks between partners in the Netherlands, De Jong and De Olde (1994) made clear that partners in general do not take these long-term accumulating consequences into account. The aim of their study of 256 male/female couples was to discover how task-division patterns developed after an important event in the household, namely the birth of a child. The emergence of a traditional pattern appeared to be the most probable case: the male assumed the role of the only or main breadwinner and the female took on the responsibilities of the main care provider. Later on in their marriages, many of these "traditional" women indicated regret about the separate spheres of responsibilities that had emerged between them and their partners in the intervening years.

After years of specialisation, however, the division of tasks could hardly be changed. Strategically, the message of this research is clear. If women and/or men want to share tasks and responsibilities of the work at home, they have to prevent traditional patterns from emerging and stabilising. This requires a lot of rational thought at a time when emotions normally have the upper hand, namely the time after the birth of a child. The – understandable – short-term thinking at this moment seems to provide an explanation for the persistent patterns of unequal division of unpaid work between males and females who share their lives. Of course, this short-term thinking often has a strong foundation in economics: most women do earn less than men and more women than men find themselves in jobs with low mobility opportunities. But economic rationality is not the whole story as far as task divisions in domestic labour between the sexes are concerned. More subtle mechanisms have been revealed by studies based on the gender perspective.

IV. The Gender Perspective: The Reality of Definitions

A central perspective in feminist research on the division of paid and unpaid work between women and men, is that of gender. Gender here refers to sex as a socially constructed reality rather than as a biological definition. Gender is seen as a social and normative construction, in which traditional task divisions along the lines of the sexes are considered and defined as natural and taken for granted. Gender, feminist theory claims, is continuously being constructed in the way men and women define themselves and each other. "Doing gender" refers to interactional processes in which individuals claim a gender identity for themselves and convey it to others. This emphasis on social constructions – norms, meanings, and definitions about what is "normal" and "natural" behaviour for women and men as moral categories, and not just as descriptions of the social reality at hand – link feminist studies theoretically with sociological insights which have already been formulated by classic sociologists like Thomas and Meas, and which have been elaborated on by, for instance, Berger and Luckmann (1967).

An interesting question is why connections between symbolic-interactionist and feminist theories have, in general, got so little attention in the history of social sciences. Two reasons could be the rather voluntary approach used by symbolic-interactionist thinkers and the relatively little attention they pay to differences in power between people. The questions of whose definitions dominate and who has the burden of proof to show that traditional divisions of tasks need to be changed, are sociologically speaking, fascinating ones. They are even more provocative if the division of tasks between women and men are at stake. Men's work and women's work are not neutral categories, after all. Ferrée (1990) made clear how in many dual-earner families in the United States, the wife's income was defined and qualified as merely supplementary to that of her husband, even if the wife earned her income in a full-time job.

Women, in general, do not define themselves as co-providers, but more likely as providers of a – welcome – supplement to the income of the breadwinner. Husbands are likely to agree. This type of definition prevents men from giving up their privileges as breadwinners and women from easily transferring household duties to their husbands. Many women – as well as men – seem to think that household duties are simply part of a woman's responsibilities, even if the woman contributes substantially to the household income. This taken-for-granted assumption and symbolic construction of household work as "women's work" and as an expression of love towards her husband and family, make a sharp articulation of a change in the order in household work rather unlikely. Most women try to prevent conflicts over household tasks. The (emotional) costs of this kind of conflict are high and its effects are, generally speaking, small. Using more formal economic terminology it could be said that the minimalisation of conflicts is a highly important utility function for many women. Conflicts are costly and marital harmony is a valuable aim. In the name of this harmony, many attempts to change the traditional patterns of the division of household tasks, are nipped in the bud. This very fact provides a viable explanation for the lasting inequality between women and men in the pattern of the division of domestic labour. It goes beyond economic rationality. This reality of social definitions needs to be taken into account in order to get a more complete insight into the division of tasks between men and women.

V. Different Types of Welfare States: The Role of Unpaid Work

Up until now, not much attention has been paid to the specific social-economic and political circumstances of the different welfare states in which divisions of household tasks are realised. This more-or-less abstract approach to domestic labour so far, seems to be in line with the overwhelming similarity in the household-labour patterns in European countries. The differences are not as striking as the fact that domestic labour is apparently predominantly a woman's affair in all Western countries. Although there are significant differences in the way European countries have organised their welfare states and although these different institutional arrangements have an impact on the degree to which women are integrated in the paid-labour market, household labour and its division seem to be rather "welfare state resistant". This is an interesting phenomenon, which cannot be explained if the underlying implicit assumptions on unpaid work in the different types of welfare-state arrangements are not given more precise attention. Esping-Andersen's typology of welfare states (1990) seems to be useful for this exercise.

In Esping-Andersen's typology, a distinction is made among three types of welfare-state regimes: the liberal, the conservative/corporatist and the social-democratic welfare states (1990). Welfare states, according to Esping-Andersen, are not merely variations of a common denominator, but are clustered around certain principles, of which issues of social stratification, employment and de-commodification – described as the degree to which people are independent of pure market forces – are the most important. The emphasis Esping-Andersen places on stratification has much in common with a basic presumption of feminist work, namely that welfare states are based on and contribute to norms and values of femininity and masculinity, and thereby structure gender relations (e.g. Plantenga & Van Doorne-Huiskes 1992). In spite of its usefulness for feminist research, Esping-Andersen's typology has received lots of criticism from that sector. One of the main objections is that his notion of de-commodification focuses entirely on the relationship between the market and the state and that, as a consequence of this approach, no systematic attention has been given to the roles of women, families and unpaid work in societies. The worker Esping-Andersen had in mind was male, as Lewis argued (1993). Women can only enter his typology when they enter the paid-labour market. Based on the work of Esping-Andersen, but giving more attention to the interrelations among the market, the state and the family, the social-democratic welfare state regime can be described as one that promotes equality among its citizens and that is committed to a full-employment guarantee for men as well as for women. The costs of having a family, therefore, are largely socialised to maximise the capacities for individual independence. An elaborate system of public services, like childcare, health care and care of the elderly, ensures that everyone who is able to participate in the labour market does in fact participate. In this welfare-state regime, the state also plays an important role as employer, especially within the service sector.

When it comes to gender, believers in the social-democratic welfare-state regime regard men and women as equivalent. The tax system is individualised and the government takes a neutral position vis-à-vis the choice of a particular lifestyle and/or division of roles. The emphasis on equal opportunities does not necessarily mean, however, that the outcomes are also equal. The labour market is highly segregated along gender lines, because women to a large extent work in public services. In addition, the fact that women do most of the (remaining) unpaid labour is not challenged. What this regime does try, however, is to make the combination of paid and unpaid work less difficult for women (Lewis & Aström, 1992; Siim, 1991). Within the European Union, Denmark and Sweden come nearest to this particular welfare-state regime.

Within the conservative/corporatist welfare-state regime, the state is willing to replace the market as a welfare provider, but there is a strong emphasis on upholding status differences which makes its redistributive impact rather small. In this welfare-state regime, the family plays an important role as a source of social stability and individual happiness. In contrast to the social-democratic welfare state, this welfare-state regime is more a (financial) compensator than an employer. This welfare-state arrangement takes care of financial compensation when the outcomes of the market are deemed unacceptable or when labour-force participation is considered undesirable. This role as compensator reveals itself in an elaborate system of breadwinner facilities within the social-security and tax systems. Also, in contrast to the social-democratic welfare-state regime, the conservative/corporatist welfare-state regime does not treat men and women as equivalents. Whereas men are seen as workers, women are seen primarily as wives and mothers. This results in two different kinds of citizens: men as breadwinners and women as caretakers. Because the emphasis is on the preservation of the traditional family and not on participation in the labour force by all citizens, childcare and/or parental-leave facilities are underdeveloped. Within the European Union, Germany and Italy come nearest to this kind of welfare-state regime.

In the liberal welfare-state regime, means-tested assistance and modest social-security plans predominate. There is a great belief in the strengths of the market and in its self-regulating capacity. The state functions only as a saviour of last resort; entitlement rules are strict and often associated with a stigma. Whereas one can say that the social-democratic welfare-state regime treats men and women as equivalents, and the conservative/corporatist regime treats them as different, the liberal welfare-state regime treats men and women as equals and makes no attempt to adjust for women's (in general) heavier care responsibilities. A working mother, therefore, does not really exist in this regime and the necessity of childcare or parental-leave facilities are more-or-less denied. Of course this greatly influences the labour-market positions of women. Because liberal welfare-state regimes only have a limited system of breadwinner facilities, however, the labour-force participation of women is still rather high. This particular welfare-state regime applies in particular to the United States. Within the European Union, the United Kingdom comes nearest, especially since Thatcher.

The welfare-state arrangements as described in this typology have a significant impact on the degree to which women are integrated in the paid-labour market and subsequently on the degree of social inequality between women and men. In Section VI, these connections between welfare-state policies and the social positions of men and women will be elaborated on briefly. The influence of welfare-state institutions on the degree to which domestic labour is assigned to women, seems to be much smaller. All welfare-state regimes were originally based on what has long been considered as a "natural" division of tasks: men primarily as breadwinners and women primarily as caretakers. This division has not really been challenged until recently. No government has attempted to attach a significant value to the unpaid work women do in caring for a family, as Lewis (1993) argued.

The figures in Table 1, however, give some evidence that the social-democratic – or maybe more precisely, the Scandinavian – welfare-state model provides the most egalitarian division of household labour. Danish men, though none too busy with household work, participate relatively speaking more often in domestic chores than men from other countries. This is partly due to the relative low amount of work that Danish women do. Neither Danish men nor Danish women seem to be as involved in domestic labour as couples from the other countries represented in Table 1. Unfortunately, no more recent comparative figures are available at this time to support this possible connection between welfare-state arrangements and the division of unpaid work between men and women more strongly. Apparently faced with the same lack of "hard" figures, Lewis pointed to attitude surveys that showed that virtually all Swedish men between the ages of 21 and 60 at least felt that they should participate in unpaid work (Lewis & Aström, 1992). It could be argued, at least theoretically, that there is a relation between welfare-state institutions and the degree of (in)equality in the division of domestic work between women and men. But given the fact that most welfare-state institutions are based on traditional divisions of tasks and that they approach people primarily as paid workers, this relationship is rather weak. The impact of welfare-state institutions on (in)equality in paid labour between the sexes can, it seems, be more convincingly demonstrated.

VI. Different Types of Welfare States: Paid Work and Social Inequalities Between Women and Men

Influenced by the increasing availability of international-comparative data, growing theoretical attention has been paid in sociological and economic research to the relationship between institutional arrangements in countries and these arrangements' impact on relevant social phenomena. One of the relevant social phenomena studied from this institutional point of view, is the level of inequality between the sexes. In an international-comparative research project, Chatab, Van Doorne-Huiskes and Ultee (1987) tried to prove the relationship between institutional arrangements and the extent and quality of female employment. They started with the assumption that if a country had a higher level of economic development and had experienced a social-democratic government for a longer period of time, there would be less inequality between men and women. The economic hypothesis was taken from the theory of industrial societies (Kerr et al., 1960). An industrial society, it was stated, would not be able to function without a well-educated labour force. As the level of education rose, the income differences would most likely diminish. This would not only affect wage differences within the male working population, but also wage differences between men and women. The political hypothesis was based on the conviction that social-democratic parties would put a stronger emphasis on equality than confessional or liberal parties did. An empirical test, based on data from 22 countries, proved them to be right: countries with a higher level of economic development had smaller differences between men and women - both in activity rates and in levels of remuneration. The same relationship is found between the duration of a social-democratic government and the differences between men and women: the longer countries experienced social-democratic governments or political coalitions in which social-democratic parties were represented since World War II, the smaller were the inequalities between women and men.

A study by The European Network of Experts on the Situation of Women on the Labour Market (1994) revealed, on a less abstract level, the relationship between specific institutional arrangements in a country and the chance of pay equity between men and women. According to that study, a general minimum-wage level system seemed to help close the gender pay gap. The same applied to a relatively centralised and integrated collective-bargaining system. Within firms, transparent pay systems which minimised the scope for managerial discretion also constituted a favourable condition for more equality in the remuneration level between women and men. In addition, it appeared from this comparative European study that the more that women were involved in the process of collective-pay determination, the larger the chance of pay equity became.

The Human Development Report 1995 of the United Nations, specifically written for The Fourth World Conference on Women held in Beijing in September 1995, gave much attention to gender disparity. An important conclusion was that even at the end of the twentieth century most women's work remained unrecognised, undervalued and unpaid. This not only applied to the developing countries, but also to the industrial countries in the Western world. In developing countries, more than three-fourths of men's work is involved with economic activities, which are officially counted. The share of women in these activities is 24%. In the Western world these figures are a bit more equal: men allocate 66% of their time to paid economic activities, while women do so for 34% of their time. So world-wide, men receive the lion's share of income and recognition for their economic contributions. In terms of total workload, females in developing countries account for 53 percent of the total working time spent on all economic activities – the "official" and "unofficial" ones. Males account for 47 percent of this time. In the Western world, that proportion is 51/49.

Table 2 shows, for a number of industrial countries, the time allocations of women and men, divided between the time that has an official place in economic statistics and the time that has not.

Table 2. Time Allocation by Women and Men in 13 Industrial Countries (as a Percentage of Total Work Time)

		Total work time		*Female*		*Male*	
	Year	*official*	*non official*	*official*	*non official*	*official*	*non official*
Australia	1992	44	56	28	72	61	39
Austria	1992	49	51	31	69	71	29
Canada	1992	52	48	39	61	65	35
Denmark	1987	68	32	58	42	79	21
Finland	1987-88	51	49	39	61	64	36
France	1985-86	45	55	30	70	62	38
Germany	1991-92	44	56	30	70	61	39
Israel	1991-92	51	49	29	71	74	26
Italy	1988-89	45	55	22	78	77	23
Netherlands	1987	35	65	19	81	52	48
Norway	1990-91	50	50	38	62	64	36
United Kingdom	1985	51	49	37	63	68	32
USA	1985	50	50	37	63	63	37
Average		49	51	34	66	66	34

Source: Human Development Report 1995, same as on page 218.

In order to refocus on the impact of institutional welfare-state arrange-

Table 3. Gender-Related Development Index (GD) for 10 Countries and Its Separate Indicators Per Country

GDI rank	*Gender related development index (GDI)*	*Share of earned income (%)*		*Life expectancy (years) (years) 1992*		*Adult literacy rate (%) 1990*		*Combined primary, secondary and tertiary gross enrolment ratio (%) 1992*	
		Female	*Male*	*Female*	*Male*	*Female*	*Male*	*Female*	*Male*
1 Sweden	0.919	41.6	58.4	81.1	75.4	99.0	99.0	79.3	76.7
2 Finland	0.918	40.6	59.4	79.6	71.7	99.0	99.0	100.0	90.6
3 Norway	0.911	37.8	62.2	80.3	73.6	99.0	99.0	88.6	86.4
4 Denmark	0.904	39.8	60.2	78.2	72.5	99.0	99.0	85.6	82.3
5 US	0.901	34.6	65.4	79.3	72.5	99.0	99.0	98.1	91.9
6 Australia	0.901	36.0	64.0	80.6	74.7	99.0	99.0	80.3	77.5
7 France	0.898	35.7	64.3	80.8	73.0	99.0	99.0	87.5	83.5
8 Japan	0.896	33.5	66.5	82.5	76.4	99.0	99.0	76.3	78.4
9 Canada	0.891	29.3	70.7	80.7	74.2	99.0	99.0	100.0	100.0
10 Austria	0.882	33.6	66.4	79.2	73.0	99.0	99.0	82.0	85.9

Source: Human Development Report 1995, same as on page 218.

ments and the degree of social inequality between women and men, two indexes from the Human Development Report 1995 will be presented. One is the gender-related development index (GDI), which is based on four indicators: the share of earned income by females, the life expectancy of men and women in years, the adult literacy rate for men and women, and the combined primary, secondary and tertiary gross-enrolment ratio per country, divided by sex. Table 3 shows the GDI-index for 10 – all Western – countries.

The four Scandinavian countries turn out to be the countries with the least social inequality between the sexes. Although more precise analyses of the relationship between national-institutional characteristics and the degree of inequality are needed, this outcome certainly can be considered as a consequence of specific welfare-state institutions and political measures.

In terms of empowerment and social integration of women, the Human Development Report 1995 constructed a so-called Gender Empowerment Measure (GEM). This index is also based on four indicators: the number of seats women hold in parliament, the percentage of female administrators and managers, the percentage of female professional and technical workers, and women's share of earned income. The overall GEM and individual countries' ranks are shown in Table 4.

Table 4. Gender Empowerment Measure (GEM) for 10 Industrial Countries and Its Separate Indicators Per Country

GEM rank		*Gender empowerment measure (GEM)*	*Seats held in parliament (% women) 1994*	*Administrator and managers (% women) 1992*	*Professional and technical workers (% women) 1992*	*Earned income share (% women)*
1	Sweden	0.757	33.5	38.9	63.3	41.6
2	Norway	0.752	39.4	25.4	56.5	37.8
3	Finland	0.722	39.0	23.9	61.4	40.6
4	Denmark	0.683	33.0	14.7	62.9	39.8
5	Canada	0.,655	17.3	40.7	56.0	29.3
6	New Zealand	0.637	21.2	32.3	47.8	30.9
7	Netherlands	0.625	29.3	13.5	42.5	25.2
8	USA	0.623	10.3	40.2	50.8	34.6
9	Austria	0.610	21.1	16.4	48.0	33.6
10	Italy	0.585	13.0	37.6	46.3	27.6

Source: Human Development Report 1995 by the United Nations Development Programme. Copyright © 1995 by the United Nations Development Programme. Reprinted by permission of Oxford University Press, Inc.

It is interesting to note that the Scandinavian countries take the first four places in this index as well. Once again the conclusion can be drawn that institutional welfare-state arrangements are responsible for this order.

VII. Discussion

The Scandinavian, or in terms of Esping-Andersen the social-democratic welfare-state, model seems to offer the best conditions for social equality between women and men. This does not mean, however, that full social equality has already been realised, not even in this relatively "women-friendly" part of the world. The most important reason for this is the rather traditional pattern of division of domestic tasks, which is still a reality in Scandinavian countries, as well as in all other countries in Europe.

Unpaid work in the household seems to be influenced far less by the nature of welfare-state regimes than by the patterns of paid labour by women. This is primarily because the notions of "masculinity" and "femininity" continue to play important roles in the division of work between the sexes. In particular, unpaid work in the household is considered by most people to be specifically a woman's responsibility. This "logic" is deeply ingrained, in both the institutional and psychological sense, in all European countries. Breaking out of that traditional pattern will take time. The relative success of the Scandinavian welfare states in achieving the integration of women in society makes it likely that a similar political-social-cultural arrangement will provide the best chance for more equality in the distribution of household tasks.

An important question, however, is whether this Scandinavian welfare-state model can withstand the pressure of rising competition brought on by world-wide economic developments. An important conclusion, so far, is that women benefit from welfare-state regimes with extensive public facilities and a strong regulating capacity. At the same time, it is to be expected that, faced with the pressure of international developments and their effects on national economics, governments will be more inclined to reduce rather than increase the number of public facilities. The legitimacy of public facilities will come under fire and the relative degree of this process will be influenced by the extent to which the idea of public care is rooted in society. In the Netherlands, for example, some of the public questioned whether the recently established facilities for parental leave should be abolished in view of the high costs involved. The same question was raised about childcare facilities. The opinion that care the sole responsibility of parents is gathering strength. It is to be expected that such discussions will not surface quite as rapidly in the Scandinavian countries, where such provisions have been the governments' responsibilities for decades. But even there a movement toward austerity in the welfare-state regime is more likely than a continuation of the status quo. As governments become more inclined to turn public facilities that until now have been financed by public funds over to the marketplace, the chance of social inequality among citizens will increase. The recent Inquiry into Income and Wealth (Hills, 1995) clearly showed this trend in the United Kingdom. An increasing inequality among citizens will also take its toll on the inequality between men and women. The most likely development accompanying an increased liberalisation of welfare states, will be that the degree of inequality between women and men will become even more disproportionate. Some women will command enough social position and status to achieve an equal division of domestic tasks. For many other women, however, a more traditional arrangement seems more likely: women will get less-important and poorer-paying jobs and bear the greatest responsibilities at home, while men will remain the primary breadwinners and will have relatively few responsibilities in the home.

References

BECKER, G. S.: "A theory of the allocation of time", *The Economic Journal,* 80 (1965), pp. 493-517.

BERGER, P. L. and TH. LUCKMANN: *The social construction of reality,* New York (Doubleday & Company) 1967.

BULLETIN ON WOMEN AND EMPLOYMENT IN THE EU: *The European Network of Experts on the Situation of Women in the Labour Market* (October 1994).

CHATAB, J., J. VAN DOORNE-HUISKES and W. C. ULTEE: "Ongelijkheden tussen mannen en vrouwen; enige verklaringen van verschillen tussen geïndustrialiseerde landen getoetst" (Inequalities between men and women; a test of some explanations of differences between industrialised countries), *Sociale Wetenschappen* 30 (1987), pp. 279 -300.

ESPING-ANDERSEN, G: *The three worlds of welfare capitalism*, Cambridge (Polity Press) 1990.

EUROPEAN FOUNDATION FOR THE IMPROVEMENT OF LIVING AND WORKING CONDITIONS: *"The Changing Use of Time". Report from an international workshop*, Dublin (Loughlinstown House Skanhill, Co) 1991.

FERREE, M. MARX: "Beyond Separate Spheres: Feminism and Family Research", *Journal of Marriage and the Family* 52 (November 1990), pp. 866-884.

GERSHUNY, J., S. JONES S. & P. BAERT: *The time economy of the economy of time: an essay on the interdependence of living and working conditions*. Dublin, European foundation for the improvement of living and working conditions, (Universities of Oxford and Bath) 1991.

HILLER, D.V. and W. W. PHILLIBER: *Equal partners: Successful women in marriage*, Newbury Park, CA (Sage Publications) 1989.

HILLS, J: *Income and Wealth. Volume 2: A summary of the evidence*, York, UK (Joseph Rowntree Foundation) 1995.

HOCHSCHILD, A.: *The Second Shift*, New York (Avon Books) 1989.

Human Development Report 1995, Published for the United Nations Development Programme (UNDP) Oxford (Oxford University Press) 1995.

JONG, A. DE; and C. DE OLDE: *Hoe ouders het werk delen, SoZaWe*, The Netherlands (Vuga Uitgeverij B.V.) 1994.

KERR, C., J. T. DUNLOP and C.A. MYERS: *Industrialism and industrial man*, Cambridge, Mass. 1960.

LEWIS S. J. (Ed.): *Woman and Social Policies in Europe*, Hants, UK (Edward Elgar Publishing Ltd.) 1993.

LIPPE, T. VAN DER: "Scarcity of time of women in European Countries", EU Report, Forthcoming.

LIPPE, T. VAN DER: "De verdeling van huishoudelijk en betaald werk in Nederland", *Mens en Maatschappij* 67 (2) (1992) pp. 128-139.

LIPPE , T. VAN DER & J. J. SIEGERS: "Division of household and paid labour between partners: effects of relative wage rates and social norms", *Kyklos*, 47 (1994), pp. 109-136.

PLANTENGA, J. and J. VAN DOORNE-HUISKES: "Gender, citizenship and welfare; An European perspective", Paper presented at the first European Conference of Sociology, Vienna, August 26th to 29th, 1992.

ROY, C.: *Evolution de emplois du temps des citadins en France entre 1975 et 1985*, Paris Cédex (Institut National de la Statistique et des Etudes Economiques. Insee.) 1991.

SIIM, B.: "Welfare State, Gender Politics and Equality Polities: Women's Citizenship in the Scandinavian Welfare States"', in: E. MEEHAN and S. SEVENHIJSEN: *Equality Politics and Gender*, London (Sage) 1991.

WYATT, S.: "Tijdsregistratie bij huishoudelijk werk: winst en verlies voor vrouwen", *Mens en Maatschappij* 67 (2) (1992), pp. 106-127.

Chapter 12

Social Rights in a Gender Perspective

Arnlaug Leira

I. Introduction: A «Woman-Friendly» Welfare State?

In Scandinavia the crisis of the welfare state is much discussed and questions concerning the future of the welfare state have been given new impetus during a period of prolonged economic problems, with unemployment reaching the highest levels in the post-war years. Moreover, the negotiations concerning Sweden, Norway and Finland's membership in the European Union actualised questions about the construction and content of the social rights of citizens. Public debate voices more disagreement over welfare state expenditure and over the egalitarian concept of the welfare state embedded in the Scandinavian political tradition. A stronger demand for privatisation and a broader desire to limit public spending is also sharpening political discussions over the welfare state. At the same time, the demands of an ageing population and of the employed-mother family have turned the public provision of caring into a hot political topic, and the welfare state is criticised for doing too little. The future of the welfare state is discussed not only in terms of social security and maintaining the welfare state as a safeguard against the perils of the market, the public provision of caring is also important when welfare state legitimacy is the issue. Although the conceptualisation of «state» and «individual» has changed, the present debate thus has revived interest in one of the main themes of political theory, concerning the character of the relationship between the state and the individual.

The economic problems of the welfare state, but also issues concerning class, gender, ethnicity and race have added to the debate. Addressing in particular what Pateman (1987) refers to as Wollstonecraft's dilemma: Whether women's social rights should be granted on their similarity to, or difference from, men, feminist scholars have explored the relationship between the welfare state and women. Feminists in the 1970s and 80s also offered two distinctly different interpretations: In Anglo-American research it was often pictured in terms of patriarchy (e.g. Eisenstein 1979; Brown 1981), while Scandinavian social scientists more often have discussed the relationship as an alliance, even as a partnership (e.g. Hernes 1984; Borchorst and Siim 1987). Although not uncontested, the idea of the welfare state as woman's (best) friend seems to have gained ground in Scandinavia. In the early 1980s, a well-known welfare state analyst, Helga Hernes, characterised the Norwegian welfare state as «tutelary» in its dealings with women. By the late 1980s she was emphasising the «woman-friendly» potentialities of the Nordic democracies, envisioning a state form in which «. . . injustice on the basis of gender would be largely eliminated . . . » (Hernes 1987, p. 15).

The increasing representation of women in Scandinavian top politics suggests a power base to build a woman-friendly state, or more precisely, a base from which to advocate women's interests. In Norway and Sweden women now make up close to 40% of the Members of Parliament, and almost half of the Cabinet Ministers are women. During the greater part of the past decade the Prime Minister of Norway has been a woman. Not surprisingly, the meaning and effect of women's representation in politics is much debated (see for example Haavio-Manilla et al. 1985; Hernes 1987; Siim 1987; Skjeie 1991). What does this political development signify? The emergence of a partnership – a «woman-friendly» state? – or does the patriarchal imprint still prevail?

The relationship is, of course, more complex than is captured by the «patriarchy»/«partnership» dichotomy. Conceptualising the welfare state as basically non-repressive is not uncontroversial. Analytically the concept of the «woman-friendly state» is difficult, as it glosses over the fact that women have both similar and different aims. Women in Scandinavia disagree among themselves on how to define women's best interests, for example with respect to those issues that Hernes regarded as important, such as motherhood and childcare policies, women's access to formal employment, women's participation in politics and public life. Still, precisely for its utopian ring, I think it is important to retain a vision of the woman-friendly potentialities of the Nordic welfare state.

In this chapter I argue that if we are to explore «the woman-friendliness» of welfare states, access to social rights provides one starting point. The gendering of social rights is commonly associated with the gendered division of labour. As the employment-relatedness of welfare states is comparatively well-documented, the case may be argued that the theoretical challenges represented by the organisation of social reproduction, for example as seen in the provision of vitally necessary care, needs more attention in welfare state analyses. Examinations concerning the different mixes of state, market and family provisions in different welfare states should also expand on the systematic comparison of processes that generate a differentiation of access to welfare state burdens and benefits.

The idea of a «woman-friendly» welfare state is linked with two processes of comprehensive social change: one, which I have termed «the modernisation of motherhood» is seen in the rapid growth in mothers' labour market participation. The other, the «collectivisation of childcare», is evidenced in the increasing public provision of day care for children (Leira 1992). Discussing these processes, an American social analyst, Alan Wolfe (1989), argues that the Scandinavian welfare states are creating a new family form, «the public family», in which both parents are in paid work, while the children are cared for in public day care centres. He regards this family experiment as a highly problematic, and foresees a fragmentation of traditional family values and commitments. Analysing processes of social change covering a longer span of time Anthony Giddens (1992) suggests that the emergence of new family forms and patterns of cohabitation are evidence of a democratisation of the relationship between genders and generations. However that may be, both concepts, «the woman-friendly welfare state» and «the public family,» imply a renegotiation of the division of labour and of the boundaries between the public and the private, a restructuring of the relationship between state, family and labour market along gender lines.

In the following, I briefly outline some main characteristics of the Scandinavian welfare states in order to give an idea of the political culture from which the concept of a «woman-friendly» welfare state emerged. I then go on to discuss policies of special importance to mothers (and fathers) who combine work and family obligations, and contrasting employment-related and caring-related entitlements. In the final section I return to questions concerning the character of the relationship between the welfare state and women, and I discuss the gendering of citizenship. I shall mention but three processes that are of particular importance to women' social rights: access is differentiated by the state-family division of labour and responsibility; access is differentiated by the welfare state definition of care as predominantly a private responsibility; and consequently, since caring is for the most part ascribed to women, access is differentiated by the gendered division of labour. The core material for my presentation is based on the Norwegian experience. I use Swedish and Danish data as a contrast rather than as a direct comparison (for a more comprehensive discussion see Leira 1992; 1993).

II. Welfare States – the Scandinavian «Model»

The term «welfare state» commonly identifies those states in which, to a varying degree, the responsibility of the state to contribute to the welfare of citizens is acknowledged, and in which «welfare», according to specifications, is formulated and interpreted as individual rights. Political sociology, following the terminology first suggested by Wilensky and Lebeaux (1958) distinguishes between «institutional» and «residual» (or «marginal») welfare states or between those providing mainly universal or selective services and benefits. The form of the welfare state known as «the Scandinavian model» is usually classified as institutional, in that it provides a wide range of services and benefits that are commonly universalist in orientation, and are perceived as citizens' entitlements. In Scandinavia, welfare state policies were aimed not only at providing a safety net for the poorest, but also at creating a more egalitarian society (Esping-Andersen and Korpe 1987; Esping-Andersen 1990; Hernes 1988; Siim 1987). The importance of equality as a social value and political norm in Scandinavia is captured for example by Stephen Graubard (1986), the editor of Dædalus, who chose "The Passion for Equality" as the title for an anthology he edited on the Nordic countries. In Scandinavia the state is expected to provide a redistribution of economic resources, power and influence between social classes and regions. Since the 1970s equal status policies added to the tradition of state intervention to promote greater social equality: the egalitarian tradition has been broadened to address also sexual or gender differences.

More recently, in the much debated book The three worlds of welfare capitalism, Gösta Esping-Andersen (1990) offers a new typology of welfare states, taking into consideration also the arrangement between state, market and family. He identifies three different clusters of welfare states: the «liberal», the «conservative» and the «social democratic», outlining the ideological driving force, so to speak, underlying different forms of the welfare state. Esping-Andersen classifies for example the United Kingdom as liberal and also, increasingly, residualist, and Germany and Italy as corporate and conservative, whereas the Scandinavian states are predominantly social democratic. The importance attributed to the principles of universalism and equality is a characteristic of the social democratic welfare state, which also serves to secure its legitimacy; «All benefit; all are dependent; and all will presumably feel obliged to pay» (p. 28).

It should be added, too, that in the Nordic social democratic tradition, the state is not regarded as inherently oppressive. Interestingly, Scandinavians (especially the Swedes) often refer to the welfare state as a «folkhem», literally «a people's home». The metaphor identifies the welfare state as «people-friendly», made by the people for the people, especially the «small» people of the working classes. Thinking about the state in such terms may be unique to Scandinavia. Obviously, it may reflect a certain naiveté, perhaps also unique. I will not dwell here upon the political tradition from which the idea of «a people's home» emerged. It does, however, illuminate aspects of a political culture in which thinking about the state as «woman-friendly» does not appear as all that strange. In Scandinavia the state is expected to provide a redistribution of economic resources, power and influence between social classes and regions. Since the 1970s equal status policies add to the repertoire of state intervention to promote greater social equality: The egalitarian tradition has been broadened to address also sexual or gender differences.

1. The Construction of Social Rights

From the Bismarckian reforms of the last century, the history of the welfare state is commonly analysed as a series of compromises between capital and labour, and between welfare and control. What is less often observed is that welfare states also represent different compromises between women and men, mediated via their relationship to the welfare state, family and labour market.

Following T. H. Marshall (1965) modern political theory often conceptualises citizenship as consisting of three elements; civil rights, political rights and social rights. Welfare state entitlements, or social rights, are commonly formulated as rights that in principle are equally available for all citizens. In practice, however, citizenship is differentiated. Mainstream political analysis has been concerned with the effect of social class on citizenship. Feminist research introduces gender as an important, but often neglected dimension to the discussion of social inequality and social rights (Hernes 1987; Pateman

1987; Lister 1990), and shows how expansion of entitlements, even when formally gender-neutral, has different consequences for women and men. My main concern in this chapter is with the gendering of the social rights of citizens; I do not discuss the differentiation produced by class, race or ethnicity.

The social rights of citizenship are constructed differently in different forms of the welfare state and the ways in which women are integrated as citizens also differ. This is not always spelt out clearly. For example, the main concern in Esping-Andersen's analysis is with the wage-workers' welfare state, and his analysis of welfare «regimes» is closely linked with the analysis of labour market regimes. Like many social analysts he observes that the social democratic welfare state has created a large public sector labour market, which has served to recruit women to formal employment, offering both jobs and services. He does comment upon the persistent division of labour by gender within the labour market, but, as feminist critique emphasises, he ignores the persistent division of labour by gender in market-external activities. Although his classification of welfare states acknowledges the influence of the family, he does not really account for the significance of the family or other informal contributions to welfare provision. The analysis therefore misses the importance of unpaid work and of the gendered division of labour to both welfare state and labour market functioning, and neglects the gendering of citizens' entitlements. In a citizenship perspective it is not sufficient to examine the arrangement between state, market and family only; it is important also to consider how different arrangements interact with the gendered division of labour to produce a gendering of citizenship. (For a more comprehensive critique and discussion see e.g. Lewis (1992); Orloff (1993); Plantenga and van Doorne-Huiskes (1992).

To illustrate some of the gender presumptions included in a social democratic welfare state design, I shall give some examples from the Norwegian National Insurance Scheme, commonly considered to be one of the cornerstones of the Norwegian welfare state. The language of the National Insurance Act is gender-neutral. However, as the life course of women and men is still relatively different, their participation in the scheme also differs. In this chapter I do not give a complete assessment of the significance for different groups of women and men of the comprehensive social policy reforms in the period of the modern welfare state in Norway. Nor do I discuss the reconceptualisation of the state-family relationship implied in the introduction of caring-related benefits. In order to clarify some of the differentiation processes stemming from the construction of the Scheme, I shall present some of the main employment-related and caring-related rights. The caring-related reforms have been regarded both as efforts to modify the impact of the gendered division of labour, and also as a wish to encourage its continuation.

2. The National Insurance Scheme

All persons resident or working in Norway are compulsorily insured under the National Insurance Scheme. Those with cover are entitled to a range of temporary and permanent Among the more important cash benefits are the following: old age, survivors' and disability pensions, occupational injury benefits, benefits to single parents, benefits in case of sickness and unemployment, parental leave schemes. Some of these benefits are for everyone, some are reserved for those in employment, some, like the survivors' benefits, replace maintenance by family members, and some are aimed at those who do unpaid caring work. Contribution rates and state grants are decided by Parliament. (For details see the Ministry of Health and Social Affairs 1995).

The National Insurance Scheme established a two-tier system which combines a range of universally orientated measures with a series of earnings- or employment-related benefits. Formal employment is in some cases a precondition for access to an entitlement; in other cases it gives a more generous deal. Formal employment is a precondition for access to some transitional benefits such as sickness and unemployment payment. For example, a mother who wishes to return to employment when her children are grown, is not entitled to unemployment benefits if she cannot find a job.

The permanent pensions, such as old age or disability pensions, are in the main made up of two parts, a basic (or minimum) pension and a supplementary pension. Entitlement to the basic old age or disability pension does not depend on previous individual contributions. All residents, whether previously employed or not, whether married or unmarried have the right to a basic pension. The supplementary pension is earnings-related and also graduated according to the number of years spent in formal employment. Given this preference for formal employment it is hardly surprising that women make up the large majority of those who are entitled to a minimum pension only. However, women who have had little or no formal employment have benefited from the universality of the scheme, which has been interpreted as a redistribution from men to women. This perspective easily overlooks the contribution of unpaid labour to income-generating work, e.g. of wives' unpaid labour to husbands' wage-working capacity. More generally, the importance of the organisation of social reproduction to that of production is often neglected.

Since the mid-60s, Norway as the only Scandinavian country has included benefits for single providers in the National Insurance Scheme, thus offering single parents, of whom approximately 90% are women, an opportunity to opt out of employment while their children are very young. This transitory benefit is interpreted as support for mothers' care for children at home. Alternatively it is regarded as the state replacing the father as provider.

In recent years, the social rights of informal carers have been expanded. Since 1992, a remarkable change in the National Insurance Act offers unpaid carers the right to earn entitlements to A supplementary pension if they do the practical, unpaid caring work for children under seven, or for old, sick or handicapped people. The reform was not made retroactive. Thus, it so far is not cost-demanding. For present-day mothers of young children this entitlement may mean a better pension some 20-30 years ahead (see Koren 1995) for an overview of the effects on women's pensions). Symbolically, however, the reform is important in acknowledging the importance to society of informal care and reducing some of the differences between wage-workers and informal carers regarding access to entitlements. The introduction of caring-related benefits has also met with different interpretations; it has been conceptualised as a «reward» for traditional family forms and divisions of labour and as a compensation for the loss of income inflicted upon informal carers, who are predominantly women.

In different ways women have gained from the National Insurance Scheme. So far, however, the construction of the scheme has clearly favoured citizens as full-time, life-long wage-workers, and therefore men's «typical» career patterns over women's.

3. Parental Leave

The schemes for paid parental leave provide perhaps the most striking restructuring of the public/private responsibility for caring obligations. From the mid-1970s, Scandinavian policies introduced an important reconceptualisation of the state/market/family relationship, in the form of expanded entitlements for maternity, paternity and parental leave. These rights establish the primacy of parental obligation to children's care over the demands of the workplace, and facilitates the combination of work and family obligations.

The right to parental leave is interesting also because fathers as well as mothers are included in legislation that interlinks the concepts of «worker» and «carer».

In Norway since 1993, employed parents are entitled to a leave of absence for 42 weeks with 100% wage replacement or 52 weeks at 80% compensation, while retaining job security and social security rights. In addition, fathers are entitled to two weeks of paternity leave in connection with the birth. After parturition, six weeks of the parental leave are reserved for the mother. From 1993 four weeks of this leave are reserved for the father, and transfer to the mother is not allowed. This experiment with mildly «enforcing» fatherhood is interesting, considering that only 1-2% of the fathers have used the right they already have to share parental leave on a voluntary basis. So far, the introduction of the «father's quota» seems a success, in that close to one-third of the fathers have taken it up. Parental leave also includes the right to paid leave from work in order to care for a sick child (for details see Leira 1995). These rights obviously are of great importance to the parents of young children, since the great majority of mothers and fathers are in the work force.

Generous leaves of absence in connection with giving birth are important for the mother's recovery and may offer parents and child a better start together. However, in both Norway and Sweden there is concern that if only women take a prolonged leave of absence their opportunities in the labour market may be impeded.

III. Combining Work and Family: Mothers in Employment

The combination of motherhood and employment is a characteristic feature of the present-day welfare states in Western Europe. In the 1970s in Norway, mothers of pre-school children became one of the fastest growing groups in the labour market. By now, 70-80% of Scandinavian mothers of pre-schoolers are in employment. This is still higher than in most European Union member states, although the combination of motherhood and employment is becoming increasingly common all over Western Europe. Scandinavian women in the 1980s and 1990s command a much greater control of their labour than in earlier generations, and they have also gained greater reproductive control, facilitated by access to oral contraception and the right to abortion on demand. Norms regarding family formation and parenthood have changed, as cohabitation has become popular, and divorce rates are increasing. In 1991, 43% of the children born in Norway were born out of wedlock. Smaller families and increased educational attainment facilitated women's employment. These processes are evidence of comprehensive cultural, economic and social changes. However, they are not special to Scandinavia. Similar processes are witnessed in many countries in Western Europe.

Table 1 gives an overview of the labour market participation of mothers in Western Europe in the late 1980s.

Table 1. Labour Market Participation of Mothers With Children Aged 0-9/10 Years. Scandinavia and the EC-Member States, Per cent. Data Recorded in the Late 1980s, in Different Years.

Country	*Labour market participation, per cent*
Norway, Sweden, Denmark	70-80+
Portugal	60-69
France, Belgium	50-59
United Kingdom, Italy, Greece	40-49
Germany, the Netherlands, Luxembourg	30-39
Spain, Ireland	20-29

Source: EC-member states: Moss 1990; Table 1, p. 6. Data apply to employed women with children aged 0-9 years.

Norway, Sweden: data apply to women in the labour force with children aged 0-10 years.

In the late 1980s in Scandinavia, mothers' labour market participation almost equalled that of fathers'. Two features of the work/family relationship are particularly interesting: Firstly, women's high participation rate has not resulted in integration in the labour market on equal terms. On the contrary, vertical and horizontal segregation prove resistant to change. Second, the dual-earner family is not a 'dual-carer' family. Gender differences in the mix of paid and unpaid work are decreasing, but still striking. According to time use studies women on the average work as long a day as do men, but get paid for a smaller proportion of their work. Women's use of part-time work is generally considered as one way of dealing with the incompatible demands of labour market and family organisation. Part-time work is important for

Norwegian mothers' labour market adaptation, for fathers' overtime is (Ellingsæter 1990).

The expansion of welfare state services is usually considered to have promoted women's employment in Norway. In a sense, this is correct. New jobs spread in areas commonly identified as typically «women's work»; in education, health and social welfare. In Norway this entry of women did not represent a challenge to men's traditional jobs, which may be one reason why women's employment was not more strongly opposed (Leira 1992).

When mothers went out to work, fathers did not return to the home in equal numbers. Moreover, Norwegian mothers took up formal employment well ahead of large-scale public funding of childcare and well ahead of generous parental leave. The public provision of day care for children lagged behind, but is now commonly regarded as a national concern and is incorporated as part of the welfare state service system in the Scandinavian countries. Table 2 shows the provision of publicly funded childcare for children aged 0-6 in Denmark, Norway and Sweden.

Table 2. Children in Publicly Funded Childcare, Denmark, Norway and Sweden 1990. Per cent of All Children in Age Group.

	Denmark		*Norway*		*Sweden*	
Form of	*Age of child*		*Age of child*		*Age of child*	
childcare	*0-2*	*3-6*	*0-2*	*3-6*	*0-2*	*3-6*
Family day care	28	7	1	1	10	18
Centre care (full time)	19	51	9	31	19	46
Centre care (part-time)	0	8	2	26	-	15

Source: Yearbook of Nordic Statistics 1992, NORD 1992: pp. 316-17.

The figures are not directly comparable because of differences in entitlements to parental leave, and some differences in registration procedures.

Public investment in day care for children is more comprehensive in Sweden and Denmark than in Norway (Leira 1992). In 1993, close to 43% of the Norwegian children under school age, that is, children aged 0-6 years were accommodated in state-sponsored day care. Increasingly in Scandinavia the public provision of childcare has come to be regarded as a means of facilitating the combination of paid work and caring for children. Moreover, access to high-quality state-sponsored day care has come to be regarded as part of children's democratic rights.

IV. State Feminism -Promises of a «Woman-Friendly» State?

From the mid-1970s, legislation that embodied new images of women and motherhood was introduced in Scandinavia. Of particular importance to women was the legalisation of abortion on demand, legislation concerning gender equality and increased public support for childcare. The revival of feminism and its elaboration in Scandinavian equal status legislation – often referred to as «state feminism» – charged the government with the responsibility of promoting equality between women and men. Twenty years later, the relationship between the sexes is profoundly changed, but it is still not equal. However, as women have come to make up a «critical mass» or more in the labour market and in politics, the significance of equality and difference takes on new meaning. Yet, some of the «old» women's issues are still important in the 1990s, for example questions concerning the division between women and men of time, money, power and care that remain unresolved. Violence towards women and children by men has not been eradicated.

In the 1980s, the high proportion of women in the Norwegian national assembly has not produced broad, cross-party agreement for example on the interpretation of women's best interest when it comes to how to reconcile work and family commitments (Hernes 1987; Skjeie 1991). State support for families with young children is commonly accepted, but political parties disagree over the form of such support, whether as cash transfers, or as provision of childcare services. Should the use of the public purse support the families where mother is employed, or the one where she stays at home? In the early 1990s parties to the Centre and Right in Norway advocate an increase in direct economic subsidies to families with young children in order to increase parental choice with regards to childcare. The subsidies, it is argued, would lessen the need for two incomes, thus one of the parents could stay at home with the children. Even if couched in a gender-neutral language, there is concern among women that this type of reform will keep mothers at home, reinforcing a well-known division of labour between mothers and fathers. The Social Democrats and other parties to the Left generally argue more strongly in support of women's rights to economic independence and in favour of high-quality, state-funded childcare both as a means to that end, and as a means of enhancing equal opportunities for children.

Certainly, I do not want to minimise the importance of the welfare state in improving the general standard of living, or its contribution to women's welfare in Norway. On the contrary, the welfare state set the general frame within which women developed new approaches to womanhood and motherhood. In material terms, the welfare state in Norway has brought real gains for women. Welfare state reforms have increased women's «property in their persons», to use Carole Pateman's (1988) formulation, in two fundamental ways: women have gained control over fertility and biological reproduction, and women's economic dependence on individual men has substantially decreased. As wage-workers in public sector employment, and as pensioners, receiving a state-guaranteed income, women have come to depend more on the state for their personal income. Women have strongly opted for this shift in economic dependence.

Still, it seems to me that terms like the «woman-friendly» state, or the «public family», exaggerate the impact of the welfare state. Women are not integrated into the welfare state on equal terms with men, unless they behave like men with respect to work and family obligations, something that very few women actually do. This is because of three interrelated elements in the basic welfare state design:

- the importance accorded to formal employment over other forms of work,
- the definition of essential parts of social reproduction as a private responsibility,
- the division of labour by gender, which ascribes the greater part of time-consuming unpaid care and domestic work to women.

Welfare state benefits are structured according to a general set of premises in which formal employment is more favoured than informal caring. In interplay with the gendered division of labour, this differentiation produces a gendering of citizens' entitlements, available as of right. This, of course, is not special to the social democratic welfare states in Scandinavia. Processes excluding women from some of the social rights of citizenship may well be more characteristic of other forms of the welfare state, for example the liberal and the conservative.

In the 1980s and 1990s, a gender dimension to the political conflicts over the future of the welfare state is increasingly recognised in Norway. Surveys show that young women are more likely than young men to vote for parties to the Left and to support welfare state provisions (Aardal and Valen 1991). Considering the argument that I have developed, that men generally have struck a better deal with the welfare state, this «gender gap» may appear strange. However, women now may have more to lose if the welfare state is fragmented. The future strategies of the welfare state are of particular importance to women as public sector employees, and as clients and consumers of welfare state services and benefits. These are not only indicators of dependence, but show that women in Scandinavia hold a strategically important position in society. As a «carer state» the Norwegian welfare state depends on women's labour, paid and unpaid. Increasingly the political parties have also come to see women's paid and unpaid caring work as essential to the functioning of the welfare state and its legitimacy.

The restructuring and overhauling of the Scandinavian welfare states have caused heated political debate. In Norway, however, some benefits have also been expanded, such as the caring-related rights, particularly parental leave mentioned above, and state support for childcare services is kept up. At the same time, privatisation of services is much discussed, as is the scaling down of some benefits or introducing greater selectivity in some universal schemes. Public debate shows strong disagreement over measures proposed or taken to «shrink» benefits, and there is profound concern with the future of the welfare state. In the 1990s, the political agenda in several respects shows a return to classical issues of the Scandinavian welfare states: whether to uphold commitment to solidarity and to egalitarian principles and whether to acknowledge a collective responsibility for individual social rights based on universal citizenship.

References

AARDAL, B. O. and H. VALEN: "Velgere, partier of politisk avstand", *Sosiale of økonomiske studier* nr. 69., Oslo (Statistisk sentralbyrå) 1989.

BORCHORST, A. and B. SIIM: "Women and the advanced welfare state. A new kind of patriarchal power" in: A. S. SASSOON (Ed.), *Women and the State,* London (Hutchinson) 1987.

BROWN, C.: "Mothers, fathers, and children: From private to public patriarchy", in: L. SARGENT (Ed.), *Women and Revolution,* Boston (The South End Press) 1981.

EISENSTEIN, Z.: "Developing a theory of capitalist patriarchy and socialist feminism" in: Z. EISENSTEIN (Ed.), *Capitalist Patriarchy and the Case for Socialist Femi-*

nism, New York (Monthly Review Press) 1979.

ELLINGSÆTHER, A. L.: "Fathers Working Long Hours. Trends, Cause and Consequences", *ISR – working chapter* 90:2., Oslo (Institute for Social Research) 1990

ESPING-ANDERSEN, G. and W. KORPI: "From poor relief to institutional welfare states: The development of Scandinavian social policy" in: R. ERIKSON et al. (Eds.), *The Scandinavian Model: Welfare States and Welfare Research*, New York (M.E. Sharpe, Inc.) 1987.

ESPING-ANDERSEN, G.: *The Three Worlds of Welfare Capitalism*, Cambridge (Polity Press) 1990.

GIDDENS, A.: *The Transformation of Intimacy*, Cambridge (Polity Press) 1992.

GRAUBARN, S. (Ed.): *Norden – the Passion for Equality*, Oslo (Norwegian University Press) 1986.

HAAVIO-MANNILA, E. ET AL.: *Unfinished Democracy*, Oxford (Pergamon Press) 1985.

HERNES, H. M.: "Women and the welfare state. The transition from private to public dependence" in: H. HOLTER (Ed.), *Patriarchy in a Welfare Society*, Oslo (Universitetsforlaget) 1984.

— *Welfare State and Woman Power*, Oslo (Norwegian University Press) 1987.

— "Scandinavian Citizenship", *Acta Sociologica* 31, 3 (1988), pp. 199-215.

KOREN, C.: *Trygd og omsorgsarbeid*, Oslo (Institute for Applied Social Research) 1995.

LEIRA, A.: *Welfare States and Working Mothers. The Scandinavian Experience*, Cambridge (Cambridge University Press) 1992.

— «The 'woman-friendly' welfare state? The case of Norway and Sweden», in: J. LEWIS (Ed.), *Women and Social Policies in Europe. Work, Family and the State*, London (Edward Elgar) 1993.

— «Parents, Children and the State» in: J. MILLAR (Ed.), *Defining Family Obligations in Europe*, University of Bath (forthcoming).

LEWIS, J.: «Gender and the development of welfare regimes», *Journal of European Social Policy*, vol. 2, no. 3 (1992), pp. 159-173.

LISTER, R.: «Women, Economic Dependence and Citizenship», *Journal of Social Policy*, vol. 19, no. 4 (1990), pp. 445-467.

MARSHALL, T. H.: *Class, Citizenship and Social Development*, New York (Anchor Books) 1965.

MOSS, P.: *Childcare in the European Communities 1985-1990, Women of Europe Supplements* no. 31., Brussels (Commission of the European Communities) 1990.

THE NORWEGIAN MINISTRY OF HEALTH AND SOCIAL AFFAIRS: "The Norwegian Social Insurance Scheme. A survey 1992", *Norway Information*, Oslo (1992).

NORD 1992:1: *Yearbook of Nordic Statistics 1992*, Stockholm 1991.

ORLOFF, A. S.: «Gender and the Social Rights of Citizenship», *Am. Soc. Rev* 58,3 (1993), pp. 303-329.

PATEMAN, C.: "The patriarchal welfare state» in: A. GUTMANN (Ed.), *Democracy and the Welfare State*, Princeton (Princeton University Press) 1987.

PATEMAN, C.: *The Sexual Contract,* Cambridge (Polity Press) 1988.
PLANTENGA, J. and VAN DOORNE-HUISKES: "Gender Citizenship and Welfare", Chapter presented at the European Conference of Sociology, Vienna (1992).
SIIM, B.: "The Scandinavian welfare states. Towards sexual equality or a new kind of male domination?", *Acta Sociologica,* vol. 30, nos. 3/4 (1987), pp. 255-270.
SKJEIE, H.: «The Rhetoric of Difference. On Women's Inclusion into Political Elites», *Politics and Society* 19 (1991).
TITMUSS, R. M.: *Commitment to Welfare,* London (George Allen & Unwin) 1971.
WOLFE, A.: *Whose Keeper? Social Science and Moral Obligation,* Berkeley (University of California Press) 1989.

Chapter 13

Does the Welfare State Destroy the Family?[1]

MICHAEL OPIELKA

The relation between the state and the family has always been put into question. Both elements of this relation are prototypical for social systems and both of them have undergone deep transformations in that recent period of history that we call modernity. For Aristotle (in his theory of friendship and „oikos") and still for I. Kant (in his „Recht der häuslichen Gesellschaft") personal and material spheres were still integrated. Starting with J.G. Fichte and especially with G.W.F. Hegel, family itself becomes explicitly conceptualised as a juridical relation. In his „Philosophy of Rights" Hegel puts the role of family and marriage into the centre of his social theory. For him, family is the starting point of „civil society" („bürgerliche Gesellschaft") and in so far a „second root of the state" (cf. Weber 1986). In contrast to Kant's concept of „morality", Hegel's idea of „Sittlichkeit" tries to overlap the private and the public sphere, the individual and the collective aspects of social life. „Family" is a centre of this overlapping consensus („das Sittliche der Ehe besteht im Bewußtsein dieser Einheit als substantiellem Zweck", B 163).

Hegel's theory of the family marks the deep shift from traditional to modern thinking in the relation between family and public life, especially the state. Family, marriage, church, state – all of these institutions have been put in question with the rise of Enlightenment and capitalism. Family relations became latently unstable, they became more and more dependent on societal conditions. Referring to Hegel this instability destroys neither society nor the

1 Revised version of a paper presented at the SEEP conference, September 8-10, 1995, Forschungsinstitut für Philosophie, Hannover (Germany). The translation gained helpful support from Kurt P. Bierschock (ifb).

family, due to the „sittliche Auflösung der Familie“ (B 177) as it is marked by the self-constituency of the child, which has been educated as a free personality. The internal dynamics between formation and dissolution of the family enables society – Hegel's concept of „corporations“ („Korporationen“) should be called to mind – to encapsulate the idea of the family within its own structure.[2]

These introductory remarks on some roots of modern social theory could lead the way to our complex question on the relation between the welfare state and the family. The juridical perspective of Hegel highlights that family is a dynamic entity, which logically by its very structure contains continuity and delusion, stability and change. This dynamic perspective is a very actual one. When emphasising the changes in the history of the family, one of the leading German sociologists of the family concludes that, in the light of his findings, it would be better to talk not of „family“, but of „familial forms of living“ (Kaufmann 1995, p. 5).

Kaufmann puts a further argument concerning the relation between family and welfare state, that shall serve as a starting hypothesis in the present paper: he argues that family is a „policy resistant area“ (ibid., p. 9) – resistant against direct and intentional efforts of influencing families by interventionist state politics, i.e. solely motivated by demographic concerns. This hypothesis provokes a preliminary answer to the central question of this paper: the welfare state cannot destroy the family, but it can improve families, if its interventionist logic fits their needs. By conceptualising the relation between family development and family policy that way, it could hardly become a destructive, but under certain circumstances a constructive relation. Is this realistic?

I. Family Change: Destruction or Transformation?

In modern industrialised societies we cannot find by definition the „traditional“, preindustrial family, which is basically understood as the „household family“, a family type centred around economic functions but in so far holistic as the family fulfilled in a traditional subsistence economy a wide set of

2 I labelled this sociological „idea“ of the family as a community type within society as „structural institution“ (cf. OPIELKA 1996).

non-economic functions as well. In addition, long-term historical comparisons indicate that the family has always been constituting a changing social institution and that, empirically speaking, family never existed as a uniform pattern. In most cases, in history and in cross-cultural comparison different family forms can be found, even when, at a given point in history, a particular family type was in a dominant position. We can also conclude from long-term historical comparisons that there have ever been certain historical periods during which the portion of children being born out of wedlock was much higher than (in most countries) today. By the same means, we can detect that the portion of married individuals among all marriageable individuals was significantly lower than it is today. Thus, one cannot speak of a historical and geographical universality of the „modern family" so „familiar" to us.

Following the tradition of Talcott Parson's theory of differentiation, generations of family sociologists have been defining the „modern" family with its origin in the first part of the 20th century as being characterised by a – compared with traditional societies – reduced set of functions, especially the economic ones (cf. Parsons 1970, Parsons/Bales 1956). The so-called „Parsonian normal family" (cf. Tyrell/Herlth 1994), the „nuclear family", centred around basically two subsystems, the parents subsystem and the parent-child relationship, wherein it made sense to distinguish the mother-child and the father-child relationship. There exist many reasons for interpreting the development from the traditional to the modern family as an evolutionary universal phenomenon of modernisation. Some scholars at the end of the 20th century anticipate that this evolution has not yet come to an end: they regard the „modern family" – the Parsonian „normal family" – as becoming further dissolved into so-called „non-conventional forms of living" (cf. Schneider 1995), i.e., one-parent families, step-family and foster-family systems, unmarried partnerships, artificial reproduction and so on. It seems to be unclear, whether this development can be interpreted as just another change, even as further „modernisation" of the family, or whether it is a kind of signpost to the destruction of the family in its current form.

As one of the first arguments in favour of a negative correlation between the expansion of the welfare state and the stability of the family, the Moynihan report („The Negro Family") in the 1960s has been the subject of stormy political controversies (Moynihan 1965). But in the meantime, it is seen by some authors as a „prophetic document" (cf. Neckerman et al. 1988, p. 397). Since then the proportion of out-of-wedlock birth among black Americans has risen to 57 percent in the 1980s.[3] Family instability, originally regarded in the United States as a problem of the black community, became increasingly common among the white population. The larger proportion of female-headed families among the poor, the „feminisation of poverty", life-long welfare dependency, and teenage pregnancy are further aspects of these destructive processes (cf. Kamerman/Kahn 1988).

Charles Murray became one of the most prominent exponents in the Reagan era of the 1980s concerning the view that liberal social welfare policies of the Great Society era have reduced the incentive to work and to maintain stable two-parent families. In his book „Losing Ground" (Murray 1984), he argued that policies intended to reduce poverty have instead created more poverty, because the disadvantaged reject the traditional avenue of mobility in favour of short-term gains derived from welfare and crime. Murray claimed that work incentive programs under the Aid to Families with Dependent Children (AFDC) lured the „working poor" into welfare. Moreover, AFDC regulations did not permit payment of welfare benefits if the couple were to share a household, regardless of their civilian status. Murray's and other authors similar claims regained political support within the framework of the „conservative revolution" of the Republicans in the mid-Nineties and stopped any efforts of the Clinton administration to reform welfare policies (cf. Murswieck 1996). But empirical evidence for those claims is nevertheless at least mixed, as Neckerman et al. demonstrate: „although welfare may play a minor role in marital break-up and a more significant role in single mothers' decisions to establish independent households, by itself it cannot account for the marked shift to single-parent families among blacks or whites" (Neckerman et al. 1988, p. 406). Instead, the authors point to the problem of male unemployment especially among black Americans as a much more significant cause for the reluctance of men to take over responsibility for their children and their families.[4]

3 This is a higher percentage than in the „leading" European society, the Swedish one, with a proportion of 48 percent (cf. LEWIS 1993, p. 7; see table 2), although one has to take into account that welfare conditions in Sweden are quite different from those in the United States.

4 This interpretation is at least ambiguous. A study on Dutch single mothers in shelters for battered women showed, that the welfare state took over the role of a breadwinner in replacement for a male partner. This supplementary function of the welfare state (mainly by its non-discriminatory programme of social assistance) reduced obviously the necessity for the women to get married (cf. VAN STOLK/WOUTERS 1987).

One of the most prominent representatives of the „communitarian" movement, the sociologist Amitai Etzioni broadens this scope by generally criticising the „parenting deficit" in American society at all. Parents dramatically reduced their time investments for their children within the past thirty years. Instead, both parents go to work with increasingly more working hours within jobs with lower pay. They deposit their children (in the United States) in day care centres with insufficiently educated and low income personnel: „The community – that is, all of us – suffers the ill effects of *absentee* parenting" (Etzioni 1993, p. 69). Although citing a 1990 Gallup poll which found that one-half of those households with working mothers would want the mother to stay home if „money were not an issue", he nevertheless recognises major ramifications for a political and cultural agenda, concerning a „revaluation of the importance of children (...). First, potential parents must consider what is important to them: more income or better relationships with their children. Most people cannot 'have it all'" (ibid., p. 64). Etzioni criticises the „consumerism" and the „careerism" of modern American culture, which inherently devalues children and family and weakens all structural and traditional orientations towards community and care. Thus, he identifies the destructive tendencies affecting the family not primarily within the welfare state – on the contrary, he argues for a pro-active European style family policy (ibid., pp. 70ff.) –, but within an anti-communitarian, anti-moralistic and in so far anti-social economic culture.

One could add similar findings and interpretations of destructive tendencies for families within the European context. However, most of them lack a honest reference to their indicators: are the tendencies mentioned above indicators for destruction or indicators for change? The reference point for the first position is a certain concept of „normality", an idea how families should be like in order to maintain their functions optimally and, in most cases, an idea of optimised parenting. The reference point for the second position is „individualism", a certain kind of relativism, which interprets these facts from the perspective of autonomy, predominantly the autonomy of women. In a similar manner, Lüscher distinguishes two family models in family rhetoric: „family models which in principle assume an institutional or 'natural' determination of a correct family form and others which in principle assume an individualistic or subjective openness" (Lüscher 1995, p. 62).

An empirical point of view may help to come to realistic interpretations – and at the same time would reduce some of the dramatising. Burkart, using German data, shows that, statistically speaking, a „pluralisation of living arrangements" can be identified only within the age cohort between 26 and

29 years: „The different living arrangements (living with one's parents; living alone; living in a liberal union; being married; living with children) are roughly equally distributed among this age cohort. Among the younger age cohort (up to 25 years of age), living in the family of origin predominates, whereas among the older age cohort (starting with 30 years of age) living in a family which they founded themselves predominates" (Burkart 1995, p. 6). He summarises: „The fear or hope – which expression one employs depends on one's point of view – that large numbers of people turn away from marriage and family, has not been verified. But families change their appearance: They get smaller, family formation occurs later in individuals' biographies, and they get dissolved more often" (ibid.). In her brilliant book on the „post-modern" „brave new families" in the Silicon Valley Judith Stacey adds to this picture the important aspect, that „post-industrial transformations encouraged modern, working-class families to reorganise and diversify themselves even more than middle-class families" (Stacey 1991, p. 254).

Further on, these empirical sketches put the evolutionary question into mind, whether the transformation of the family – with its potentially destructive aspects – has been caused by the development of the modern welfare state, the development of social security systems, especially of the old age pension plans, or whether the making of the modern family has been the outcome of social changes in subsystems of society other than the state, i.e., within the economical system, the cultural system or the legitimisation system (esp. religion).[5]

An alternative argument for blaming the welfare state for family change would point to the genetic role of capitalism in the evolution of the modern family by demanding mobility and by destroying the very prerequisites of subsistence economy, dissolving local markets by integrating them into the a single world market, followed by the „commodification" of the labour force as dependent workers into the labour market. Empirical evidence for supporting an *economical argument for family change* can be found not only in the literature on past societies, e.g. in the writings of Marx on the English working class of the 19th century, but equally in the peripheries of today's megalopolises like Mexico City, Calcutta, or Cairo with their dramatic disruptions of traditional familial norms resulting in crime and anomie. The differentiation of submarkets (for production, labour, consumption etc.) and the

5 To a certain degree the differentiation of society as an all-embracing social system into four subsystems, to a certain degree, follows Parson's AGIL-scheme (economy, polity, societal community, fiduciary system) (cf. OPIELKA 1996).

residual role of the modern family within all of these markets holds another set of arguments concerning the economical framework.

A third evolutionary framework contains *cultural arguments for family change.* They point to the processes of individualisation and to the „cult of the individual“ as a cultural concept of modernity. This concept has been evolved not only by economical and political (esp. democracy and human rights) change, but also by the Western Culture, i.e., with Hollywood's modernised idea of romantic love or the world wide pop culture ranging from the Beatles to Madonna. The cultural individualism includes fundamental antipathies towards all types of community, which, in turn, claim continuity, obligation and other-centredness. These cultural changes – combined with modern reproductive technologies (esp. birth control) – deeply question the traditional role of women and erode the traditional patriarchal supremacy of men. As a consequence, the family model based on sexist forms of the division of labour has been regarded as being questionable, too. Research on the historical decline in the birth rate within the European cultural hemisphere as well as research on the development of the birth rate in Third and Fourth World countries can be summarised altogether in one formula: „The higher the educational level among women, the weaker the traditional definition of gender roles, the lower, in turn, is the number for children and the lower, as a consequence, is the importance of the family“ (Burkart 1995, p. 8). If one considered the inclusion of girls and women into the educational system as welfare state politics, one could argue that the welfare state distracts the family by means of educational measures, it nevertheless seems to be more precise to regard this correlation as a cultural source of family change.

We should note a fourth source of family change, which can be found within *legitimisation arguments for family change.* This framework of arguments highlights the process of secularisation and the loss of spiritual-religious foundations of family models. Although there exist „counterrevolutions“ within this type of change, i.e. the rise of fundamentalist efforts to foster Islamic or other traditionalist modes of legitimisation being a case in point, one can diagnose a complex legitimisation transfer from religion („holy family“) towards secular institutions on this societal level, i.e. constitutional courts, social sciences and so on. The goal of the new procedures of legitimisation is „individual autonomy“, not only with respect to cultural practices and the questioning of traditional community bonds, but with reference to a concept of individual freedom and responsibility which is unprecedented in human history. Anyway, it is very difficult to judge whether the legitimisation change of the family implies destructive or – on the contrary!

– constructive tendencies. One could argue, that the value changes help „the family" – understood as an ideal type of community between parents and their children – to survive under new social conditions, as a non-traditional community of individuals. I will pick up this line of arguments at the end of the paper.

Therefore, from a sociological point of view, it would be simple reductionism to blame the welfare state as the one and only catalyst of family destruction or at least family change. In summary, modern family development seems to be more intelligible when considered as „a *horizontal differentiation* of familial living forms as a reaction to complex societal changes" (Vaskovics 1994, p. 89).

II. Achievements of Families After Modernisation

The current demographic situation of the modern family in the Western World has been described as a result of a „second demographic transition" (cf. Lesthaeghe 1992) since the 1960s towards a „below-replacement fertility". This transition can be clearly distinguished from the demographic changes in fertility and nuptiality that formed the „first demographic transition" in the 18th and 19th century. Alongside with the influence of economic factors, the recent demographic changes are also closely interconnected with the rise of individual autonomy; the demographic change could be paralleled with the value change explained i.e. by the concept of the „silent revolution" of Ronald Inglehardt. One of the most obvious aspects of this transformation is marked by the *loss of the plausibility of marriage as an institution and by a biographical disposability of parenthood.* Marriage and family became a topic of decision of the individual or the couple, respectively. Parenthood lost its automatism and became one, although very favoured option among others. With respect to the welfare state: continuous partnership and parental care are no longer a familial contribution to society without saying.[6]

Differences in national (and religious) cultures in Europe (which are even more marked in a world-wide comparison) result in demographic forms of family development which are typologically distinguishable (cf. Roussel 1992):

6 This effects of demographic change do not necessarily mean that marriage and parenthood are less important for individuals nowadays, but could be interpreted as an enforcement of commitment towards partner and child.

a) the Southern European model (Spain, Italy, Greece, Portugal) is marked by the following characteristics: low fertility; low or high divorce rates; low number of liberal unions; very low number of out-of-wedlock births.
b) the „softened" model (Austria, Germany, Belgium, Luxembourg, Switzerland) showing these characteristics: low fertility; average or high divorce rates; low number of liberal unions; very low number of out-of-wedlock births.
c) the Scandinavian model (Sweden and Denmark) showing the following characteristics: fertility rate conditionally high; very high divorce rates; very high number of out-of-wedlock births.
d) the liberal model (France, Great Britain, Norway, the Netherlands) displaying the following features: fertility rates conditionally high; very high divorce rates; average number of liberal unions, very high number of out-of-wedlock births.

Roussel is more in support of the thesis of a demographic rupture emerging in the 1960s which is held by Lesthaeghe and others. He assumes that all Central European states will have joined the „softened" model at the beginning of the 21st century. In the future, family development in Europe will be characterised by the following changes: the number of marriages will continue to decline, relationships prior to cohabitation will be more unstable than marriages, and it will no longer be feasible to measure the frequency of separation in accordance to divorce rates alone, because separations of unmarried couples will have to be taken into account (cf. Salzmann 1994, p. 40).

One might wonder why a liberal society is so much concerned with private facts as the family. We can call this a liberal paradox. With reference to their stability, families must be *self-centred* systems, who follow their own *communitarian logic*. Family is a prototype of a societal community (cf. Parsons 1979, chapter 8), by quoting Hegel: of „sittliche" community, which at the same time is consciously self-centred and – at least unconsciously - society-centred. This resolves the liberal paradox. The public interest concentrates on the consequences, which are the products of familial activities concerning education, health maintenance for their members and the founding of solidarity orientations. The welfare state is profoundly interested in the continuous maintenance of certain functions of the family.

Within the body of literature on family politics and policies a variety of definitions of the functions of the family can be found. Due to the lack of (consent) theory on a macro-social level, their differentiation is subject to free choice. In order to give an example: a „recreational function" and a „placement function" (the latter being related to status) has, in part, been placed on equal footing with a „household function", a „generative function" and a „educational function" (i.e. Bethusy-Huc 1987, pp. 8ff.). Kaufmann argues for a division of the familial functions into five categories: „cohesion and emotional stabilisation", „procreation", „caring and educating children", „household maintenance, health and recreation" and „mutual help" (Kaufmann 1995, pp. 34ff.). In table 1, I systematically relate these partial functions to four functional categories which, in turn, are systematically related to the areas of intervention of the welfare state: the economic functions regarding household and practical mutual help (*„support"*), the field of generative and educational functions (*„education"*), the functions of mutual emotional support, recreation, cultural and moral action carried out by means of *„communication"*, and those functions aiming at the maintenance of structural patterns and at the feedback of familial action by means of supra-individual values (*„legitimisation"*).

In most European welfare states the majority of transfers seem to complement – at least quantitatively – the economic support functions of the family (on level 1). Therefore, family researchers argue that the household functions of the family have become less important in favour of its educational (level 2) and communicative-emotional (level 3) functions. Empirical evidence, however, for this line of argument is difficult because a simple loss-and-gain pattern does not properly take into account that the functions of the family themselves have changed within the framework of their dialectical relations with welfare state interventions and other societal changes mentioned above. Additionally, the functions of the family have changed because of new needs fulfilled and functions gained, especially in the field of communication, education and so on, but also on the level of support/household functions (i.e. in the field of private consumption or management of household technologies). It would be necessary to reconstruct the changes of functions on each of the four levels in order to come to precise results. This task, however, cannot be performed here, since it goes beyond the scope of this presentation.

The tendency in family sociology to view the family exclusively in the light of its functions should be rendered as problematic, because this notion straightforwardly deconstructs the family into its functions (i.e. Meyer 1993). Under certain circumstances, however, the disintegration of certain functions considerably influences their performance. Two well-known examples for the ambivalent effects this tendency has should be mentioned here. First, the differentiation of care services for the elderly, which are relocated from of the family context to professional service providers. The transfer of old family members to old age homes and other institutions and the evacuation of infirmity and death from the life world of younger people connected to it also causes – alongside with significant costs for the public – that the older generation is less and less perceived as a productive resource for the community. The second example deals with filiation, which is a familial core function. In Germany joint custody is about to be implemented by law as an automatic procedure after divorce as well as for unmarried couples upon their request. In this case, too, the empirical evidence is ambivalent: a „normal family" either dissolved by individual choice or constituted in an informal way only, nevertheless is treated as a normal family proper. Whereas joint custody for liberal unions is likely to have an impact on the stabilisation of this form of living - in addition, it might enforce the perception of this form of living as a „transitory stage" toward marriage (cf. Vaskovics/Rupp 1994) –, it is likely that the post-divorce stage will become even more complicated. At least, if no relevant mechanisms for safeguarding children's rights were integrated. The very tendency of detaching functions from the concrete family (as an institution) constituted by individuals is a prerequisite for the conception and justification of implementing an automatism in joint custody.

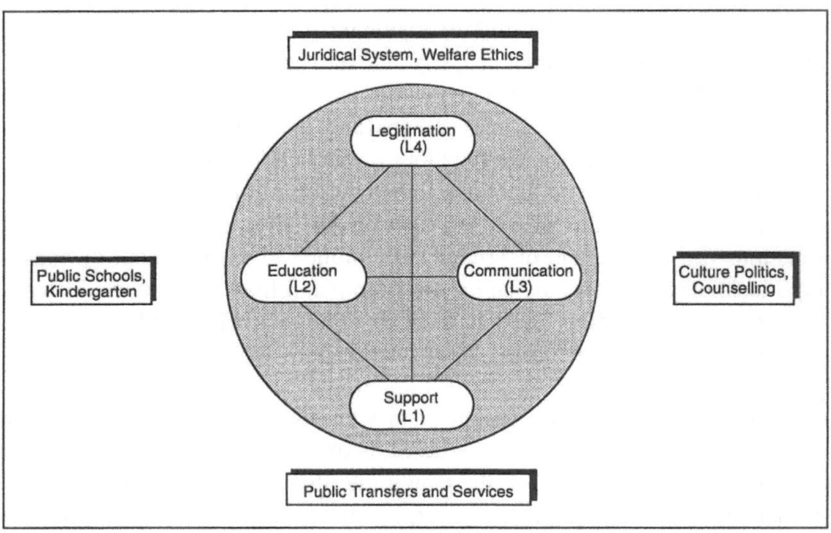

Figure 1 : Family Functions and Fields of Intervention of the Welfare State.

Regardless of how these functional areas are defined and valued: the familial achievements can no longer be taken for granted. „The arrival of children is less and less a natural event, but a consequence of the stabilisation of the contexts of partnership" (Kaufmann 1995, p. 10). The future of families will very much depend on whether the cultural and economic conditions for a widespread stabilisation of continuous partnerships can be developed. With respect to the cultural changes, this necessitates the *chance for gender partnership,* while in the economic sphere this task necessitates the *chance for parenthood without enormous disadvantages* concerning self-fulfilment of mothers and fathers – what is still the discouraging reality. But how could those goals, which would profoundly affect personal behaviour, be achieved without political mobilisation and state intervention?

III. Relative Autonomy and Societal Institutionalisation of the Family

When making an interim conclusion on whether the welfare state does or does not destroy the family from a sociological point of view, we come upon a dynamic relationship, a dialectics between „autonomy" and „institutionalisation" of the family. The hypothesis of the autonomy of the family with regard to welfare state intervention, which is at least a relative one, characterises, among other issues, the discussion on the emergence of the so-called „post-modern" family (cf. Lüscher et al. 1990). This notion asserts that, due to the dissolution of cultural prescriptions as well as due to other societal evolutions, the degree of institutionalisation of the family should considerably decline and should yield to a patchwork of family types which could be summarised at most under the label of „private living arrangements" (cf. Schneider 1994, Meyer 1993).

In the meantime, though, this kind of notions referring to the theory of individualisation, have been qualified or even discarded by their advocates. E.g., Lüscher concedes that families are „post-modern in a relative manner only" (Lüscher 1995a, p. 246), because their realities are constructed not only from aesthetic and cultural facts (which might possibly be de-constructed). Rather these realities are predominantly constituted by the shaping of economic and social functions.

Thus, those notions approaching the family from a sociological perspective of institutionalisation are more plausible. From this perspective, the phenomena of juridification, continuity, and social acknowledgement taking the forms of norms, moral standards and collective ascription of meaning can be analysed. In one of those attempts, so (regrettably) uncommon to sociological writing, to respond to the question whether family can be conceived as a societal partial system in a sociologically systematic manner, Kaufmann opens his notions with a presumption which is important for our discussion here: „The legitimisation of family politics as a specific area of politics does imply the recognition of the family as a macro-systematic structure“ (Kaufmann 1994a, p. 42). Referring to the systematic contributions of Talcott Parsons and Niklas Luhmann, he investigates those functions of families in global society which „they, to a large extent, fulfil exclusively and whose aggregated effects are considered as being indispensable“ (ibid., p. 50). He makes a strike at the functional category of *procreation* which is characterised, despite the obvious liberalisation of partner relationships, by an increase in the normative obligations of parenthood in the course of the 20th century. The „binary code“ (Luhmann), which is accepted by society as a whole, can be founded under the dichotomy „kin/nonkin“ and has, in turn, been standardised by family and marital law as well as by the law of inheritance (cf. Price 1995). From this point of view, the juridical construction of family becomes the central linkage between family and society, and between family and (welfare) state. Therefore, it is feasible to put forward the hypothesis, that the effectiveness of interventions by the welfare state correlates with their opportunity to be codified in laws.

This macro-sociological background given, institutionalisation implies losses in autonomy. At least this is the case, when families fail to represent their very own interests, as specifically embedded in the partial system „family“, against the welfare state system and its actors in an effective way. Doing so, however, requires a variety of politically powerful organisations as well as stable institutions which are oriented toward central functional areas in society. Due to different traditions of the welfare state, in Europe the actual situation is extremely diverse, displaying a large spectrum which ranges from highly institutionalised family politics in France, over rather rhetoric family politics in Germany, to the virtual lack of family politics explicitly labelled as such in Great Britain. We should, however, not be deceived by the political power of resistance of the family and its relative autonomy of the familial partial systems against welfare state interventions, as it has been postulated by Kaufmann. On the contrary, we should bring our full attention to the latter: if it were not feasible for the welfare state to destroy the family, it could at least substantially obstruct it. In due course, we will consider if and how the state could *support* the family.

IV. Welfare State and Family Policy

Is it possible to think of modern societies not being welfare states at the same time? For systematic reasons, societies which are highly differentiated, pluralistic and democratic, are welfare states, i.e., the societal subsystem of the state does not restrict itself to its autopoiesis, but this subsystem is structurally coupled with other subsystems. On one hand, the politics of the welfare state substitutes support in situations of risk which, to a varying scope and degree, were delivered by community systems in earlier times. On the other hand, the welfare state absorbs new risks for which there exists no social experience in non-state coping. With the exception of some ideologists belonging to „neoliberal" circles (who owe their raison d'être to special, mostly vested interests), no honest social scientist would, therefore, argue for an abandonment of social policy. Thus, I start this section with the hypothesis, that in a world market society the lack of a welfare state indeed destroys the family, because founding and forming family became a question of personal choice for individuals who depend to a more or less significant degree on welfare state resources. At the same time, families do not only depend on protection by the state, they – themselves – also protect the welfare state: The welfare state would become unsustainable without stable marriages and families. Research results demonstrate, that the costs for unemployment, health maintenance or care for the elderly are dramatically higher for persons at risk without close familial network.

What kind of *quality* of welfare state interventions concerning family is needed? Familial work in the field of care concentrates in modern families (as in traditional families) nearly exclusively on women. The moral obligation connected with family work disadvantages women against men in all extra-familial spheres of life. A total economisation of familial functions and products is practically impossible and would have, if state agencies would try to do something like that, dramatic negative effects on familial cohesion. Gender partnership, therefore, necessitates a much stronger *inclusion of men* into the context of the non-market community work within the family. Men should participate more actively in the tasks of caring for and educating the children, doing household work, and caring for the elderly, if a (re-)stabilisation of the family should succeed.

Traditional (social democratic) welfare policies have been concentrating on social inequalities resulting from class differences and - pragmatically - from labour market problems. This has been characterised as a „commodifying", paid-labour-centred logic of the social security state, which, despite some fundamental criticism concerning the role of women or visible minorities, has been viewed as at least an unavoidable step in the evolution of welfare societies (cf. Offe 1990; Esping-Andersen 1990). But as the integration of women into the labour market becomes more and more normal, the *number of children starts to become a new central element of social inequality* – a quite recent phenomenon, which marks the societal role of children as a „public good".[7] Kaufmann discovers a significant correlation between the birth rate and the relative public expenditures for families among the member states of the European Union, but no correlation at all between birth rate and social expenditures of the welfare states (see). He resumes: „The higher the proportion of social expenditures, which is spent towards the families, the higher the birth rate" (Kaufmann 1995, p. 194). Kaufmann goes on by saying: „The individual economic utility of children in favour of their parents tends today towards zero, because they do contribute neither to the family income nor to the cost of living in old age. Paradoxically, children therefore become a public good: sufficient offspring is in the interest of everybody, but everybody, too, has the individual choice to opt out of the necessary expenses. This is a typical situation, which necessitates state intervention" (ibid.).[8]

At least, it can be doubted whether welfare states, their current state of the affairs given, are in a position to address effectively the enormous chal-

7 Although the duality of public-private is sub-complex it may help economists to understand the sociological findings; similar proto-economic arguments within the debate on family policy occur around conceptions like „human capital" used within the 5th Report on Families for the German Government (BUNDESMINISTERIUM FÜR FAMILIE UND SENIOREN 1995).

8 NETZLER employs a broader societal definition of „risk" with similar results: „The 'structural inconsiderateness' (Note: this term was introduced by KAUFMANN into the German discussion on family politics: M.O.) toward families is not primarily constituted by assessing the family as an 'private issue' (which does not contradict its simultaneously accepted quality as a 'common good'), but is constituted by the non-perception of a risk incline of family vis-à-vis individuals without children caused by the lack of taking into account maintenance responsibilities in the case of need-oriented social transfers which, in turn, put a significantly heavier burden of losses in welfare when risks occur" (NETZLER 1995, pp. 44f.).

lenges of politics and policies, which should lead to family stabilisation and, at the same time, to individual and communal options of action. Even when limiting the focus to the EU member states indicates that there are considerable differences between them. As mentioned above, there is a great variation in family development in Europe due to differences in national cultures. Systematic comparative studies on family politics and policies in the EU member states did not exist before the 1990s. With regard to the genesis of this field of research, the contributions of Bahle should be mentioned (Bahle 1995). This work has been continued with an international research project on family changes and family policies in the Western World (cf. Rothenbacher 1995a). The study of Neubauer et al. (1993) provides a good overview. It is, however, limited to a description of political measures, of the representatives of these measures as well as to the discussion on family politics and policies. This fact is even more applicable for the valuable contributions of the „European Observatory on National Family Policies" (cf. Dumon 1992, 1994) which was co-ordinated by W. Dumon and whose present coordinator is J. Ditch. It has rightly been pointed out that comparative research is still in the beginning, provided that family politics and policies are to be regarded not only as a more or less institutionalised area of isolated political measures, but also as a problematic interrelation between the opportunities of family development and the shaping of the conditions of political frameworks (cf. Kaufmann 1994, p. 147).[9]

Taking this into account, the comparative overview (Table 1) on the correlation between some demographic key variables (fertility rates, divorce rates and rates of illegitimate births) on the one hand and the portion of expenditures for family and motherhood, all other social security expenditures and the national income on the other hand should only be regarded as an illustration. Statistical inconsistencies significantly impede cross-national comparison (cf. Rothenbacher 1995), because particular data is missing, e.g., data concerning the commonness and duration of liberal unions. The latter have often been considered as a substantial indicator for the weakling of marriage as an institution. With regard to the comparison of family policies, similar problems do exist: Especially the portion of expenditures for family and motherhood is highly influenced by different statistical demarcations. In addition, the actual effectiveness of a political measure (involving costs) obviously depends on its combination with other forms of regulation issued by social politics, the industry and private action. The high portion of pri-

9 For a positive example see Gauthier (1993).

vately owned housing in the Netherlands, e.g., has not been included in this table, whereas family-related rent rebates in Germany have increased the portion of family-related support payments. Similarly, the same holds for the lack of countable periods of raising children in Denmark and the Netherlands, which, however, does not harm the women in question because the popular pension plan in these countries does not start out from participation in the labour market.

When we focus the central question of whether the effects of the respective welfare state on the family are deconstructive or constructive, definite results are hard to reach at. At first glance, a simple correlation between the expansion of welfare state payments related to family policy and family development does not seem to be an easy one, even more so because the basic indicators for family development employed in table 1 do not allow for an unambiguous assessment of the stability of the family, as already discussed above. A high portion of illegitimate births, at the same time, could be a sign of the breaking-up of the two-parents-family as well as it could indicate an increase in the number of liberal unions which, in turn, do not have to take second place in their quality to married individuals. A kind of welfare state evaluation with more precise answers on the question about its destructive/constructive tendencies can only be obtained within the context of careful research including the respective social-ecological framework. The latter, in turn, dramatically aggravates the comparability of the results. In our context here, it should be sufficient to outline some exemplary problems with those four countries in Europe which are most like to be influential for socio-political developments in the future: France, Germany, Sweden, and Great Britain (cf. Kaufmann 1994, pp. 155).[10]

France has the longest tradition in family policy, fuelled by the motive of family as an institution (i.e., a „familialist“ notion) and by motives originated in population policy (i.e., a „natalist“ notion). These motives are represented by actors related to it: the social doctrine of Catholicism and the nationalist bourgeoisie (cf. Schultheis 1988). This results in a system of day-care institutions for small children and pupils which has the highest density in the European Community and in policies safeguarding a guaranteed minimum income, especially for single parents and low income families. Today, France – which

10 With regard to the the demographic models mentioned above, it has to be noted that the „Southern European model“ does not correspond with welfare patterns discussed here. Thus, it is not perceived as being influential for future European family policies.

Table 1. Basic Indicators for Family Development and Family Policy in EC-Countries (In 1988; Numbers In Brackets Indicate the Rank of Each Country; a = 1991, b = 1989, c = 1987 – the Respective Category is Called "Families and Children", * = Not Available)

	Total fertility rates		*Divorce rates (per 1000 existing marriages)*		*Illegitimate birth rates (births outside marriages/ 1000 total births)*		*Social Expenditures in % GDP*		*Expenditures for Family/Motherhood in % GDP*		*Expenditures for Family/ Motherhood in % of Social Expenditures*	
Belgium	1.57a	(8)	8.4	(7)	106.7	(10)	27.7	(5)	1.8	(8)	8.4	(6)
Denmark	1.56	(9)	13.1	(1)	446.8	(2)	29.3	(2)	3.5	(1)	11.6	(2)
Germany	1.42	(10)	8.7	(6)	156.9	(6)	28.3	(4)	2.1	(6)	7.7	(7)
France	1.82	(5)	8.4	(7)	263.3	(5)	28.0	(3)	2.8	(3)	9.8	(5)
Greece	1.40	(12)	6.0	(10)	20.6	(14)	16.5	(12)	0.2	(12)	1.6	(12)
Ireland	2.17	(1)	0.0	(14)	118.7	(9)	22.4	(8)	2.6	(3)	11.9	(1)
Italy	1.34	(12)	2.1b	(11)	58.3	(13)	23.1	(7)	1.1	(10)	4.6	(10)
Luxembourg	1.64	(6)	10.0 b	(4)	120.8	(8)	26.2	(6)	2.4	(4)	10.5	(4)
Netherlands	1.61	(7)	8.1	(9)	101.5	(11)	30.9	(1)	1.9	(7)	5.3	(9)
Portugal	1.42	(10)	*	(12)	137.1	(7)	17.0	(11)	1.2	(9)	6.4	(8)
Spain	1.28	(14)	*	(12)	91.2	(12)	17.2	(10)	0.3	(11)	1.7	(11)
Great Br.	1.84	(3)	12.3	(2)	251.4	(4)	22.1	(9)	2.3	(5)	10.6	(3)
Norway	1.84	(3)	9.37	(5)	360.0	(3)	25.4c	(7)	3.1c	(3)	11.6c	(3)
Sweden	2.10a	(2)	10.7	(3)	483.8	(1)	35.2c	(1)	4.2c	(1)	12.1c	(1)

Source: Lewis 1993, pp. 6-7; Kaufmann 1994, p. 149; Salzmann 1994, p. 27; Neubauer et al. 1994, p. 168; Social Security in the Nordic Countries 1990.

had the lowest birth rate in Europe between 1830 and 1950 - has the second highest birth rate in the EC. Also, the portion of large families with three or more children is higher than in other EC-countries. Due to liberalisation in the 1980s, the number of out-of-wedlock birth strongly increased raising to 28.2 % in 1989. The vast majority of these children has been acknowledged by both parents. In 1989, the Constitutional Court has ruled that liberal unions and marriages are equal in law. In addition, the labour force participation of women in the child-bearing age between 25 to 50 years is high ranging between 75 to 80 per cent. Kaufmann values France as a „model of successful family policies which succeeded in the attempt to bring the modernisation of familial living conditions into line with the economic, social and demographic needs of the country to a large extend" (Kaufmann 1994, p. 158).

Family policy in *Germany* is rooted in an institutionalistic understanding which defines (quite Un-Hegelian!) marriage and family as an epitome of privacy (cf. Gerlach 1996, Münch 1990). After the World War II, an open debate with arguments taken from population policy were made taboo because of the family policy of the Nazis motivated by race theory and eugenics. Alongside with grounds based on the family as an institution – which were investigated by Lüscher (cf. Lüscher 1995) under the term „family rhetoric" – and beginning at the end of the 1960s, motives concerning policies for women and children increasingly emerged as well as the socio-political motive of compensating social disadvantages deriving from parental responsibilities. As a result, there exists the concept of „burden payments for families" („Familienlastenausgleich") which is unique to German family rhetoric (cf. Pechstein 1994, Netzler 1995). Due to the federal organisation of the state and to the delegation of responsibilities for social services to the municipalities and federal states, there are significant regional differences in the supply of pre-school care. On a national level, following the changeover of power to a liberal-conservative government in 1981, family policies concentrates on monetary transfers, in particular such ones which should safeguard the temporary leave of employed women for raising their children in their first three years of age. It is characteristic of German family policy that it is highly isolated from other political areas (cf. Kaufmann 1994, pp. 159f.).[11] Empirically speaking, Germany has one of the lowest fertility rates

11 At the State Institute for Family Research at the University of Bamberg (ifb), we currently attempt to analyse in a systematic way the impact of political processes not typically assigned to family policy under the project title „Continuous Observance of Politics and Policies Related to the Family".

in Europe, a low rate of gainful employment of women, and a relatively low number of out-of-wedlock births. In the discussion on family policy, these facts are persistently traced back to the incoherence of a practice of family policy which can hardly be covered by ambitious platforms. At the same time, we have, here in Germany, the most intensive discussion on „crisis" and „dissolution" of the family (cf. Burkart 1995, Lüscher 1995a), which is perhaps surpassed only by the debate in the US. This German discussion has been exaggerated simultaneously by a frivolous delight at the potential degrees of freedom of „individualisation" and by a romantised mourning for the end of communal living forms, for which family was regarded as being prototypical (cf. Opielka 1996). Empirical studies (most prominently among them: the German „Survey on Families"), however, show that in Germany – in West Germany as well as in East Germany – the family is not an „endangered species", but these studies indicate that familial orientations are of a central importance for the overwhelming majority of the population, not only in their normative meaning but also for their practice of everyday life (cf. Bertram 1991, 1992).

In *Sweden*, for historical reasons, the constellation in family policy is completely different from both France and Germany. Very early in recent history, a high priority was given to the extension of women's rights and, thus, to equal treatment of both sexes, which has formally achieved as early as during the 1920s. At least during the 1930s and 1940s, Swedish family politics and policies contained a component which was markedly oriented toward population policy and partially oriented toward eugenics justified by paternalistic-economic reasons, even among the dominating Social Democratic Party. This was an attempt to keep the community of the „people's home" homogeneous (cf. Myrdal 1941, Henningsen 1986, pp. 96ff.). After World War II, Swedish family policy turned its attention simultaneously to affirmative action for the equalisation of both sexes in the labour market and to a diminution of the effects of marriage by a far-reaching equalisation of married couples and liberal unions, by separated and independent parental power for both parents as well as by an individualised taxation and individualised social security. Today, Sweden possesses the highest labour force participation rate among women in Europe – with an extraordinarily high portion of part-time work among women, though – and the highest birth rate in Europe. This unusual combination is generally said to be caused by the extended infrastructure of day-care institutions and by the generous possibilities of reducing work time existing for both parents. By international comparison, Sweden holds a top rank in parental leave by men, even if the number of men taking this leave does not significantly exceed 10 % of all leaving periods taken of women and men.

It is also astonishing that family structures in Sweden basically remained the same, despite of all the efforts to reduce the importance of marriage. Although one out of two children is born out of wedlock, outside of a formal marriage, most children grow up with both parents. Marriage, which eventually occurs quite often in long-lasting liberal unions seems to be entered into for the perspective of mutual support in old age.[12] In a way, the Swedish model of family policy – which, by the way, is only occasionally addressed under this label – seems to have transformed the agrarian-productivistic concept of two partners being actively involved in a process of production for a modern industrial society; there is, at least, no room left for a housewife marriage (still so predominant in Germany). In this regard, the Swedish model also differs from that of France (or the US) where an exclusive concentration on women on family work is quite acknowledged. Despite of reservations, especially by conservative Europeans elsewhere, a destruction of the family cannot be detected in Sweden.

In *Great Britain,* the situation differs from all examples cited above. The term „family policies" is not employed there, too. There are two reasons for the fact that portion of expenditures for families and mothers in relation to total social expenditures is above the average of the EC (cf. table 1): First, social expenditures are understood in a significantly individualised manner. Second, considerable allowances are made for the benefit of families in need. The background for this is a concept of the welfare state aiming at fighting poverty, with the consequence that low income families - even with breadwinners among them – and single parents get allowances, whereas families whose income is above the poverty line (as defined by social assistance agencies) are extremely disadvantaged (if compared with people without children). This, in turn, has the consequence of a high rate of female gainful employment with the most likely motive of securing families' livelihood. It is remarkable that there is a strong emphasis on policies related to children and that there exist diverse movements dedicated to children's' rights. Other-

12 The high degree of voluntary activities in Sweden (and, more generally, in Scandinavia), which topples the degree of such activities in other European countries might serve as an illustration for a considerable orientation toward community not restricting solidarity and mutuality to familial contexts. Vice versa this orientation, at the same time, supports the (communal) idea of the family (cf. WOLFE 1989, pp. 168f.).

wise, a reductionist concept of the state's tasks and the handing over of safeguarding subsistence to the market logic and the individuals (including the abandonment of legal protection of motherhood and a thin supply of day-care institutions) corresponds with an ideology of privacy.

The four welfare states that have been discussed above with reference to their profile in family policy in a certain way constitute ideal types for principles of construction because, in my opinion, they allow for interesting points of reference with regard to the future shaping of family policy in Europe. For the purpose of conciseness necessary in this contribution, I shall outline their major features only. In doing so, I fall back upon a proposal made by Claus Offe[13] who differentiates between four political-ideological pushes in the recent discussion on the welfare state in Europe (which also occur in North America): „Privatisation", „inclusion", „exclusion", and „guarantism" (cf. Offe 1990, pp. 185ff.). Offe argues that these four strategies are sufficiently closely related to four political main currents which are predominant at the end of the 20th century: the liberal one, the social democratic one (i.e., the „traditional socialists"), the (right-wing) „conservatives", and the „green-alternatives".[14]

In historical terms, the policy of „inclusion" which has been used for the inclusion of individuals into the systems of social security which were outside that net before, has been predominant during this „social democratic century" (Ralf Dahrendorf). The concept of „inclusion" characterises the traditional social democratic model of the welfare state. From this view of view, inclusion was understood as a „de-commodification" (cf. Esping-Andersen 1990, pp. 44ff.), i.e., as a liberation from the total dependence on

13 OFFE's proposal starts with the assumption, that the welfare state sorts the population into three main categories: (a) people who, due to stable incomes from market participation or property, do not depend on transfer payments (be it money, goods, or services), (b) the core group consisting of the clientele of the welfare state who enjoys being legally entitled to portions of societal "transfer capital" (DE SWAAN) and (c) a residual category of those people who only – if at all – have access to welfare state payments under the precondition that they must meet certain behavioural standards.

14 In a similar attempt, GÖSTA ESPING-ANDERSEN differentiates between three welfare state regimes: (a) the liberal one, (b) the conservative (and strongly „corporatist") one, and (c) the social democratic welfare state (ESPING-ANDERSEN 1990, pp. 26ff.). As he concentrates on political economy, he neglects the „green-alternative" approach directed towards the legitimising bases of modern welfare states.

the employer-worker relationship by means of strengthening the position of the wage earner. It is questionable whether this strategy has met its definite ends – as it is frequently argued nowadays – or whether it suffers from deficits in its legitimacy, because of the competition wage-earning workers experience from additional socio-political actors. From a family policy perspective, this position is a problematic one anyway, because mechanisms of social security remain conceivable only within the context of gainful work.

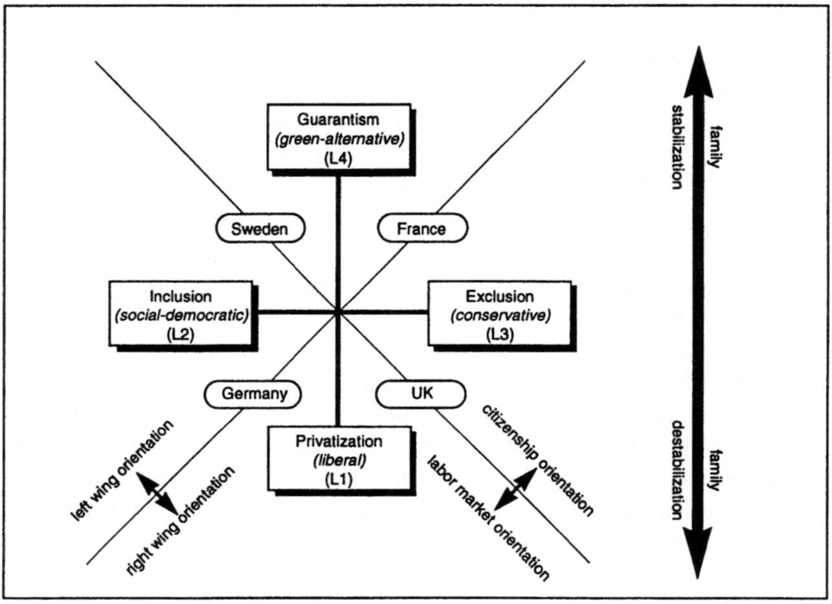

Figure 2. Four Welfare State Options in Europe

In figure 2, I have graphically arranged the four options of the policy of welfare states. In this regard it should be noted that particular political strategies have been assigned to the four European welfare states. The political strategies never are clear-cut ones, though, but the respective countries constitute mixtures of these ideal types.[15] From a family policy perspective, I

15 The structure of the figure follows a systematic logic which has been leaned against the AGIL-scheme of TALCOTT PARSONS, which cannot be discussed here comprehensively (cf. OPIELKA 1996).

place the German model of the social welfare state into the field of interpenetration between „inclusion" and „privatisation". Germany belongs to the „inclusion" type due to its social democratic tradition, which, in terms of family policy, can be proven by the important safeguarding measures against the risks surviving dependants might have to cope with in the context of the pension system. At the same time, there exists a strong tendency to comprehend family not as a societal task, but primarily as a private task, which, in turn, finds its expression - among others aspects - in the principle of „subsidiarity", in extremely limited systems of public day-care for children, in the lack of out-patient care for the elderly supporting the family, and in the taxation model of „Ehegattensplitting" (i.e. the tax load is unequally distributed among married couples with dual income in disadvantage of the wife). These disadvantages given, it would be more adequate to provide parents with direct transfer payments or to take affirmative action in the labour market policy favouring women (as mothers) (cf. Ostner 1995).

Traditionally, the welfare state model of „privatisation" has been supported by the employers' camp. Under the current conditions of both a heavy burden upon individual incomes caused by incidental labour costs and of the significant indebtedness of public budgets, this model meets significant response again and again. With regard to the effects on families, this approach is not very problematic under the precondition that incomes from participation in the labour market and property respectively are distributed relatively equally in society as well as between different types of families and households and between parents and people without children, resulting in similar prerequisites for conducting one's life: If these preconditions were not met, one could assume that familial living forms with their higher degree of vulnerability, which is due to the care for dependants (in most cases: for children) could be destabilised by a lack of welfare state interventions. I have indicated this dynamics in figure 2 by an arrow positioned on the right side.

The third type of the welfare state could be labelled „exclusion". There is a close connection to the „inclusion" approach discussed above sharing the same assumption that the „latent functions of socialisation and normalisation of the welfare state can only be fulfilled under the preconditions that 'inclusion' does not go 'too far' and that the 'second best' solution (more concrete: paying a visit to the social security office) is considered as a significantly worse solution and thus being a deterrent one" (Offe 1990, p. 193). At least in its present form of post-Thatcherism, the British welfare state is oscillating between a conservative option of restricting welfare state payments to core groups of the welfare state itself (according to the „Beveridge" tradition, parts of the lower classes belong to these core groups[16]) and an ideologically even more accentuated liberalistic renunciation of welfare state intervention at all.

Contrary to this position, the fourth position, i.e., the position of „guarantism", is attached to a time-honoured motive of the trade unions, which perceived a „de-commodification" of mechanisms safeguarding the individual's subsistence in society as being most likely guaranteed by universalistic systems of regulation, which in turn should be independent from participation in the labour market. Only when this precondition is met, „normal" wage earners can get a feeling of security as they would not be threatened by a competition on undercutting wages provoked by groups with disadvantages in the labour market (women, young people, persons unemployed for long terms). From the point of view of family policy, Offe's analysis of the approach of „guarantism" offers important hints for a strategy in order to stabilise families. "The improvements and guarantees for women with an 'incomplete' educational and professional biography as well as for mothers and widows – it is remarkable that these laws have been driven toward by a liberal-conservative government – are suitable for lifting out their material situation of the grey area of family subsidiarity and welfare payments, at least with regard to those forms stipulated by social security legislation. Of course, the principle of guarantism constitutes the core of a widely discussed outsider's opinion arguing for a decoupling of the participation in the labour force from the legal right to obtain a modest, but nevertheless sufficient payments by means of a guaranteed basic income for all citizens" (Offe 1990, p. 195).

The welfare cultures in Sweden and France approach the model of „guarantism" from different sides. As Sweden is concerned, this is true in so far as a unique combination of guarantist elements (most prominently among them: basis income in old age, child care, and care support), which are cushioned by corporatism, and inclusive elements oriented towards the labour market can be found there (e.g., with reference to transfer payments, parental leave is safeguarded within the context of gainful work; this approach is contrary to that in Germany). The French model, in turn, combines in its family policy guarantist elements independent from labour market impact with a con-

16 An element of „guarantism" originating in the „Beveridge" model does exist in the British tradition of social policy. It can be detected in the policy concerning poor people and the state-controlled health system, but it does not seem to be a prominent feature in British social policy.

servative orientation leading to significant socio-political discrimination against non-integration in the labour market if this occurred outside acknowledged traditional family roles.

With regard to all the other implications of the axes illustrated in figure 1, I only go into the assumption contained in the marking on the right corner, that a „guarantist“ family policy most likely has positive effects on family stabilisation. Whereas – as already indicated above – the opposing assumption of destructive tendencies of liberalist policy, i.e., of a renunciation of the welfare state proper, cannot be proven easily, astonishing evidences may be found for the assumption that social policy in general and family policy in particular are more likely to bring about constructive effects when they are shaped by „guarantism“. How else could the demographic „record of success“ shown for countries like Sweden and France in table 1 be interpreted?

The exemplary discussion of four welfare state models and their stance toward families allows for a single, yet incomplete, answer to our central question: the family cannot be destroyed by the welfare state (at least: not yet). The vast differences in family development seem to be interrelated with the national cultures of the welfare state – this is an interrelation on which research in family science did not cast much light up to now. This allows for the conclusion that our introductory hypothesis stating that the family is a „policy resistant area“ is hardly tenable; it might be of some use as an optimistic negative assumption: the welfare state cannot destroy the family, but it is able to influence the family development and concrete family forms to a considerable degree.[17]

V. The Constructive Welfare State – Some Outlines

What kind of welfare state intervention is most promising to support families – and not to destroy them? Living as a family – and this means basically: raising up children – should be viewed as *one sustainable way of living.*

17 It is possible to put forward a sociological assumption for this fact by referring to the predominant structural medium of the welfare state, i.e., the medium of the law. In modern democracies, the law posits every individual as an irreducible subject of law. As long as the family, in turn, is the birthplace of the individuals, for the sociological and systematic reasons mentioned above, the welfare state as a constitutional state could destroy the family at the expense of self-destruction only.

Netzler proposed the concept of „value equivalence" (Netzler 1995) to argue for family oriented transfer systems, which transform familial work to the effect of having an economic outcome not equal to the participation in the labour market, but sustainable. Child rearing should become a biographical period with a set of differentiated rights, because (only) rights can be granted by the welfare state: rights of a sustainable income guarantee at least on a level which is markedly above the poverty line; rights of participation in different public spheres by return guarantees into the labour market; rights for further education to maintain and update one's labour market competencies, and so on.

The socio-political increase in value of parenting from a parents' point of view should constitute the core concept of the continuing development of the welfare state as indicated against the background of the analytical reflections discussed above. I have, however, attempted to demonstrate that the function of parenting cannot be perceived as being isolated from other familial functions. This is especially true for the state support of marriage. Here in Germany, a discussion is going on whether the marriage should no longer be considered as a fact deserving state aid (e.g. by abolishing the „Ehegatten-spitting" in tax law).[18] In contrast to that, it should be taken into consideration that the marriage – if understood by both partners as an enduring relationship of living together – constitutes an important economic and socio-emotional factor of stabilisation in itself, especially when it remains childless or when the children left their parents' home („empty nest"). The realistic socio-political standpoint given that informal support systems are imperative for the welfare of the individual and of society as a whole, the welfare state should support the social institution of the marriage. Otherwise the welfare state would be obliged to construct it in case it wouldn't exist (which indeed is the case to an increasing degree). This is not meant, however, as an argument against the socio-political recognition of non-marital living arrangement since these liberal unions in general are living arrangements „similar to marriage", at least with regard to mutual expectations of support (cf. Diewald 1993).

Especially from a communitarian standpoint the call was pronounced that strategies in social policy and legal policy should be designed in order to soften the considerable consequences of divorces, in particular for women and

18 Some authors (among them: BORCHERT 1989) argue that transfers directed to the family should not be linked to the marriage status but should be assigned to the support obligations towards children.

children. It has been argued that the best ways to prevent these consequences simply are the prevention of divorce itself and the stabilisation of the two-parents-family (cf. Galston 1995). Mary Ann Glendon, a law professor, argues for taking the principle of „children first" into account by employing the socio-political argument alongside with other arguments, that the long-term effects of families breaking up are alarming for society (Glendon 1987). It is obvious that the honouring of the two-parents-family owed to the still prevailing marital basis of the family seems to conflict to a certain degree with the interest in the liberalisation of the relations between the sexes and, most prominently, with women's rights. In particular, the misinterpretation might emerge that liberal unions do not have to cope with such problems. This, however, is not the case, especially when children at minority age exist. Even in this case, the loss of one parent following the dissolution of the liberal union reduces the children's bonding competencies. Therefore, prohibiting divorces would not constitute a sensible and useful perspective for a continuing development of family policy. Instead of this, Amitai Etzioni proposes a bundle of measures for supporting the future spouses by educational and other means before marriage, because he argues: „to avoid the rush to divorce, we need to further slow the rush to marriage" (Etzioni 1993, p. 78).

It is astonishing, indeed, that future parents are not instructed by societal institutions, especially by the schools, preparing them for their tasks, despite the high and complex expectations from the family fulfilling its functions. In order to stabilise families, there would be opportunities for individual tests, for a conscious development of an individual concept of the prospective family. Under the conditions of the modern times, family development and development of the personality are more closely interrelated than ever before. Although welfare state policy can not provide for a common daily meal as it is recommended by Bellah et al.: „The family meal (....) is the chief family celebration, even a family sacrament. (....). We can be sure that having a common meal, and one to which all contribute, results in a warmer family and an enhancement of everyone's capacity for attention" (Bellah et. al. 1991, p. 260). In indirect ways, however, social policy contributes to the fact that common meals resulting in family encounters and communication are obstructed or prevented by inflexible work hours or by a political culture of ignoring families as such.

As a conclusion, yet another perspective will be taken into account by discussing the construction principles of the welfare state according to their relation with the family. I fall back upon Hegel's considerations, mentioned in my introductory remarks, on the differentiation between functions of the state on one hand, and the dialectical relationship between the state and the family on the other hand.

In a discussion about the ethical premises of the „post-modern social state" Koslowski criticised Hegel's idea of the state as all-embracing umbrella of modern society: „Because Hegel's dictum - that what is rational is actual, and what is actual is rational - is not correct, it can also be said that the actuality of the state is not the actuality of the moral idea, but the struggle to actualise this idea in an ever deeper way. (...) The state and the churches present and keep alive the content of moral idea" (Koslowski 1990, p. 37).[19] Koslowski's approach neither to super-elevate the state nor to demand too little of it and to emphasise the interpenetration of the different spheres of society by the state and by the different state functions (i.e. social security state, cultural state or territorial state) merits attention. Koslowski's systemic view on the modern welfare state corresponds to a certain degree with the Post-Parsonian approach employed in the present paper, especially when it comes to the anchoring of its ethical principles and, in my words, its legitimating functions. In the latter perspective, however, Koslowski's approach seems to be uncompleted: not only the (Christian) churches, but a set of different subsystems have taken over the function of legitimisation in modern societies, i.e. the scientific institutions as well as those institutions, which foster the mixture of secular and religious rituals of modern societies that Robert Bellah has called „civil religion" (cf. Opielka 1996). This multidimensional view on society holds for some reluctance toward Koslowski's ethicist advocating within a duality of individual vs. state, „that the mixture is too strongly on the side of the state bureaucracy, that this gives rise to crises in social insurance and in the relationship between the generations, and that therefore we must come to see the need for restructuring the way social insurance is weighted and for a greater degree of provision based on personal responsibility" (Koslowski 1990, p. 43). On the contrary, I have tried to argue above that in modern welfare states the sources for income, services and welfare at all are manifold and should by no means reduced to „personal responsibility" – understood as reliance on market income – and state provi-

19 I cannot discuss the philosophical presuppositions of KOSLOWSKI's Anti-Hegelianism in this context, but one may suppose that KOSLOWSKI tends to replace the "state-ism" of Hegel with a certain kind of (Catholic) „church-ism", resulting from a misunderstanding of Hegel's dialectical theory of society (for a better understanding of Hegel's social theory see TAYLOR 1979).

sion only. This differentiation is needed, because the modern welfare state penetrates and regulates nearly all spheres of welfare production, at least to a certain degree. Consequently, non-regulation or deregulation have to be scored critically whether they improve or worsen the living conditions of certain groups in society.

The influence of the welfare state on the process of family development – from a micro-perspective as well as from a demographic macro-perspective – seems to find its most clear-cut expression (historically as well as currently) within the system of old age pension plans. Although there is not very much evidence for a direct statistical correlation between the establishment of pension plans and the amount of pensions on the one hand, and, i.e., the fertility rate of a certain population on the other hand, one may wonder whether the socialising of making provisions has any effect on family planning. Some authors are confident about offering evidence for such a connection and speak of a welfare state illusion: "The social insurance system is leading to decreasing investment in future in the form of children. It is reinforcing the trend towards childless marriages or marriages with few children" (Koslowski 1990, p. 48).[20] The arguments are convincing at first glance: "The modern 'contract between the generations' sets the traditional scheme of things on its head. Parents are no longer acquiring capital as they once did to provide for themselves and their children, but rather, the children, via the state's system of compulsory savings through social insurance, are providing for their parents, for themselves and for their own children, i.e., for their grandchildren" (ibid. p. 50). Following this argument, childlessness becomes rewarded. Another "welfare state illusion" should be added: "the older, working generation have a distorted perception of reality and systematically overestimate the value of their assets in the form of their accumulated pension entitlements" (ibid.). Consequently, this line of argument concludes in a call for a "new subsidiarity", where "the family will play the primary, but not the only role" (ibid., p. 55). Following a broad discussion in Germany on the reform of the Bismarckian pension plan, Koslowski argues for a contributory basic pension and for the abolishment of the compulsory, income-related pension system for wage earners. The economic

20 For further references on the discussion on this issue in Germany see BORCHERT (1989), who criticises that the reform ideas on the social security system presented by the established social actors might initiate "social reforms bound for catatrophe", as it is suggested by the subtitle of his book.

assumption behind this is "that provision for retirement can be made very largely by acquiring private capital (ibid., p. 45).

The whole argument lacks, however, the insights of a realistic systemic approach to the inner differentiation of modern societies. First of all, the assumption that the decision for having children is, to a relevant degree, influenced by long-term considerations about economic support by one's children in the period of old age has very little empirical evidence. On the contrary, those industrialised countries, esp. in Southern Europe, with a low extension of old age pension plans seem to have a low fertility rate as well. More important, however, is the evidence that the decision for having children in modern societies has become much influenced by the support systems within the period of active parenthood (parents' leave, children allowances, and above all, a well-established system of public child care). The most striking examples for that case are France and the Nordic countries, esp. Sweden.

Secondly, it does not seem very convincing to escape from both the all-embracing world-wide division of work and the multidimensional interconnection of the modern world by returning to a simple do-ut-des-principle, which has never been valid in pure fashion within traditional societies either. Quite the reverse, the modern welfare state with its socialising effect concerning provisions for a large scale of risks appears to be entirely adequate to a differentiated society (only very few fundamentalists want to get rid of the latter). Nevertheless, our discussion on advantages and disadvantages of the different types of welfare states has clearly demonstrated that according to the respective model families seem to gain more less support by society. A liberal economism, i.e., which overemphasises the market forces of individual wages and properties, turns out to be subcomplex and therefore anti-familial.[21]

The welfare strategy called "guarantism" has proven to be successful in the field of family development; an outcome which a traditional economic thinking does not expect. If we think about the outline of the future welfare states, we should take into consideration that family is made up of individuals but it is also part of society. In order to survive productively in a modern society, the individual needs the shelter of the small community - the family – as well as the shelter of the great community – society. "Guarantism" will

21 This has been discussed quite clearly in a recent book on "the missing child in liberal theory", focusing on to the situation of families and family policy in Canada (O'NEILL 1994).

be put into effect by concrete political measures, i.e. by a basic pension system as it is working in the Nordic countries, in the Netherlands or – to a certain degree – in Switzerland (cf. Opielka 1996a).[22] The principle of guarantism would translate into action to an even greater extent, if a "guaranteed income" would be implemented. There are many reasons in favour of such an unconditional entitlement for all members of a given society, and, of course, a lot of scepticism concerning its implementation has been expressed (cf. Opielka/Vobruba 1986, Scharpf 1994). Very little research has yet been done on the effects of such a social reform on families. From the point of view of the existing "guarantist" welfare politics and their results, one might hope that those effects will be quite positive. However, the multicomplexity of familial change on the way to modernity calls for multicomplex welfare reforms as well. The very question in debate is their direction.

22 Concerning the critical discussion with KOSLOWSKI it should be mentioned, however, that his proposal of a contributory basic pension seems to accept, by effect, at least partially the societal presuppositions of a policy of "guarantism".

References

BAHLE, THOMAS: *Familienpolitik in Westeuropa*, Frankfurt/New York (Campus) 1995.

BELLAH, ROBERT N. ET AL.: *The Good Society*, New York (Alfred Knopf) 1991.

BERTRAM, BARBARA: „Die Wende, die erwerbstätigen Frauen und die Familien in den neuen Bundesländern", in: BERNHARD NAUCK/NORBERT SCHNEIDER/ANGELIKA TÖLKE (Eds.): *Familie und Lebensverlauf im gesellschaftlichen Umbruch*, Stuttgart (Enke) 1995, pp. 267-284.

BERTRAM, HANS (Ed.): *Die Familie in Westdeutschland. Stabilität und Wandel familialer Lebensformen*, Opladen (Leske + Budrich) 1991.

BERTRAM, HANS (Ed.): *Die Familie in den neuen Bundesländern. Stabilität und Wandel in der gesellschaftlichen Umbruchsituation*, Opladen (Leske + Budrich) 1992.

BETHUSY-HOC, VIOLA GRÄFIN VON: *Familienpolitik. Aktuelle Bestandsaufnahme der familienpolitischen Leistungen und Reformvorschläge*, Tübingen (Mohr) 1987.

BORCHERT, JÜRGEN: *Innenweltzerstörung. Sozialreformen in die Katastrophe*, Frankfurt (Fischer) 1989.

BUNDESMINISTERIUM FÜR FAMILIE, SENIOREN, FRAUEN UND JUGEND (Ed.): *Fünfter Familienbericht. Familien und Familienpolitik im geeinten Deutschland - Zukunft des Humanvermögens*, BT-Drucksache 12/7560, Bonn 1995.

BURKHART, GÜNTER: „Zum Strukturwandel der Familie. Mythen und Fakten", *Aus Politik und Zeitgeschichte*, B 52-53 (1995) pp. 3-15.

DEUTSCHE NATIONALKOMMISSION FÜR DAS INTERNATIONALE JAHR DER FAMILIE: *Familienreport 1994*, Bonn 1994.

DEUTSCHER BUNDESTAG (Ed.): Zwischenbericht der Enquete-Kommission „Demographischer Wandel", Bonn 1994.

DIEWALD, MARTIN: „Netzwerkorientierungen und Exklusivität der Paarbeziehung", *Zeitschrift für Soziologie*, Vol. 22, 4 (1993), pp. 279-297.

DUMON, WILFRIED ET AL.: *Europäisches Observatorium für nationale Familienpolitik. Nationale Familienpolitik in den EG-Ländern in 1991*, Brüssel (Kommission der Europäischen Gemeinschaften) 1992.

DUMON, WILFRIED ET AL.: *European Observatory on National Family Policies. National Family Policies in the Member States of the European Union in 1992 and 1993*, Bruxelles (European Commission, Directorate General V) 1994 (= V/5005/95-EN-FR).

ESPING-ANDERSEN, GÖSTA: *Three Worlds of Welfare Capitalism*, Cambridge et al. (Cambridge University Press) 1990.

ETZIONI, AMITAI: *The Spirit of Community. Rights, Responsibilities, and the Communitarian Agenda*, New York (Crown Publishers) 1993.

ETZINOI, AMITAI (Ed.): *Rights and the Common Good. The Communitarian Perspective*, New York (St. Martin's Press) 1995.

GALSTON, WILLIAM A.: „A Liberal-Democratic Case for the Two-Parent Family", in: ETZIONI (1995), pp. 139-149.

GAUTHIER, A.H.: *Population, Family and Women on the Political Agenda:* Oxford (Oxford University Press) 1993.

GERHARDT, UTA ET.AL. (Eds.): *Familie der Zukunft. Lebensbedingungen und Lebensformen,* Opladen (Leske + Budrich) 1995.

GERLACH, IRENE: *Familie und staatliches Handeln. Ideologie und politische Praxis in Deutschland,* Opladen (Leske + Budrich) 1996.

GLENDON, MARY ANN: *Abortion and Divorce in Western Law,* Cambridge, Mass. (Harvard University Press) 1987.

HENNINGSEN, BERND: *Der Wohlfahrtsstaat Schweden,* Baden-Baden (Nomos) 1986.

HOFFMANN-NOWOTNY, HANS-JOACHIM: „Ehe und Familie in der modernen Gesellschaft", *Aus Politik und Zeitgeschichte,* B 13 (1988), pp. 3-13.

HOFFMANN-NOWOTNY, HANS-JOACHIM/HÖHN, CHARLOTTE/FUX, BEAT (Eds.): *Kinderzahl und Familienpolitik im Drei-Länder-Vergleich,* Boppard (Boldt) 1992.

KAMERMAN, S./KAHN, A.F.: „Social Policy and Children in the United States and Europe" in: PALMER, J.L. et al., I.V. (Eds.): *The Vulnerable,* Washington 1988, pp. 351-380.

KAUFMANN, FRANZ-XAVER: „Familienpolitik in Europa", in: BUNDESMINISTERIUM FÜR FAMILIE UND SENIOREN (Ed.): *40 Jahre Familienpolitik in der Bundesrepublik Deutschland,* Neuwied/Darmstadt (Luchterhand) 1994, pp. 141-167.

KAUFMANN, FRANZ XAVER: „Läßt sich Familie als gesellschaftliches Teilsystem begreifen?", in: HERLTH, A. et al. (Eds.): *Abschied von der Normalfamilie?,* Berlin et al. (Springer) 1994, pp. 42-63.

KAUFMANN, FRANZ XAVER: *Zukunft der Familie im vereinten Deutschland,* München (Beck) 1995.

KOSLOWSKI, PETER: „Der soziale Staat der Postmoderne. Ethische Grundlagen der Sozialpolitik und Reform der Sozialversicherung", in: SACHBE/ENGELHARDT 1990, pp. 28-70.

KÜNZLER, JAN: *Familiale Arbeitsteilung. Die Beteiligung von Männern an der Hausarbeit,* Bielefeld (Kleine) 1994.

LESTHAEGHE, RON: „Der zweite demographische Übergang in den westlichen Ländern: Eine Deutung", *Zeitschrift für Bevölkerungswissenschaft,* Vol. 18, 3 (1992), pp. 313-354.

LEWIS, JANE (Ed.): *Women and Social Policies in Europe. Work, Family and the State,* Aldershot (Edward Elgar) 1993.

LEWIS, JANE: „Introduction: Women, work, family and social policies in Europe", in: *ibid.* pp. 1-24.

LÜSCHER, KURT ET. AL. (EDS.): *Die „postmoderne" Familie. Familiale Strategien und Familienpolitik in einer Übergangszeit,* Konstanz (Universitätsverlag Konstanz) 1990.

LÜSCHER, KURT (1995a): „Was heißt heute Familie? Thesen zur Familienrhetorik", in: GERHARDT ET AL. (1995), pp. 51-66.

LÜSCHER, KURT (1995b): „Postmoderne Herausforderungen der Familie", *Familiendynamik*, 3 (1995), pp. 233-251.

MEYER, THOMAS: „Der Monopolverlust der Familie. Vom Teilsystem Familie zum Teilsystem privater Lebensformen", *Kölner Zeitschrift für Soziologie und Sozialpsychologie*, 45 (1993), pp. 23-40.

MOYNIHAN, DANIEL P.: *The Negro Family. The Case for National Action*, Washington, D.C. (Department of Labor, Office of Policy Planning and Research) 1965.

MÜNCH, URSULA: *Familienpolitik in der Bundesrepublik Deutschland*, Freiburg (Lambertus) 1990.

MURRAY, CHARLES: *Losing Ground: American Social Policy, 1950-1980*, New York (Basic Books) 1984.

MURSWIECK, AXEL: „Sozialpolitik unter der Clinton-Administration", *Aus Politik und Zeitgeschichte*, B 8-9 (1996), pp. 11-21.

MYRDAL, ALVA: *Nation and Family. The Swedish Experiment in Democratic Family and Population Policy*, London 1941.

NECKERMAN, KATHRYN M./APONTE, ROBERT/WILSON, WILLIAM JULIUS: „Family Structure, Black Unemployment, and American Social Policy", in: MARGARET WEIR/ ANN SHOLA ORLOFF/THEDA SKOCPOL (Eds.): *The Politics of Social Policy in the United States*, Princeton (Princeton University Press) 1988, pp. 397-419.

NETZLER, ANDREAS: *Wertäquivalenz familialer Leistungen und Risiken: Pozialpolitische Situation, Perspektiven und Konsequenzen*, Bamberg (Staatsinstitut für Familienforschung an der Universität Bamberg) 1995 (= Forschungsbericht Nr. 1).

NEUBAUER, ERIKA ET AL.: *Zwölf Wege der Familienpolitik in der Europäischen Gemeinschaft*, Stuttgart et al. (Kohlhammer) 1993 (= Schriftenreihe des BMFuS, Bd. 22.1).

OFFE, CLAUS: „Akzeptanz und Legitimität strategischer Optionen in der Sozialpolitik", in: SACHBE/ENGELHARDT (1990), pp. 179-202.

— „A Non-Productivist Design for Social Policies", in: PHILIPPE VAN PARIJS (Ed.): *Arguing for Basic Income*, London/New York (Verso) 1992, pp. 61-78.

— „Wohlfahrtsstaatliche Politik in nachkommunistischen Gesellschaften", in: *ibid.* (1994): *Der Tunnel am Ende des Lichts*, Frankfurt/New York (Campus) 1994, pp. 95-134.

O'NEILL, JOHN: *The Missing Child in Liberal Theory*, Toronto et al. (University of Toronto Press) 1994.

OPIELKA, MICHAEL: „Das garantierte Mindesteinkommen - ein sozialpolitisches Paradox?", in: THOMAS SCHMID (Ed.): *Befreiung von falscher Arbeit*, Berlin (Wagenbach) 1984, pp. 99-120.

— „Der Wandel im Verhältnis der Geschlechter", in: WILL CREMER/ANSGAR KLEIN (Eds.): *Umbrüche in der Industriegesellschaft*, Opladen (Leske + Budrich) 1990, pp. 101-136.

— *Gemeinschaft in Gesellschaft*, Diss., Berlin (Humboldt-Universität) 1996 .

OSTNER, ILONA: „Slow Motion: Women, Work and the Family in Germany", in: J. LEWIS (1993), pp. 92-115.

— „Sozialstaatsmodelle und die Situation der Frauen", in: WERNER FRICKE (Ed.): *Jahrbuch Arbeit und Technik,* Bonn (Dietz) 1995, pp. 57-67.

— „Wandel der Familienformen und soziale Sicherung der Frau oder: von der Status- zur Passagensicherung", in: DIETER DÖRING/RICHARD HAUSER (Eds.): *Soziale Sicherheit in Gefahr,* Frankfurt (Suhrkamp) 1995, pp. 80-117.

OSTNER, ILONA/VOGES, WOLFGANG: „Verschwindet der Ernährer-Ehemann? Wandel der Familienformen und soziale Sicherung der Frau" in: KARL-JÜRGEN BIEBACK/HELGA MILZ (Eds.): *Neue Armut,* Frankfurt/New York (Campus) 1995, pp. 93-106.

PARSONS, TALCOTT: "The Normal American Family", in: M. BERASH/A. SCOURBY (Eds.): *Marriage and the Family,* New York (Random House) 1970, pp. 193-214.

PARSONS, TALCOTT: *The American Societal Community,* unpublished Manuscript, Harvard University Archives 1979 (= HUG (FP) 42.45.1, Box 1-2).

PARSONS, TALCOTT/BALES, ROBERT F.: *Family. Socialization and Interaction Process,* in collaboration with James Olds, Morris Zelditch and Philip E. Slater, London (Routledge & Kegan Paul) 1956.

PECHSTEIN, MATTHIAS: *Familiengerechtigkeit als Gestaltungsgebot für die staatliche Ordnung,* Baden-Baden (Nomos) 1994.

PEIL, IRIS: *Akzeptanz familienpolitischer Maßnahmen in der Bundesrepublik Deutschland - Ein Ost-West-Vergleich,* Wiesbaden (Bundesinstitut für Bevölkerungsforschung) 1996 (= BIB-Materialien Heft 85).

PRICE, CYNTHIA J.: „The Effect of Welfare Laws on the Family", *Marriage & Family Review,* Vol., 21, No. 3/4 (1995), pp. 217-237.

ROTHENBACHER, FRANZ: *Familienberichterstattung in und für Europa,* Mannheim (MZES) 1995 (= Forschungsarchiv EURODATA / Nr. 6).

ROTHENBACHER, FRANZ: „Household and Family Trends in Europe: from Convergence to Divergence", *Eurodata Newsletter,* 1 (1995), pp. 3-9 (=1995a).

ROUSSEL, LOUIS: „Le futur de la famille", in: EUROSTAT (Ed.): *Human Resources in Europe at the Dawn of the 21st Century.* Conference Proceedings, Luxembourg 1992, pp. 185-208.

ROUSSEL, LOUIS: „Läßt sich die Familie definieren?", *Familiendynamik,* 4 (1995), pp. 419-437.

SACHBE, CHRISTOPH/ENGELHARDT, H. TRISTRAM (Eds.): *Sicherheit und Freiheit. Zur Ethik des Wohlfahrtsstaates,* Frankfurt (Suhrkamp) 1990.

SALZMANN, BRUNO: „Voraussichtliche Entwicklung der demographischen Struktur in den europäischen Ländern: Konvergenz und Divergenz", in: BRUNO SALZMANN (Ed.): *Demographie und familiale Aspekte von Arbeitskraft und Wohnungsbau München,* (DJI) 1994 (= Materialien zum 5. Familienbericht, Band 1), pp. 9-64.

SCHARPF, FRITZ W.: „Negative Einkommensteuer – ein Programm gegen Ausgrenzung". *Die Mitbestimmung,* 3 (1994), pp. 27-32.

SCHEIWE, KIRSTEN: „Labour Market, Welfare State and Family Institutions: The Links to Mothers' Poverty Risks", *Journal of European Social Policy*, 4, No. 3 (1994), pp. 201ff.

SCHMID, JOSEF: *Wohlfahrtsstaaten im Vergleich*, Opladen (Leske + Budrich) 1996.

SCHNEIDER, NORBERT F.: *Familie und private Lebensführung in West- und Ostdeutschland*, Stuttgart (Enke) 1994.

SCHNEIDER, NORBERT F.: „Nichtkonventionelle Lebensformen - moderne Lebensformen?", in: HEINZ, SAHNER/STEFAN SCHWENDTNER (Eds.): 27. *Kongreß der Deutschen Gesellschaft für Soziologie*, Halle an der Saale, Opladen (Westdeutscher Verlag) 1995, pp. 109-116.

SCHULTHEIS, FRANK: *Sozialgeschichte der französischen Familienpolitik*, Frankfurt/New York (Campus) 1988.

SCHULZE BUSCHOFF, KARIN: *Familie und Erwerbsarbeit in der Bundesrepublik. Rückblick, Stand der Forschung und Design einer Lebensformentypologie*, Berlin (WZB) 1995 (= FS III 95-402).

SOCIAL SECURITY IN THE NORDIC COUNTRIES: *Scope, expenditure and financing 1987*, Copenhagen (Nordic Statistical Secretariat) 1980 (= Statistical Reports of the Nordic Countries 51).

STACEY, JUDITH: *Brave New Families. Stories of Domestic Upheaval in Late Twentieth Century America*, New York (Basic Books) 1991.

STOLK, BRAM VAN/WOUTERS, CAS: „Die Gemütsruhe des Wohlfahrtsstaats: Der Staat als Ernährer, in: *ibid.*: *Frauen im Zwiespalt. Beziehungsprobleme im Wohlfahrtsstaat*, Frankfurt (Suhrkamp) 1987, pp. 71-87.

TAYLOR, CHARLES: *Hegel and Modern Society*, Cambridge et al. (Cambridge University Press) 1979.

TYRELL, HARTMANN/HERLTH, ALOIS: „Partnerschaft versus Elternschaft", in: HERLTH, A. et al. (Eds.): *Abschied von der Normalfamilie?*, Berlin et al. (Springer) 1994, pp. 1-15.

VASKOVICS, LASZLO A.: „Rolle der Familie und der Familienpolitik in der gegenwärtigen gesellschaftlichen Realität", *Deutsche Nationalkommission 1994*, pp. 85-93.

VASKOVICS, LASZLO A./RUPP, MARINA: *Entwicklungspfade nichtehelicher Lebensgemeinschaften. Forschungsbericht nach Abschluß der dritten Datenerhebungswelle*, Bamberg (SOFOS/Universität Bamberg) 1994.

WALTER, WOLFGANG: „Familienberichterstattung und familienpolitischer Diskurs", in: GERHARDT ET AL. 1995, pp. 81-98.

WEBER, MARTIN: *Zur Theorie der Familie in der Rechtsphilosophie Hegels*, Berlin (Duncker & Humblot) 1986.

WOLFE, ALAN: *Whose Keeper? Social Science and Moral Obligation*, Berkeley et al. (University of California Press) 1989.

WOUTHNOW, ROBERT: „Between the State and Market: Voluntarism and the Difference It Makes", in: ETZIONI, pp. 209-221.

Part V

Theory and Critique of the Welfare State

Chapter 14

The Justification of Welfare Rights

PER BAUHN

I. Introduction

The welfare state has for many years been the unquestioned triumph of a long era of social engineering. It has been so widely accepted that its administrators might never have felt the need to justify it in moral terms. Things have changed, however. Today the welfare state is more and more considered as a tax-payers' burden, something that has grown too big and too expensive. The public sector has even been blamed for contributing to a decrease in industrial investment, and hence, at least indirectly, to be responsible for the present economic depression, both by means of legislation (regulation of environmental and other conditions of work) and by means of taxation (redistribution of wealth).

The defenders of the welfare state, on the other hand, have been at a loss for arguments. There is often a reference to "solidarity" as a moral base for the welfare state, but the extension of that term is left undetermined. This leaves the field open to the anti-welfarists, who demand that every fiscal infringement of the tax-payer's right to his property must be justified, and who generally assume that redistributive taxation is as wrong as forced labour. The onus of proof that the welfare state is morally justified rests, they claim, with the welfarists.

In this chapter I will try to develop an argument for welfare rights which, I believe, will save the most central aspects of what has been called the welfare state. This argument will defend an equality of opportunity rather than an equality of outcomes. Its conclusion will be in line with some influential contemporary conceptions of human goods and entitlements, such as the conception of human development advanced by the United Nations Development Programme. According to the UNDP,

> *Development must enable all individuals to enlarge their human capabilities to the fullest and to put these capabilities to the best use in all fields – economic, social, cultural and political . . . . This equity is, however, in opportunities – not necessarily in final achievements. Each individual is entitled to a just opportunity to make the best use of his or her potential capabilities.*
>
> (UNDP, p. 13)

The argument contains a refutation of the libertarian ideas of Robert Nozick (*Anarchy, State, and Utopia,* 1974), but also a refutation of the egalitarianism of John Rawls (*A Theory of Justice,* 1972). It will defend a theory of rights, originally developed by Alan Gewirth (*Reason and Morality*, 1978), which combines both libertarian and welfarist aspects, and provides a model for ranking these two aspects when they conflict.

II. Different Meanings of "Rights"

Any discussion of welfare rights presupposes a discussion of rights in general. What does the term "right" mean, and how can we establish the truth of the proposition that rights exist?

The first part of this double question seems to be the more tractable one, since even those who deny that rights exist may accept that the term "rights" has a meaning. Even if we do not believe that unicorns exist, we still know what the word "unicorn" means.

For reasons of clarity, we should distinguish, on the one hand, between legal and moral rights, and, on the other hand, between positive and normative conceptions of moral rights. In this chapter I intend to discuss moral rights, not legal rights. Moral rights are rights that persons should have, according to some moral principle. Legal rights are those rights that persons actually have according to the law of the land. Legal rights are the outcome of a political process: they reflect the views of the current legislative authority. Legal rights can be assessed from a moral point of view. It can be argued, for instance, that the legal rights in question are too few or too limited in their possible application. Laws can be considered morally wrong, no matter whether they are supported by a majority of the citizens or not.

Moral rights, on the other hand, can be viewed in either positive or normative terms. The positive conception of moral rights is the one that people actually have: the rights they believe they are entitled to. The normative conception of moral rights is the one they should have, if their moral beliefs were justified.

In the best of all possible worlds all these categories would coincide, so that the legal rights are those rights that people believe that they are morally entitled to, and the moral beliefs of the people in question are justified. In the actual world, however, we often find reason to criticise legal rights for being morally insufficient (as the American Civil Rights movement did). Likewise, we often find reason to criticise the moral views that people hold (such as the views of racists, that their own race is superior in rights to other ethnic groups).

The theoretically most important category is, consequently, that of the normative conception of morality. If we can establish what rights people should have, we are able to examine critically both the moral conceptions that people actually have, and the legal rights their states offer to maintain and protect (or refuse to maintain and protect).

A moral right is, then, a normative property, something that someone should possess, and which nobody else is permitted to interfere with. More formally, a rights relation can be depicted as follows: A has a right to X against B by virtue of Y, where A designates the subject of the right (the right-holder), X the object of the right, B the respondent of the right (the one who is obligated not to interfere with the right-holders having X), and Y the justifying ground of the right (Gewirth, 1992:1104).

Now, why should anyone claim a right in the first place? A right-claim implies that the claimer regards the object of her claim as something necessary and indispensable to her. A right-claim expresses the claimer's view that she must have this object, and that she cannot accept that anybody else interferes with her having it. To be more precise, since the object in question is an object of value to the claimer, and at the same time is believed by her to be necessary, the object of her claim is, in her eyes, a necessary good.

But why should B accept and respect A's right-claim? Anyone could claim a right to anything that she considers to be a necessary good. But why should other people care?

III. The Normative Structure of Action

In his much discussed book *Reason and Morality,* Alan Gewirth develops a careful answer to this question, by exploring the logical implications of agency. Action has, according to Gewirth, a normative structure: we act in order to achieve something that we regard as good (Gewirth, 1978: 48ff). We would not have moved from a state of non-action to one of action, had it not been for the value we assign to some goal that we intend to achieve by our action. It should be noted that Gewirth is not claiming that an agent's trying to achieve some end E proves that E is good; what Gewirth claims is that it proves that the agent thinks or holds that E is good (1978:51; 160). Nor should we assume that E is necessarily in the agent's interest, in the sense that it, for instance, contributes to her having a long and good life. E might be to light today's twentieth cigarette, which clearly will not promote the agent's health. Still, since the agent voluntarily controls her behaviour with the intention to light the cigarette, we must assume that she assigns at least some value to that purpose. Gewirth is careful to point out that we should distinguish between wanting to do something in the inclinational sense, and wanting to do something in the intentional sense (1978:39-41). To want to do p in the inclinational sense would be to feel a desire for doing p, to want to do p for the sake of the pleasure that one expects to get from doing p. To want to do p in the intentional sense, it is sufficient that the agent forms an intention to do p. It is not necessary that she even likes to do p: she may want to do p because she believes it to be her duty, or because doing p is instrumental to some other purpose of hers.

When Gewirth claims that every agent regards the ends of her actions as good, he assumes only that the agent wants them in the intentional sense. The agent expresses by her action a preference for a state of affairs in which her goal is achieved, over one in which it is not. More than this need not be involved in the claim that every agent necessarily regards the goals of her action as good.

It should also be clear, that by action is meant voluntary and purposive behaviour, i.e., behaviour that is controlled by the agent with a view to achieve a purpose of her own (1978:27). Behaviour that is caused by reflexes, intoxication, hallucination, hypnosis, insanity, or other causes beyond the agent's control, do not count as actions.

Agency hence involves valuation. This valuation extends beyond the agent's immediate end, to the action-related necessary conditions of her achieving that end. Now, different ends of action require different sets of necessary conditions. A person who wants to climb mountains needs a physical ability that is not necessary to another person who just wants to collect stamps. But common to all agents are certain conditions that are necessary for all successful action in general, and hence must be considered as necessary goods by all rational agents, no matter their different ends (1978:58-59).

By successful agency, Gewirth means agency in which the agent both avoids losing what she already has and regards as good, and gains new objects that she regards as good. The necessary conditions of successful agency in general involves more than the basic preconditions of action (being alive, free, and healthy); it also involves the conditions necessary to maintain and improve one's level of goods (not being lied to, not being cheated, not being robbed, enjoying self-esteem, having access to education, and being able to support oneself by one's own productive work). We can sum up these conditions, as Gewirth does, as freedom and well-being.

When Gewirth argues that all agents must consider the necessary conditions of successful action as necessary goods, he does not intend this to be a phenomenological claim about what agents actually say or believe. Instead it is a logical and conceptual point about what follows from the concept of agency. A rational agent, i.e., an agent who reasons according to the canons of deductive and inductive logic, including the evidence of empirical facts, will indeed accept that the necessary conditions of successful action are necessary goods for her, as she knows what conditions are causally necessary to all action, and also knows that since she values her goals and her ability to achieve these goals by her own action, she must, on logical grounds, also value the conditions that are necessary to have for her and all other agents in order to be successful in action.

Since the rational agent must accept that freedom and well-being constitute necessary goods to her, she cannot consistently accept that other agents interfere with her having these goods. To accept such interference would be equivalent to deny that they indeed are necessary goods, and that she must have them. An agent who accepts such interference would involve herself in a contradiction, by both affirming and denying that freedom and well-being are necessary goods to her. Hence, in order to avoid contradiction, the agent must accept the following statement: "All other persons ought to refrain from interfering with my freedom and well-being". But this strict ought-judgement is equivalent to a right-claim: "I have rights to freedom and well-being" (1978:78-80).

So far, the ought-judgement and the corresponding right-claim are not of the moral kind: they express only the self-interested attitudes of the individual agent: from her point of view, others ought not to interfere with her freedom and well-being. But this self-interested right-claim implies a universal right-claim, since the sufficient reason, or ground, for her claim is that she is an agent with purposes to achieve. It is because she views herself as an agent, that she considers herself having rights to freedom and well-being. Hence, she must hold that all agents have rights to freedom and well-being (1978:109-112).

To make this logical reasoning quite explicit: the agent's claim "I have rights to freedom and well-being" should be understood as "I have rights to freedom and well-being, because I am an agent", which in turn implies the claim "All agents have rights to freedom and well-being". This last claim is a moral one, since it is about all agents and not confined to the speaking agent's self-interest.

Freedom and well-being, being the generic features of all successful action, constitute the objects of what Gewirth has called the generic rights of agents. Hence, every agent must, on logical grounds, accept the Principle of Generic Consistency (PGC), which has the following content: "Act in accord with the generic rights of your recipients as well as of yourself" (1978:135), The PGC thus prescribes an equality of generic rights among agents.

IV. The Justification of the Welfare State

Now, in order to maintain the equality of generic rights, certain institutions are instrumentally justified (Gewirth, 1978: ch. 5). The minimal state with its criminal law is justified to the extent that it prevents people from violating each other's rights. But sometimes agents may be unable to secure for themselves their rights to freedom and well-being, not because of the criminal activities of other agents, but because of their own inability to acquire, for instance, an education and a work from which they can earn an income. In a society where some persons cannot supply themselves with food, clothes, and shelter because they, through no fault of their own, lack the necessary economic resources, while other persons are wealthy enough to buy themselves the education they want, and to go on expensive holidays abroad, there is no equality of generic rights. The poor agents are left in a position where their very status as (successful) agents is endangered. The wealthy persons, on the other hand, could help the poor without impoverishing themselves. Hence, the wealthy agents, who as agents must accept the PGC, cannot without violating that principle refuse to help the poor agents to secure their basic welfare rights.

To refuse to assist the poor and disabled would be to deny their right to basic well-being. It would be just as refusing to help a drowning, when you can help him at no comparable cost to yourself. It would be to hold that not all agents have a right to basic well-being, which would involve the wealthy agent in a contradiction, since she, as an agent, must accept that all agents have this right. It should be noted, however, that the PGC does not require anyone to make herself a pauper in order to help the poor. The PGC prescribes that you shall act in accord with the rights of your recipients as well as of yourself, not that you shall sacrifice your own basic rights for the sake of protecting the basic rights of your recipients. If you cannot swim, you are not expected to throw yourself in the water to help the drowning. And it is not the fact that you are rich and your neighbour is poor that makes it a duty for you to help him. Instead, it is the fact that he is so poor that he cannot secure his most basic rights, and that you are so rich that you can help him to do so without any comparable cost to yourself (i.e., it will not cost you your basic rights to help him to get his basic rights satisfied), that ground your duty.

A libertarian objection could be raised here. If a rich person, Smith, has earned his wealth by his own hard labour, without ever exploiting or cheating other people, why should he not be left in peace to do what he wants with his money? After all, it is his own money. What right could anyone else have to his property? Even if Jones is without means to support himself, that is not through any fault of Smith's. If Smith is forced to give up some of the wealth he has earned by his own work for the benefit of Jones, is that not equal to forcing Smith to work n hours for Jones without pay? In short, is not redistribution of wealth morally equal to forced labour (Nozick, 169)?

This objection presupposes that a person's right to his property is an unrestricted, non-overrideable one. Libertarians tend to assume that there is such an unrestricted right to property, but they have been unable to give any convincing argument for it. To be sure, the PGC does imply that there is a right to property, but it does not imply that this right is an unrestricted one. According to the PGC, all agents have rights to freedom and well-being. Property is relevant to both these general rights. As a part of the right to freedom, agents have a right to do what they want with things they own. As a part of the right to well-being, agents have a right to acquire wealth, since wealth tends to improve their capabilities of action. But these rights could be overridden by more important rights.

Since the PGC is derived from the conditions of agency, these conditions will also determine the ranking of rights (Gewirth, 1978:343-344). Some objects of the generic rights are causally more important to the possibility of successful action than others. Life, physical and mental health, are more important than, for instance, promise-keeping and wealth. If someone breaks a promise to you, it will normally frustrate only certain particular actions of yours. But if you are killed, you are deprived of all further possibilities to act. Hence, it would, according to the PGC, be morally right to break a promise, if doing so would be necessary to prevent a killing. In a similar way, Smith's right to all of his wealth can be overridden by Jones's right to more basic goods, such as food, clothes, and shelter.

In a realistically conceived society the problem of establishing and maintaining an equality of generic rights will require an institutional solution. There will, in all probability, be many persons, and not just Jones, in need of some assistance to have their rights secured. Since it is a question of rights, we cannot leave it only to voluntary associations to provide the help needed. Partly this is a question of efficiency. Voluntary associations may be efficient at a local level, but assistance may be needed everywhere. Hence, the responsibility for protecting welfare rights ought to be left with the state, which is the only institution that, per definition, is supposed to be able to exert control over a whole political community.

Another reason, besides that of efficiency, why the state and not private philanthropists should be responsible for basic welfare, is that the benefits of supportive arrangements should be impartially distributed to those who need them, without discrimination based on the preferences of private providers (-Gewirth, 1978:315). Another moral reason for state-managed protection of welfare rights is that all agents who have the sufficient means, not only the philanthropists, should contribute to the establishing of an equality of generic rights prescribed by the PGC. By taxing the affluent, the state can see to it that nobody shirks this duty.

In this way, the PGC justifies welfare rights and a welfare state. Some aspects of the welfare state should be carefully noted. A right to welfare should not be interpreted as a right to whatever people may happen to want or whatever will make them happy. According to the PGC, the objects of welfare rights are restricted to the necessary conditions of successful action, including the conditions for maintaining and improving one's level of goods. That is, every agent has a right to have her life, health, and means of self-development protected. Accordingly, she has rights to food, clothes, shelter, medical care when needed, a healthy environment, including healthy conditions of work, education to the limit of her capacities, and a productive work whereby she can support herself. Where these objects are absent, or unequally distributed, the state should encourage and support their production and equal distribution. The state should promote the increase of wealth generally in society, in order to provide the resources necessary to secure to each citizen her generic rights.

Another thing to be noted is that only those who are unable to secure their generic rights by their own efforts can claim a right to state assistance. There is a morally relevant difference between Colin, who cannot support himself because there is no work available for him, and Dexter, who cannot support himself because he does not want to work, although he is offered good jobs. Only Colin can claim a right to support here, since it is only about him that it would be true to say "Unless he is given support, his generic right cannot be maintained." In Dexter's case this is not so, since he will be able to support himself (though he does not want to) even if he is given no state support.

The whole point of having a supportive state, according to the PGC, is to help people to maintain their status as agents, i.e., to help them to be and to continue to be self-controlling, purposive, creative, and self-developing persons. The point is not to promote dependency or to create permanent recipients. Hence, the kind of support favoured by the PGC is directed at developing the abilities of persons to support themselves: training and education, rather than just giving money, should be the policy of the welfare state.

The PGC also justifies measures to regulate conditions of work, as well as environmental protection more generally. (For applications of the PGC, see Gewirth, 1982.) To endanger the health of workers and consumers is to violate their rights to the most basic part of the generic rights. Hence, production must be carried out in a safe manner, and consumer's goods must not be harmful. External harmful effects of industrial production, such as pollution of air and water, must be prohibited. In traditional political and economical reasoning it is common procedure to weigh such harmful effects against the expected economic benefits from the production in question. A certain increase in cancer or allergic diseases could, according to such reasoning, be balanced by the opportunities for employment offered by the polluting factory, and by the increase in tax revenues that may be expected.

The PGC cannot justify such reasoning, however. Nobody is allowed to expose other people to poisonous chemicals, just in order to secure an income, or a profit, for himself. The PGC does not prohibit anyone from risking his own health, if he freely chooses to do so, but when the risks are not restricted to those who have consented to them, they are not morally acceptable. Pollution of air and water clearly affect the rights of other agents than those who are immediately involved in the production that causes the pollution.

The closing down of polluting factory plants must be coupled with state efforts to encourage other forms of production which both offer opportunities for productive and remunerative employment, and are free from harmful external effects.

Likewise, the PGC would justify legislation that prohibits excessive use of cars in city areas, at least as long as cars are dependent on fuel the burning of which produces emissions of hydrocarbons, and other cancer-producing substances. Car producers should be encouraged to fabricate vehicles that do not need petrol for fuel. Meanwhile, the public transportation system should be expanded in order to compensate those people who no longer can use their own cars (either because these are prohibited or because they are taxed so severely that people no longer can afford them). It is indeed a freedom right to be able to move around, but this right is not violated because you no longer can move around in a car of your own.

V. Equality of Opportunity, Not Equality of Results

The PGC prescribes that there should be an equality of generic rights among agents. This does not imply, however, a prescription that all agents should earn the same income, live in the same type of house, and be equal in wealth and material possessions. The PGC does not prescribe an equality of results; rather, it prescribes a certain minimum (the necessary goods of successful agency) which all agents should have in order to maintain their opportunities for successful agency. Above this minimum level, there may well be differences in wealth. In this way, the PGC is not like John Rawls' Difference Principle (DP), which prescribes that all distribution of social and economic benefits and burdens should aim at equality, unless an unequal distribution benefits all affected (Rawls, 76-80). This means that if the alternative to an equal distribution between A, B, and C is one where A and B get a bigger share, while C remains as before (getting neither more, nor less than before), then this second alternative is ruled out, since it is not the case that all benefit from that unequal distribution.

One objection to the DP is that it dogmatically assumes that a just distribution should always benefit all affected, ignoring that people may differ in talent and energy, and hence may deserve unequal shares, at least when the inequality in question does not imply that some are deprived of objects to which they have rights, i.e., according to the PGC, objects necessary to successful agency in general.

Rawls defends the DP by arguing that it is the outcome of a procedure that is just in itself; hence, the DP must also be just, and morally right. The procedure in question is a hypothetical contract situation, an "original position", in which persons who have no particular knowledge of themselves or each other (which would have tempted them to design principles in their own favour) are to agree on which principles should guide the community in which they all expect to live. The DP would be one of these principles, according to Rawls.

Maybe persons without particular knowledge about themselves (being behind what Rawls calls a "veil of ignorance") would choose the DP. Maybe not – it would depend on their attitudes to equality, and on how willing they are to take chances: after all, not knowing whether I will be in A's or in C's position above, I might just take a chance that I will be in A's position and opt for a less egalitarian principle than the DP. But no matter how people behind a veil of ignorance would choose, the basic question is: why should we, persons who are not behind a veil of ignorance, be committed to principles that such persons have chosen? Why should people with full rational abilities be bound by principles chosen by people with less than full rational abilities?

Rawls' answer is that the conditions of the original position are in fact conditions that we already accept as generating just outcomes. He argues that his decision procedure, prescribing conditions of restricted knowledge about ourselves and others, actually catches our intuitions about how to achieve fairness (p. 21). Now, it is always hazardous to let one's argument depend on intuitions when one is trying to defend moral principles. What if one's intuitions are contradicted by the intuitions of other people? For instance, Rawls seems to be convinced that we should exclude knowledge about our natural assets from the original position. But Robert Nozick, another moral intuitionist disagrees:

"[W]hy should knowledge of natural endowments be excluded from the original position? Presumably the underlying principle would be that if any particular features are arbitrary from a moral point of view, then persons in the original position should not know they possess them. But this would exclude their knowing anything about themselves, for each of their features (including rationality, the ability to make choices, having a life span of more than three days, having a memory, being able to communicate with other organisms like themselves) will be based upon the fact that the sperm and ovum which produced them contained particular genetic material. The physical fact that those particular gametes contained particular organised chemicals (the genes for people rather than for muskrats or trees) is arbitrary from a moral point of view; it is, from a moral point of view, an accident. Yet the persons in the original position are to know some of their attributes" (Nozick, 226-227).

Rawls tries to secure an egalitarian outcome of the original position by prescribing an equality of (lack of) knowledge in the contracting individuals. The egalitarian conclusion of his argument hence depends on the egalitarian premises he has introduced, and these premises in turn are left without independent justification. Rawls can only offer us an intuition about the validity of the egalitarian restrictions on the knowledge admitted to the individuals in the original position, and if this intuition is rejected his argument can proceed no further. Hence, the DP cannot be considered as a rationally justified normative principle.

The PGC, however, is such a rationally justified normative principle, provided that we accept the logical relationship between agency and right-claims. (For a further discussion and defence of the PGC, see Beyleveld, 1991.) From the PGC welfare rights can be derived, and the supportive state can be defended as necessary to maintain these rights. Such a defence would be based on a strict logical line of reasoning, and hence offer an argument that should be convincing even to those who are emotionally indifferent to all forms of welfarism. It would also point to the possibilities of a fruitful combination of philosophical argument and political reform, possibilities that may well be of further significance.

References

BEYLEVELD, DERYCK: *The Dialectical Necessity of Morality* , Chicago (The University of Chicago Press) 1991.

GEWIRTH, A.: *Reason and Morality*, Chicago (The University of Chicago Press) 1978.

— *Human Rights*, Chicago (The University of Chicago Press) 1982.

— "Rights", in: *Encyclopaedia of Ethics* (Ed. Lawrence C. Becker), New York (Garland) 1992, pp. 1103-1109.

NOZICK, ROBERT: *Anarchy, State, and Utopia*, New York (Basic Books) 1974.

RAWLS, JOHN: *A Theory of Justice* , Oxford (Oxford University Press) 1972.

UNITED NATIONS DEVELOPMENT PROGRAMME: *Human Development Report* 1994, Oxford (Oxford University Press) 1994.

Chapter 15

Risk, Justice and Social Policies

SERGE-CHRISTOPHE KOLM

I. Introduction

Justice probably demands that the most unfortunate citizens be protected one way or the other, at a cost paid by more fortunate persons. However, these situations result in particular from risk-taking, and individuals may want to try their luck at obtaining a good situation at the risk of ending up among the losers. Therefore, a policy motivated by justice may violate individuals' liberty to take the risks they want – in particular, risks that concern only themselves and may even imply actions favourable to others. This policy may indeed also, for this reason, cut down incentives to enterprise, innovation, investment, research, etc., and hence reduce employment, productivity, the social output and growth. If all individuals prefer ex ante to take the risk, in a democracy they would rule out the justice policy considered, by unanimity (this is, however, unanimity *ex ante*, rather than ex post, since ex post the unfortunate persons regret the protection if it does not exist). The same logic underlies the debate about whether certain insurances should be free or should be compulsory, and this includes in particular the question of the status of "social insurances" (health, unemployment, etc.) which concerns both a notable part of GNP and major social questions, and for which various countries and societies choose opposite solutions. This interference between justice and risk, and the resulting possible opposition between justice on the one hand and liberty, efficiency and democracy on the other hand, thus seem to cover a number of the most crucial problems of modern societies. Furthermore, social policies commonly want to compensate for certain handicaps, yet not for all characteristics of the individuals, and this begs the basic question of how this separation can be made.

It so happens that the basic framework necessary for the analysis of these problems has been set up by John Harsanyi in the early fifties, albeit in models which present themselves as something completely different, namely proofs of utilitarianism (inadvertently in a sense). These models, indeed, do not even mention liberty, responsibility or compensations, and utilitarianism is classically seen as the very opposite of the consideration of such entities as end-values. Yet we will see that this is precisely what these models are about.

Now, for their specific purpose and methods, John Harsanyi's works from 1953 and 1955 are among the most famous contributions to Normative Economics and Social Ethics of the twentieth century. They introduced two innovations in the methodology of normative proofs: risk-consistency and the theory of the Original Position (the name later coined by John Rawls).[1] They have drawn enormous attention and innumerable comments, and also criticisms which were neatly answered. The proofs of utilitarianism they provide have haunted Political Philosophy and Normative Economics for the last few decades. And this may be understandable: the 1955 piece, for instance, *deduces utilitarianism from Pareto-efficiency*; or again, both theories can be seen as *deducing utilitarianism from freedom of choice*! These are "Harsanyi's enigmas" referred to in the title of the present essay, and the first things we propose here is to show their actual meaning and to elucidate their apparent mysteries.

Nevertheless, I will argue that the actual interest of these striking and celebrated theories has been definitely *under*rated, and that they are still much more important than they are generally thought to be, yet for a reason which is different – and indeed rather opposed – to that held by common opinion, and because they have not yet been considered under their most fruitful angle. This requires that one takes a new view of Harsanyi's constructions. The classical question about them is: Do they prove utilitarianism? By contrast, I will propose that their much more important contribution is that they prove, in the neatest possible way, the crucial importance of the central questions of Social Ethics and the theory of justice: responsibility, accountability, liberty, equality, the possible conflict between justice and freedom, and the question of the self. Now, they raise these issues in an ethic which is otherwise completely welfarist (the term coined by Hicks in 1959), and this is precisely that which is needed by welfarism, inherited from classical utilitarianism, which has been so important in English-language philosophy and aca-

1 The suggestions by VICKREY will be recalled below.

demic Normative Economics. These conclusions stand out strikingly when Harsanyi's models are considered in the light of the general theory of justice (see Kolm 1990, 1993a and c, 1994a, b, and d, 1995a and c 1996).

In order to focus on this most important aspect, I will completely accept Harsanyi's basic assumptions without discussing them here (they are discussed elsewhere): for both theories, an uncertainty-rational evaluation of risks by expected values of utilities, and interpersonally comparable " fundamental" utilities (see Kolm 1966a, 1971, 1994c, 1995d); and, for the theory of 1955, the additional assumptions of a social ethical evaluation function [2] with a similar evaluation of risks, probabilisable risks with "objective" probabilities, and a sufficiently large domain of risky prospects.

The theory of 1955, which can be labelled " ex-ante respectful consequentialism," will be considered first. The following lines of argument will be developed:

1. The case of a single individual shows that the theorem is primarily about non-paternalism in risky situations, rather than primarily about utilitarianism.
2. Yet, uncertainty might provide a reason based on justice in favour of paternalism, as a simple example shows.
3. The general theory of justice emphasises the rationality of prima facie equality, the crucial question of the assignment of accountability, and the roles of responsibility and liberty.
4. The respect of individuals' ex ante preferences means that the individuals are accountable for the effects of the occurrence of the risky event onto themselves. Utilitarianism is the particular social ethic where the assignment of this accountability between the individuals and the justice-motivated policy makes no difference.
5. Given the otherwise completely welfarist conception, this accountability of the individuals should probably be justified by their responsibility.
6. Yet, responsibility requires free choice, and hence the individuals should also be responsible for the rest of their preferences, which leads to a social ethic of equality of liberty (rather than of the sum of utilities).

2 For a criticism of this widespread assumption, see KOLM (1992, 1994b, 1995 a and b).

7. The theory of 1953 will then be considered. It will be pointed out that it can be defended as the rational theory of the Original Position. Yet, this kind of theories raises serious questions concerning justice, responsibility and the self.
8. However, theories of the "partially original positions" lead to the theories of "fundamental insurance" and of "partial welfarism" which provide the solutions to the problem of the definition of just compensations for specific disadvantages, handicaps or other characteristics, with solutions which rest on morals of either (implicit) liberty or individual welfare.

II. Risk-Paternalism and Justice

1. The Case of One Individual: Non-Paternalism for Risk

In all the following, we consider risky prospects in a domain sufficiently large to guarantee the properties that will be stated (our concern here is the meaning of these properties).[3] The risks are assumed to have "objective" probabilities and E denotes the mathematical expectation operator.

We begin with a single individual with a utility function in certainty u, and a social ethical evaluation function which respects this individual's preferences in certainty, $W(u)$ with W increasing. We also consider that both the individual and the social ethical evaluation appraise risky prospects through the mathematical expectation of values of evaluations in certainty, and we choose as specific u and W specifications of the corresponding von Neumann-Morgenstern cardinal utility and social ethical evaluation function.

For a risky prospect, u is stochastic and hence so is $W(u)$, and the ex ante social ethical evaluation is $EW(u)$. It is straightforward to show that *the ordering of the risky prospects by $EW(u)$ coincides with that by Eu if and only if the function W is affine increasing,* that is, $W(u) = au + b$ with con-

3 A literature has emphasized this assumption: see the references to works of Mongin, Weymark, Fishburn and Domotor. It seems that Harsanyi's theorem of 1955 is not much weaker if we assume maximal variability of risky prospects, as long as one does not consider a theory of tangible reasons for the limitation of their domain.

stant a and b and $a > 0$. One can for instance note that this coincidence implies the existence of an increasing function V such that $V(Eu) \equiv EW(u)$, with $V \equiv W$ from the cases with certainty, and hence $W(Eu) \equiv EW(u)$, from which the result can be drawn.

This property means that the social ethical evaluation respects the individual's preferences for risky prospects, that is, preferences ex ante, and not only ex post. Other forms of the function W represent *paternalism* with respect to risk.[4] For instance, a strictly concave W means that the social ethical evaluation is more cautious or risk-averse for the individual, than the individual is. The quantity $R = W(Eu) - EW(u)$ measures the *paternalistic prudence or paternalistic risk-aversion*. $R > 0$ for the case just noted and actually uncertain u's.

$R \equiv 0$, and hence an affine W, means that the social ethical evaluation endorses or « respects » the individual's preferences toward risk. Then, if the individual chooses and acts, a policy which maximises the corresponding $EW(u)$ does not interfere with the individual's risk-taking, choices and freedom. Conversely, if a policy both respects the individual's free choices and maximises $EW(u)$ with a certain function W, then this function must be affine and $R \equiv 0$.

Although no utilitarianism is here yet (since there is only one individual), this case raises certain of the key issues which will be met below.

2. Risk-Paternalism Induced by Justice

The consideration of several individuals, rather than only one, introduces something new, namely one a priori possible reason for an ethical interference with individuals' preferences toward risk and free risk-taking behaviour in the name of social morality. This reason is readily seen. Indeed, the occurrence of the risky event may treat certain people badly and others much better. Don't solidarity, charity, mutual aid or simply justice demand a certain compensation of the former by the latter, in terms of the presently relevant items which are welfares? Should not this be implemented by social policy, either by ex ante actions, or by ex post compensations which amount to the latter if they are foreseen ex ante for each of the possible occurrences? How-

4 Note that, as it is standard in this kind of use, "paternalism" means "father knows better what is good", rather than the possible opposite meaning "father is kind and hence respects the individual's wishes".

ever, this may lead to allowing less risk than the individuals desire ex ante. Indeed, certain individuals, or all of them, may prefer to take the risk of ending up with a poor situation in exchange for the hope of a larger chance of having a still better situation if they happen to be fortunate. The described policy amounts to a forced mutual insurance. If the risk results from individuals' choices, this policy constitutes a limitation of their liberty. Yet, this refers to individuals' preferences ex ante rather than ex post. Indeed, in the absence of this policy and ex post, the least fortunate individuals regret that the risk has not been reduced directly or by a guaranteed assistance. And if the policy limits the misfortune of the least lucky individuals without affecting their relative situation, ex post these individuals appreciate this policy. If the individuals are sufficiently audacious, they may all oppose this policy ex ante. Hence, this "ex post moral" policy may be Pareto-inefficient. This, however, is *ex ante* Pareto-inefficiency, rather than an ex post one. Ex post, indeed, the least lucky individuals regret the policy in its absence, or appreciate its presence if they would also have been the unlucky ones in its absence. Unanimous ex ante opposition is not unanimous regret. Now, a welfarist ethic, such as the one considered here, is a priori ex post.

An elementary example can illustrate this crucial point. Assume there are two individuals who evaluate risk by expected utility and have comparable (fundamental) utility for which we choose the same specification of the von Neumann-Morgenstern cardinal utility (more details will be provided in the next section). A pair of numbers represents these individuals' utility levels, one for each individual, in a given order of the individuals. There are two prospects. One is a risky prospect with two possible occurrences giving the utility levels (10,0) and (0,10) respectively, each with probability 1/2. The other prospect is a sure one with utility levels (4,4). The first prospect leads to situations with – let us assume – "very low" lower welfares and "very unequal" distributions of welfare. A social policy may prefer the sure prospect where no one is miserable (say) and welfares are equal. For example, social ethical evaluation functions which are the sum of the square roots of the individuals' utilities, or the sum of the logarithms or the product of these utilities, or the lowest utility level, lead to this social choice. Now, the risky prospect provides each individual with an expected utility level of 5. Therefore both individuals prefer the risky prospect to the sure one. Both prefer to take the risk to have 0 for the chance to reach 10, rather than the safe and acceptable but mediocre 4 (compared to 10). In a democratic system, they choose the risky prospect by unanimity and overrule other moral considerations and policies. However, in this case they are *responsible* for this choice and for the risk it entails, and the individual who ends up with a zero level of utility has no moral right to complain about this social choice.

3. A Brief Reminder of the General Theory of Justice

Understanding the problem at hand requires one to recall the relevant basic aspects of the general theory of justice, concerning rationality, equality, accountability, responsibility and liberty.[5]

Social ethics is the science of what should be done in society. Its part of what is concerned with the situations of "justiciable" social entities is the topic of justice. These entities are often individuals and we focus on this case here. Justice thus is a justified answer to the question of what these situations should be. "Justified" is synonymous with "rational" in the normal sense of "for a reason", or "non-arbitrary". This implies that when the relevant facts are the same, the conclusion should be the same. In particular, when the relevant characteristics of individuals are the same, the relevant aspects of their situations should be the same. This is all at once allocating according to a rule, or "rule-equality", the "rule of law", "equal treatment of equals", "impartiality", "to or from each according to x", etc. This per se implies an equality of the appropriately chosen items. If, for instance, we re-define these items as being the preceding rule, we must have strict identity for all the individuals. We have a formally identical case when, with the former variables, the relevant characteristics of the individuals is their mere existence. Therefore, justice is equality, from the mere requirement of rationality (a particular aspect of the manifestation of this necessity will be presented with examples below). Then, the nature of the equalizand is the question.

The basic choice of a particular conception of justice consists of a dichotomy of the items of the world into those that are the concern of an active policy and those for which the rule is "to each according to how things happen to be". The latter domain is classically justified by concepts such as "natural" (e.g. Locke), "spontaneous" (Hayek), "respect", "non-interference", agents' responsibility or liberty, etc. There, the social ethics considered underwrites facts, or acquiesces to them. Practically, this corresponds to an absence of active justice-motivated policy, and, notably, redistributive policy. The only justified, and possibly necessary, policies in these domains are things such as the protection of rights (including, possibly, the implementation of implicit

5 The full presentation can be found in Kolm (1995d).

contracts ("Liberal social contracts": see Kolm 1985, 1987a and b, 1991c). The other cases imply active, and possibly redistributive, policies in the name of justice. Certain social ethics attribute everything to the "spontaneous" domain [full process liberalism: (Kolm 1985, 1987a and b, 1991c), and, if they are ethical conceptions, neo-libertarianism and classical Public Choice]. Others attribute most of the field to it (Hayek, M. Friedman). Other widespread or famous conceptions of justice want to reduce it to individuals' preferences, tastes or ends (ideals of reduction of inequalities in income or in consumption, views of Tobin, Rawls, Dworkin or Walzer, the theory of efficient super-equity, see Kolm 1991b, 1993c, 1995c and d, 1996). Ideals of "equality of opportunity" add various possible individual capacities to the preferences of the latter case. Still other moral conceptions restrict this "spontaneous" domain to nothing, and this is the case of full individual welfarism; then individuals' freedoms can be recommended only as means for the implementation of the policy, and all inter-individual differences are considered for compensation.

This delineation of the domains of active and passive or acquiescent justice implies the choice of the end-values of active justice, which are respectively, for instance, in common-life ethics or in classical theories, individuals' welfare, basic rights, opportunities, incomes, consumption goods either specifically (Tobin) or within broad "spheres of justice" (Weber and Walzer), "primary goods" (Rawls), resources (Dworkin), the satisfaction of various needs, etc. All these are cases of "respectful justice" for which the social ethical end-values are desired by the concerned individuals.

From the above, justice implies an ideal equality of its similar end-values appropriately defined attributed to the individuals.[6] "Ideal", or, equivalently, "prima facie" means in the absence of an overpowering reason against it.[7] This reason can be impossibility, or the effect of other criteria deemed to be also relevant, possibly other criteria of justice when their own ideal equalities conflict with that of the considered items. One such criterion can be Pareto-efficiency. Others can refer to interpersonal comparisons of gains and losses. The task of a conception of justice, after it has defined its domain of active policy and its end-values, consists in defining the adjustments among its criteria if their ideals conflict. This is done according to various possible

6 This can be equality of items (e.g. rights, welfare, income, etc.) or of rules (e.g. to or from each according to his needs, means, contribution, merit, and so on).

7 The classical analysis of the use prima facie properties in ethics is that of Ross (1930).

structures such as compromises, priorities, "super-imposition" (i.e. one criterion is applied from the outcome of the application of another), etc.[8]

The delineation between the domains of acquiescence or " spontaneity" and of active policy also takes the form of *accountability*. A conception of justice deems the individuals to be *accountable* for the effects onto themselves of the items which it accepts and hence does not try to influence, correct or compensate for. Symmetrically, this conception sees itself as accountable for the final situation of the end-values of its active policy. Indeed, since it seeks to intervene so as to influence this final situation by action, intervention, correction or compensation, and this is intentional and purposive action, the policy is even more or less *responsible* for the (final) state of these items.[9]

All the above-mentioned common or scholarly social ethics constitute examples of the described general structure of conceptions of justice. Another such instance is provided by "Harsanyi's problems", and their consideration from this angle provides the meaning of these problems and the answer to the questions they raise. This also leads to the solution of important questions of justice and of social policy. We now turn to this application.

III. Social or Private Risk-Bearing

1. Application of the General Theory of Justice to Harsanyi's Problem

We consider here social ethics that take as end-values individuals' welfares, that is, which belong to welfarist justice. The welfare of individual i is represented by a utility index v_i. We take for the v_i the same specification of

8 The analysis of the various modes of adjustment of criteria is provided in KOLM (1990).

9 The crucial concepts of responsibility and accountability are considered in more detail below, and fully in KOLM (1995d).

a fundamental utility (see Kolm, 1966a, 1971, 1994c, 1995d).[10] Hence, these v_i are comparable and defined up to the same transformation. There results that the objectives of the ethics are symmetrical in the v_i (invariant to permutations among the v_i). From the preceding section, rational justice implies a prima facie reason for the equality of the v_i. Yet, other reasons may be introduced by the structure of the set of possibilities and by moral or other considerations. Denote $v = \{v_i\}$ and let us describe the ethical choice among several possible v by the maximisation of a social ethical evaluation function $V(v)$. The function V is symmetrical from the above. We furthermore assume another criterion, unanimity in Pareto's sense, with priority, which means that the function V is increasing. The v_i and V are a priori ordinal (co-ordinal for the v_i), and if the v_i are replaced by an increasing function of themselves, the function V as a function of the v_i incurs the corresponding co-variation.

We furthermore consider the possibility of probabilisable risks with "objective" probabilities. We consider that both the individuals and the social ethical evaluation evaluate risky prospects by the mathematical expectation of indices of utility or of evaluation. Let u_i denote the same specification for all i of the von Neumann-Morgenstern cardinal specification of the fundamental utility, W denote a specification of the von Neumann-Morgenstern cardinal index for the evaluation function, and E denote the mathematical expectation operator. We can then take ex ante the occurrence of the risk, Eu_i as v_i and EW as V. Let $U = \{u_i\}$ denote the vector of the u_i and $EU = \{Eu_i\}$. The u_i and W are cardinal (co-cardinal for the u_i), and if the u_i incur an increasing affine transformation of themselves, the function W as function of U or of EU (see below) incurs the corresponding co-variation. These are but Harsanyi's assumptions, albeit more explicitly and cautiously stated.[11]

We consider now a risky prospect. One cause of the situation of the world and, for our present concern, of individuals' welfares, is the occurrence of the risky event. We thus consider two conceptions of justice. Both are welfarist, but one feels the policy to be responsible for the consequences of the risky event whereas the other deems the individuals to be accountable for them.

10 This theory of fundamental utility provides the justification for writing $v_i(x) = f(y_i,x)$, where x denotes the object of the preferences, y_i denotes a sufficient set of characteristics of individual i, and f denotes the fundamental utility function. This function is a priori ordinal, but we use below a cardinal specification.

11 Fundamentalism is explicit in HARSANYI (1953), and it is required in HARSANYI (1955) by the assumption of symmetry which transforms a social ethical evaluation by an affine function of individual utilities into a social ethical evaluation by their sum.

Their ex ante evaluations are respectively the following. For the former conception, an evaluation ex post is *W(U)*. Ex ante, it faces the uncertainty of the effects of the risky event on *U* and hence on *W*, and its evaluation is *EW(U)*.

The second conception, on the contrary, does not care a priori and directly for the consequences of the risky event, that is, for the *U* which occurs. Hence the policy should not try to influence the justice of the situation which results from each occurrence, that is, of the possible distributions of the u_i for all *i* in each case. It does not try, for instance, to augment the lowest u_i. The effects of the occurrence of the risky event are left to the charge of the individuals, they are considered to be a purely private business of theirs, outside the scope of the social ethical evaluation (the question of the justification of this position will be discussed in the next section). Since this social ethical evaluation is not directly concerned by the occurrence of the risky event, it cares only for the situation ex ante. And since it remains welfarist, it cares for the ex ante welfare of the individuals, that is, the Eu_i. Hence this ethic is not directly concerned with risk, it is only concerned with the sure ex ante welfare of individuals who are concerned with the risk they face. This social ethical evaluation function is thus *W(EU)* (the particular cases where the prospect is not actually risky confirm that the same function *W* is to be considered in both cases).

The difference in conception between these two cases, and their common welfarism, imply that the item which is charged to the policy in one case and to the individuals in the other is the dispersion of *U* around *EU*, and hence, for each individual *i*, of u_i around Eu_i. But when the accountability for the stochastic variable $u_i - Eu_i$ is shifted from the concern of the active justice policy to individual *i*, for all *i*, the effect of these variables on justice, in each occurrence, ceases to be a concern at all, since the individuals do not have, by construction, an objective concern for the justice of the inter-individual distribution (each individual *i* cares only for his/her u_i and Eu_i).

Therefore, these two ethical conceptions lead a priori and in general to very different policies. In the former case, the policy is directly concerned by the ex post values of the u_i, and hence by the justice of their distribution over the individuals in each possible occurrence, even though it considers ex ante all the possible occurrences (and certain policy choices may jointly affect several of them). By contrast, in the latter case the policy is only concerned by the Eu_i and hence by the justice of their distribution. Hence, as just noted, the dispersion of u_i around Eu_i, for each *i*, is a concern of the policy in the former case but not in the latter case. Notice that in the former case the policy is a priori also concerned by the correlation among the u_i. Notice also that we do not distinguish here between the various types of implementation of the policy. If its actions are ex post, they are foreseen ex ante for each of the possible cases of occurrence. But there can also be actions ex ante for choosing among various risky prospects, for instance in influencing the cause of the risk, the protection of the individuals, their insurance coverage, etc.

These two conceptions amount to the same when $EW(U)$ is indifferent to the dispersion of the u_i around the Eu_i, and hence when W is an affine function (if this holds for a sufficient domain of probabilities), which amounts to Σu_i since W is symmetrical, increasing and cardinal. Indeed, $EW(U) \equiv F(EU)$, where F is a function of n variables, implies that F is affine since, taking the probabilities as basic variables, a function of affine functions is itself affine if and only if it is an affine function of these functions (for a sufficient domain); then also, $F \equiv W$ (consider notably the particular cases with certainty). A remarkable consequence is that the *social ethical indifference to the stochastic dispersion of each u_i around Eu_i is equivalent to the social ethical indifference to the distributional dispersion of the certain ui around their average $\Sigma u_i/n$* (note that the symmetry of W is necessary for this result). This case, with its utilitarian form, can be called the specific Harsanyi's case.

In the other cases, the specifications of the ex ante evaluation function that are to be compared in the two alternatives are $EW(U)$ and $W(EU)$ since they are identical for sure prospects. The difference

$$R = W(EU) - EW(U)$$

is the *ex ante social cost of the occurrence of the risky event.* It is due to the dispersion of each u_i around Eu_i. For a given occurrence U, one can have $W(U) \gtrless W(EU)$. But $EW(U) < W(EU)$, or $R > 0$, for all actually risky prospects, is the very definition of the strict concavity of the function W. Now, a strictly concave, symmetrical and increasing W is the natural structure that expresses the prima facie reason for equality presented above, or particular concerns for the lowest individuals' welfares (increasingness expresses the priority of the unanimity-Pareto criterion).[12] Then, $R > 0$ means that the

12 An increasing symmetrical strictly concave W is also strictly Schur-concave (see KOLM 1966a and b), hence it takes a higher value for interpersonal distributions U that have a higher concentration curve (i.e. a concentration curve somewhere above nowhere below), and in particular, for distributions that have the same Σu_i, that is, that are equivalent for utilitarianism, this W takes a higher values for distributions that have a higher Lorenz curve (with the same definition of "higher"). In particular, a transfer of an amount of utility from a higher u_i to a lower one of less than the difference augments W. All these properties are meaningful from the co-cardinality of the u_i.

direct social ethical endorsement of the concern for the occurrence of the risky event (and hence, ex ante, for the dispersions of individuals' welfares – the end-values – that result from it) lowers an ex ante social ethical evaluation with this structure.

$R = 0$ for a sure prospect or for a utilitarian W. The extreme opposite obtains when the only property which is deemed to be able to interfere with the prima facie or ideal equality is the priority to the unanimity or Pareto criterion. This is *Practical Justice* (Kolm 1971) with $W = \text{Min } u_i$ (this was more specifically a leximin in fundamental preferences or utilities;[13] note that this W is no longer an increasing function in all the u_i). Then,

$R = R_0 = Min\ Eu_i - E\ Min\ u_i.$

For all concave W, $0 \leqslant R \leqslant R_0$.

There can also be intermediary conceptions of justice, where the individuals are deemed to be accountable for the fraction a of the ex ante social cost due to the occurrence of the risky event, while the justice-abiding policy is deemed to be responsible for the rest. The corresponding ex ante social ethical evaluation function then is

$$EW(U) + aR = aW(EU) + (1 - a)\,EW(U),$$

with $0 \leqslant a \leqslant 1$, which gives the two cases discussed for $a = 0$ and $a = 1$ respectively.

This function *does not actually depend on this choice of assignment of accountability* if the social ethical evaluation is *utilitarian*, and only in this case for a sufficiently large domain of risky prospects (that is, in Harsanyi's case).

In particular, the cardinal function $W(U)$ has the form $W(U) = \Sigma w(u_i)$ when the evaluation $W(U)$ classifies the set of u_i for the $i \in I$ independently of the given u_i for all $i \notin I$, for all subsets I of individuals (it suffices that this holds for all pairs $-|I| = 2$) (see Kolm, 1966a, 1977, the symmetry and cardinality of W being added for the present property). The function w is cardinal and increasing. Then, $R = \Sigma r_i$, where $r_i = w(Eu_i) - Ew(u_i)$ is the "parternalistic prudence" considered in Section 2, for individual i. Strict concavities of W and w imply each other, $r_i > 0$ for a strictly concave w and an actually risky prospect for u_i. The paternalistic prudence is now justified by rational justice.

13 This has a priori nothing to see with RAWLS' (1971) "difference principle" which is emphatically not concerned with utilities but with "primary goods" (income, wealth, power, positions, and self-respect or the means to it).

2. Responsibility

The right assignment of accountability for the consequences of the occurrence of the risky event cannot be told without more information. It will a priori not be the same for all actual risky situations. If the individuals can in no way influence the consequences of the occurrence of the risky event on their welfare, then, since both ethics considered see the policy as responsible for the effects of everything else onto the individuals' welfares, consistency provides a prima facie case in favour of the conception of justice that also takes responsibility for the considered consequences, that is, in favour of the evaluation function *EW(U)*.

However, individuals can generally more or less influence these consequences by influencing or even choosing the risk or by more or less protection, avoidance, insurance, etc., and even by mastering their minds toward appreciation and equanimity. Then, they are more or less responsible for these consequences onto their welfare. The concept of responsibility, let us recall, implies by definition two things that relate the responsible person respectively to the causes and to the consequences of the fact considered. First, the responsible person can or could influence wilfully that which he/she is responsible for. Second, responsibility implies accountability for the consequences. Responsibility can of course be shared among joint causes, and hence between the individuals considered and the justice-oriented policy (and among several of these individuals), which entails the corresponding accountabilities. Note that individual responsibility is not only a possible reason for departing from full responsibility of the policy, it indeed requires such a departure. The only way to avoid this conclusion and to stick to integral welfarism when there is individual free choice is to deny responsibility in denying the existence of freedom of the will. This is indeed the neatest case of paternalism.

Now, to acknowledge an individual's responsibility for consequences on his welfare amounts to the respect of his corresponding freedom, that is, to the classification of the corresponding acts and of their effects in the domain of respected "spontaneity" (in Hayek's sense).

Then, however, the end-values of active justice become individuals' means of these free acts, and these means are not the expected utilities which are the end-values in the alternative ethic of maximising *W(EU)*. If D_i denotes the domain of this free choice for individual i, the ideal or prima facie equality is that of the D_i, and a social ethical evaluation function is

$\phi(D)$ where $D = \{D_i\}$ is the set of the D_i, and the function ϕ is symmetrical in the D_i. One cannot, in general, separate the choice of the stochastic variable $U - EU$ from the choice of EU, particularly for individuals who determine $U - EU$ in maximising each Eu_i (in individual or collective choices), but also for the justice policy which maximises $EW(U)$ or $W(EU)$. Then, each individual i chooses one possible alternative within D_i, and these choices determine the (generally) risky prospect. If an individual's choice affects the prospect or situation of another, there is a matter for agreement and cooperation between these individuals. If an agreement failure for whatever reason results in a Pareto-inefficiency, this constitutes a case for a public policy correcting this inefficiency by the usual means such as the setting up of institutions for enforcing promises or promises conditional on promises,[14] or the vicarious implementation of the putative agreement (a "liberal social contract", see Kolm 1985, 1987a and b, 1991c). These devices determine the resulting distribution of individuals' welfares by principles which are "liberalisms" rather than "welfarisms".

The foregoing remarks result from the fact that the accountability which is disputed between the two ethics considered is that of the dispersion of individuals' welfare around their expected values Eu_i, whereas individuals' actual choices generally affect by assumption these expected values. For example, in the case which is the closest to the choice of a pure risk where individuals receive incomes y_i which they choose to invest in risks with fair gambles for the stochastic incomes x_i with $Ex_i = y_i$, and assuming away the classical possible reasons for limiting gambles (addiction, mistaken evaluation, excessive risks, external effects on family, etc.), the social ethic should reject the evaluation function $EW[\{u_i(x_i)\}]$ because of individuals' responsibility (there is no reason to limit this freedom or to impose that the lucky people compensate the unlucky ones). It should choose as end-values the means of action y_i rather than the expected utilities $Eu_i(x_i)$ or their lower bounds $u_i(y_i)$ – since not gambling is a possible alternative for individual i. The point is that each individual i chooses jointly both the dispersion of $u_i(x_i) - Eu_i(x_i)$ and $Eu_i(x_i)$ itself, given y_i. If individuals face the same possibilities of choice of risks, the ideal is equality of the y_i. Note that the choice of $u_i(y_i)$ as social ethical end-values has the advantage of introducing a certain compensation for differences in the functions $u_i(\ )$, but the relevant val-

14 The possibility to enforce promises and promises conditional on promises suffices to solve situations such as those of the prisoner's dilemma type (see KOLM (1995d), chap. 1).

ues are the $u_i(x_i)$ for all values x_i. We face here the classical difficulty or impossibility of distinguishing choice from evaluation in the case of choices driven by the individual's evaluation.

However, if the individuals are seen as *irresponsible* actors, who obey mechanically their given and irrepressible tastes, the policy may have to be fully welfarist and maximise $EW[\{u_i(x_i)\}]$, possibly in choosing itself the individuals' gambles. If $W(U) = \Sigma w(u_i)$ and if the function w is sufficiently concave so that the functions $w \circ u_i$ are concave, then the optimal policy forbids gambles and the social evaluation is $\Sigma w[u_i(y_i)]$.

Yet, in particular examples the problem can be presented as the ethical choice between the alternatives considered. The following example thus extends the example of Section I.2 so as to add the question of prima facie equality.

3. A More Complete Example

We consider two individuals with the same co-cardinal fundamental and von Neumann-Morgenstern utilities as above, written in a fixed order in a pair (u_1,u_2). We now consider eight prospects labelled from A to H, shown in the following table. Prospects A, B, C, D and H are sure. Prospects E, F and G are uncertain with two eventualities with probability 1/2 each. The three lines give the utilities for each eventuality and the expected utilities.

A	*B*	*C*	*D*	*E*	*F*	*G*	*H*
4,6	5,5	6,4	16,0	0,14 18,0	0,16 16,0	0,18 14,0	0,16
				9,7	8,8	7,9	

The comparison between prospects B and F is similar to the comparison discussed in Section I.2, with the same results for functions W which are, for example, $\sqrt{u_1} + \sqrt{u_2}$, or $u_1 u_2$, or Log u_1 + Log u_2, or Min $\{u_1,u_2\}$.

How would justice choose among A, B and C? Assume that one and only one of the three has to be picked up, and recall that no other characteristics of the individuals than their utility levels is deemed to be relevant (and known). Alternative B is chosen, rather than either A or C, for reasons of "fair balance", "just middle", "equitable compromise", "symmetry", "not yielding completely to one individual", etc., by most people (all people ? all "normal" people ?). The basic reason behind such a choice is probably simply rationality in the normal and common sense of "for a reason". Indeed, when asked "why don't you rather choose A?", most people answer: then, if A, why not C which is identical from the objective standpoint (it is not for the concerned individuals). And, truly, one can provide no reason for the choice of A rather than C, or the converse, in the pair (A,C). Only the choice of B, in the triple (A,B,C), does not elicit such a lack of rationality.[15] Then, if (5,5) is deemed to be more just than both (4,6) and (6,4), by continuity the same holds if the utility levels of 5 are reduced by the same sufficiently limited amount, down to a certain level. Now, $W(5,5) > W(4,6) = W(6,4)$ for any strictly concave, symmetrical (increasing) function W.[16]

If the individual's ex ante evaluations Eu_i are the end-values of a conception of justice, then prospect F is to be chosen in the triple (E,F,G) for the same reasons as those presented above for the choice of B in the triple (A,B,C). This choice maximises $W(Eu_1, Eu_2)$ for any strictly concave, symmetrically (increasing) function W.

If the end-values are the final welfares of the individuals, the prospects (E,F,G) provide each individual with 0 with probability 1/2, and with (14,16,18) and (18,16,14), respectively, with probability 1/2. Then, the same as above certainly leads to the choice of F in this triple. The maximisation of $EW(u_1,u_2)$ leads to this result for any strictly concave, symmetrical (increasing) function W.

Furthermore, one can check that $EW(u_1, u_2)$ takes a higher value for any of the certain prospects A, B and C than for any of the risky prospects E, F

15 Note that the recourse to a lottery for the choice between A and C, or among A, B and C, would elicit a similar question for the choice of the probabilities and, for instance, for the justification of using equal probabilities (furthermore, to rely on an irrelevant process of chance is certainly second rate rationality). Note also that, as it was pointed out, the reasons for equality are always prima facie ; for instance, the impossibility to choose between (4,6) and (6,4) may not be a good reason for preferring the equal (3,3), if this was the alternative, since this latter solution is dominated by unanimity by any of the former (priority to unanimity or to Pareto efficiency would be violated) – then, the choice between (4,6) and (6,4) by an equiprobable lottery would be appropriate, the equality of probabilities being justified by a reasoning akin to the one used above.

16 Here, as in the following, in parentheses are properties of the function W which are not necessary for the specific result stated.

and G for a class of such functions W which includes again, for example, $\sqrt{u_1} + \sqrt{u_2}$, $u_1 u_2$, $\text{Log } u_1 + \text{Log } u_2$ and $\text{Min}\{u_1,u_2\}$. However, the individuals evaluating by Eu_1 and Eu_2, respectively, both prefer any of the risky prospects E, F or G to any of the certain prospects A, B or C. Note, finally, that alternative B maximises $EW(u_1,u_2)$ over the whole set of prospects for these particular functions W.

Finally, consider alternatives D, F and H. In all cases (and in all eventualities for the risky prospect F), ex post one individual has 0 and the other has 16. Since, from the objective point of view, the individuals are not relevantly discernible, these cases amount to the same. Any symmetrical function W gives to $EW(u_1,u_2)$ the same value $W(16,0) = W(0,16)$ in the three alternatives. If, however, the ex ante view were relevant, the pairs (Eu_1,Eu_2) would respectively be (16,0), (8,8) and (0,16) in the three alternatives, and reasoning similar to that presented above leads to the choice of the intermediary alternative F. This preference was for instance expressed by Diamond (1967). This alternative also gives the highest value of $W(Eu_1,Eu_2)$ for any strictly concave, symmetrically (increasing) function W. However, the ethical relevance of the Eu_i meets the difficulties which have been discussed in the preceding section.

IV. Original Positions, Fundamental Insurance, Partial Welfarism

1. The Original Position

All the foregoing concerns Harsanyi's paper of 1955. His contribution of 1953 is a completely different theory as regards the logical reasons for utilitarianism. However, from the point of view of the social, economic and ethical meaning, which we consider here as the important aspect of these theories, we will see that the preceding discussion enables one to see that the theory of 1953 is in fact a particular case of the model of 1955, with a particular choice among the two possible ethical alternatives, and that this provides a basis for an evaluation. We will also point out that, between the two opposed theories of the Original Position, Harsanyi's and Rawls', rationality (non-arbitrariness) favours Harsanyi's, but all such theories are objectionable, yet they can lead to theories of "partially original positions", or "fundamental insurance" (Kolm 1985), which, along with their dual "partial welfarism", solve an important problem in the formulation of social policies.

We consider the same individuals' utilities and evaluation of risks as above. Let x denote the state of society to be chosen. This is the argument of the individuals' utility functions: $u_i = u_i(x)$. Let us also make explicit the fundamental utility in writing $u_i(x) = u(y_i,x)$, where y_i is the set of characteristics of individual i that determines his preferences and the function $u(\, , \,)$ is the fundamental utility function.[17]

Harsanyi (1953) now assumes that the individuals face only one uncertainty, albeit a major one: they do not know which of the n individuals they are, or, as the stories of the Original Position go, they have not yet been allocated their « selves » and they do not know which of the n actual individuals they will become. They even have an equal probability to become any of the n individuals, which I propose to justify by complete ignorance about this event plus the Laplace (Bayes, Condorcet) basic principle of the definition of probabilities (this ignorance may result from complete ignorance about which of the $n!$ possible assignments of the "selves" to the individuals will prevail). The "selves" are here relevantly and sufficiently described by the set of characteristics y_i. Hence, the individuals in the original position are identical and face the same uncertain utility $u(y,x)$ for each x where y is a stochastic variable which can take any of the n values y_i with the probability $1/n$. Each, therefore, evaluates the situation by $E_y u(y,x) = (1/n) \Sigma u(y_i,x) = (1/n) \Sigma u_i(x)$, and hence, since the number n is given, by $\Sigma u_i(x)$.

This model is a particular case of the one discussed in the previous sections: the risky event is the "allocation of the selves", ex ante is the original position, ex post is real life, and the choice of the risky prospect is described by the choice of the instrumental variable x. Let us therefore apply the results of the previous sections to this case.

With full welfarism, the end-values of justice are $u_i(x)$, and a social ethical evaluation is $W[\{u_i(x)\}]$ where W is a function which is increasing because of the priority of unanimity (a Pareto principle), symmetrical because the levels u_i encompass all the items that relevantly distinguish the individuals, and strictly concave in order to express the prima facie reason for equality given the symmetry (see Section III.1).

---

17 A discussion of the meaning of the function u, and of its relation to the society of individuals considered and to "human nature", can be found in Kolm (1966a, 1971).

If the individual's ex ante evaluations are the relevant end-values, this social ethical evaluation function becomes $W(\{e_i\})$ with $e_i = (1/n)\ \Sigma u_j$ for each i, which classifies the x as Σu_j does since the function W is increasing.

Therefore, the social ethical maximand is either $W(\{u_i\})$, in the former case, or Σu_i, in the latter case. From the discussion of the previous sections, the former case is the correct one if the individuals are not *accountable* for the assignment of their preferences, and the latter case is the correct one if they are (preferences are the only relevant part of the "selves" here). The latter case is a logically meaningful utilitarianism (since the u_i can be added because they are co-cardinal). The result is that utilitarianism is the welfarist social ethics which is not concerned with the utility functions of the specific individuals. This seems paradoxical in the light of the classical discussions of utilitarianism. We will indeed emphasise in the next paragraphs that this case is that of the social ethics which are the classical opponents of utilitarianism, which deepens the paradox. Yet, we will come to question the theories of the Original Position, while finding importance and interest in more partial and modest devices of this family.

The view that the individuals are *accountable* for their own preferences and tastes for questions of distributive justice is by very far much more common than the opposite position. This is for instance the view of all social ethics that advocate liberties of any kind for their intrinsic social ethical value, or the ideal equality of any items other than welfares, more generally of those that take as end-values various possible freedoms, powers, rights, opportunities, consumption levels, incomes, resources, etc., and hence of those that value lower inequalities in incomes, wealth, rights, liberties, opportunities, powers, various consumption goods or resources, etc. This includes, for instance, the defences of the Rights of Man, or of the free market in the name of freedom of exchange and enterprise (this is the historically most important social ethics of modernity, including Locke's view, that which was called "political economy", the positions of contemporary scholars such as Hayek, Friedman or Nozick, and finally the theory of complete full-process liberalism with a public sector implementing "liberal social contracts" – see Kolm 1985, 1987a and b, 1991c, 1995d). This also includes the views of the "libertarians", of the school of Public Choice and of Gauthier (1986), which differ from the former ones by an absence of a priori rights. But this also includes the rather opposite views of "egalitarians" whose ideal equalities are not those of welfares or of process-freedoms but, for example, of incomes (a widespread view, implied by the analyses of income inequalities and notably the elaborate ethically-based analyses initiated with Kolm

1966a), of consumption goods (also a widespread view for specific goods, advocated for all goods by Tobin, 1970, and implicit in the analyses of multidimensional inequalities initiated in Kolm 1977), of resources (again a widespread view for various types of resources, extended systematically to all resources but consumptive capacities or needs by Dworkin, 1981), of Rawls' "primary goods" (1971), or of items in Weber or Walzer's (1982) "spheres of justice", etc.

This constitutes an extremely large and diverse set of non-welfarist social ethics, often strongly opposed among themselves on other grounds, and which relegate welfarism to a secondary, minority and marginal position. However, the reasons for the exclusion of individuals' tastes or preferences from the direct concern of active ethical policy are often not stated explicitly. Note first that this reason is not a priori responsibility, although this term is sometimes mistakenly used in this context for accountability (responsibility implies accountability but the converse is not true, and responsibility implies being caused by the agent's will by acting or by abstaining from action – by "commission or omission"), and although responsibility has a couple of roles to play here, as we will see. The central reason is that an individual's preferences or tastes are seen as belonging to his "private sphere", and even as constituting it in a number of views. As a consequence, for instance, my tastes are seen as unsuitable to provide a basis for a reason why you or I should receive more or less income, goods or liberties. A rather elaborate defence of this kind of view is notably provided by Dworkin (1981). On the other hand, individual preferences can also be seen just as the description of free choice, and an individual is responsible for his free choice. This would describe the view of most liberty-based conceptions, and also that of Rawls (1971). This conception, however, does not explain why the intensity of preferences, for instance the capacities to enjoy or to endure, are irrelevant for active justice. It thus probably needs to resort to the former reason (the "private sphere" view) to answer this question. The idea that individuals can more or less wilfully control or influence their own preferences, tastes or consumptive capacities, and hence that they can be held responsible – and hence accountable – for them to this extent, is not very important in this specific context (although it is for other philosophies and ethics, such as Sartre's existentialism with its over-extensive conception of responsibility).

Individuals' accountability for their own preferences, however, provides *the reason for choosing* $E_y u(y,x)$ as the ethical maximand, but not, it seems, a reason to restrict the values of the random variable y to the actual y_i 's (with probability $1/n$ for each). The distribution of y should probably extend to all "possible" values. However, which values (that is, which individual preferences or utility functions) are a priori possible or plausible is not something given. Certain are a priori very unlikely. Thus, there should be something like an a priori distribution of individual preferences. Yet, that is not a priori given. Indeed, the only really sure thing is that the actual preferences are possible. But this does not seem to be a sufficient reason to restrict the distribution to them.

One should, however, consider the specific reasons which are provided for resorting to theories of the Original Position. The basic intent is to guarantee some sort of impartiality among the actual individuals. Rawls (1971), who is more explicit – and coins the expression – says that the individuals' choices "in the original position" should be considered since, there, the individuals first do not tend to favour their later actual embodiment since they do not know it, and second are not endowed with different bargaining powers as the actual individuals are.[18] The reference to the bargaining power is redundant since the individuals in the original position propose the same thing since they have identical objectives and information. Furthermore, Rawls, in opposition to Harsanyi, considers that the individuals in the original position envision that they could have any psychologically possible "life plans" (which we describe here by the preferences that lead to their choice), rather than only those of the actual individuals. However, since the aim is to grasp impartiality *among the actual individuals,* Rawls' hypothetical uncertainty is in a sense more than is needed for this objective, and hence rationality in the normal sense of "for a reason", or non-arbitrariness, applied to the choice of this conceptual tool (the hypothetical uncertainty) favours Harsanyi's choice to restrict "original" uncertainty to the actual preferences (the "thin veil of ignorance" as opposed to Rawls' "thick" veil, in the classical vocabulary of the theory). Then, complete uncertainty among these known preferences leads to equal probabilities from the very basic axiom of the definition of a probability (Bayes, Condorcet, Laplace). If we now add the possible reasons for a choice in uncertainty by the highest expected utility, we obtain

18 RAWLS sees furthermore a third interest in his theory of the Original Position: its use as a heuristic device in a dialectical discovery of the specifics of justice, for testing "ethical intuitions" or for obtaining them. In his view, the original position is not a priori given, as regards the crucial parameter which is the individuals' information: it suffices that there exists a "veil of ignorance" (a structure of individuals' information in the original position) which leads to the stated principles of justice. Hence this theory is not a strictly deductive one.

Harsanyi's theory. Note, however, that from the foregoing its justification rests on *non-welfarism* rather than on welfarism.

However, the choice of a x that maximises $\Sigma u_i(x)$, by the "individuals in the original position", may well lead to " very" low $u_i(x)$ for certain i. This happens when this x makes other $u_j(x)$ sufficiently high in sufficiently large numbers. This seems prima facie unfair or unjust toward an actual individual with a very low welfare. Specifically, the choice of the policy instruments x attributes goods to actual individual j rather than to actual individual i because individual j's capacity to enjoy them is higher, with the possible final result of a u_j "much" higher than u_i. This criticism rests on the use of individuals' welfares and consumptive capacities by utilitarianism, and hence it is in a sense a criticism of welfarism after all, yet only of this particular extreme aggregative and anti-egalitarian form of welfarism,[19] as opposed to rational and hence ideally egalitarian welfarism. Yet, if the actual individual with a particularly low welfare level is *responsible* for the choice of the individuals in the original position, he has to accept this outcome and cannot complain. The individuals in the original position are all identical by definition and they all make the same first best choice. If one of them *is* actually the actual individual considered, then this individual is actually responsible for the choice he "made", and he just lacked luck in the drawing of the lottery he has himself chosen and set up in choosing x while knowing perfectly all the odds. However, this lottery by definition allocates the very characteristics that distinguish the individuals from one another in the question considered. For a given actual individual, one can thus hardly consider that an "individual in the original position" is "himself", and in particular that he is himself rather than any other actual individual, and thus that he has defended his interests rather than those of any of his competitors in the overall allocation. The "individuals in the original position" do not even have a particular and identifiable "self" distinct from that of others for the relevant items (the preferences). One can thus hardly maintain that the chain of the self, which would permit the assignment of responsibility, has been maintained. Then, there is no reason to hold that a miserable actual individual is morally bound by the putative choice of "individuals in the original position".

19 The equality of weights in the sum does not consitute an egalitarianism if the end-values are individuals' welfares (it could be called a "marginal egalitarianism" in the sense that the highest sum leads to equal marginal utilities for a divisible and transferable private good, but the relevant individual welfares are global rather than marginal).

Of course, the original position is imaginary and counterfactual, and therefore a moral conclusion based on its assumption may not be binding at any rate. However, the "veil of ignorance" is a device which guarantees "impartiality" or the "objective standpoint", and any judgement or reasoning concerning justice implies that one takes such a point of view one way or the other. The usual method consists either in disregarding one's own particular self-centred interest or preferences ("self-centred" is not "selfish", it may imply specific altruism, such as toward one's family), or in choosing a judge or arbitrator who is not personally concerned by the issue. Assuming people who "do not know who they are" (*existential ignorance*) and, still more, who "do not know who they will be" (the Original Position), seems weirder than other philosophers' elaborations on the "impartial spectator" (A. Smith), the "impartial observer" (e.g., J. S. Mill) or the "objective standpoint" (e.g. Nagel 1986, 1991). The most serious problem, however, arises with the next step which consists of defining the optimum by the self-interested choice in this uncertainty, in assuming that the chooser is going to become any of the actual individuals (or still others). As we have explained, this can yield, for the actual individuals, results which may seem unfair and cannot be justified by responsibility. This device differs much from the normal mind-process of the determination of the just solution for the actual individuals, which leads, as we have seen, to prima facie equalities and to the adjustments among various such ideals if required. The reduction of the social optimum to a single person's interest "does not take seriously the division of society into individuals", as Rawls says of utilitarianism.[20] From the classical iconography of Justice, the Original Position keeps the blindfolding but forgets the balance.

Finally, the theory of the Original Position, suggested by Vickrey (1945, see also 1960, 1961), and proposed fully by Harsanyi (1953, see also 1977a, 1977b, 1992) and more elaborately, with opposite conclusions, by Rawls (1971) does not provide a convincingly rational ethical method.[21] This does not imply, however, that it is uninteresting, since we will see that neighbouring theories, yet more discerning and subtle ones, provide the solution of an important problem in the theory of justice: the definition of the just compensation for certain relative handicaps whereas the individuals remain accountable for the rest of their personal characteristics. These theories are those of

20 The questions raised by RAWLS' own theory are not our topic here (see KOLM 1985, Part 5, and 1995d, Chapter 8).

21 The same applies, for the same reasons, to the theory proposed by VARIAN (1980).

the "partially original position" and of "fundamental insurance" (Kolm, 1985). Before we consider this topic, let us recall that we have emphasised the duality of aspect of the theory of the Original Position. On the one hand, it is a theory of a putative collective unanimous agreement (a Social Contract); on the other hand, it purports to encompass the notion that the individuals are accountable for their own preferences (this is both Rawls' view and is implied by Vickrey and Harsanyi taking, as ethical end-values, individuals' evaluation ex ante the allocation of preferences). These dual aspects coincide for the theory of the Original Position, yet we will see that they lead to two different solutions for the "intermediary cases" we consider now.

2. The Partially Original Position and Fundamental Insurance Versus Partial Welfarism; Equity and Adequacy

We seek the solution of two problems. One is the practical problem of defining compensations for certain handicaps or groups of handicaps while individuals are deemed to be accountable for their other characteristics, for example their tastes or preferences. The second question is the theoretical problem of the theory of the Original Position which cannot be justified by responsibility because of the lack of maintenance of identifiable selves from the original position to the actual situation. Indeed, we have noted that even if the objective standpoint, which is necessary in all theories of justice, is defined by the particular device of an original position, then the loss of the identity of the self prevents the concept of responsibility justifying the solution. This prevents this theory from being an instance of a classical Social Contract.[22] However, a number of social policies aim to compensate for handicaps of various kinds, without putting into question the identity of the individuals, and without compensating for all interindividual differences. For instance, classical social policies intend to compensate for a number of effects of family environment and in particular for their consequences on education, information or motivation, or for poor health in the sense of propensity to sickness, without compensating for all tastes and capacities to enjoy.

We then dichotomise the set y of characteristics of an individual into two sets, $y = (s,t)$, where t denotes the set of characteristics for which compensa-

22 A general theory of Social Contracts is provided in KOLM (1985), Chapter 23.

tion is considered, and s represents the rest (which can for instance include, among others, the characteristics that are seen as defining the core "self" for the question and situation considered).[23] Let s_i and t_i denote the values of s and t for individual i. Let c_i denote the policy tools relative to individual i, such as various possible subsidies, taxes or specific compensatory measures. Since rationality implies equal treatment of equals (see Section II.3) and y constitutes by assumption a sufficient set of characteristics, one has $c_i = c(y_i) = c(s_i,t_i)$. The fundamental utility is now $u[s,t,c(s,t)]$. The problem consists of the determination of the *function $c(s,t)$ which provides a compensation for the inter-individual differences in t, while leaving each individual accountable for his own s.* This can be done according to two ethics, one based on liberty (a process-liberal, or "liberist", solution), and the other based on welfare.

The former solution is the theory of the **fundamental insurance** (see Kolm, 1985; a neighbouring concept is suggested by Dworkin, 1981).[24] One considers the hypothetical situation where the s_i are allocated while the t_i are not "yet" and are uncertain, and the individuals set up a mutual insurance by a collective voluntary agreement among themselves, as an insurance for the cases where they receive unfavourable t_i 's. Fundamental insurance is a particular case of a "liberal social contract" (Kolm, 1985, 1987a and b), where the impediment to free exchange is that it should have taken place before the considered adult individuals existed. The collective choice is that of the function $c(s,t)$. The ex ante expected utility of individual i which corresponds to the situation is $E_{t_i}\, u[s_i,t_i,c(s_i,t_i)]$. The same justification as that provided in Section IV.1 for Harsanyi's uncertainty of the y_i in the original position leads one to consider that each individual can receive any of the n t_i with the same probability $1/n$. Individual i's expected utility is then $(1/n)\Sigma_j u[s_i,t_j,c(s_i,t_j)] = u'_i$. The full determination of the function $c(s,t)$ then requires a theory of bar-

23 Such a t represents directly a consumptive capacity or handicap, but various models can make it also represent productive capacities (which, for instance, influences earned income which influences consumption bought with it).

24 DWORKIN does not define precisely his concept. More basically, this kind of concept is in contradiction with DWORKIN's basic intent. Indeed DWORKIN's conception of justice is a resourcism, with an ideal of equality of resources, and the proposal is suggested as implementing this ideal for the resource or handicap t. Now, this device is on the contrary a "liberalism" or process-liberalism based on a free exchange (although an hypothetical and putative one). DWORKIN's ideal is in fact implemented by our other proposal, "partial welfarism", which also answers the reproaches that ROEMER (1986) addresses to DWORKIN.

gaining for which more information on relative bargaining powers is needed. The particular case where $y = t$ and there are no characteristics s is the theory of the Original Position (in Harsanyi's form); then all the u_i^t are the same and there is no actual bargaining, and utilitarianism is the unanimous desire. Note that the outcomes of bargaining situations, and of arbitrations to which they often resort, commonly add ethical concepts (to settle for a "fair deal" may be no less important than to obtain a "good deal"). Then, a natural solution is the equality of the u_i^t , at least if it can be Pareto-efficient, or, if this prima facie equality meets a situation of asymmetrical trade-offs, the maximisation of a function $W(\{u_i^t\})$ which is increasing, symmetrical and concave (for the prima facie equality and the priority of the unanimity-Pareto criterion).

However, welfarism expressing that the individuals are accountable for their own characteristics s and only for these and applied in a theory of the Original Position type where the individuals do not know their own characteristics (as it was done for the full original position earlier), leads to a different solution which is also quite natural, **partial welfarism**. This method consists of considering that the characteristics s_i are uncertain and, if this is described by a randomisation, in taking $E_{s_i}u[s_i,t_i,c(s_i,t_i)]$ as the relevant social ethical welfare index for individual i. The same reason that was used for y_i in the original position (in order to justify Harsanyi's theory), and for t_i above, leads to the consideration that each stochastic $\tilde{s}_i$ can take as a value any of the n actual s_j with the same probability $1/n$. Hence, the preceding expression becomes $u_i^s = (1/n)\Sigma_j u[s_j,t_i,c(s_j,t_i)]$. This means that the relevance of the s_j is removed, for the justice-motivated policy which chooses the function $c(s,t)$, by averaging each individual's utility over the values that it would take if his s were each of the individuals' s_j. Then, the ideal equality of rational justice is that of the u_i^s for all i, with an ethical evaluation function $W(\{u_i^s\})$ with an increasing, symmetrical and concave function W if one adds a priority to Pareto-efficiency and the possibility of relevant non-symmetrical trade-offs.

In the particular case where $y = s$ and there are no characteristics t, all the arguments of the function W are the same and are the utilitarian sum, and the policy amounts to the maximisation of this sum, that is, this is utilitarianism (note that this case is obtained with $y = t$ for the fundamental insurance, that is, the full Original Position case). The particular case where $y = t$ and there is no characteristics s is just the fully welfarist position where the policy excludes no characteristics from compensability.

If W were a utilitarian sum (or an affine function), it would amount to $\Sigma u_i^s = \Sigma u_i^t$. If the priority to the unanimity-Pareto criterion were the only relevant obstacle to the ideal equality of the arguments of W, the maximand would be $\text{Min}_i u_i^s$.

Denoting $u_{ij} = u[s_i, t_j, c(s_i, t_j)]$, we have $u_i^t = (1/n)\Sigma_j u_{ij}$ and $u_j^s = (1/n)\Sigma_i u_{ij}$ (and hence $\Sigma u_i^t = \Sigma u_i^s$).
When the prima facie equality is not possible or not the best for whatever reason, the maximisation of a $W(\{u_i^s\})$ first requires the specific choice of such a function W. One way of avoiding this choice consists of resorting to the classical criterion of "*equity*",[25] if it permits the satisfaction of the other requirements, that is, to choose a system of compensations $c(s,t)$ such that $u_{ii} \geqslant u_{ij}$ for all i,j. If, for example, s is the parameter of tastes or preferences, and t is a parameter of "handicaps" of any (other) nature, "equity" means that, *with the compensation rule adopted*, each individual, characterised and "defined" by these preferences, prefers his overall situation to that of any other or is indifferent between them. This defines an "equitable" or fair compensation rule. This criterion implies $u_{ii} \geqslant u_i^t$, that is, an equitable compensation rule weakly unanimously dominates its evaluation in the corresponding situation of fundamental insurance. This also implies $\Sigma u_{ii} \geqslant \Sigma u_i^t = \Sigma u_i^s$ and hence it is not possible that $u_i^s \geqslant u_{ii}$ for all i and $u_i^s > u_{ii}$ for at least one i: the average u_i^s cannot Pareto-dominate the actual u_{ii}.

An alternative criterion to be used for the same purpose is "*adequacy*", that is, the compensation rule is such that its application entails that *each "handicap" is allocated to the individual whom it hurts less* (or one of these individuals). Formally, this is: $u_{ii} \geqslant u_{ji}$, for all i,j (see Kolm 1971, 1991a). These conditions define an "adequate" compensation rule. This criterion is in a dual relation with equity; in the matrix of the u_{ij}, the first diagonal dominates in rows in one case and in columns in the other. Adequacy implies $u_{ii} \geqslant u_i^s$ for all i: an adequate compensation rule weakly unanimously dominates the corresponding individual averages. This also implies $\Sigma u_{ii} \geqslant \Sigma u_i^t$, that is, the fundamental insurance evaluations of an adequate compensation rule cannot Pareto-dominate the actual evaluations. The relation between equity and adequacy concerning existence is the following: if a compensa-

25 Noted by TINBERGEN (1946) and FOLEY (1967), and the topic of elaborate analyses initiated in KOLM (1971).

tion rule satisfies one of the properties but not the other, no other re-assignment between the s_i and the t_i satisfies this other property (with a finite number of individuals; from Kolm 1971, see also 1991a).

V. Conclusions

The welfare state is a policy of justice toward the major risks of life. The combination of risk and justice raises logical problems that determine, notably, the political implementability and sustainability of this system. In particular, a policy that implements a welfarist justice, wants to help the most unfortunate, and more or less favours lower resulting inequalities, is necessarily defeated ex ante by the unanimity of votes by certain alternative proposals. Therefore, such a system tends to be unimplementable and unsustainable in a political system of competitive electoral democracy. Hence, democracy tends to eliminate ex post welfarist justice (care for the unfortunate and lower inequalities) from the principles that rule public institutions and notably social insurances. There remains, of course, the simple insurance that can be organised by institutions of various statuses, and political decisions taken ex post. The latter applies in particular to the effects of "bygone hazards" that allocated items "before" the individuals can take insurance, such as inequalities in natural endowments or in the effects of education and motivation received in the family. The corresponding "fundamental insurance" (or "partial original position") constitutes one possible principle of justice of social policies, based on an extended "liberal social contract". This differs from the corresponding "resourcism" of "partial welfarism" which equalises by compensation the benefits from the corresponding human resources. We thus provided the precise determinations of social policies when compensation is deemed to be relevant for certain characteristics (such as handicaps, possibly of social origin) while it is not for others (such as tastes).

References

ATKINSON, A. B. and F. BOURGUIGNON: "The Comparison of Multi-Dimensioned Economic Status", *Review of Economic Studies*, 49 (1982), pp. 183-201.

BROOME, J.: *Weighting Goods*, Oxford and Cambridge, Mass. (Basil Blackwell) 1991.

DALTON, H.: "The Measurement of the Inequality of Incomes", *Economic Journal*, 30 (1920), pp. 348-361.

DIAMOND, P.: "Cardinal Welfare, Individualistic Ethics, and Interpersonal Comparison of Utility: Comment", *Journal of Political Economy*, 75, no. 5 (October 1967), pp. 765-66.

DOMOTOR, Z.: "Ordered Sum and Tensor Product of Linear Utility Structures", *Theory and Decision*, 11 (1979), pp. 375-99.

DWORKIN, R.: "What is Equality ? Part I: Equality of Welfare; Part II: Equality of Resources", *Philosophy and Public Affairs*, 10 (1981), pp. 185-246 and 283-345.

EICHORN, W. (Ed.): *Models and Measurement of Welfare and Inequality*, Heidelberg (Springer-Verlag) 1994.

FEIWEL, G. R. (Ed.): *Arrow and the Ascent of Modern Economic Theory*, London (MacMillan) 1987.

FISHBURN, P. C.: "On Harsanyi's Utilitarian Cardinal Welfare Theorem", *Theory and Decision*, 17 (1984), pp. 21-8.

HAMMOND, P. J.: "Utilitarianism, Uncertainty and Information", in SEN and WILLIAMS (Eds.): *Utilitarianism and Beyond*, Cambridge (Cambridge University Press) 1982.

HARSANYI, J. C.: "Cardinal Utility in Welfare Economics and in the Theory of Risk-taking", *Journal of Political Economy*, 61 (1953), pp. 434-5.

HARSANYI, J. C.: "Cardinal Welfare, Individualistic Ethic, and Interpersonal Comparison of Utility", *Journal of Political Economy*, 63 (1955), pp. 309-21.

HARSANYI, J. C. (1975a): "Non-linear Social Welfare Functions", *Theory and Decision*, 6 (1975), pp. 311-332.

HARSANYI, J. C. (1975b): "Can the Maximin Principle Serve as a Basis for Morality? A Critique of John Rawls' Theory", *American Political Science Review*, 69 (1975), pp. 594-606.

HARSANYI, J. C.: *Essays in Ethics, Social Behaviour and Scientific Explanation*, Dordrecht (Reidel) 1976.

HARSANYI, J. C. (1977a): *Rational Behaviour and Bargaining Equilibrium in Games and Social Situations*, Cambridge (Cambridge University Press) 1977.

HARSANYI, J. C. (1977b): "Morality and the Theory of Rational Behaviour", *Social Research*, 44 (1977), pp. 623-656.

HARSANYI, J. C.: "Bayesian Decision Theory and Utilitarian Ethics", *American Economic Review*, Papers and Proceedings, 68 (1978), pp. 223-228.

HARSANYI, J. C.: "Von Neumann-Morgenstern Uilities, Risk Taking and Welfare", in G.R. FEIWEL (Ed.) 1987.

HARSANYI, J. C.: "Game and Decision Theoretic Models in: Ethics", in R. AUMAN and S. HART (Eds.), *Handbook of Game Theory with Economic Applications,* Volume 1, 669-707, Amsterdam (North-Holland) 1992.

HAYEK, F. A. (1976a): *The Mirage of Social Justice; Law, Legislation and Liberty,* London (Routledge and Kegan Paul) 1976.

HAYEK, F. A. (1976b): *Law, Legislation and Liberty,* Vol. 2, Chicago (The University of Chicago Press) 1976.

HICKS, J.: *Essays in World Economy,* Oxford (Basil Blackwell) 1959, preface, reprinted as «A Manifesto» in *Wealth and Welfare,* Oxford (Basil Blackwell) 1981, pp. 135-141.

KOLM, S.-CH. (1966a): "The Optimal Production of Social Justice"; International Economic Association Conference on Public Economics, Biarritz, 1966 (proceedings ed. by H. Guitton and J. Margolis, *Economie Publique*, Paris: (CNRS), 1968, pp. 109-177, and *Public Economics*, London (MacMillan) 1969, pp. 145-200).

— (1966b): *Les choix financiers et monétaires (théorie et technique modernes)*, Paris (Dunod) 1966.

— *Justice et Equité,* Paris: CEPREMAP, 1971; reprinted Paris: CNRS, 1972.

— (1973a): "Super-équité", *Kyklos*, vol. XXVI, fasc. 4 (1973), pp. 841-843.

— (1973b): "More Equal Distribution of Bundles of Commodities", CEPREMAP, 1973.

— "Sur les conséquences économiques des principes de justice et de justice pratique", *Revue d'Economie Politique*, 1 (janvier-février 1974), pp. 80-107.

— "Multidimensional egalitarianism", *Quarterly Journal of Economics* 91 (1977), pp. 1-13.

— *Le Contrat Social Libéral (theorie et pratique du libéralisme)*, Paris (Presses Universitaires de France) 1985.

— (1987a): "The Freedom and Consensus Normative Theory of the State: the Liberal Social Contract", in: P. KOSLOWSKI, (Ed.): *Individual Liberty and Democratic Decision-Making (the Ethics, Economics and Politics of Democracy)*, Tübingen (J.C.B. Mohr [Paul Siebeck]) 1987, pp. 97-127.

— (1987b): "Public Economics", in *New Palgrave Dictionary in Economics,* J. Eatwell et al. (Eds.), London (MacMillan) 1987, pp. 1047-55.

— *The General Theory of Justice*, Paris: (CERAS), 1990.

— (1991a): "The Normative Economics of Unanimity and Equality: Equity, Adequacy and Fundamental Dominance", in: K.J. ARROW (Ed.): *Markets and Welfare.* London (MacMillan, for the International Economic Association) 1991, pp. 243-86.

— (1991b): "Super-Equity", CERAS, no. 98, German Bernacer Lecture, University of Alicante (1991b).

— (1991c): "Full Process Liberalism", IMF working paper and CGPC 1991.

KOLM, S.-CH.: "What Sense Social Choice ?" CGPC 1992.

— (1993a): "Distributive Justice", in R. GOODIN and P. PETTIT (Eds.), *A companion to Political Philosophy*, Oxford (Blackwell) 1993.

— (1993b): "The Impossibility of Utilitarianism", in: P. KOSLOWSKI and Y. SHIONOYA (Eds.): *The Good and the Economical*. Berlin, Heidelberg, New-York (Springer) 1993.

— (1993c): "Efficient Economic Justice", CGPC 1993c.

— (1993d): "Equal Liberty", CGPC 1993d.

— (1994a): "L'égalité de la liberté", *Recherches Economiques de Louvain*, vol. 1 (1994), pp. 81-86.

— (1994b): "Rational Normative Economics against Social Choice and Social Welfare", *European Economic Review* (1994), pp. 721-730.

— (1994c): "The Meaning of Fundamental Preferences", *Social Choice and Welfare*, 11 (July 1994), pp. 193-198.

— (1995a): "Rationalities in Social Choice" in: D. ANDLER and P. BANERJEE, (Eds.): *Facets of Rationality*, Delhi (Sage) 1995.

— (1995b): "Rational Just Social Choice", in K. ARROW, A. SEN and K. SUZUMURA, *Social Choice Re-examined*, London (MacMillan) 1995.

— (1995c): "Economic Justice: the Central Problem", *European Economic Review* (July 1995), pp. 661-673.

— (1995d): *Modern Theories of Justice*, Cambridge, Mass. (The MIT Press) 1995d.

— "The Theory of Justice", *Social Choice and Welfare*, 1996.

MONGIN, P.: "Harsanyi's Aggregation Theorem: Multi-Profile Version and Unsettled Questions", *Social Choice and Welfare*, 11, 4 (1994), pp. 331-355.

NAGEL, T.: *The View for Nowhere*, Oxford (Clarendon Press) 1986.

NAGEL, T.: *Equality and Partiality*, New York, Oxford (Oxford University Press) 1991.

RAWLS, J.: *A Theory of Justice*, Cambridge, Mass. (Harvard University Press) 1971.

ROEMER, J.: "Equality of Resources Implies Equality of Welfare", *Quarterly Journal of Economics* (1986), pp. 751-784.

ROSS, D.: *The Right and the Good*, 1930.

TINBERGEN, J.: "Welfare Economics and Income Distribution", *American Economic Review*, 47 (1957), pp. 490-503.

TOBIN, J.: "On Limiting the Domain of Inequality", *Journal of Law and Economics*, 13 (1970), pp. 363-78.

VARIAN, H.: "Redistributive Taxation as Social Insurance", *Journal of Public Economics*, 14 (1) (August 1980), pp. 49-68.

VICKREY, W.: "Measuring Marginal Utility by Reactions to Risk", *Econometrica*, 13 (1945), pp. 319-333.

VICKREY, W.: "Utility, Strategy and Social Decision Rules", *Quarterly Journal of Economics*, 74 (1960), pp. 507-535.

VICKREY, W.: "Risk, Utility and Social Policy", *Social Research*, 28 (1961), pp. 205-217.

VON NEUMANN, J. and MORGENSTERN, O.: *Theory of Games and Economic Behaviour*, Princeton, N.J. (Princeton University Press) 1944.

WALRAS, L.: *Etudes d'Economie Sociale*, Lausanne (F. Rouge) and Paris (F. Pichon) 1898; new edition 1936.

WALZER, M.: *Spheres of Justice*, Oxford (Blackwell) 1983.

WEYMARK, J.: "Harsanyi's Social Aggregation Theorem and the Weak Pareto Principle", *Social Choice and Welfare*, 10 (1993), pp. 209-221.

WEYMARK, J.: "Harsanyi's Social Aggregation Theorem with Alternative Pareto Principles", in W. EICHHORN, (Ed.): 1994.

Chapter 16

Sweden: Towards a 21st Century Post-Modern People's Home?

SVEN E. OLSSON HORT

«What was accomplished in this small country in this period was one of the most instructive and civilising experiences. . . not the Keynesian but the Swedish revolution.»

J K Galbraith: *A Journey Through Economic Time – A Firsthand View*, Houghton Mifflin, Boston, 1994

I. Introduction

Already in the mid 1930s Sweden was presented, in particular to North Americans but also in other parts of the Western world, as a "middle way» between unbridled capitalism and totalitarian socialism. During the depression of the 1930s, to the proponents of a New Deal in the United States, Sweden and the political-administrative solutions adopted at that time in this country, fitted into their image of a better and more just society. In terms of democracy and welfare – thus, in terms of civil, political and social rights – Sweden became an example for other countries. At a time when most advanced countries were threatened by the prospects of authoritarian rule, the ethics of the social policies discussed and partly also adopted in this remote Northern European country received considerable global attention. However, it was not until the 1960s, after the demise of the Beveridge model in its native country, the UK, that the flower of the Far North fully blossomed. This institutional or universal welfare model has later also been dubbed a Social Democratic model of social policy. Here, it is important to emphasise that this moral approach to social policy had broad popular support from most sectors of society.

What can be said about this Linnean wild flower today, as history turns to an end and we are approaching the beginning of a new century? As late as 1990, a decade after the double failure of the Reagan Revolution and the Thatcherite counter-revolution against welfare state developments, Sweden was – despite substantial revisionist academic writings – still upheld as an example of a model welfare state. A year after the fall of the Wall and the end of the second world within sight, there was still a possibility of a «third road» – as the Swedish model was called by its domestic reformers from the early 1980s. However, at the turn to the last decade of the 20th century, there were significant signs of breakdowns in Sweden, and the first half of the 1990s has been a decade of tremendous change, in particular from full employment to a European average level of unemployment as well as the rise of a burdening public deficit.

In this chapter, a short historical sketch is given in order to bring the present problems into focus, and make possible a discussion of the possibility of something as insane as a post-welfare state, even post-modern, people's home?

II. History

In terms of material development Sweden, in the 19th century on and off called the poor-house of Europe, made an industrial take-off in the last quarter of that century. In the decades prior to this upheaval, an agrarian revolution had made the never feudalised independent farm landowners both better off economically, and politically stronger. Despite this increasing power of the farmers, Sweden was in no sense a popular democracy as the franchise was among the most limited in Europe, and at this time many capable non-prosperous individuals left the country to seek their fortune in North America. Hence the old nobility – and its most significant adjacent institutions such as the Military, the Church, etc. – was constantly under pressure, both from the domestic semi-popular forces but also from outside as Norway was a non-integrated part of the Kingdom of Sweden after the Napoleonic wars. This forced union was from the outset contested by a Norway similar to the French 18th century «third estate».

The emergence of the welfare state in Sweden developed through conflict, compromise and collaboration across interest groups and political lines. In the 1880s, the urban liberal welfare intelligentsia in civil society became a strong proponent of state reform, and managed to secure support from the independent farmers. In civil society, the temperance movement as well as the revivalist movement were instrumental in forging a new social ethic. These socio-political collaborations formed the early foundation for the moral philosophy of universality and solidaristic social policy ethics. The first welfare provisions were developed either in the form of flat-rate pension benefits available to all and everybody above the age of 67, or based upon compensation for loss of income during previous periods of gainful employment, a form known as occupational injury insurance. These endeavours were part of the early 20th century Parliamentary and democratic breakthrough which was most consistently backed by the rural Liberal party and the emerging Social Democratic working class movement.

The political regrouping in the early 1930s, in particular the election of the Social Democratic Party government in 1932, and the compromises between farmers, labour and capital formed throughout that decade, not only in politics but also on the labour market, prepared the ground for the agreements in the field of welfare reform that followed from the mid-1940s onwards. The economic upswing of the 1940s and 1950s provided the foundation for the expansion and development of the social responsibility of the state for citizens' welfare. During this era of full employment and economic progress, much of what is known as the Swedish welfare state was structurally developed. The intent was to provide universal benefits not only for all citizens but also for all workers and salaried employees based on those which had been previously available only to white-collar groups through the private sector. The ambition was to extend the notion of solidarity beyond exclusive group interests.

Collaboration between the trade unions, the agrarian movement and political forces formed a favourable alliance upon which to build a system of social security, health services, housing, and elderly care. Support of a domestic agricultural policy was crucial for the success of this system. Through the 1940s universal benefits were expanded and in the 1950s benefits which tied to the labour market were created. Universal child allowances, housing subsidies, and a national health system were created. The universality of the benefits from the welfare system, through income transfers, social security schemes and health benefits, aided in maintaining the popularity and legitimacy of the system as well as reducing the suspicion of welfare fraud. Further the strong relationship between employment and benefits reduced the suspicion of free-ridership and more or less eliminated the possibility of «moral hazard».

Throughout its development, the traditional Swedish welfare state came to be identified by the following characteristics:

1. An active manpower policy keeping unemployment at a low level (compared to international rates);
2. A comprehensive social security network closely related to active labour force participation;
3. A large public service sector in the spheres of health, education, and personal social services;
4. Significant public regulations and subsidies in such areas as agriculture and housing;
5. A system of extensive resource extraction – i.e. taxation – as a basis for financing 1-4 above.

In the administration of these services, the public sector expanded rapidly from the early 1940s through the 1980s. During this time, many women entered the employment arena, and thus became eligible for benefits which were directly linked to employment. Many of these new employment positions involved care-taking roles and often on a part-time basis. However, these roles had now become a legitimate part of the labour market.

In the late 1960s, criticism of the welfare system as being an oppressive and unresponsive social force began to occur. Criticism arose concerning the rigidity of social services legislation and the inability of the administrative agencies to respond to individual needs. Discussions concerning a radical change in social service legislation ensued, particularly around the issue of decentralising services to the local level and the over-professionalisation of the public sector. As is usual in Sweden, a national investigative committee was established to examine these issues which recommended sweeping changes in social welfare legislation. In many cases, changes had already been implemented when the law was finally passed in Parliament.

Amidst the critical examination of the legislative and structural aspects of the welfare bureaucracy came the recession years of the early 1970s which had a political as well as economic affect on Sweden. In 1976, after 44 years of unbroken Social Democratic rule, a coalition of non-socialist parties came into office. During their six years in power, movements to increase the independence and responsibility of local governments continued as well as early discussions of privatisation. Unemployment began to rise, however, and the concern over the increasing public deficit became more pronounced. Social reform through state intervention in the process of distribution in the welfare state strategy became troublesome in conjunction with weak economic growth and mounting public deficits.

Although the centre-right rule was short-lived, many of the trends initiated during that time remained in active debate even when the Social Democrats regained power in 1982. They were also forced to deal with shrinking resources and pressure for fiscal reforms. Public spending and welfare policy had become politically controversial in Sweden. Concern with the state budget deficit and the national debt continued to grow. In response to many of the criticisms of the traditional bureaucratic system, the Social Democrats continued a theme of decentralisation and increasing local autonomy in order to avoid further privatisation. Several legislative developments strengthening local and regional responsibility for welfare led to the current structural division of the different realms of welfare.

From 1982 onwards, legislative changes provided the foundation for a restructuring of welfare from centrally steered bureaucracies to more local control and autonomy. At the same time, the ethical foundation of the new Social Services legislation concretised the values of a «right» to welfare services during times when individuals cannot provide for themselves through other means. The legislation, as a heuristic framework, did not specifically outline the services to be offered, but squarely placed the responsibility on the local authorities to provide for citizens' well-being through the philosophy of welfare «entitlement».

The provision and delivery of direct welfare benefits for citizens, much of what is known as social services, health care and elderly care, came to be shared between 286 municipalities and 25 county councils. The county councils administer health and medical services while the local municipalities are in charge of basic and secondary education, housing development, and personal social services. The national government on the other hand, takes on responsibility for full employment and partly also social security such as pensions and other social insurances (parental, daily sickness, occupational injury, and disability benefits, etc.).

The increasingly larger role that local authorities and regional authorities play in delivering services can be seen as one of the more important transitions that the welfare state has gone through since the 1970s. The re-invention of municipal institutions has provided the bridge between state and civil society, which has undoubtedly had an effect on the negligible growth of the private sector. Demand-driven privatisation has been an issue only in specific areas such as home-help services for the elderly and some forms of care for children and adolescents, such as group homes and day-care, but even these are limited.

III. Problems

As Sweden entered the 1990s, problems with the economy rose to a crisis. The currency devaluation policies of the 1980s – a solution adopted by cabinets of whatever leaning – had little impact on the slow economic growth though for a while employment grew considerably. In the early 1990s, however, unemployment rose beyond all previous levels and pressure to decrease public spending put the welfare state in direct attack. Growing consumer dissatisfaction over freedom of choice in services as well as with control over the types of services offered came to a head in the early 1990s. Although the welfare state had been built on the principles of 'equality' and 'quality', creating one standard of high-quality care for all, this philosophy appeared increasingly out of step with consumers' growing desire for '-choice' and 'influence' over public welfare services. Many consumers felt they had little to no say in the quality and content of the services offered. By the 1990s, demographic changes and technological advances had altered the needs of various client groups, such as an increasing elderly population, and new forms of health care as well as women's increasing participation in the work force, put pressure on the welfare state to respond to many new client demands. Nevertheless, the legitimacy of the core welfare programs remained high and constant.

A political crisis in early 1990 added to the tensions when disagreements between the reigning Social Democratic party and its traditional ally, the labour unions, more or less exploded. By the end of 1990, agreement that change was necessary was a consensus among the political parties. However, all major players involved disagreed as to the course and emphasis that the changes should take. During the 1991 election campaign, the non-socialist parties took the position of significant structural change, increased privatisation, cuts in public expenditure, and increased freedom of choice. The Social Democrats, while also arguing for greater flexibility in the welfare system, held closer to the status quo, although they started the reduction of generous cash benefits already in 1990.

The results of the election in the fall of 1991, when a coalition government of four non-socialist parties replaced the Social Democrats, reflected dismay over the Swedish economy and partly also citizens' growing dissatisfaction with the public service monopoly status quo. The Social Democrats received the lowest proportion of votes since 1928, only 37.6 per cent, which was a significant reduction from the average 42-45 per cent that the party had received during the post-war decades. Instead of a crisis of the welfare state, in the early 1990s it was probably more correct to talk about a crisis of Social Democracy, in a longer perspective maybe even a crisis of democracy or political representation.

As of late 1991 a non-socialist minority coalition cabinet, comprised of the Conservative party, the Liberal party, the Centre party, and the Christian Democrats, ruled the country for three years. However, in order to govern it needed the support of a new right-wing populist party, New Democracy. The necessity of this support caused a lot of internal strains within the government as the Liberal Party was fiercely anti-racist and pro-welfare. For three years, however, this coalition cabinet managed to stay together and run the daily business of national administration. It had to face the difficult task of combating raising unemployment as well as other problems related to the severe economic downturn in the first half of the 1990s. It particular a series of attacks on the currency made bipartisan agreements with the opposition Social Democrats necessary. These «crisis agreements» across party lines resulted in significant reductions in social benefits and they reflect the difficulties which the welfare state of the 1990s faced. Overall, replacement levels in social insurance were lowered from 90 to 80 per cent of previous earnings.

Nevertheless, the new cabinet set out to restructure the public sector and to allow more private – for profit as well as non-profit – initiatives in the realm of welfare. Thus, this government brought a new ethical dimension to the provision and delivery of welfare in Sweden. Actually, the government explicitly declared a «revolution in welfare policy». Even for-profit business, in particular those run by women, would be encouraged in earlier sacred sectors of human services. However, the government still adhered to the principle of public financing, basically tax financing, of such services and businesses. Furthermore, it did not abandon the principle of regulating local government, and imposed a number of welfare rights that these levels of government had to fulfil. In focus of these fairly costly reforms were such issues as equality between men and women and such groups as children and persons with functional disabilities. For instance, all regional county boards had to open up an expert position on gender issues. Both children and handicapped got their own ombudsman, which already existed for gender equality. The task of the new Children's Ombudsman is to make sure that Sweden complies with the United Nations Convention on the Rights of the Child while the task of the new Handicap Ombudsman is to promote and protect the interests of physically and mentally disabled persons.

As mentioned previously, municipalities are responsible for the majority of personal social services, such as day-care, elderly care, social welfare assistance, education, among others. However, as of 1991, a tax ceiling was imposed on the municipalities in an effort to reduce the overall tax burden on individuals. At the same time, state grants to local governments were once again reduced significantly. Thus, many municipalities have been forced to reduce services, in particular care of the elderly, close schools and child day care centres, as well as overall reduce the number of municipal employees. Although the municipalities have a legislated duty to assist those citizens who are in need within their area of jurisdiction, many are finding that it is impossible for them to carry out this responsibility to the same extent as previously. In order to continue to provide services, most local authorities are increasing the fees paid by consumers for services, such as child day-care. While this may not on the surface appear to affect the availability of services, it nevertheless affects the distribution of services as lower-paid workers may find themselves unable to pay the increased fees.

Furthermore, the fate of the national social security system is uncertain. For example, a new pension system is underway, and unemployment insurance was made mandatory for a while (1993-94). Sickness and work injury insurance is under review. As earlier in Swedish social policy history, there is a mix of conflicts and compromises. Presently, the Employers Confederation, supported by a neo-liberal intelligentsia, is pushing for not only cutbacks in welfare benefits, but for a much more market-oriented social security system, while the trade union movement is on the defence. In the 1991-93 government, the Liberal party stood out as the main defender of a fairly generous universal welfare system, although not as generous as the previous one. Also within the other parties in government there was fairly strong support for a universal system, but in particular among the Moderates there was a highly articulate neo-liberal wing inspired by Anglo-Saxon, anti-etatist free market economics. In opposition, the Social Democratic Party was trying to locate a balance between what was deemed possible versus desirable. Again in power as a minority government, the latter party will have to consider many tough decisions.

IV. Challenges

While the bipartisan agreements from the first half of the 1990s indicate a preparedness for change, recent trends do not yet indicate a substantial threat to the foundation of universality in the welfare state – or the moral philosophy of Swedish institutional welfare policy. Although the reductions within the benefit and service delivery system are significant, they do not yet seem to represent an increasing trend toward a two-tiered system of welfare. Integration is still high on the socio-political agenda, and segregation is pointed out as a high-risk negative phenomenon targeted for greatest possible elimination.

In order to maintain legitimacy in the face of both increasing privatisation and decreasing resources, the central task of the public sector for the immediate future is to increase both the productivity and efficiency of its activities. This is easier said than done but was partly the force behind the Social Democrats' decentralisation reforms in the 1980s. The most recent privatisation movements in Sweden have most often been in the form of private service delivery, or the contracting out of services funded by the public sector.

Many of the municipalities had begun to contract out the delivery of services to the private sector, such as elderly care and home-help care in the 1980s. Currently, however, many municipalities are also raising various fees, such as for child day-care, as well as creating new fee-for-services where possible. The introduction of transfers for private schools and the encouragement of the development of private alternatives, such as child day-care, has also resulted in a partial change in the structure of welfare services. Continuation of cutback in services and increase in fees may, as the municipalities continued to be squeezed between rising costs and decreased public revenue, open the door for privatisation to «fill in the gaps» left behind by the public sector.

Because many of the benefits of the welfare state are based on labour market participation, the «Swedish model» has more aptly been described as an achievement model, based on a close relationship between welfare provisions and participation in the labour market. With the growth of unemployment, an increasing group of previously employed individuals has become marginalised within the system. This tendency towards growing marginalisation and segregation may be one of the greatest challenges to the current Swedish model.

The role of women in modern society and the effects of the current social policy modifications have also had much recent discussion. Women were originally marginal to the welfare state as fewer women were gainfully employed during the early 1940s and 50s. Many of the benefits created, since they were tied so closely to employment such as pensions, benefited men to a greater degree. Women were drawn into the labour market in the development of the public sector, often on a part-time basis. From 1965 to 1990, the labour market participation rate for women between the ages of 20 to 65 increased from 45 per cent to 83 per cent. As the public sector is reduced, the employment opportunities for women are also affected and thus their level of benefits within the welfare state. Women are also affected by the cuts in services, as often this returns the burden to women to provide the substitute care-taking, at their expense, both professionally as well as personally.

Furthermore, although internationally Sweden has been rewarded for its fairly progressive immigrant policies, domestically these policies have come under increasing fire. In 1991, an anti-immigration party entered Parliament, although it did not manage to keep its seats in the subsequent election three years later. However, a 1993 survey indicated that 66 of 100 Swedes were still dissatisfied with the way in which refugees were accepted and handled in Sweden. The rising unemployment rate has resulted in a discussion by some circles, most notably at the National Labour Board, to advocate for a more stringent refugee policy based on the argument that employment cannot be guaranteed to those refugees granted permanent residency permits. This has sparked further debate in the area of unemployment among immigrant groups, which is significantly higher than for Swedes. Further problems such as the exorbitant costs for refugee accommodations through contracts with the private sector as well as the comparatively low quality of some of the housing, has been of recent debate. In the context of ethnic considerations it should also be pointed out that Sweden recently has had some difficulties in implementing the international charter of the Rights of Indigenous Peoples. This refers exclusively to the Sami population of the sparsely populated Northern mountain regions, the majority of who are living above the Polar Arctic circle, but it has brought into focus the difficulty of balancing modern social rights and cultural traditions and customs now considered as rights. Hence, it is an issue that for centuries has poisoned relationships between a native minority and, in a world human history perspective, the majority of newly arrived southerners and more or less repressive state agencies.

A final future challenge is worth mentioning: Sweden's role in the European Union has been a much discussed issue since the Social Democrats applied for membership in mid-1991. Although many representatives within the EU have indicated that they looked forward to Sweden joining the EU for Sweden's advanced views on women, social policy and welfare issues, right-wing pro-European Swedes within the former right of centre coalition cabinet instead looked to see what areas of the welfare state needed to be reduced to bring Sweden financially «in line» with Europe. These discussions have revolved around such issues as what reduced taxes, services and legislative changes will mean for the overall structure of the welfare state. During the fall 1992 currency crisis, the Conservative Prime Minister explicitly stated that the drastic changes in the welfare state were ultimately necessary to prepare Sweden for membership in the European Union. However, during the campaign leading up to the referendum on membership in November 1994, these fears were downplayed by the Yes-proponents in order to clear the way for an overall majority.

The economic crises of the early 1990s within both Sweden and the European Community has contributed to the increase in opposition, as well as the recent uncertainty surrounding the Maastricht Agreement, in particular the social charter, and the prospects for a European Monetary Union. The proportion of the population most opposed to entry into the European Community were those living in northern Sweden, women in all age brackets, and youth between the ages of 16 and 29. The Conservative and Liberal parties were the ones with a majority of members supporting membership, and opposition was substantial within all other major political parties.

V. Conclusions

What about the possibility of a post-welfare state or even post-modern home, room or apartment for the Swedish people in a wider European house?

In September 1994 the Social Democrats returned to the helm of Swedish politics, and less than two months later Sweden decided to join the European Union. These are the overall socio-political parameters within which welfare state reform will be addressed in the years leading up to the 21st century (the next regular election is scheduled for September 1998). To this should of course be added cross-border influences from the international economy.

Overall, the decisions taken during the last couple of years point towards a slimmed and somewhat more market-oriented version of the old model, and not a radically new one. More important for the fate of this model is of course if the rather recent (post-1993) trends towards an economic boom will result not only in the growth of industrial investments but also in an improved situation – if not full employment in the old, pre-1989, sense – in the labour market. It is a truism to maintaining a fairly generous welfare state, like maintaining reasonable salaries, is dependent upon maintaining international competitiveness.

The challenge to this development will be to maintain a level of solidarity and uniformity to these developments, to avoid the creation of a dual system: one for the high-level wage earners who can afford to purchase high quality services and those who will be forced to be satisfied with – an ever-decreasing level of ? – public services. Thus one can assert that although the Swedish welfare state model has survived the major crises, it is however currently in one of the most wide-spread transition periods to which it has ever been subjected. Crucial to the outcome of this transition is whether the welfare state will be regarded as promoting social justice, efficiency, security, or whether a further concretising of inequality and selectivity will reign.

The Swedish approach to welfare has, in short, attempted to maximise citizens` equality of status while attempting to minimise dysfunctional conditions manifest in a capitalist market economy, primarily those concerning the distribution of income, goods, and wealth. Hence, in vesting citizens with the basic right to entitlement, Swedish welfare systems should not only be appraised in terms of the elaborate social security benefits they offer and the social services they provide, but also – and perhaps just as importantly – in their capacity to ensure full employment and affect equitable redistribution.

This represents one of the basic dilemmas faced by this approach to welfare, and also the theoretical perspective of welfare as citizenship from whence it has evolved. Indeed the citizenship perspective has been accused by critics as merely providing a foundation of equality upon which the structure of inequality can then be built. To what extent the Swedish approach to welfare has been tainted by such a flaw remains an open question although there are indications that the Swedish welfare state may be experiencing increasing social stratification which, in turn, may represent a manifestation of conditions of income inequality and property ownership. If this is indeed a reliable indicator of present-day social conditions and trends affecting the Swedish welfare state, then a no less troubling dilemma for this approach to welfare is that of conflicting values and interests which lie behind the ethics of social policy. Although Swedish social policy has been propelled by egalitarian motives of social rights, the principle of social citizenship becomes highly charged in practice when arbitrary decisions are made concerning the kinds of goods and services and the level and means of provisions that constitute such rights.

Full employment has been the over-riding objective in Sweden and at least up to the early 1990s the government seemed to unfailingly adhere to it. However, like in Norway a few years before, there may be a change of emphasis in the years to come. Fighting inflation has evidently become of principal importance in economic policy formulation. The scarcity of labour and full capacity utilisation put up costs in the late 1980s, and the rate of inflation increased considerably. With the deep recession of the first half of the 1990s, unemployment increased to levels hitherto unknown since the 1930s. Such a dramatic development in a few years' time pose a challenge to the idea of the welfare state. In the early 1990s, Sweden reached a point where the welfare system – except unemployment insurance – stopped growing. It remains to be seen if this is just a temporary break or the beginning of a new retrenchment trend.

The 1991-94 government, like the prior non-socialist government from 1976 to 1982, did not have much of an effect on the structure of the welfare state. However, at least at the beginning of this latter period, the political climate was much different, and there were more conservative movements among popular opinion which provided the impetus for a more radical restructuring of the welfare state. Both the Christian Democrats, who advocated increasing economic support for women to leave the labour market to remain home with their children – «family values» – and the populist positions of New Democracy on welfare, immigrant and refugee policy – «less government» – represented sharp contrasts to prior Social Democratic policies. Even if New Democracy disappeared in the 1994 election, in the years to come there is nonetheless reason to believe that ethnic and racial issues will remain highly controversial in the moral domain of welfare policy.

In today's world, what kind of post-Linnean wild flower is Sweden – after the end of an era of Western welfare statism, the rise of global civil society, and during a drive towards increasing competitive world capitalism – as the century draws to an end? To invoke the North American 20th century New England Liberal – once the US Ambassador to India – quoted at the start of this article, the far from nostalgic answer is that the model residing in the Far North of Europe is still a civilised version of workfare – a universal people's home – where the full effects of European average level unemployment has not yet been truly felt. The work ethic underpinning the fairly solidaristic and egalitarian welfare system has, contrary to the opinion of many wishful opponents, not been undercut to a considerable degree. If the full early post-war dimensions of the moral logic of the institutional welfare model ever will be restored, is quite another question. Second, if it will regain the status as an alternative on a global scale, at least partially may be determined to the extent this model will be underpinned by a domestically successful moral logic.

This chapter is a result of the Research Project: European Integration and the Restructuring of the Welfare State supported by the Swedish Council for Social Research (Dnr 93-0050:2A).

Bibliographical note: This article contains a summary of research presented in several other articles and books, of which a sample in English and German is listed below. For references to particular archival data sources, see these items.

References

HORT, S. E.: «The Swedish Model» in: BERGHMAN, J., and CANTILLON, B. (Eds.): *The European Face of Social Security,* Aldershot (Avebury) 1993.

— «Freiwillige Arbeitslosenversicherung und Umfassende Soziale Sicherheit – der Widerspruch der Schwedischen Vollbeschäftigungspolitik», in: LOTTES, G. (Ed.): *Soziale Sicherheit in Europa: Renten und Soziale Versicherungssysteme im Vergleich,* Heidelberg (Physica-Verlag) 1993.

— «Sozialpolitik und politischer Wandel – Schweden nach den Wahlen im Jahre 1991», *Zeitschrift für Sozialreform,* Heft 11/12 (1992).

— «What is segregation, and why is it still an issue in Sweden?», Paper presented at the joint OECD/European Foundation for the Improvement of Living and Working Conditions Conference «Partnership for People in Cities», Dublin, Oct. 1993.

— «Sickness and Unemployment Insurance in Sweden: Recent Changes and Policy Proposals», in: E BRUNSDON & M MAGGIE (Eds.), London (Guildhall Press) 1994.

HORT, S. E. and MCMURPHY, S.: «Social Policy in Sweden: the Swedish Model in Transition», *Social Policy Review,* No 5 (1993).

HORT, S. E. and LEWIS, D.: «Swedish Welfare Reform and the Role of the Voluntary Sector Re-examined». Paper presented at the Annual Conference of the Association of Researchers in Non-profit Organisations and Voluntary Action (ARNOVA), Berkeley, Oct. 20-22, 1994.

HORT, S. E. and LEWIS, D.: «Sami welfare: Social Rights versus Indigenous Rights», in: J. DIXON & R. SCHEURELL (Eds.): *Social Welfare with Indigenous Peoples,* London (Routledge) 1995.

HORT, S. E. and COHN, D.: «A Small but growing slice of the pie», in: JOHNSON., N. (Ed.): *Private Markets in Health and Welfare,* Leamington Spa (Bergh Publ.) 1995.

OLSSON HORT, S. E.: *Social Policy and Welfare State in Sweden,* Lund (Arkiv) 1993, 2nd. ed.

OLSSON HORT, S. E.: «Welfare Policy in Sweden», in: BOJE, T. P. & OLSSON HORT, S. E. (Ed.): *Scandinavia in a New Europe,* Oslo (Scandinavian University Press) 1993.

This article was first presented as «Challenges To The Welfare System: The Case Of Sweden» at the 4th International Conference on Ethics in the Public Service, Stockholm, Sweden, June 15-18 1994. A revised version was discussed at the SEEP-Conference «Restructuring the Welfare State – Ethical Issues of Social Policy in a European Perspective» at Forschungsinstitut für Philosophie Hannover, Germany, 8-10 September 1995. I would like to thank the participants at this meeting for constructive comments and criticisms, in particular its main organizers Peter Koslowski and Andreas Føllesdal.

Chapter 17

The Social State in the Post-Modern[1]

PETER KOSLOWSKI

The crisis in social insurance systems compels us to adopt a new approach to the theory of the state and of social security systems. The crisis in the social state[1] is above all a crisis in the ethical and cultural presuppositions of social insurance. Social policy, geared to socio-technology, has underestimated the cultural and ethical conditions for social security provisions. It is emerging today that the institutions of the social state, set up as functionalist socio-technical institutions, are undermining their own ethical-cultural foundations, and are not able to reproduce, on the scale required, their ethical presuppositions: that those covered by insurance live according

---

1 In the following I shall use the English translation of „Sozialstaat" or „sozialer Staat", social state, for what in the English speaking world is usually named welfare state since the German social state was not set up originally to realize welfare but to secure social insurance against the definable risks of illness, work accidents and unemployment as well as for old age pensions. It was not designed to provide for „general social welfare". This paper is the revised and enlarged English translation of P. KOSLOWSKI: „Der soziale Staat der Postmoderne. Ethische Grundlagen der Sozialpolitik und Reform der Sozialversicherung", in: CHR. SACHSSE, H. TR. ENGELHARDT (eds.): *Sicherheit und Freiheit. Zur Ethik des Wohlfahrtsstaates*, Frankfurt a. M. (Suhrkamp) 1990, pp. 28-70.

to a sense of their own responsibility; and that there is a culture in which we make basic provisions and organise our own lives. A point is being reached where there are considerable risks in social insurance. On the one hand, these risks are finding expression in the damage to the relationship between the different generations, in the fact that justice between different generations is becoming problematical, and in the situation where there is over-provision of social security for insured parties in certain strata of society. On the other hand, they are finding expression in new poverty and under-provision of social security in other groups in society, as well as in acute financial shortfalls in social insurance.

The alternative of a post-modern social state responds to the crisis in basic provision by recalling ethics and by giving social policy an ethical aspect, and making it culture-oriented. The following reflections on the social state in the post-modern proceed in six stages. The first stage is to sketch a concept of the post-modern. The second is to describe the current post-modern situation in society, and its effect: the end of the ideologies. The third is to set down some basic ideas for a post-modern theory of state (sections III and IV), and the fourth is to analyse the current social insurance system in the Federal Republic of Germany under the concept heading, „welfare state illusion" (sections V and VI). The fifth stage is to make proposals for shaping social insurance in a new way that takes culture into account, according to the principles of a „culture of basic provision" and new subsidiarity. The final stage is to suggest a few concrete steps for pensions insurance reform in the Federal Republic of Germany (sections VII and VIII).

I. The Concept of the Post-Modern

The post-modern as an experience and a way of relating to the world begins with the newly arisen awareness of the finite nature of the world and the limited nature of its resources, an awareness that has had a decisive universal influence since 1973, owing in particular to the shock caused by the rise in oil prices. With the inception of this awareness, the utopianism and progressivist characteristic of the modern were thrown into crisis, and the notion, inherent in the modern, of endlessly progressive mastery over nature and unrestrained economic growth, became untenable (see Koslowski, 1987).

The post-modern as a philosophy departs from the modern as an ideology, but does not depart from modernity as historicity. To be modern, meaning contemporary, or „state of the art", is a requirement in any given present time, and remains so even when the modern and its ideology of modernism have been overcome. That modernity, meaning the contemporary, is required in thought and human behaviour, even under the conditions of the post-modern, results from the fact that humankind and human culture are by nature historical. We cannot forego modernity, because we cannot take leave of history. Historicity and modernity demand that we continue to think up, to imagine and to realise that which is new and modern.

The fact that we shall continue to be modern does not rule out the end of the modern as the ideology of the „New" in its conclusive and unsurpassable form. For the modern was and is the radical dissolution of historicity by geschichtsphilosophie, i. e. the type of the philosophy of history founded by Hegel and Marx. Not only did the modern seek to emancipate itself completely from its origins, and thus from history, in a religious and political sense, it also understood itself to be the ultimate healing of the geist („spirit"), to be the consummate emancipation of the human species, and to be the ultimate realm of freedom, cancelling all alienation. In spite of its name, the geschichtsphilosophie of the modern is not a philosophy of history and of historicity, rather it is a philosophy of the sublation[2] of history and the historical method. The philosophy of history of the modern denies the relentless advance of the historical epochs, and denies the uniqueness and transience of these, in favour of an ultimate worldly fulfilment and an end of history. The modern as an ideology, and modernism tell a single great myth, the total myth of progress and its fulfilment in the society of the modern, bringing history to an end. The real effect of the artificial concept of history as a worldly history of salvation, heilsgeschichte, and the ideology of the modern - according to which history itself can sublate and bring to an end the process of the sequence of historical epochs and projects – includes the end of historicity, indeed of history itself.

Yet, after the experience of the ageing of the modern, the historicity of the world can no longer be denied. The post-modern refutes the sublation of history by geschichtsphilosophie, and regains an appropriate, non-artificial concept of historicity and modernity. The one „great narrative" of *ge-*

2 The German word here is aufheben. As well as meaning to remove, this verb, esp. in Hegelian philosophy, can mean to cancel and preserve (by overcoming dialectically). Where I have thought it to be appropriate, and in an attempt to do justice to the complexity of the German, I have offered the English near-equivalent, sublate.

schichtsphilosophie, of the epic of the modern, is replaced in the post-modern by the many narratives about historical processes and changes, and by the religious view of history as heilsgeschichte.

We cannot leave historicity and modernity behind us, but we can leave behind the modern as an ideology. The post-modern, as a critique of modernism and of the artificial concept of history inherent in the modern, is the restoration of historicity, and thus of normality. It does not replace the belief of geschichtsphilosophie in the modern with a belief in the post-modern. The post-modern does not believe in history and is not the resumption of modern geschichtsphilosophie by post-modern means. It is the critique and overcoming of the modern philosophy of history, since by its rejection of modernism and with its notion of the fourth age of the post-modern, it restores human historicity to its rightful place.

Post-modernity is the position of modernity under the conditions of the post-modern, and after its passage through the modern as an ideology. Modernity in the original sense is the position of acknowledging historicity, and the willingness to create the New and take on board what is modern. Only since the modern understood itself to be the „Ultimate New", the New in its conclusive form, and to be the ultimate era, it tried to usurp the concept of modernity and to reinterpret it, changing it into a hard and fast ideology of the „modern worldview". Yet modernity cannot be restricted to a conclusive, un-historical content. Rather, it must remain open to the New and the „Unheard-of". Thus modernity today, under the conditions of the end of the modern as an ideology, is post-modernity. Post-modernity is not a process of disembarking from history and from what is modern, but of overcoming the modern and the dictates of modernism.

Philosophically, the progressivistic characterising of the modern in its relation to the world was represented and manifested in Hegel's idealist monism, and in the materialist monism of Marx. Hegelian and Marxist philosophy, the two „master stories" of the modern constituted the modern in its typical form. The French post-modern has destroyed the validity of both these monisms, which dominated the modern as an epoch, and upon which the modern as an ideology was founded.[3] The philosophical „master stories" of the modern also had a decisive influence on those world views that at first were further from them, such as evolutionism and positivism; so that now the

3 LYOTARD defines the postmodern by rejecting the master stories of Hegelianism: „In the simplest possible terms, ‚Postmodern' means that the Metanarratives are no longer credible." (LYOTARD 1979).

philosophical monisms have been made relative, evolutionism and positivism are also affected. Scientism as a whole is being subjected by post-modern philosophy to a „critique of scientific reason".

A distinction must be made between the two current approaches to a theory of the post-modern: the deconstructivist and the essentialist. Mysticism plays a very important part in both: as atheological and atheistic mysticism and gnosticism in the deconstructivist post-modern, and as theological mysticism, and Christian, theistic gnosis in the essentialist post-modern (cf. Koslowski 1989d).

The deconstruction of modern system philosophy forms the essential content of the French post-modern, which, represented by writers such as J. F. Lyotard (Lyotard 1979) and J. Derrida (especially Derrida 1995), calls itself „deconstructivism". The deconstructivist post-modern affirms the principle of deconstruction against the constructions of system philosophy; it affirms the principle of irresolvable conflict against the Hegelian principle of total sublation; and it affirms the „small narrative" against the „master narrative" of *geschichtsphilosophie* in absolute idealism and Marxism. Yet by totalising the principles of conflict, of the small narrative, and of the pluralism of what Nelson Goodman has called „ways of world making", the deconstructivist post-modern banishes speculative philosophy and the idea of totality from our thinking altogether, and seems also to seek to exclude, with the critique of modern monism, the possibility of any metaphysics, even non-totalitarian and non-monistic metaphysics. Since its deconstructivist critique of reason goes beyond even the autonomising of reason in the projects of the modern, to a human sovereignty that posits itself as an absolute, it does not overcome the „autonomy concept" of the modern, but rather it takes it further. In this respect, it is super-modern, but not post-modern.

The concept of modernity represented below follows on from the deconstructivists' calling modernity into question, and from the post-modern critique of the master stories of the modern. Yet at the same time, it strives also to overcome even the deconstructivist post-modern, and thus to arrive at an essentialist post-modern. Our thinking must arrive at an essential concept of post-modernity – one that supersedes the modern as an ideology - and at a new theory of metaphysics – one that does justice to the prefix post, as the first after-modern philosophy.[4] Our thinking must not confuse post-modernity and super-modernity. Post-modernity means working towards a specula-

4 Cf. for a social and economic theory under the conditions of the postmodern, KOSLOWSKI (1989b).

tive philosophy that is not monistic or atheistic, as the modern system is, but also does not simply lapse apologetically into dogmatic pluralism, or deconstructively into atheological mysticism and gnosticism.

For post-modern speculative philosophy, the traditional wisdom of Christian gnosis and Jewish mysticism is of great significance, its speculative, theistic and personalist character going beyond the monism of the modern, but also going beyond the traditional metaphysics influenced by Aristotle (cf. Koslowski 1989e, 1989f). As a philosophical position, post-modernity stands in opposition to the modern, and the modern view that the absolute is actualised in the iron cage of the weltgeist, or – and no distinction is made between the two – in the dialectics of history. Post-modernity as a philosophical position retains the distinction between the absolute and history against the gnosticistic negation of monistic dialectics. It maintains the singularity of the individual in thinking and in practice against the „sublation" of the finite in the infinite, and it preserves the dignity of nature against the sublation of nature in the mind or Hegelian geist. Post-modernity means imagining the interior faculty of the self, the corporeality of the mind, and acknowledging the wisdom that is in nature.

II. The Post-modern Situation: Making Society Ethics- and Culture-Oriented and the End of the Ideologies

Today's industrial society has been described as a risk society (Beck 1985), and this concept has come to have a decisive influence on our awareness. The experience of living in a risk society in fact represents a „limit experience" for the modern. It is a limit experience in two respects: it is the experience of the limits of the project of the modern; and it is the perception of the transition to an after-modern paradigm (cf. Koslowski 1989c). It has been discovered that scientific and technical progress, the notion of emancipation, and the complete pluralisation of lifestyles, as well as the economic growth that these necessitate, are not to be had at zero cost, but that the modern carries significant side-effects, costs and risks. This discovery means the end of the utopia of enduring, risk-free modernisation. The ecological and cultural risks emerging today in industrial society are forcing the modern as a worldview into the twilight, and are calling into question the claim of the modern to be the conclusive project of humankind and the ultimate Enlightenment. The discovery of the finite nature of the world, of the limited nature of its resources, and of the risks of industrial mastery over nature means, on the one hand, the disappointment of the utopian expectations held by the modern, and on the other a return to normality and actuality. The development of industrial society shows that its great risks are not only the obvious risks, such as atomic energy, and gene technology, but that they lie equally in the cultural sphere of social institutions and the way of our order of Living, at the centre of which the social state belongs.

The limit experience – the experience made by the modern in becoming conscious of the risks it carries – reveals that progress without risks is not to be had, and that the modern is a form of society that carries risks. The experience of a risk society also makes us aware of our ethical responsibility for economic and cultural development, a development that can no longer be thought to provide of itself the economic or technical impetus for its own progress. Hence, the demand for making industrial society ethical and cultural – and making ethical and cultural its social branches of economy and state – is a response to the discovery that the modern, by its nature, carries risks. The new interest in ethics results from the need to restore the ethical and cultural aspects to industrial society. Furthermore, with the experience that the concept of progress inherent in the modern has run up against its limits, this new interest signals the end of the ideologies. The recall of the ethical dimension, in, say, economy (cf. Koslowski 1988) and social policy, is a critique of the ideological ways of viewing society and economy. It shows that the ethical cannot be replaced and made redundant by organisational changes.

Ideology always sees the origin of what is evil or deficient as being a non-moral error or simply a fault in organisation. The super-elevation of the market economy to an ideology of the market explains all economic problems by claiming that not enough room has been given to the market mechanism to operate, that extraneous disruptions, etc. have entered the system, disruptions that would simply vanish if the market was allowed to operate unhindered. The only question here is, how these faults could have arisen of themselves, how the political faults – if they caused the faults in market equilibrium – could ever have got into the balanced order of the pure market in the first place. Marxist ideology, for its part, points to private ownership of the means of production as an explanation of all ills.

Explanations of social reality are ideological when they regard the ethical decision of the individual in the given conditions of an order as irrelevant for the overall result, and claim to be able to rid the economy of all ills simply by modifying a single organisational principle. The philosopher Franz von

Baader gave one of the earliest definitions of the concept of ideology when in 1836 he called „ideologues" those who deny the original sin, and in so doing deny the ethical character of all actions (Baader 1836, 130). The ideologue denies the original sin, i.e. denies the view that human weakness and moral false decisions share the blame for the ills of the world. Ideology is the expression of the tendency of the modern to remove the moral element from reality and to declare ethics to be irrelevant. Ideology and the „de-moralisation" of actuality are the perfect expression of the ethical deficit of the modern. The ideologies of the modern deny that political, social and economic actions possess an ethical dimension.

In contrast, ethics emphasises that the will of the agent in economy and policy must posit itself in a moral relationship to itself, that is to say, the will must question whether its activity is justifiable and proper. This ethical relationship of the will to itself is more easily realised in the liberal democratic and market economy order, because this order leaves more room for individual responsibility, although at the same time it does not guarantee that economic power will be used in an ethical way. The new process of making society ethics- and culture-oriented marks the transition from the modern industrial society to the post-modern cultural society. Ethics and culture, as a way of ordering the life and interpreting the existence of a society, show that what unites society can neither lie solely in the rationality or the utility of an individual, nor can it be defined, independently of the individual's self interest, as raison d'état or common good. Rationality cannot adequately be defined as a mere principle of economising, or as a functionalistic process of optimising ends and means, rather it relies on material cultural aims to provide society with a raison d'être and substance.

The unifying factor in the individual pursuit of goals is provided by the spiritual superstructure of culture, a superstructure that at once transcends and gives form to immediate self-interest. It is only possible to acquire culture if individuals act autonomously, and take up a conscious position. Culture cannot be acquired by conditioning or external moulding. It presupposes the ability to perceive, to experience, to express, to understand and to take up a position. Understanding occurs in a cycle involving personal experience, the expression of experience, and reliving the experience of another. Society wins its culture and education by acquiring inwardly the spiritual substance and the traditions developed by the culture in question (cf. Spranger 1962, 56ff.).

The industrial society of the modern has held the belief that it can replace cultural and ethical interpretations of life with the rationality of economics and technology, and replace the risk of ethics with socio-technical functionality. It is apparent today that the risk believed to have been banished once and for all is returning in the form of the large-scale technical risks, loss of cultural identity, and the crisis of social insurance as a system for collective security. The risks in the modern are compelling post-modern cultural society to work at regaining a culture capable of providing unity, and to work at new forms of basic provision – a new shape for the moral idea.

III. Post-modern Theory of the State: Against Super-elevating and Demanding too Little of the State

State and church are the institutions for representing and progressively actualising the ethical idea. The ethical idea is the model developed by a society of a right way for its members to live. The state is not, as Hegel supposed, already the actuality of the moral idea, nor can the state, as Hegel also believed, represent the moral or ethical idea, alone and without the religious community of the Church, because this idea is never fully actualised under conditions of human finiteness and fallibility. What is rational, is, wrote Heinrich von Treitschke in his dispute with the pulpit-socialists (Kathedersozialisten) (Treitschke, 1874). What is rational, what is moral, has Being and in Being there is the rational, but what is actual is not what is rational. Because Hegel's dictum - that what is rational is actual, and what is actual is rational - is not correct. The actuality of the state is not the actuality of the moral idea, but the struggle to actualise this idea in an ever deeper way. The substance of the moral idea goes beyond the sphere of immanence into the transcendence of the absolute. So, it is only together that state and church can represent, and offer the chance to realise this idea: the idea of what people in one area, in a particular historical situation, conceive to be the correct way of life for them. The state and the churches present and keep alive the content of the moral idea, the idea of an order for the life of a people or several peoples within a state, and their common interpretation of their existence. State and church must seek to realise this idea in the life of a society.

The idea of the right way of living must be the guiding star for the legislative, the executive and the administration of a state.[5] The constitution is the

5 Cf. St. Koslowski (1989) for the difference between the executive power and the administration adopted in this case by Lorenz von Stein.

legal codification and the blueprint of those institutions in which the common idea of the right way of living is to be actualised. The moral idea is not identical with the changing majority will of Parliament, but at the same time, it is not independent of this will. The majority will is rather the means of arriving at an ever more profound definition of the moral idea as history continues onward. The democratic legislative is not the master, but the organ of the general will.

Recourse to the ethical and religious substance of the idea to be realised in state, church and society is necessary as a beginning to observations on the ethical foundations for social policy. This is because the task of social policy can only be defined in the context of the overall aims of the state; and because achieving the purpose of state social policy depends upon those who shape the policy, and those affected by it, recognising a state's ethical substance and actualising it in the way they conduct their lives.

IV. The Social Task in the Teleological Structure of the State's Provision of Goods and Services

Social policy is only possible as part of an overall policy that is at once an economic, cultural, and foreign policy, because the social policy makers depend on the achievements of the economy – the production of goods; on the achievements of culture – a symbolically and linguistically common understanding of the world; and on the achievements of foreign and defence policy – securing territorial integrity. Social security achievements are only possible within an overall framework that teleologically harmonises the achievements of the branches of state policy. The actions of the state form an integral working structure that must in turn be placed in a relationship of concordance with society, the economy, and the non-state culture. The outward organisation of the state, and with it the outward organisation of the social insurance institutions proceed from the aims of the teleologically organised body politic and what it demands in terms of achievements; and the body politic must define and harmonise the priorities, function, structure and shaping of the institutional branches.

The organisations of the state, each having a different purpose, refer to, and rely on a common ethos, an idea of customary morality, which embraces at once the order of life, the order according to which we live, and the way we interpret our existence. The moral idea is the idea of an ethic that embraces both, the exterior mores, custom and ethos, the ethics of culture, and the interior moral faculty independent from outward mores - the ethics of conscience. Ethics as a theory investigates both aspects of ethical actions. The ethic includes the morality of conscience or inner morality, which is expressed in the demands – to be realised by the individual – of the supra-empirical and internal moral law; and ethic is a critique, representation, and manifestation of the sphere of mores and culture, a sphere shaped by the expectations of mores, customs and conventions regarding the behaviour of an individual. It is not possible for any state or any society to realise the good way of life unless there are, present in the branches of society and state, mores and morality, a cultural order for the way we live, and an individual inner morality.

That the state is not the actualisation of the moral idea, but that it depends on customary morality applies to one sphere of state action more than any other: to the transfer of benefits in social policy, where the definition of needs is always dependent also on what is imagined to be reasonable and fair. The sphere of social policy presupposes an ethics and culture of basic provision.

The ethical bases for social policy consist firstly in observing rules from a sense of morality, in refraining from exploiting loopholes in the law, and in behaviour that cannot be imagined without the moral decisions governed by the individual's conscience. Social policy cannot dispense with conscience.

The bases for social policy embrace, secondly, the mores, conventions and habits whereby benefit is claimed and delivered under a system of social insurance, i.e. the culture of the social fabric.

The ethical attitudes and mores presupposed if the fabric of social insurance is to function, cannot be guaranteed merely by the law and its sanctions. Basic social state provision presupposes a culture of the conduct of life in which the individual is conscious of the way he or she leads his or her life, and consciously provides basic provisions for the future. The social state or welfare state presupposes a culture and morality whereby the individual is responsible for, and organises his or her own life, and which social policy cannot create and maintain by technocratic organisation and administration alone.

Responsibility and the culture of the self – the cultura animi and care for oneself – are not primarily the object and findings of objectifying, empirical science. Rather, they are the result of those forms of knowledge that include a relationship of the thinking individual to himself, a moral relationship to oneself and to the outside world. The self-referential, non-objectifying ways of knowing and finding oneself are religion and philosophy. The modern state cannot, in its social and cultural policy, define the praxis of religion, which in Christianity also presents itself as church, but it can support religion and philosophical ethics as the culture of knowing and finding oneself. Why must the state today also have an interest in a philosophical and religious culture of the self? It must take this interest because it relies on its citizens leading their lives consciously and responsibly. Today the people's claims for basic provision, and thus the claims directed at the government, have risen to a point where they can only be met if the people, for their part, foster a culture of self-responsibility in which there is basic provision, and in which the individual leads his life responsibly.

Modern social policy, geared exclusively to socio-technology, has overlooked the ethical and cultural presuppositions of the basic state provision emphasised by a post-modern social theory geared to ethics and culture. It has presupposed and taken for granted the cultural conditions for comprehensively securing our existence – these conditions being the culture in which the individual cares for himself and leads his life responsibly. Yet these conditions are not fulfilled eo ipso, rather they presuppose a culture for the way we conduct our lives that must be fostered and cultivated, and wanted by its subjects. A system of social insurance that, like the current, very comprehensive system of compulsory insurance in Germany, fails to pay heed to the cultural and ethical presuppositions of social insurance, and does not promote the cultivation of individual responsibility, is thrown into financial difficulties owing to a „cultural and ethical deficit", notwithstanding its socio-technical perfection.

The cultural and ethical deficit of the modern social insurance system is inextricably linked to the ethical deficit of the modern. The modern social policy of the welfare state has underestimated the moral presuppositions of social security just as much as it has overestimated the socio-technical capacity of the welfare state. The theorists of the welfare state in the modern saw social policy as being either the technocratic solution to the residual problems created by the market economy and democracy of liberalism, or else the emancipatory overcoming of the entire parliamentary-capitalist constellation. Both factions of „welfarism" failed to acknowledge either the ethical and cultural substance of the social state or the ethical and cultural presuppositions of the social insurance system. Also, the fascination of the „secular" eschatology and salvation implied by the concept of „welfare" had its effect even in the moderate socio-technical faction among the „welfare politicians".

Because „welfare" was supposed to be actualised already in this world by large-scale organisations established for that purpose, the welfare utopia left little room for the ethical and cultural presuppositions of the social state.

If a welfare state programme dangerously super-elevates what can be demanded and expected from state policy, and turns „welfare policy" into a sort of worldly and secular strategy for salvation, it has to be said that the concept of a state solely centred on social insurance is, in fact, in danger of underestimating the capacity and potential of the state as a whole, in danger of going to the other extreme where the state has only superficial significance. The state is based not only and not primarily on social justice, but rather on the rule of law. The social aspect, along with the purpose of social security, is only one of the purposes pursued within the teleological structure for the achievements of the state. This is already apparent from the fact that the functions of providing social insurance can be performed in part by bodies other than the state, for example by private insurers.

In its evaluation of the state, the modern has, since the Enlightenment, swung remarkably between, on the one hand, super-elevating the significance and worth of the state, and on the other, falling short of it. In Hegel's idealist monism, states are vessels inhabited by the weltgeist as it moves through world history, and the state is the actualisation of the moral idea. In the materialistic, evolutionist view of doctrinaire liberalism, on the other hand, the state is merely one manifestation of free-market society which has to be overcome. Finally, in the monism of dialectical materialism, the state is an obsolete stage in history, withering away as the forces of production evolve.

A post-modern theory of the state and society stresses, rather, the indispensable nature of statehood and the organisational unity of the functions of the state. Social security is just one among these functions. Post-modern state theory neither turns the state into a vessel for the absolute or ascribes to it qualities of supra-individual intellect, as Hegel did, nor does it reduce the state to a mere agency for social services. The state is the central organ of society for the observation and recognition of the social reality, for reaching agreement, taking decisions about that reality, and for implementing them in social life: in securing our existence, in culture and the economy and for the outward assertion of the body politic.

Therefore the state is not a social security state, but rather a state having social attributes, in just the same way that it has other attributes as a promoter of culture and, externally, as preserver of its territory. In pursuing social, cultural or territorial-security purposes it does not become a social security state, a cultural state or a power state. Rather, the concepts of the state as social security state, cultural state and power state, each considered individually, are one-sided representations of state purposes derived from a single aspect of the teleological structure for the achievements of the state. The state can be a social security state, cultural state or territorial state only to the extent that it is all three at once and realises jointly its social, cultural and foreign-policy telos. It must preserve a balance between its social, cultural and territorial-security purposes.

In the post-modern theory of the state, what characterises the current development of states and societies is the permeation of state functions, not their differentiation or separation. In the state in the post-modern, the social, culture-oriented and territorial purposes of the state permeate one another, and in this process it is, above all, the reciprocal permeation of the social and cultural purposes of state action which is significant for the post-modern state. Permeation is a spatial analogy for the synthesis and the simultaneous realisation and differentiation of qualities. In the case of the state, its social qualities and tasks and those which are geared to the furtherance of culture must permeate one another.

In the post-modern, just as the tendency towards one-sided representation of the state's purposes has been reversed, so the opposition between liberalism and socialism has moved into the background. In today's conditions, the false dichotomy between full personal responsibility and full state provision and care, which was linked to this opposition, is becoming obsolete.

Full personal responsibility and full state provision are equally abstract extreme positions. A sensible social security policy will strive to achieve a mixture of personal responsibility and state provision. The question for the social state in the post-modern and for Germany's social security today is not „Should we have personal responsibility or should the state provide for our existence?", but rather: „Have we still got the right mixture of provision between that for which we take personal responsibility and that which the state administers care for?" It is the contention here that the mixture is too strongly on the side of state bureaucracy, that this gives rise to crises in social insurance and in the relationship between the generations, and that therefore we must come to see the need for restructuring the way social insurance is weighted and for a greater degree of provision based on personal responsibility.[6]

How much should the state do in comparison with the other forms of human association, in comparison with the family, the workplace and the church? The state cannot take care of individuals. Individuals can only take

6 DETTLING (1988), p. 68, makes a similar call for a „social policy mix".

care of themselves within various structures for decision-making and co-ordination. In this process the state cannot prima facie claim for itself a special position as an organisational structure. The state is not able, any more than any other organisation, to give without taking.[7]

V. Welfare State – Social State: the Bismarckian Origins

In relation to the problem of the super-elevated claim of the term welfare state already mentioned above it is useful to note the semantical differentiation between the Anglo-American term „welfare state" and the German term „Sozialstaat". The German tradition has used the term social state (Sozialstaat) in general, not the term welfare state (Wohlfahrtsstaat.). Behind this semantical difference lies a different conception of the task of the state, being the procurement of means of subsistence in the „Staat der Daseinsvorsorge", in the „state of the procurement of means of subsistence" (Forsthoff) in the older German tradition of the social state and general welfare in the tradition of the British welfare state. The older German *Sozialstaat* does not aim at „social welfare" but at „social insurance". It does not aim at redistribution but at solidarity in times of need.

The Bismarckian model in contrast to the Beverigian model has not been a model of redistribution or socialist welfare but a model of a minimalist social insurance. This should also to be taken into account against certain charges of „paternalism" raised against the Bismarckian reforms by Victor Fuchs [8] and others. In many respect the workers' insurance of Bismarck of the years 1888 following has not been paternalistic but minimalistic. It aimed at a minimal degree of insuredness against the new risks of the industrial society and of the industrial mode of production.

Bismarck in his famous speech in the Reichstag of March 15th, 1884, had a clear consciousness of the revolutionary change that the introduction of the social insurance system would make in history. He expressed his wish that

---

7 Cf. CARL SCHMITT's formulation: „Nur Gott kann geben, ohne zu nehmen." [„Only God can give without taking."]

8 Cf. VICTOR FUCHS: „From Bismarck to Woodcock: The ‚Irrational' Pursuit of National Health Insurance", *Journal of Law and Economics,* 19 (1976), pp. 347-359.

the government and the present parliament would have the merit to do at least something, to do at least the first beginning in this field and to be the leader of all the other European nations.[9] In his speech, Bismarck touches upon almost all questions we are still discussing today in social policy: the questions whether a private insurance is to be preferred to a social one, whether social policy is a task of the state at all, whether social insurance does not introduce a socialist element into the state and whether social insurance is detrimental to individual freedom or not.

In answering the objection that private insurance should be preferred Bismarck answered: "I should like to express the principle here in the name of the allied governments that we do not assume that mischief and cases of accidents are the apt basis for earning the payment of high interest rates and dividends, we rather want to provide an insurance as inexpensive as possible for the workers against these and other evils and we think it to be our duty that we lower the price for insurance as much as possible in the interest of the workers and of industry, in the interest of the employer as well as of the employed".[10]

On the question of the legitimate task of the state and against the reproach of socialism he replies: "There are aims and tasks that only the state in its entirety can fulfil. To these ultimate aims belongs national defence, the general system of traffic ... To these aims belongs also the support and help for the needy and the prevention against situations of need that are the cause of such justified reproaches that are the really useable material for exploitation by the social democracy indeed. This is a task of the state which the state in the long run cannot escape. If someone, however, replies to me that this is socialism, I am not afraid of being called so. The question is: where is the admissible limit to the socialism of the state? Without such a socialism of the state we cannot develop the economy. Every ‚legislation against poverty' is socialism" (*ibid.*, p. 98f.).

Bismarck delineates his understanding of the task of the state and distinguishes it from the one that he ascribes to the social policy of France which believes to be able to do without laws against poverty: „In Léon Say we see expressed the French conviction that every French citizen has the right to die

9 OTTO VON BISMARCK: „Rede vor dem Reichstag vom 15. März 1984 (Speech in the Reichstag of March 15th, 1884)", in: OTTO VON BISMARCK: *Werke in Auswahl,* 7, Darmstadt (Wissenschaftliche Buchgesellschaft) 1981, p. 92 (my translation).

10 *Ibid.*, p. 97.

from starvation and that the state has no obligation to prevent him from the exercise of this right!" (*ibid.*, p. 99).

Bismarck clearly agrees to the socialist element in social insurance legislation: „The member of the opposition has it called something very new that we introduce a socialist element into legislation. I have already anticipated that by admitting that the socialist element is nothing new and that the state cannot even exist without a certain degree of socialism" (*ibid.*, p. 101).

Against the objection "that the organisation of the social insurance proposed does not harmonise with the word ‚free'," Bismarck replies: „Gentlemen, freedom is a weak notion; the freedom to die from starvation is of no use for anybody ... There is hardly any word nowadays that is more misused than the word ‚free', and it has even more charm when it is placed in front of any other adjective." (Bismarck refers here to the word „freisinnig" [free thinking, free minded] as the synonym for liberal.)

According to Bismarck, he who talks about freedom in general is only aiming at putting the importance of his or her own person above the common weal, „under the pretence that this is demanded by freedom. In our German history this is more clearly the case than in the history of any other country. How sharply and eagerly has not been accentuated the Germanic freedom in all the centuries of the decline of the German empire! What had to be understood by that? The freedom of the princes from the empire and the rule of the nobility over the serfs! They wanted to be free themselves; and that implied that ‚to be free' for them meant nothing else than ‚ruling', they did not feel free unless they ruled others" (*ibid.*, p. 103).

Bismarck compares the introduction of social insurance with a 'voyage of discovery in an unknown land' (*ibid.*, p. 104), and at the end of his parliamentary speech, he emphasises: „I have only to add my request that the gentlemen of the opposition support the government and serve them as a pathfinder in an unknown land that to enter we consider to be a duty for the government" (*ibid.*, p. 107).

Bismarck's social insurance reforms aimed at the introduction of an insurance of minimal extension against the risks of the industrial society, they did not aim at redistribution measures and „general welfare".

PETER KOSLOWSKI

VI. On the Situation of Social Insurance in the Federal Republic of Germany

The social insurance system of the Federal Republic of Germany changed this picture. The reforms made after the Second World War at the Reichsversicherungsordnung (Social Insurance System) introduced by Bismarck in 1888 extended the categories of people covered by insurance and increased the scope of insurance benefits. By doing so they have created a national insurance system for almost all citizens out of what was, in the nineteenth century, a provision limited to workers. In the present system virtually the entire population is entitled to standardised insurance benefits.

The social insurance system in the Federal Republic of Germany is a radical extension of the workers' insurance scheme under greatly changed conditions and with different objectives. The former worker's insurance system was extended and the social insurance system of the Federal Republic was created in a climate marked by the large-scale destruction of private assets through the ravages of the Nazi era and the Second World War, as well as by two preceding periods of inflation. In post-war Germany the only remaining system for social and retirement insurance was the collective one because private assets had been wiped out.

The welfare state depends on sociological and demographic changes and therefore on history. It is a misguided form of universalism to abstract from the historical conditions of welfare states. In times of general need, other schemes of social insurance are required than in times of long periods of peace and of the formation of private capital. The pay-as-you-go pension system introduced in Germany after the destruction of World War II and after the destruction of the private wealth of ten million Germans being expelled from East German lands has been inevitable since one could not rely on private capital formation and private pension funds in a situation where there was just no private capital left.

The close relationship between historical conditions and forms of institutions of the social state implies, however, that the institutions of social insurance must be revised when the social and historical conditions change. This is the case in Germany today where after a long period of private wealth formation the social insurance system must now be down-sized. We note, however, a „ratchet effect" in social insurance: it is easy to extend the degree of social insuredness but it is hard to reduce it. Adaptations in social insurance are very flexible towards higher social benefits but are very inflexible and inelastic towards their reduction.

The two conditions for establishing collective social insurance on the scale of the system in the Federal Republic of Germany no longer apply today. On the one hand, the conditions prevailing in the nineteenth century, those of mass poverty and deprivation, which necessitated a system of compulsory insurance for workers, do not obtain today, or affect only a marginal group among those covered by social security. On the other hand, the post-war situation, in which most sections of the population had suffered from the loss of assets, due to the war or to expulsion from their native lands, has been transformed into a new prosperity marked by the widespread wealth creation and acquisition of assets. In this new situation, in contrast to the immediate post-war period, the ownership of private houses and apartments has played an important role.

The creation of private assets and recourse to private insurance mean that there is a new social situation, different to that of the post-war period, and requiring a new structure for social insurance. The increased level of wealth, the improved standard of education and the increased potential for personal responsibility which that entails demand a „decollectivisation" of provision for old age and a redefinition of the risks and the population groups to be covered by social insurance. Today the acquisition of private assets has increased [11] – this has happened even among the less well-off who have acquired durable consumer goods [12] – and the improvement in educational

11 Personal savings deposits within Germany amounted, in themselves, to some DM 679 530 million in 1987; in 1982 the figure was still less than DM 500 billion (*Statistisches Jahrbuch* 1988, p. 316). To this must be added building society credits of around DM 120 billion. The building society savings account in particular is a classical form of savings for the „ordinary man". Of the 2,685,000 new building society savings accounts opened in 1987, 2,216,000 were for blue-collar or white-collar employees, pensioners, people in receipt of a social security pension, housewives or people without a trade or profession (*Statistisches Jahrbuch* 1988, p. 319). Securities held by private individuals within Germany had a nominal value of DM 143 billion in 1987 (*Statistisches Jahrbuch* 1988, p. 324). In 1987, 67,795,000 life insurance policies had a total value of DM 1,190,434 million (*Statistisches Jahrbuch* 1988, p. 326). These figures represent some of the major credit items in the net asset position of households.

12 Cf. on the acquisition of private capital *Statistisches Jahrbuch* 1987, p. 475 (for 1988: *Statistisches Jahrbuch* 1988, p. 465).

standards has enabled more people to take their own responsible decisions about the level of insurance they require. So what is called for now is a reduction in the scope of compulsory insurance and an increase in individual freedom to decide what form insurance should take.

This pressure for change applies above all to retirement insurance. In retirement insurance the element of risk and uncertainty about the insurance benefits which will be required in the future is a less important factor than it is in sickness and unemployment insurance. Retirement insurance is less an insurance against risk than an institution through which, in the course of time, the individual's source of income changes. This means that provision for retirement can be made very largely by acquiring private capital. Thus retirement insurance must be the first point of reform in a „decollectivisation" of insurance systems in favour of their subsidiary organisations.

The aim of social insurance in Germany is to secure income in the event of sickness, unemployment or old age. The system ensures that those covered by it will have a replacement income from the onset of the insured risk. In the case of sickness and unemployment, this income is proportionate to the average income of the preceding years, subject to a deduction. In the case of retirement, the replacement income, i.e. the pension, is calculated according to the insured person's relative gross income and the length of the term of insurance and payment of contributions to the system (cf. Schmähl 1983). Thus it increases in proportion to the length of time over which contributions have been paid and to the amount of income earned over the person's lifetime, up to a fixed limit for assessment. Social insurance pensions ensure an income in old age of up to 72 or 73 per cent of the net average income of the years preceding retirement, if insurance contributions have been paid over 45 years. In the event, only 24.3 per cent of the insured population meets this ideal requirement. If contributions have been paid over 40 years the level of pension will be 63 per cent of the net average income (Institut der Deutschen Wirtschaft 1985, table 35b). This is a very high rate for a compulsory social insurance scheme. The comparable pension level under the English social insurance system, for example, is only 30 per cent of average male income (cf. Cairncross 1985). A pension level of 70 per cent of previous net income also represents a high degree of protection when we consider that the older person, unlike the young family, has already made specific investments in consumer goods (furniture, kitchen equipment etc.), and moreover, that they no longer have to bear the costs of maintaining their capacity to work - costs estimated at around 10 per cent of income (cf. Albers 1985).

Between 1957 and 1985 the pension level increased from 66.6 per cent to

72.9 per cent, a rate of growth somewhat higher than that of incomes. This increase over and above the increase in incomes is unjustified in terms of the principle upon which social insurance is built. It can be explained only by the widening gap which growing social burdens have created between the gross income of people in employment – against which pensions are calculated – and their net income. If we further consider that the age of retirement is coming down and that increased life expectancy means people are drawing pensions over a longer period of time, it becomes clear that the balance has shifted considerably to the advantage of pensioners and the disadvantage of the working population. In terms of the Federal Statistical Office „shopping basket", the real purchasing power of pensions has more than doubled. In 1984 the average pensioner could afford 2.64 times as much as his counterpart in 1959.[13] Pensioners' assets have been maintained and consolidated. People who have been in continual employment have achieved an almost even distribution of income throughout their lifetime.

Should the state set itself the goal of maintaining, through pension payments, an equal distribution of disposable income over the life cycle at all income levels, as it is in Germany today? And should it use compulsion on all its citizens to achieve that goal? What sort of pensions legislation can be made binding and enforced by the state? The state can enforce only those laws which can claim to be in the general interest, i.e. those which may be considered to be acceptable to everyone. The state cannot legislate for the good or ill fortune of its citizens. Therefore, what can be made binding through a general system of social insurance is not comprehensive insurance – i.e. the arbitrary life-pattern in which income is distributed almost evenly throughout the different phases of life – but rather insurance against basic risks, i.e. a basic form of insurance (cf. Koslowski 1982a, Chap. 5). The workers' social insurance of the Bismarckian tradition was a basic or minimum insurance which was implemented by means of legal compulsion. By contrast, present-day social insurance obliges almost all citizens to have comprehensive insurance. Making comprehensive insurance compulsory in this way imposes upon the citizen a form of insurance unacceptable to a certain sort of individual who is prepared to take risks; and it is not legitimate for the state to do this.

13 Calculated according to *Statistisches Jahrbuch* 1985, p. 516. On social benefits cf. *Statistisches Jahrbuch* 1987, p. 405 ff.

The social insurance system presupposes that all members of the population wish to distribute their income evenly throughout the different phases of their life. But such an even distribution is at odds with the natural economic cycle of the family. A scheme which supports young families, who have to make substantial investments in setting up a home, and which reduces the income of those households comprising people aged fifty and over, can more legitimately claim to be reasonable and in the general interest. Such a scheme corresponds to the way people distribute their lifetime's income through private and voluntary savings: young families get into debt when they are starting out and clear that debt when the children grow up and leave home. Pensions insurance is based on the notion of a single individual who lives only for himself and wishes to have the same opportunities for consumption throughout all the phases of his life. It is not surprising, therefore, that the social insurance system fosters the spread of a corresponding type of marriage. It favours childless marriages in which both partners are earners and it places the family at a disadvantage.[14]

When it comes to pensions insurance, the German social insurance system is geared not towards protecting against risks and neediness, but towards protecting acquired assets and benefits (Besitzstandswahrung). This goal is a legitimate one for the individual, but it does not justify a generalised and legally compulsory system, because the negative effects of protecting assets on the life of the community are too great. These negative effects make themselves felt in the falling birth rate and in what I have called the „welfare state illusion" (Koslowski 1986).

VII. The „Welfare State Illusion" and the Question of Justice Between Generations

The social insurance system is leading to decreasing investment in the future, in the form of children and it is reinforcing the trend towards childless marriages or marriages with few children. This situation of declining investment in the future arises from illusions about the value of assets in the

14 Cf., on the financial life-cycle of an average working person, KÖHLER (1989) and GBUREK/KÖHLER (1989).

form of pension entitlements. Our present situation can be described – in analogy to the public debt illusion associated with David Ricardo[15] – as one of „welfare state illusion". The idea of public debt illusion discussed in public finance is the following: when the state becomes indebted a distortion occurs in the way economic decision-makers perceive actuality. These decision-makers can no longer recognise their financial position in an adequate and realistic way and they overestimate the extent of their assets because, when the state finances its spending through debt issue, they do not take account of their future payment obligations and the servicing of interest on the national debt as a drain on their budget. Rather, they perceive their disposable income as being greater than it is. Unlike public financing from tax revenue, which immediately reduces people's disposable income, financing by means of public debt leads to a lack of transparency as regards future payment obligations, with the effect that individuals consider themselves richer than they are (see Buchanan 1976, Cavaco-Silva 1977).

In contrast to one major opinion in present-day public finance, which sees financing through taxes and through public debt as being equivalent, tax financing and debt financing are not equivalent. The two alternatives might be equivalent for the state's purely financial decision but they are not equivalent in their real effects on the consumption versus investment decisions of the individuals. Rather, financing through public debt leads to a higher proportion of the disposable national income being expended on consumption than is the case with financing through taxation. Financing through public debt also leads to a comparative reduction in investment and in growth. When public spending is financed by means of public debt rather than by increased taxation, actuality becomes less clear, opaque, and its correct perception more difficult if not impossible.

15 To most readers, the „Ricardian equivalence theorem", will be familiar. RICARDO assumes that financing public expenditurs by public debt or by taxes is equivalent for the state. RICARDO (1821), pp. 247, adds, however, that: „From what I have said, it must not be inferred that I consider the system of borrowing as the best calculated to defray the extraordinary expenses of the state. It is a system which tends to make us less thrifty – to blind us to our real situation." This conclusion of Ricardo is very often overseen. Cf. BARRO (1974) and ABEL (1987), p. 174-179, for the thesis that the Ricardian equivalence theorem must be derived from RICARDO. For the opposite thesis that the theorem of public debt illusion must be deduced from his reasoning cf. BUCHANAN (1976) and CAVACO-SILVA (1977). Ricardo's preference for tax versus debt financing of public expenses is also expressed in RICARDO (1820), p. 186.

A problem of illusion analogous to that of public debt illusion, and one which also arises from a lack of foresight about the obligations entailed in servicing the debt, is apparent in the present state pensions insurance system of compulsory pay-as-you-go governmental social insurance. Modern state pensions insurance involves elements of indebtedness. Specifically it is tantamount to the present generation becoming indebted to the next generation. If the number of pensioners rises relative to the number of people in employment or if the length of time over which pensions are paid increases, then the generation in retirement becomes indebted to the working generation, without any possibility of repaying the debt. If the number of children declines, reducing the generation of children in comparison to that of their parents, because working parents do not raise enough children, then the parents' generation becomes indebted to the children's generation, with an equal impossibility of repaying the debt. Within the German social insurance system, factors are at work which foster illusion. They are as follows:

- There is a lack of transparency about future payment obligations, i.e. transparency for the individual about the extent to which his generation, that of the young parents, has become indebted to the following generation of the current children generation either by raising too few children or by increasing their own life expectancy.
- Insufficient consideration is given to the future obligations of children to pay for their parents, or these obligations are underrated.
- There is a corresponding distortion of decisions as between consumption and the formation of capital.

Why is pension insurance in the welfare state equivalent to a debt issue to the next generation, if the relationship between the generations shifts to the disadvantage of the younger generation? Surely the generation in employment goes on paying into the social insurance system. The present working population is earning the pensions of the people who were in employment in the preceding period. But the pensions of the people in employment today will be earned by the generation which will be working in the period that follows. The modern „contract between the generations“ sets the traditional scheme of things on its head. Parents are no longer acquiring capital as they once did to provide for themselves and their children, but rather, the children, via the state's system of compulsory savings through social insurance, are providing for their parents, for themselves and for their own children, i.e. for the grandchildren. As yet insufficient attention has been paid to the historic importance of this change in terms of the way the social world develops and to its huge effects on the relationship between generations.

Increasingly, the young generation is refusing to assume the task of rearing children in the numbers needed to ensure security for the old. They are refusing – understandably, because they bear a double burden – to perform the increasingly necessary task of accumulating capital and savings to bring up children and to keep pensioners. Because they are compelled to set aside growing portions of their income to secure the retirement income of the generation that worked before them, they are no longer prepared, to the extent they were previously, to maintain a constant rate of reproduction. The birth rate is declining, and with it the rate at which capital, in the form of human capital, is accumulated. The drop in the reproduction rate of „children as human capital" is conditioned by the social insurance system and the way it sets on end the duty of provision for the future. The system of provision for old age rewards childlessness.[16]

This process is intensified by the welfare state illusion. The currently working generation have a distorted perception of reality and systematically overestimate the value of their assets in the form of their accumulated pension entitlements. If the levels of contributions to the social security system remain constant, social insurance benefits can be financed only when the age structure of society does not change – when family size and life expectancy remain constant. If the number of children per family declines or if life expectancy increases without a change in retirement age, or if, as is happening today, these two parameters shift simultaneously in their separate directions, then either contributions must be raised or benefits must be cut.

Only in theory can the state counter this welfare state illusion by means of ever-increasing social insurance contribution levels or tax incentives for larger families. For, on the basis of current demographic trends, unchanged rates of benefit and a constant level of state subsidy for financing pensions insurance, the level of contributions required to cover pension payments would have to rise from 18.7% in 1989 to 35% in 2030.[17] The average working family could not be expected to pay such a level of contributions.

---

16 Cf. NELL-BREUNING (1960), p. 186: „Wer keine Kinder aufzieht, baut seine Zukunft auf den Kindern anderer Leute auf." [„People with no children are building their future on the children of others."]

17 According to FINK (1988 a), p. 9, in 1988 two employed people were paying for every pensioner; in 2030 there will be one person paying contributions for every pensioner.

Regarding the financing problems caused by population decline, the opinion is often expressed in public finance that the population problem itself is a problem exogenous to the economic and social security system and that it cannot be tackled by institutional reorganisation. The decline in the child population is, in fact, a problem affecting all the Western democracies (cf. Clark/Kreps/Spengler 1978). Germany, however, has one of the lowest birthrate of any democratic country and this problem has been remedied only very partially by the huge influx of immigrants. The fall in the number of births is a problem of our welfare institutions because our social insurance system includes no incentives for people to have children, but rather, contains clear disincentives, elements which deter people from having children. Removing those elements of social insurance which deter people from having children would not constitute a policy for population increase, but a policy of equal treatment for the family and of making those responsible for the declining number of children and future contributions to the transfers of the pensions internalise the costs of this phenomenon.

According to the principle that those who cause a problem should be responsible for its solution, those who have no children should bear more of the cost of population decline, while families who contribute to securing pensions should get more relief from the financial burdens of child-rearing. The current system of provision for old age places the burden of children in the private domain, while children as an asset are nationalised in the so-called contract between the generations - a contract between adults and other people's children. Justice demands that if children as an asset are nationalised, then the burden of children should also be nationalised to a greater extent: this may involve – in the process of securing financial parity between couples with children where only one partner is in paid employment and childless couples where both partners work – making deductions to take account of the joy which children give their parents. Thus, Germany has the choice either to move into the direction of Sweden and socialise the costs of child-rearing or to move into the direction of England and reduce the level of pension payments and of compulsory contributions to the pension system.

VIII. A Culture of Basic Provision and a New Subsidiarity

The social insurance system weakens that element of basic provision which serves to impart meaning and to create social community, what W.

Sombart has called the culture function of seeking a living. The process of seeking and making provision for our living is not just an economic phenomenon, but also a cultural one, because it influences the way we lead our entire economic, family and spiritual life. Providing for our living and our existence on the basis of personal responsibility is always conditioned by culture, and its effects are felt on the way we lead our lives in more than the economic sense. To take personal responsibility for acquiring capital and savings means that a person is acting and taking decisions on their own cognisance. Acquiring capital is the result of a process of individual recognition, decision-making and responsibility which leads to the choice of the best possible alternative. This responsible choice which I make for myself cannot be fully taken over by state agencies without eliminating precisely that element of individual optimisation, of making the best decision for each person.[18]

Compulsory state insurance eliminates the cultural function and the meaningful aspect of provision by imposing a system of compulsory savings which are then redistributed on the basis of contributions made. Provision for old age is removed entirely from the realm of structuring one's own life in a personally responsible way. In such a centrally important area of life as caring for old age – and thus caring for life in its entirety – the individual is reduced to the status of an object to be administered, a child who must be taken care of. The consequence is the danger that the German population becomes a nation of infants in an idyllic cabbage patch under the total care of the state.

To cut provision for, and anticipation of old age out of the lives of working people is to induce a frivolous attitude to life, not only as regards provision for old age, but also in relation to responsibility for the way life is led in its entirety. People will turn to the playgrounds of life in search of seriousness and challenge, to activities like sport, mountain-climbing or sailing or to adventure safaris, but they will no longer seek these qualities in the way they shape their own lives or in the life of their family.

Taking away personal responsibility for old-age provision by means of a collective system of compulsory insurance removes the necessity for people to perceive life in its entirety, the necessity to recall the warning given by

18 Increasing awareness of this problem is apparent. The growing number of life insurance policies being taken out (*Statistisches Jahrbuch* 1988, p. 326) is a clear indicator that people are increasingly prepared to make private arrangements for basic provision. However, those in the lowest income brackets are still heavily reliant on state pension insurance.

Solon of Athens - that we cannot count any man happy before the end of his life. Comprehensive insurance makes the perception of life in its entirety superfluous.

General, comprehensive state insurance is so expensive that it can be financed only in conditions of economic growth, for only then can we guarantee the state subsidies that have become increasingly necessary for social insurance. Comprehensive state insurance forces the economy along a growth path, the costs of which, in terms of the environment and the hectic pace of economic life, could be greater than the security to be gained through general, comprehensive insurance. A system of provision for old age cannot be predicated on growth in the economy as a whole, because economic growth is precarious, has too many side effects and may not be sustainable in the long term. The system of security for old age must function even when the economy is static, not growing, because otherwise it bases itself on something which is too insecure and encumbered with too many side-effects, namely continual growth.

Financial shortfalls in pensions insurance are making social security reform unavoidable. Certain changes are apparent already. Within a few years the pension funds will have a financial shortfall of DM 50 billion. This „gap“ cannot simply be „plugged“ by increased federal subsidy because the federal authorities cannot go on forever putting vast sums of money into subsidising pensioners' consumption without taking account of overall economic justice and overall social priorities. Today we need to restructure social insurance and to redistribute the weight on the so called „three pillars" of the social security system – i.e. compulsory state insurance, corporate insurance or occupational pensions, and private insurance – towards the last two of these. This reform and reweighting must restore the individual's learning and decision-making capacity within the system of collective and individual provision; as well as restoring the meaningfulness of basic provision in the real world and its cultural character. It must dispel the welfare state illusion of state provision, the idea that social security can be achieved without regard to justice between the generations.

The guiding principle in the reform of social security must be the principle of subsidiarity (cf. Utz 1956 and Rauscher 1989), the principle that the system of basic provision must follow the meaningful structure of the social world and the system of the social relationships of the people in society. The principle of subsidiarity leads to increased transparency and brings basic provision closer to the individual concerned. It restores the individual's awareness of the connection between security for old age and family development;

between social security and the culture of the provision securing income for retirement and of provision for our living. Cover for life risks must be provided through institutions, in which one can experience a sense of social and cultural meaning and can develop personal relationships which involve loyalty and responsibility.

Nowadays sociology talks of the classical family losing ground to a 'pluralisation of lifestyles' such as open long-term relationships, single-parent families and so on. This development can either be welcomed or rejected. However, with regard to social policy and security, this development is alarming if the cost of pluralising lifestyles is externalised or nationalised and is simply loaded onto the welfare state. For example, if social aid is claimed by single-parent families or for alternative lifestyles, „alternativeness" being financed from a fund which is actually set up for emergency cases, the cost of which is borne by all members of society.

In the new subsidiarity, the family will play the primary, but not the only role. The family is the original and natural institution which provides basic provision. Since the family income is, however, so heavily dependent on the market and therefore on its fluctuations and since the cohesion of the extended family is reduced by geographical, professional or social mobility, the family alone is no longer in the position to deliver basic provision. Corporate and occupational pension institutions must work in conjunction with the family. In this process, a reduction in state responsibility for social benefits must not be limited to purely financial restructuring. The ever more important area of care services can also increasingly be taken over by non-state institutions (cf. Fink 1988a; Dettling/Jaekel/Munder 1988; cf. also Fink 1983).

The principle of subsidiarity calls for a distinction to be made between the kind of risks which can only be borne by the larger community and those which can be borne by smaller, subsidiary communities. Compulsory state provision ought to provide only basic insurance, protection from neediness, and not protection from poverty in old age. Only this kind of insurance constitutes a general purpose of the state; one can thus assume that the public would agree to it. At this point, it is valid to differentiate clearly between the state's objective of providing protection from neediness in old age and that of protecting from poverty in old age. The proposal from the Greens' parliamentary group in the German Lower House, to introduce a „basic pension", financed by taxation, in order to avoid poverty in old age, implies as an objective of state provision something which is unattainable. The state cannot eliminate poverty, but only vital neediness, because poverty is a relative concept. Poverty is a disparity between means available and perceived needs and requirements. A rich man, whose annual income falls from DM 300,000 to DM 30,000 will feel poor but will not be in need. If there is relative poverty during working years then there will also be poverty during retirement. The state cannot eliminate relative poverty, neither during active, working life nor during retirement.

Nor is it the task of state provision to avoid every relative increase in poverty during retirement. The protection which social insurance aims to achieve, namely that in old age no insured person ought to fall from his previous social stratum, is one which should be critically questioned. Protecting the assets of relative income positions may well be an interest of the individual, and accordingly, he or she can privately insure this interest. However, protecting assets is neither a means towards the state objective of protecting the citizen against neediness, nor is it a state objective in itself. For, if it were an aim of the state, the state would then be favouring and establishing an existing stratification of income and society. The state governed by the rule of law and the social state should be neutral towards the distribution and stratification which emerges from the free play of society's forces, and it should intervene structurally in distribution, only on the margin of the social spectrum, in the case of neediness or when riches and power are being monopolised.

Even if the state were to set itself the goal of protecting a certain level of income in retirement, related to the level of income during working life, it certainly could not realise that goal, because the retired generation as a whole can only protect their capital assets and income when the age structure of the population is constant or is becoming ever younger. If the entire society is ageing, securing a constant level of real income for the older members is only possible through the worsening of the relative position of the younger members. This problem of inter-generational justice, that is, justice between the generations, is the ultimate cause of the current crisis in insurance for old age.

It is unjust for the state to guarantee a constant level of disposable income even for retirement incomes, without taking into account the changed conditions as regards the population structure and life expectancy. However it is also unjust to carry out large-scale, discretionary devaluation of the claims to pension payments acquired by the life-long contributions to the social security system during the active work life. What is just is that a balance of interests is achieved through impartial consideration of the issues and of the entitlements of the generations affected. It is precisely as unjust to establish the entitlements of one generation when circumstances have changed as it is to undermine people's entitlements in a discriminatory way by devaluating their benefits.

In any event, justice between generations can only be realised to a limited extent. When someone is born largely defines their fate (cf. Künzel-Schön 1986, 102 ff). The person who is old enough to have lived through two world wars and two inflationary periods in Germany experiences a fate different to someone who was born well after the war. However, for the past fifteen years the generation born in the high birth-rate years of the „baby boom" has been economically worse-off than their parents' generation at the same stage in life (cf. Baby Boomers 1986).

To want to establish in detail equal conditions in life between generations would be to remove the uncontrollable nature of birth and of fate, and to want to play God. Here the state can only strive for something approaching justice. It must also be noted that in a democracy with an age structure in which the older age groups are particularly strong, there is no danger that the young will be privileged; the privileged group will rather be the old. Currently in Germany the 45-and-over age group has an absolute majority over the younger age cohorts[19], so that this age group, if it is as united as the younger one, is capable of politically pushing through amendments to the law in favour of improved provision for old age.

IX. A Proposal for the Reform of the Social Insurance System: Contributory Basic Pension

The task of basic provision by the state is to provide basic security for old age, not full security in the sense of protecting assets. This view is represent-

19 On 1 January 1985, 45-and-over age group: 22.74 million, 18-45 age group: approx. 22.0 million; figures based on INSTITUT DER DEUTSCHEN WIRTSCHAFT (1985), table 4. Cf. also HAUSER (1982), p. 441. According to reliable estimates, in the year 2000, one in four Germans will be over 60, and if current trends continue the ratio will be more than one in three in 2030. The fact that senior citizens set up their own party, the Graue Panther, in July 1989 shows that political debate and even party formation already target age groups, and that „age-group classes" are beginning to shape parties. The creation of „class-based parties", with age as the factor defining class, and the dangers of an emergent „class struggle between age groups" are already looming.

ed by two very different groups of authors in two draft reforms. Both the draft reform from the Green party group in the German Lower House and that of the Institut für Wirtschafts- und Gesellschaftspolitik (IWG) [Institute for Economic and Social Policy] (by Meinhard Miegel and Stephanie Wahl) question the principles of protecting assets and of dependency on contributions, upon which the current pensions insurance law is founded.

The Greens' draft proposes a citizen's income of DM 1000 which would be financed from tax revenue and index-linked, as well as a compulsory additional pension (Die Grünen/ Graue Panther 1985). Miegel and Wahl's draft for the IWG proposes a basic insurance, which would amount to 40 per cent of the given average net wage of all non-self-employed workers, i.e. around DM 800 at present, and would be fully financed from tax revenue. It ought to be possible to complement this basic insurance with a voluntary and private supplementary insurance (Miegel/Wahl 1985, p.10).

One objection to the Greens' draft is that it proposes such a high basic pension that a compulsory additional pension would be utopian. The citizen's income system would not change the current comprehensive insurance system, but would only shift the financial burden off the system which has run up until now, involving a combination of the socially insured individual's contributions and state subsidies, onto the state alone.

But the level of basic security or basic pension should not be the central issue here. More important are systematic objections to tax-financed basic security. If one of the key problems in state provision up to now has been that it does not take into consideration the real economic side effects of the way provision for old age is organised on the population structure, on the behaviour of different generations and on the capacity for personal responsibility [20] then it is surely an even greater problem for drafts which throw the baby out with the bath water, calling for and advocating even less personal responsibility. With a tax-financed basic pension income there is no remaining incentive to look after the culture of basic provision, because even personal work performance no longer has an influence on security. Incentives to renounce consumption, to work more economically and to sensibly acquire savings become completely irrelevant. Except for the very affluent classes,

20 Here again we must reject the widespread view that population development is a variable completely exogenous to the organization of the national economy and the institutions for basic provision, and that it is not affected by the organizational principles of social insurance. Rather, population development must be endogenized as a variable in the system of old-age insurance.

there is no longer any incentive to save. Saving is enforced by means of taxation, but in a situation where basic insurance is financed through taxation and where there is a lack of incentive to work and to invest because of high taxation, the level of taxes necessary for the basic pension may not even be being earned any more.

The concept of basic pension was introduced in the proposal of the Greens' parliamentary group and the senior citizens' protection association, Graue Panther in 1985, and was based on the argument that more and more work is being done by machines and that we are running out of work as it were evident from the high unemployment figures. Therefore society must maintain those who cannot find work. In reply to this it can be said that a machine tax is effectively a tax on those who own machines, and thus it raises production costs just as much as employment-related social contributions, and like the latter, it has potentially negative repercussions on employment and social security.

The argument that unemployment and unemployment benefit as a replacement income represent a disconnection in the link between work done and the entitlement to income, and that this disconnection can be applied to the entire retired population is untenable. This disconnection between work and income applies at present, at a time of great national economic pressure, to about 10 per cent of the working population in Germany (a figure equivalent to the number of unemployed). Society is affluent enough to be able to bear this disconnection between work done and the entitlement to income. However, an analogous total break between work and income in old age would only be possible if the national economy were able economically to bear an even higher rate of unemployment without material difficulty. This, however, is highly unlikely. It is astonishing that millions of unemployed can successfully be maintained over a long period of time without a collapse of the national economy, but it does not justify extending the phenomenon of the non-work-related income for the unemployed to turn it into a general pension for everyone independent of work and of contributions.

It may be justified to add a thought on long-term unemployment to these considerations on the problem of basic income. Current long-term unemployment is not, like the mass unemployment of the nineteenth century primarily a question of distribution, but is rather a cultural problem. It is not subsistence protection of the unemployed which is called into question but the protection of their right to participate in the society's culture, a culture which is transmitted through work. Because work has a cultural function and at the same time offers participation in the creation of the values of a culture, the unemployed are excluded from a part of society's culture. The same is true for women not working. The feelings of demoralisation experienced by many housewives who are not in work, do not arise from an objective income crisis, but from the feeling of having limited participation in society's culture.

The solution for long-term unemployment cannot only be envisaged through redistribution of work, because work is not a homogeneous good like money which can be distributed better by transfers. Unemployment comes about precisely because the production factor labour is not homogeneous and particular forms of work are no longer required, i.e. they are no longer sufficiently productive or are not taken on by the workers. The solution for long-term unemployment must rather be sought in a new „culture of employment" within companies, which does not instantly make less productive jobs redundant, but attempts to keep them in the company, and which also has the possibility of reducing wages for less productive work. The state should even out some of the loss in productivity due to less productive workforces, by transfer payments to the companies.

This kind of culture of employment would prevent employers from being able to externalise completely their obligation to provide for the welfare of their employees and would stop them from shifting it onto the state social insurance. Care for the unemployed cannot be externalised completely from the companies to social insurance. The fight against unemployment must be at least partly internalised inside the companies again and the state must support this internalisation in a subsidiary way. The social issue of the present day is the co-existence of long-term unemployment in particular sections of the working population and a boom in the national economy. This social issue is primarily a cultural one. It puts to society and the economy the cultural demand of permitting everybody to participate in the creation of society's cultural and economic values which are transmitted through work.

Returning to the problem of basic security in old age: those who advocate a basic pension guaranteed by the state and financed by taxation, base this call on the argument that the basic pension would have to be introduced without a compulsory contributions scheme, in order to prevent a large number of pensioners from drifting over to social aid and to stop the „stigmatisation" associated with this from arising at all in the first place. The reply to this is that the distinction between normal and abnormal, between responsible and irresponsible behaviour is not a „stigmatisation" of, nor a mark of Cain on those acting irresponsibly. It is what it is: a factual distinction. The difference between a self-earned entitlement and social aid cannot be abolished just so that no one need any longer be ashamed to claim social aid. The ethos of personal responsibility cannot be abolished so that those acting irresponsibly need no longer feel any ethical reproach. Normality cannot be abolished so that there is no longer any anomaly. The distinction between social insurance and social aid cannot be abolished either, just because people who occasionally find themselves needy are ashamed to claim social aid. If someone finds himself in neediness through no fault of his own, he must not, indeed ought not to be allowed to be ashamed to claim social aid. If he must claim it through his own fault, then it is right that his conscience pricks when he makes the claim.

Unfortunately there are many forms of neediness which fall between those which arise through one's own fault and those which arise through no fault of one's own, and these ought to be dealt with cautiously when moralising about lifestyles. However, taking people seriously as responsible beings requires that the ethics of responsibility as well as the question of blame cannot be completely divorced from the economic question of maintenance. To divorce the question of responsibility from the distinction between personally earned entitlement and social aid granted from the national income would not only be an injustice to that majority which live their lives responsibly, it would also be a denial of the central identity and values of the individual who may have made one mistake and who would only be regarded to an even greater extent as an object without awareness, if this mistake were not also accounted to him.

Most people want to be recognised as personally responsible individuals, and also want to be recognised by the state. Therefore most people do not want to receive their pension as a good-Samaritan allocation, but as an entitlement acquired through contributions. They regard their payment of contributions as buying an entitlement. They are buying a feeling of entitlement to a claim. However, those entitled to pensions will have to learn that their contributions are not buying them future benefits on a basis of equality of value and counter-value, of deposit and withdrawal, but that they are merely „acquiring" pension payments which are just, are in relation to contribution payments and commensurate with the relationship between the generations. Under changing environmental and generational relationships, for which the individual is not responsible, the contributions cannot buy a particular pension, but only the entitlement to a just pension benefit. Pension entitlements are a relationship of just reciprocal services, not of contractual equality. Talk of the contract between generations is misleading. By definition generations cannot make contracts because everybody who ought to enter into such a contract is not present simultaneously. I do not have a contract with my parents to be born, because they cannot ask me if I wish to be born.

Similarly, a younger generation, decreasing in number because part of the parental generation found raising children too troublesome, could not be asked to agree to the pension contract. And they certainly would not have agreed to maintain more and more retired people and pensioners when there are fewer and fewer employed people. The legal form of the civil law contract is based on the equality of the reciprocal performance of a contract, as long as it is not a gift contract. Relationships based on mutuality are however relationships of reciprocity which are socially standardised and ethically influenced, and which, taking a long-term perspective, may sometimes be equal, but at least are fair in the long run, as regards the balance between the reciprocal elements of performance. In pensions insurance there is a relationship based on mutuality, not a contract. Thus, if the circumstances change, then the relationship of reciprocity must also change. The balance of burdens between the generations is not an equal reciprocal performance, or an equal deposit and withdrawal which is defined by contract, but it is a just two-way balance of justified claims which generations have upon each other.

If the life span of old people increases and the number of young people decreases then there should be a fair and balanced decline in the claims of the old, while the performance of the young should increase. The burdens must be fairly distributed. It is not absolutely necessary for the balance to be equal according to numbers or percentages, as intended by the Social Democrat Party (SPD) proposal for reform. According to this proposal, pensions should be reduced by the same percentage as that by which working people's contributions and government subsidies to pensions insurance go up. It is doubtful whether a just or equal distribution of burdens is thus achieved. Because the government subsidies are paid by tax-payers and therefore (because pensioners pay no direct taxes) paid by workers, and because the pensioners' level of wealth is often higher than that of younger families, this solution is too elegant and too numerical in fact to be just.

Performances based on complete mutuality are only possible in families and between friends, but not between people who are not acquainted and between the members of an entire population. A population is not bound together to that extent. Basic provision by the state based on mutuality is therefore not possible in the form of a citizen's income nor as a general basic pension financed by taxes, but can only be organised on a contributory basis and not including full cover for income in old age according to the relative level of wealth in the income pyramid during the working years. The dynamic state pension of recent decades which protected a particular level of assets, was linked to one-off historical conditions: i.e. the baby boom generation with its increasing number of contributors, the high level of economic growth during these years and the low starting level for pensions in 1957. These conditions no longer apply today.

The reform of social security should provide for a basic pension financed by contributions under state management, and should direct claims to protection which exceed this to private and company insurance. There are two principles in this which ought to be decisive and at the same time they should establish the line of continuity which provides the link to the current system of insurance for old age. These are the compulsory nature of basic protection for everyone and the financing of the basic pension through contributions.

The model of state basic pension takes into account the fact that not all members of society can insure themselves privately for basic risks, but that a general compulsory insurance cannot constitute protection of assets, but only a basic insurance. The model of financing through contributions emphasises the difference between a personally earned entitlement to insurance for old age and the granting of social aid, which is not worked for. The formulation of the basic pension financed by contributions could look like this:[21]

- The state-enforced, legally organised insurance for old age, invalidity and dependants would be exclusively a basic insurance.
- This basic protection or basic pension would be financed by compulsory contributions from everyone, including the self-employed. Everyone would be entitled to this basic pension in old age.
- The basic pension would amount to 40 - 50 per cent of the average net remuneration for work of all non-self-employed people in a given period.
- The basic pension would be financed by contributions from everyone. In periods which count towards pension, but for which no payments are made, the state would pay the contributions in the place of the insured party, particularly for housewives when they are raising children.

21 The proposal, the essential features of which are oulined here, contains elements of the IWG draft proposal for a basic pension (H MIEGEL, S. WAHL) and elements of R. HAUSER and G. WAGNER'S Voll Eigenständiges System der Absicherung; cf. WAGNER (1986). My proposal differs from that of the IWG in that basic pension would be funded by contributions, and from Wagner's proposal in that it places greater emphasis on the character of the basic pension and on balancing out the costs of having children.

- The distinction between basic pension financed by contributions and social aid would continue to be maintained.
- The contributions paid by the state from tax revenue for periods during which women work as housewives and which count towards pension, but for which no payments are made, would be financed from an energy and resources tax, with the aim of reducing the use of non-renewable resources which will no longer be available for future generations and of using the money from the resources tax towards new life and towards making it easier to raise children.
- The basic pension would realise equality in old age protection between married couples with children in which only one parent works, and married couples without children in which both parents work.
- The basic protection financed by contributions would be introduced within a period of 30 years, during which acquired pension and maintenance entitlements would be safeguarded. In protecting pension entitlements acquired up until now, there would be a percentage reduction in the level of pensions to date, which would be approximately equivalent to the percentage rate by which the relationship between the number of employed people and the total population had declined.
- Company and co-operative insurance systems and procedures to protect capital as part of company profit-sharing and share-ownership schemes for employees, which would be able to supplement the basic pension, should be promoted to a greater extent.
- Private acquisition of capital for security in old age, by means of home owning, among other things, should also be made easier than before for those with lower incomes.

The transition from the present system, with its very predominant proportion of state provision, to a mixed system of personal responsibility and basic state protection poses political and technical problems of financing for the legislator, because expectations have been created and accumulated entitlements to social insurance exist which are like wealth, and which require a longer transitional period. However, it must be made clear that the entitlement to an unchanged level of pensions insurance and the protection of the trust of today's pensioners can only be acknowledged on condition that the average duration of retirement, pension payments to those who are entitled to them, and the relationship between the number of actively employed and the number of those who receive pensions remain unchanged. If this constant is not true, as is the case today, then either reductions in pensions must be fixed according to the changed relationship in numbers between the generations, or the pension age must be shifted upwards. Decreases in pensions based on reasons of this kind can facilitate the transitional phase from the current pension system to the system of a basic pension financed by contributions.

The model presented here is not a revolutionary break with the system which has been in place until now, as would have been the case with a basic pension financed by taxation. But rather, it follows the line of continuity from the pension system in the past. It is making use of the financial crisis in the social security systems of Germany as an opportunity for a reform, which will lead to a better combination of personal responsibility and basic provision by the state.

X. Individual Responsibility for Social Security

The state system of compulsory comprehensive insurance weakens the cultural and meaning-imparting function of provision in that it takes provision right out of the hands of the citizens. The current pension system enforces full cover through compulsory contributions. It lays down the level and duration of payments by legal obligation and fixes the relative levels of pensions according to these two yardsticks for all income groups. Because the current pension system makes compulsory the method and the scale of protection for old age for everyone, but of necessity cannot put a time limit on pension payments in retirement according to their duration nor make them legally binding, this system finds itself between the frying-pan and the fire: between decreasing receipts from contributions as the working population is on the decline and increasing pension payments when the period of retirement – of pension entitlement – increases in duration. In the administered system of compulsory contributions in which the individual has no influence whatsoever on the ways and means of acquiring and eroding capital, he will not be induced to be independent to the extent of creating capital for himself and his children, will he be led to a communal, „contextual" matching of his provision with the people in his area. He will, rather, be kept in the position of a cared-for and administered member of the compulsory insurance system.

The removal of personal responsibility for old-age provision by means of a system of collective comprehensive social security does away with the necessity to see one's life as a whole and to have old age present in youth as well, in that anticipation of the mind which Heidegger called „running forward in thought towards death“ (cf. Heidegger 1956, p. 68 + 75). Comprehensive social security eliminates the individual's incentive to provide care for him- or herself.[22] However it cannot eliminate the economic necessity that a general culture of basic provision must exist amongst members of society because the means for securing an existence must still be efficiently obtained. To experience the run-up to old age with an attitude of responsibility means uniting all one's life in a single point of view, that as unity it will be a success and can be justified. The consideration of the entirety of life under the perspective of securing oneself against the basic risks of existence – for which the individual takes responsibility – is an essential part of successful human activity. Social responsibility for social security and for basic provision cannot remove the necessity for individual ethical responsibility for the entirety of the individual life and its individual security. Rather it must promote the cultivation of individual responsibility within the subsidiary forms of insurance against risks provided by private, corporate and occupational, and governmental schemes.

22 Cf. also KOSLOWSKI (1987) on the culture in which the individual provides care for himself.

References

ABEL, A. B.: Article „Ricardian equivalence theorem", in: J. EATWELL, M. MILGATE, P. NEWMAN (Eds.): *The New Palgrave. A Dictionary of Economics*, Vol. 4, London (Macmillan) 1987, pp. 174-179.

ALBERS, W.: „Die Strukturreform der sozialen Sicherung - eine sozialpolitische Aufgabe", *Wirtschaftsdienst*, 65 (1985), pp. 601-608.

BAADER, F. VON: *Vorlesungen über speculative Dogmatik.* Viertes Heft (1836), Sämtliche Werke, Vol. 9, Aalen (Scientia) 1963.

[BABY BOOMERS]: "Growing Pains at 40. As they approach midlife, Baby Boomers struggle to have it all", *Time-Magazine*, 19 May 1986, pp. 38-50.

BARRO, R. J.: „Are Government Bonds net Wealth?", *Journal of Political Economy*, 82 (1974), pp. 1095-1117.

BECK, U.: *Risikogesellschaft. Auf dem Weg in eine andere Moderne*, Frankfurt a. M. (Suhrkamp) 1985.

BUCHANAN, J. M.: „Barro on the Ricardian equivalence theorem", *Journal of Political Economy*, 84 (1976), pp. 337-342.

CAIRNCROSS, F.: „Social Studies: A moving Target", *Times Literary Supplement*, 20 September (1985), p. 1025.

CAVACO-SILVA, A. A.: *Economic Effects of Public Debt*, London (Robertson) 1977.

CLARK, R./J. KREPS/J. SPENGLER: „Economics of Aging: A Survey", *Journal of Economic Literature*, 16 (1978), pp. 919-962.

DERRIDA, J.: *Die Schrift und die Differenz*, Frankfurt a. M. (Suhrkamp) 1985.

DETTLING, W.: „Jenseits von Markt und Macht", in: U. FINK (ed.) (1988a), pp. 65-69.

DETTLING, W./M.JAECKEL/J.MÜNDER: „Zwischen Geld und Güte. Auf der Suche nach einem optimalen Ordnungsrahmen für soziale Dienste", in: U. FINK (ed.) (1988a), pp. 65-79.

FINK, U. (Ed.): *Keine Angst vor Alternativen. Ein Minister wagt sich in die Szene*, Freiburg i. Br. (Herder) 1983.

FINK, U. (Ed.) (1988a): *Der neue Generationenvertrag. Ich für Dich. Die Zukunft der sozialen Dienste*, München (R. Piper) 1988.

FINK, U. (1988b): „Der neue Generationenvertrag. Die Zukunft der sozialen Dienste", in: U. FINK (Ed.) (1988a), pp. 9-22.

GBUREK, M./W. KÖHLER: „Reichtum nach Maß. Vermögensplanung", *Wirtschaftswoche*, Nr. 12, (17 March 1988), pp. 42-58.

DIE GRÜNEN/GRAUE PANTHER (Ed.): *Grundrente statt Altersarmut*, Essen (Klartext) 1985.

HAUSER, R.: „How to Guarantee West German Public Pension Payments During the Next Fifty Years", *Zeitschrift für die gesamte Staatswissenschaft*, 138 (1982), pp. 440-468.

HEIDEGGER, M.: *Existence and Being*, translated by D. Scott, R. Hull, and A. Crick, Chicago (Vision Press) 2nd ed. 1956.

INSTITUT DER DEUTSCHEN WIRTSCHAFT (ED.): *Zahlen zur wirtschaftlichen Entwicklung der Bundesrepublik Deutschland*, Köln, 1985.

KÖHLER, W.: „Planvoll zum Ziel. Vermögensplanung (11)", *Wirtschaftswoche*, Nr. 13, (24 March 1989), pp. 124-130.

KOSLOWSKI, P. (1982a): *Gesellschaft und Staat. Ein unvermeidlicher Dualismus*, Stuttgart (Klett-Cotta) 1982.

— (1982b): *Ethik des Kapitalismus, mit e. Kommentar von James M. Buchanan*, Tübingen (J.C.B. Mohr [Paul Siebeck]) 1982, 5th ed. 1995. English translation: *Ethics of Capitalism and Critique of Sociology. Two Essays with a Comment by James M. Buchanan*, Heidelberg, New York, Tokyo (Springer-Verlag) 1996 (= Studies in Economic Ethics and Philosophy, Vol. 10).

— „Versuch zu einer philosophischen Kritik des gegenwärtigen Sozialstaats", in: P. KOSLOWSKI, PH. KREUZER, R. LÖW (Eds.): *Chancen und Grenzen des Sozialstaats*, Tübingen (J.C.B. Mohr [Paul Siebeck]) 1983, pp. 1-23. Reprinted in P. KOSLOWSKI: *Die Ordnung der Wirtschaft. Studien zur Praktischen Philosophie und Politischen Ökonomie*, Tübingen (J.C.B. Mohr [Paul Siebeck]) 1994, pp. 299-322.

— "Sozialstaat. Glück mit Illusionen", *Wirtschaftswoche*, 21 (16th May 1986), pp. 79-83.

— *Die postmoderne Kultur, München* (C. H. Beck) 1987, 2nd ed. 1988.

— *Prinzipien der Ethischen Ökonomie. Grundlegung der Wirtschaftsethik und der auf die Ökonomie bezogenen Ethik*, Tübingen (J. C. B. Mohr [Paul Siebeck]) 1988, 2nd ed. 1994.

— (1989a): *Die Prüfungen der Neuzeit. Über Postmodernität*, Wien (Edition Passagen) 1989.

— (1989b): *Wirtschaft als Kultur. Wirtschaftskultur und Wirtschaftsethik in der Postmoderne*, Wien (Edition Passagen) 1989.

— (1989c): „Risikogesellschaft als Grenzerfahrung der Moderne. Für eine postmoderne Kultur", *Aus Politik und Zeitgeschichte. Beilage zur Wochenzeitung Das Parlament*, 36/89 (1 September 1989), pp. 14-30.

— (1989d): „Supermoderne oder Postmoderne? Dekonstruktion und Mystik in den zwei Postmodernen", in: P. KOSLOWSKI (1989a), pp. 64-88.

— (1989e): „Die Postmodernität der Weisheitstradition", in: P. KOSLOWSKI (1989a), pp. 109-121.

— (1989f): „Christliche Gnosis und spekulative Philosophie unter Bedingungen der Postmoderne", in: P. KOSLOWSKI (1989a), pp. 122-150.

— *Die Ordnung der Wirtschaft. Studien zur Praktischen Philosophie und Politischen Ökonomie*, Tübingen (J.C.B. Mohr [Paul Siebeck]) 1994.

KOSLOWSKI, ST.: *Die Geburt des Sozialstaats aus dem Geist des Deutschen Idealismus. Individuum und Gemeinschaft bei Lorenz von Stein,* Weinheim (VCH/Acta humaniora) 1989.

KÜNZEL-SCHÖN, M.: *Wenn unsere Eltern älter werden. Familienbeziehungen – Pflegebedürftigkeit – Generationenkonflikt. Erfahrungen und Informationen,* Reinbek (rororo Sachbuch) 1986.

LYOTARD, J.-F. (1986): *Das postmoderne Wissen, Wien* (Edition Passagen). Original: *La condition postmoderne,* Paris (Minuit) 1979.

MIEGEL, M./ST. WAHL: *Gesetzliche Grundsicherung. Private Vorsorge - Der Weg aus der Rentenkrise,* Stuttgart (Bonn Aktuell) 1985.LL-BREUNING, O. VON (1960): *Kapitalismus und gerechter* Lohn, Freiburg i. Br. (Herder) 1960.

RAUSCHER, A.: Artikel »Subsidiarität. I. Sozialethik«, *Staatslexikon,* 7th ed., Freiburg i. Br. (Herder) 1989, pp. 386-388.

RICARDO, D.: "The Principles of Political Economy and Taxation", (3rd ed.1821), in: *The work and correspondence of David Ricardo,* Vol. I, Pamphlets and papers, Piero Sraffa (Ed.), Cambridge (Cambridge University Press) 1966.

RICARDO, D.: "Funding System" (1820), in: *The works and correspondence of David Ricardo,* Vol. IV, Pamphlets and papers 1815-1823, Piero Sraffa (Ed.), Cambridge (Cambridge University Press) 1966, pp. 143-200.

SCHMÄHL, W.: „Ist die dynamische Rente noch finanzierbar?", in: P. KOSLOWSKI/R. LÖW/PH. KREUZER (Eds.) (1983): *Chancen und Grenzen des Sozialstaats,* Tübingen (J. C. B. Mohr), pp. 177-191.

SPRANGER, E. (1962): *Das Gesetz der ungewollten Nebenwirkungen in der Erziehung,* Heidelberg (Quelle & Meyer) 2nd ed. 1965.

STATISTISCHES BUNDESAMT (Ed.): *Statistisches Jahrbuch für die Bundesrepublik Deutschland 1987,* Stuttgart (Kohlhammer) 1987.

STATISTISCHES BUNDESAMT (Ed.): *Statistisches Jahrbuch für die Bundesrepublik Deutschland 1988,* Stuttgart (Kohlhammer) 1988.

TREITSCHKE, H. VON (1875): *Der Sozialismus und seine Gönner. Nebst einem Sendschreiben an Gustav Schmoller,* Berlin (Georg Reimer), (First in: *Preußische Jahrbücher* 1874).

UTZ, A.F. (1956): *Formen und Grenzen des Subsidiaritätsprinzips,* Heidelberg (Kerle).

WAGNER, G. (1986): „Strukturreform des Rentensystems. Ein konkreter Vorschlag", *Wirtschaftsdienst,* 61 (März 1986), pp. 148-152.

Conclusion

Chapter 18

On the Moral Foundations of the Welfare State Three Research Programmes

PHILIPPE VAN PARIJS

I. Introduction

While discussing the ethical issues raised by present-day social policy and the restructuring of the welfare state, the authors of this book have been talking about the moral foundations of the welfare state in three distinct senses. I shall illustrate each of them with a number of examples, mostly borrowed from the papers included in this collection or from the discussions that followed their oral presentation. Each example is cited (usually without any specific attribution, so as to spare qualifications) because it illustrates an interesting pattern of argument and/or a promising avenue of research, not necessarily because I am committed to its validity.

II. The Moral Requirements of the Welfare State

The moral requirements of (one or other particular form of) the welfare state are those moral aspects of the motivation that underlies the private or political behaviour of the contributors and beneficiaries of the welfare state whose disappearance arguably jeopardises the latter's sustainability. By «moral», I mean here those aspects of a person's motivation that do not reduce to his or her self-interest narrowly construed.

Take, first, honesty, the disposition to abide by the rules of the game, to abstain from cheating on either the tax or the benefit side, for example by hiding some of one's income. It is clearly a virtue whose widespread and active presence greatly helps the working of a welfare state. But it is being slowly eroded, some say, by such exogenous factors as the weakening of religion-based moral codes or the increasingly anonymous character of social life. It is also quickly being undermined, others say, as the endogenous outcome of the following process. Our welfare states typically expect able-bodied claimants to be actively looking for work. But growing numbers of adults of working age have such poor skills (and skill-acquiring capacities) that there is only a very dim hope of their ever being able to get a job, as younger, more energetic and more adaptable applicants keep pouring into the labour market. Hence, they cannot realistically be expected to keep applying for jobs and constantly be on the lookout for work opportunities. Indeed, they grow indignant against a system that expects them, morally and legally, to keep looking for something they know they will never find, and they have therefore no compunction in «cheating the system» by merely pretending to be job seekers. This in turn, once realised and publicised, can only feed the resentment of those who have to work hard in order to earn wages whose post-tax levels are reduced so as to fund the benefits of the jobless. The contributors grow indignant at a system that expects them to support crowds of cheaters and have no scruples in «cheating the system» themselves by evading taxation as much as they can. As a result of such processes, the working of the welfare state will be able to rely even less on widespread honesty. The resources at its disposal will shrink, and the cost of collecting and allocating them efficiently will swell.

Secondly, take the complex formed by the work ethic («work as hard and well as you can»), the thrift ethic («save for your children and for your old days»), the health ethic («do not take unnecessary risks nor unnecessary remedies») and the family ethic («stick together and help your relatives»). As long as this complex is in place, the levels of provision to which people are entitled in case they happen to be destitute, sick, etc., can be quite generous without its making the system very costly, because people's work, saving, health and family behaviour remains essentially unaffected by the prospect of compensation. But as this complex gets eroded, whether again as a result of exogenous forces or of the social security system itself, the latter becomes increasingly vulnerable to moral hazard: the explosion of claims – by people who are, but in the absence of social security provisions would not be, unemployed, single parents, overusers of medicines, abandoned old people, etc. – goes hand in hand with a reduction in the income available to honour these claims, itself generated by people who work and save less than they would if no part of their incomes were used to finance the system.

Thirdly, let us turn from the moral motivation of individual behaviour to that of collective behaviour, and in particular to the political expression of solidarity which has made the development of the welfare state possible. This politically expressed solidarity is today under pressure for two related but distinct reasons. One is the dwindling ethnic and cultural homogeneity of the population concerned, both as the result of immigration and (prospectively) as a result of the rising scale at which redistribution will have to operate in order to be economically sustainable. The second reason is the growing potential geographical mobility of individual members of each political society: there is bound to be a big difference between the feelings of solidarity among people «in the same boat» and among people who happen to be briefly gathered under the roof of the same airport.

Consequently, whether (one or other particular form of) the welfare state is sustainable depends not only on «objective» processes, whether demographic (say, how big the baby bust is), economic (competition for both commercial outlets and taxable assets) or technological (such as the development of medical technology). It also depends on a moral evolution that affects both the cost of maintaining a certain level of provision and the politically expressed will to bear that cost.

III. The Moral Presuppositions of the Welfare State

The moral presuppositions of (one or other particular form of) the welfare state are the principles that underlie it, in the sense that they would justify its actual operation, whether or not they correspond to its proclaimed aims. Such principles can be arrived at by looking at the actual effects of particular social security institutions in particular historical contexts and spelling out their implicit (sometimes unconscious or hidden) purposes. (See Moon 1988 for an approach along these lines.)

For example, one can look at the obligation to work imposed in Northern Europe by the first Poor Laws either as a way of enforcing a religiously motivated compulsion to work, or as a screening device for the purpose of identifying the truly needy. Or one can contrast two categories of contemporary welfare states in terms of an opposition between those aiming to provide people with more options and those aiming to make them choose the right option. Or again one can try to read the history of the welfare state as an ever more ambitious attempt to suppress risk, to fully compensate whatever bad things can happen in our lives, whether caused by the actions of nature, other people or even oneself. But the most common attempt at spelling out the moral presuppositions of the welfare state is of course in terms of the contrast (and frequent conflict) between the «Bismarckian» insurance principle, which can only accommodate ex-post transfers, and the «Beveridgean» solidarity principle, which makes room for ex-ante transfers between categories of people who know in advance that it is not in their interest to pool risks of a certain sort. This distinction is made with many refinements and in a great variety of versions (see e.g. Baldwin 1990, Koslowski 1990, Euzéby 1991).

However, it leaves out an important third principle which could be called «Painean» because of its having received its first clear expression from Thomas Paine (1796). In a memoir addressed to the French Directoire, Paine argued for an unconditional cash payment made to every person, rich or poor, working or not, as (s)he reaches the age of 21, and then again, every year, as from the age of 50, to be funded out of a general land tax. The ground for the transfer, in this case, is not the materialisation of a risk, and hence cannot be derived from either insurance or solidarity as usually conceived. It is rather the right of each citizen to an equal share in the value of society's natural resources. Paine's principle has a straightforward application in Alaska's annual dividend scheme funded out of the proceeds of the exploitation of oil (see O'Brien & Olson 1990). An appropriate generalisation of it also provides the most straightforward justification for universal child benefits and universal basic pensions in those countries in which they exist, and for a universal citizen's income in those countries in which it is being advocated. One way of looking at the moral presuppositions of the evolving welfare states would therefore be in terms of the complex pattern of conflict and co-operation between these three fundamental principles (see Van Parijs 1994).

IV. The Moral Justifications of the Welfare State

Although norms are an essential component of their subject matter, research programmes focusing on the moral requirements or on the moral presuppositions of the welfare state are of a factual, empirical, social-scientific nature. One only reaches the ethical level proper as one moves on to the question of the moral justification of (one or other form of) the welfare state.

The question, then, is no longer about what is, was or can be, but about what ought to be. What sort of welfare state must we have (if any), and why?

One answer that is sometimes heard the organisation of poverty relief as the central role of the welfare state. The insurance function is best left to the private sector, with a number of constraints on who is to be taken on (to counter adverse selection problems) and on the use of insurance funds (to guarantee diversification). But poverty relief, whether motivated by self-interest (the fear of muggers and the dislike for beggars) or charity (of a genuinely altruistic nature), cannot be left to private initiatives, because of co-ordination and free-riding problems. In a «liberal social contract» (Kolm 1985), there is room for unanimous agreement on compulsory redistribution.

An ethically more ambitious answer makes social solidarity the central objective, as spelled out, for example, in Ronald Dworkin's (1981) «insurance behind a veil of ignorance» or in Serge Kolm's (1985) «fundamental insurance». Solidarity consists of being generous towards those in whose situation we could have been and who could have been expected to act the way we do now if they had been in our situation and we in theirs. It justifies transfers to the unlucky and less well endowed, including those whose only handicap resides in their having inadequate earning power.

A further answer, which seems more ambitious still, views the welfare state as an instrument in the service of equality. But equality is multidimensionally ambiguous. Firstly, what exactly is the distributive criterion that is being appealed to? Even if there is only one variable at stake (say, income), is the ideal equality at any cost? This seems blatantly absurd. Is it then the minimisation of inequality subject to the basic needs of all being satisfied ? But such minimisation can lead to different choices depending on whether, for example, the Gini coefficient, the standard deviation or the inverse of entropy is chosen as the measure of inequality. Or is it the maximin, i.e. the restriction of legitimate inequalities to those which help make the situation of the worst off as good as it can be made? This is attractive but moves us a long way from pure equality. And what if there are several variables? Should one equalise along all dimensions (consumption, paid work, domestic work, etc.)? Or should one lump together all dimensions into a single variable, as in Jan Tinbergen's (1943) conception of justice as equality of welfare? Or should one rather resist such amalgamation and adopt a weaker notion of multidimensional equality as envy freeness or, even more weakly, such undominated diversity? (See Fleurbaey 1994, Thomson 1994, Arnsperger 1994, Van Parijs 1995a: ch.3.)

Thus, many interpretations are possible at the level of the criterion. Many are also possible as regards the variable to which the criterion is meant to apply. Should outcomes or opportunities be equalised? If it is opportunities, should they be made commensurable in terms of the highest level of welfare they give access to (Arneson 1990), or in terms of the competitive value of the resources they stem from (Varian 1975), or perhaps through some counterfactual insurance procedure which would take us straight back to solidarity, as characterised above (Dworkin 1981)? If it is rather outcomes that should be equalised, are they to be interpreted as distributive shares and, if so, what is the ground for an equal claim by all members of society: the qualitative and quantitative diversity of talents (Rawls 1990), the equal right to natural resources and bequests (Steiner 1994), or perhaps the fact that without society people would have neither entitlement nor even identities(Føllesdal 1996)?

Equality indicates one direction in which one can attempt to assign an ideal to the welfare state that goes beyond both poverty relief and social solidarity. But it is not the only one. A no less ambitious ideal is the promotion of a virtuous life. As Koslowski (1996) puts it, «the idea of the right way of living must be the guiding star for the legislative, the executive and the administration of the state». In this fourth, «post-modern» (or perhaps rather «post-post-modern») perspective, the welfare state has, for fundamental reasons, an educational, possibly even a coercive, role which it cannot conceivably have in any of the first three perspectives, each of which is consistent with a liberal or «modern» conception of the state.

V. Responsibility

Against the background of this normative map, it is worth returning to the theme of responsibility that appears throughout this book, also in connection with the other two research programmes sketched above. At one extreme, an outcome-egalitarian conception of the objectives of the welfare state strives to minimise responsibility for the consequences of one's actions. The deserving of rewards or punishments has no role to play in this perspective. Unequal outcomes matching unequal efforts can at most be justified instrumentally, as a way of providing incentives, and only to the extent that the ideal of outcome equality is qualified by a minimum subsistence condition or modified into maximin outcome. Fundamentally, the less need there is for the rewarding of «deserving» behaviour, the better.

At the other extreme, one finds an odd convergence of those who ascribe the welfare state no other purpose than minimal poverty relief and of those who entrust it with the far more ambitious task of enforcing virtue. In the «libertarian» poverty-relief perspective, people are entitled to the full product of their activities but have to bear full responsibility for their own welfare, also when ill or old. It is only in residual situations that the state must intervene to help out those who cannot manage through no fault of their own. In the «conservative» virtue-enforcement perspective, living a responsible life (of work, thrift, care for one's spouse and offspring, etc.) is part of what the state must encourage or even impose if it has the power to do so, as is the case with people who are dependent on public support. Responsibility is not rewarded here for contingent instrumental reasons, or as a trivial implication of entitlements, but because it is intrinsically good.

If one judges that responsibility is not given adequate place in the current organisation of the welfare state, let alone in an outcome-egalitarian interpretation of its aims, is one forced to opt either for the libertarian or for the conservative vision just mentioned? Certainly not. For it can be said that equality of opportunities is centrally a strategy for reconciling a concern for equality with a concern for responsibility. This strategy rests on a distinction between people's opportunities, which need to be equalised, and people's (possibly risky) use of these opportunities whose good and bad consequences they can and must bear. The conception of justice as «real freedom for all» presented and defended in my recent work (especially Van Parijs 1995a) constitutes a new variant of opportunity-egalitarianism which claims to combine the appeals of liberty, equality and efficiency and to make adequate room for both individual and social responsibility. It leads to the justification of an unconditional basic income at the highest sustainable level subject to two conditions which I shall not present nor explain here.

VI. The Three Big Challenges

Instead, I would like to conclude by adding one remark about each of the three big challenges to our welfare states that keep surfacing throughout this book the ageing of the population, the dualisation of society, the globalisation of the economy.

It is clear that ageing – due to falling birth rates and rising life expectancies – raises an arithmetic problem whose acuteness varies greatly from one country to another. The extent to which this arithmetic problem is also an economic problem can be overestimated: both pension levels and tax efforts can be held constant despite growing dependency ratios if per capita earnings grow accordingly. But the extent of the economic problem can also be seriously underestimated for three distinct reasons. First, there is the possibility of a significant positive feedback loop: the pressure from increasing claims of the old on the incomes of the active population may squeeze out children even more than predicted. Secondly, the dependency ratio correctly (though always roughly) describes the depth of the problem only if most people of working age can find an unsubsidised job. But reducing the dependency ratio by postponing retirement is an illusory solution if there are already masses of adult people without jobs or with subsidised jobs. Thirdly, even with an unchanged ratio of the retired to the employed, there may be a growing problem in collecting funds because of the growing transnational mobility of high-wage workers and firms. These last two points indicate how heavily the seriousness of the first big challenge depends on the seriousness of the other two.

The fight against the dualisation of society, against the exclusion of a growing part of the adult population from participation in the main stream of paid work, can only be successful if we gradually turn the basic component of our welfare states from a net in which people get caught into a floor on which they can stand. This implies a fortiori that we should firmly resist the repeated pleas for making welfare state provisions more selective than they currently are. One way of fighting selectiveness consists turning more means-tested assistance into rights-based insurance by having the state pay social insurance contributions on behalf of people involved in caring or training activities for example. This could make their «Bismarckian» claims on contributory pensions, paid sick leave or unemployment benefits sufficiently high to render «Beveridgean» means-tested assistance less necessary. The other strategy – the only one, I believe, which gets to the root of the problem – consists of maintaining and extending «Painean» citizenship-based benefits, such as universal health coverage, family allowances or basic pensions and, more radically, an unconditional basic income for all adults. Moral argument along the lines sketched above is of decisive importance to make it politically possible.

Whether it involves a net or a floor, any generous system of social solidarity is threatened by the advent of the world market and in particular the selective mobility of taxable assets. If we don't want to go down the American road, it is urgent to broaden and deepen our common thinking and discussion on these subjects at the European level, for a number of obvious and less obvious reasons (see Van Parijs 1995b). The contribution of this book makes to this important task is one major reason for thanking the organizers of this volume and of the conference from which it stems. Another resides in the particularly favourable working conditions which we enjoyed during three intense and fruitful days. Like any other privilege, and there are quite a few even in an academic's austere life, this one generates a responsibility not just to produce scientifically reliable work along the three complementary avenues illustrated above, but also to help fight a dramatic worsening of the inequalities in life chances which will plague and destroy our societies if we do not play our difficult and crucial roles as morally committed intellectuals.

References

ARNESON, R. J.: «Liberalism, Distributive Subjectivism, and Equal Opportunity for Welfare», *Philosophy and Public Affairs* 19 (1990), pp. 158-94.

ARNSPERGER, C.: «Envy–Freeness and Distributive Justice», *Journal of Economic Surveys* 8 (1994), pp. 155–86.

BALDWIN, P.: *The Politics of Social Solidarity. Class Bases of the European Welfare State,* Cambridge & New York (Cambridge University Press) 1990.

DWORKIN, R.: «What is equality? Part II. Equality of Resources», *Philosophy and Public Affairs* 10 (1981), pp. 283-345.

EUZÉBY, C.: *Le Revenu minimum garanti.* Paris, (La Découverte) 1991.

FLEURBAEY, M.: «L'Absence d'envie dans une problématique post-welfariste», *Recherches économiques de Louvain* 60 (1994), pp. 9-42.

FØLLESDAL, A.: «Do Welfare Obligations End at the Boundaries of the Nation State», this volume 1996.

KOLM, S-C.: *Le Contrat social libéral.* Paris (Presses Universitaires de France) 1985.

KOSLOWSKI, P.: «Der soziale Staat der Postmoderne. Ethische Grundlagen der Sozialpolitik und Reform der Sozialversicherung», in: C. SACHBE and H. T. ENGELHARDT (Eds.):*Sicherheit und Freiheit. Zur Ethik des Wohlfahrtstaates,* Frankfurt a.M. (Suhrkamp) 1990, pp. 28-70.

—— «The Social State in the Post-modern. The Ethical Bases of Social Policy and the Reform of Social Security», this volume 1996.

MOON, J. D.: «The Moral Basis of the Democratic Welfare State», in: A. GUTMANN (Ed.):*Democracy and the Welfare State,* Princeton (Princeton University Press) 1988.

O'BRIEN, J. P., OLSON, D. O.: "The Great Alaskan Money Give Away Program", *Economic Inquiry* 27 (1990), pp. 604-15.

PAINE, THOMAS: «Agrarian Justice» (1796), in: P.F. FONER (Ed.):*The Life and Major Writings of Thomas Paine,* Secaucus, NJ (Citadel Press) 1974, pp. 605-623.

STEINER, H.: *An Essay on Rights,* Oxford (Blackwell) 1994.

THOMSON, W.: «L'absence d'envie: une introduction», *Recherches économiques de Louvain* 60 (1994), pp. 43-62.

TINBERGEN, J.: *Redelijke Inkomensverdeling,* Haarlem (De Gulden Pers) 1943.

VAN PARIJS, P.: «Au delà de la solidarité. Les fondements éthiques de l'Etat-Providence et de son dépassement», *Futuribles* 184 (1994), pp. 5-48

—— (1995a): *Real Freedom for All. What (if Anything) Can Justify Capitalism?,* Oxford (Oxford University Press) 1995.

—— (1995b): *Sauver la solidarité,* Paris (Cerf) 1995.

VARIAN, H.: «Distributive Justice, Welfare Economics and the Theory of Fairness» (1975), in: F. HAHN & M. HOLLIS (Eds.):*Philosophy and Economic Theory,* Oxford (Oxford University Press) 1979, pp. 135-164.

About the Authors

PETER BALDWIN is Associate Professor of History at the University of California, Los Angeles, USA.

PER BAUHN is Assistant Professor of Peace and Conflict Research at Lund University, Sweden.

FRANCES CAIRNCROSS is on the staff of The Economist, is an honorary fellow of St. Anne's College, Oxford, and a governor of the National Institute of Economic and Social Research, the United Kingdom.

PETER CURWEN is a Reader in Public Policy at the Policy Research Centre, Sheffield Hallam University, the United Kingdom.

TIBOR CZÉH is a Ph.D. candidate in international relations at the Budapest University of Economic Sciences, Budapest, Hungary.

DIETHER DÖRING is Professor of Social policy at Akademie der Arbeit at the University of Frankfurt, Germany.

YOSHIFUMI FUSHIMI is the director of the Division of Research and Development at the Social Development Research Institute in Tokyo, Japan.

ANDREAS FØLLESDAL is director of a research group on normative theory at the Program on Advanced Research on the Europeanisation of the Nation State (arena), University of Oslo, Norway.

SVEN E. OLSSON HORT teaches sociology and social policy at Stockholm University, Sweden.

SERGE-CHRISTOPHE KOLM is director at the École des Hautes Études en Sciences Sociales, Paris, France.

PETER KOSLOWSKI is director of the Forschungsinstitut für Philosophie Hannover and its Centre for Ethical Economy and Business Culture, and Professor of Philosophy and Political Economy at the University of Witten/Herdecke, Germany.

ABOUT THE AUTHORS

STEFAN KOSLOWSKI is researcher at the Institute of Philosophical Foundations of Theology at the University of Tübingen, Germany.

ARNLAUG LEIRA is Professor of Sociology at the University of Oslo, and Research Director at the Institute for Social Research, Oslo, Norway.

ELISABETH LILJA is a Fellow Researcher at the Nordic Institute for Studies in Urban and Regional Planning, Stockholm, Sweden, and a lecturer at the Department of Sociology and Department of Human Geography, University of Stockholm.

MICHAEL OPIELKA is head of the Department for Program Development and Evaluation at the State Institute for Family Research at the University of Bamberg, Germany.

KEES SCHUYT is Professor of Sociology at the University of Amsterdam, the Netherlands.

ANNEKE VAN DOORNE-HUISKES is a professor in the Department of Women Studies at Erasmus University Rotterdam, the Netherlands.

PHILIPPE VAN PARIJS holds the Hoover Chair of Economic and Social Ethics at the Université Catholique de Louvain, Belgium.

ARENA is a research program under the Research Council of Norway, providing Advanced Research on the Europeanisation of the Nation-State. The program seeks to describe, analyse and evaluate the processes of institutional, political and cultural change in Europe. ARENA is located at the University of Oslo, Norway.

FORSCHUNGSINSTITUT FÜR PHILOSOPHIE HANNOVER (The Hannover Institute of Philosophical Research), Hannover, Germany, is an institute for basic research in all disciplines of philosophy. It is funded by the Catholic Diocese of Hildesheim (Eastern and Northern Lower Saxony). The institute works in the fields of social philosophy, economic ethics, ontology, philosophy of nature, theology and metaphysics. Part of the institute is the Centre for Ethical Economy and Business Culture.

Index of Names

Page numbers in italics refer to quotations in footnotes or references

MIX
Papier aus verantwortungsvollen Quellen
Paper from responsible sources
FSC® C105338

If you have any concerns about our products,
you can contact us on
ProductSafety@springernature.com

In case Publisher is established outside the EU,
the EU authorized representative is:
Springer Nature Customer Service Center GmbH
Europaplatz 3, 69115 Heidelberg, Germany

Printed by Libri Plureos GmbH
in Hamburg, Germany